U I D E

SAN DIEGO & TIJUANA

High tide near La Jolla Cove. Debbie K. Hardin

A COMPLETE GUIDE

FIRST EDITION

SAN DIEGO & TIJUANA

Debbie K.
Hardin

The Countryman Press
Woodstock, Vermont

To my mom, Irine Axton, who always told me that I could travel around the world and never find a better place than San Diego. She was right—as usual.

ISBN 978-1-58157-035-9

Cover photo of Mission San Diego de Alcala © Bert Creighton/iStockphoto.com
Interior photos by the author unless otherwise specified
Book design by Bodenweber Design
Page composition by Chelsea Cloeter
Maps by Mapping Specialists, Ltd., Madison, WI © The Countryman Press

Published by The Countryman Press, P.O. Box 748, Woodstock, Vermont 05091

Distributed by W. W. Norton & Company, Inc., 500 Fifth Ave., New York, NY 10110

Printed in the United States of America

10 9 8 7 6 5 4 3 2 1

GREAT DESTINATIONS PUTS THE "GUIDE" IN GUIDEBOOK

Recommended by *National Geographic Traveler* and *Travel + Leisure* magazines.

[A] CRISP AND CRITICAL APPROACH, FOR TRAVELERS WHO WANT TO LIVE LIKE LOCALS.
— *USA Today*

Great Destinations™ guidebooks are known for their comprehensive, critical coverage of regions of extraordinary cultural interest and natural beauty. The authors in this series are professional travel writers who have lived for many years in the regions they describe. Each title in this series is continuously updated with each printing to ensure accurate and timely information. All the books contain more than one hundred photographs and maps.

Current titles available:

THE ADIRONDACK BOOK
ATLANTA
AUSTIN, SAN ANTONIO & THE TEXAS HILL COUNTRY
THE BERKSHIRE BOOK
BIG SUR, MONTEREY BAY & GOLD COAST WINE COUNTRY
CAPE CANAVERAL, COCOA BEACH & FLORIDA'S SPACE COAST
THE CHARLESTON, SAVANNAH & COASTAL ISLANDS BOOK
THE CHESAPEAKE BAY BOOK
THE COAST OF MAINE BOOK
COLORADO'S CLASSIC MOUNTAIN TOWNS: GREAT DESTINATIONS
THE FINGER LAKES BOOK
GALVESTON, SOUTH PADRE ISLAND & THE TEXAS GULF COAST
THE HAMPTONS BOOK
HONOLULU & OAHU: GREAT DESTINATIONS HAWAII
THE HUDSON VALLEY BOOK
LOS CABOS & BAJA CALIFORNIA SUR: GREAT DESTINATIONS MEXICO
THE NANTUCKET BOOK
THE NAPA & SONOMA BOOK
PALM BEACH, MIAMI & THE FLORIDA KEYS
PHOENIX, SCOTTSDALE, SEDONA & CENTRAL ARIZONA
PLAYA DEL CARMEN, TULUM & THE RIVIERA MAYA: GREAT DESTINATIONS MEXICO
SALT LAKE CITY, PARK CITY, PROVO & UTAH'S HIGH COUNTRY RESORTS
SAN DIEGO & TIJUANA: GREAT DESTINATIONS
SAN JUAN, VIEQUES & CULEBRA: GREAT DESTINATIONS PUERTO RICO
THE SANTA FE & TAOS BOOK
THE SARASOTA, SANIBEL ISLAND & NAPLES BOOK
THE SEATTLE & VANCOUVER BOOK: INCLUDES THE OLYMPIC PENINSULA, VICTORIA & MORE
THE SHENANDOAH VALLEY BOOK
TOURING EAST COAST WINE COUNTRY

If you are traveling to, moving to, residing in, or just interested in any (or all!) of these enchanting regions, a Great Destinations guidebook is a superior companion. Honest and painstakingly critical, full of information only a local can provide, Great Destinations guidebooks give you all the practical knowledge you need to enjoy the best of each region. Why not own them all?

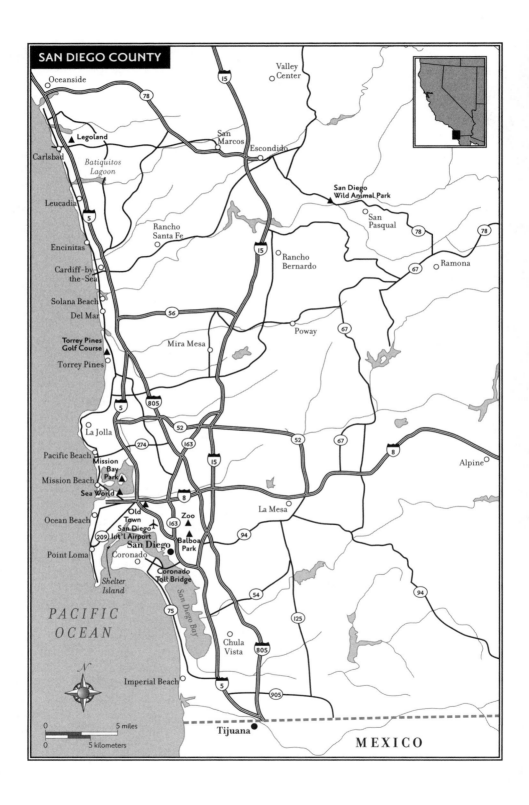

CONTENTS

Acknowledgments

I consulted many experts throughout San Diego and Tijuana when writing this book, and I am sincerely grateful to all of those who kindly answered my pleas for help and advice. Among this number are several extraordinary public relations professionals who made my work both easier and more enjoyable: Judith Adams, Rob Akins, Leslie Araiza, Sean Curry, Joanne DiBona, Lauren Clapperton, Lauren Clifford, Linda Kissam, Sara DeYoung, Vanessa Kanegai, Mikel Wadewitz, and Juan Saldana all went the extra mile for me. And a special thanks goes to Kate Buska at the San Diego Convention and Visitors Bureau, who not only helped when I asked but who anticipated my requests and answered my emails almost before I sent them.

In addition, I called on family and friends to share their favorites in San Diego and Tijuana. For their willingness to divulge their secrets and for their support as I hammered away on the manuscript, I thank Lori Boechler, Susie Bright, Karen Carriere, Swati Dalvie, Cate DaPron, Gilbert Gonzalez, Pat Gonzalez, Donna Johnson, Kevin Legg, Margie Rogers, Cindy Simpson, Sheila Spahn-Bettencourt, Joyce Teague, and Rosanna and River Weiss. In addition, I owe a special debt of gratitude to two brothers-in-law who gave me insight into their favorite sports: Larry Legg, who helped me make the fishing sections authoritative, and Joe Preimesberger, who shared his expertise on golfing.

For entrusting me with this project, I thank Kim Grant and Kermit Hummel of Countryman Press, both of whom have been supportive and exceedingly kind. I am also grateful to the efficient and cheerful production team: Chelsea Cloeter, Fred Lee, Collette Leonard, and Kelly Thompson. Special thanks go to Jennifer Thompson, who managed the project efficiently and made the production process surprisingly enjoyable.

Finally, I thank my beautiful daughter Juliane, who sets a high bar for excellence in our household, and my understanding husband Jon Preimesberger, who never complained when I dragged him along for research. Both supported and encouraged me throughout this past year; I hope this book reminds them of the good times we had exploring our hometown.

Introduction

San Diego and Tijuana have long attracted tourists and new residents who are looking for unbeatable weather, miles of sun-drenched shoreline, and a less frenetic pace than most cities of comparable size. But San Diego and its sister south of the border, Tijuana, have so much more to offer: Their rich historical heritage, geographical diversity, and blending of cultures make for thriving cities that offer a staggering variety of experiences. Where else can you kayak through ocean-sculpted caves; admire cruise ships and Navy carriers docked side by side; shop for hand-crafted silver jewelry and fine leather goods in an outdoor market; attend world-class theater in a reproduction of Shakespeare's Old Globe theater; have breakfast with a killer whale; stroll through Roy Lichtenstein's and Christo's work at the foremost contemporary art museum in California; or simply walk across the border and into a foreign country?

It's hard to miss the incredible natural beauty in the San Diego and Tijuana area: Sage-colored mountains swell up close to the sea, the Pacific Ocean glitters in the sun like a rolling blanket of diamonds, and the sun bleaches the landscape and the sky to Impressionistic hues. The explosion of flowers year-round, the imported evergreen palm trees, and the relentless sunshine confuse the seasons, resulting in a timeless quality. It isn't quite endless summer, but it's close. There is barely a day when an outdoor café is out of the question; surfers paddle out seeking the perfect wave year-round; and runners hit the pavement even in the middle of winter.

With a Mediterranean climate and abundance of outdoor activities, it is easy to characterize San Diego and Tijuana as merely resort destinations—and indeed, this embarrassment of natural riches *does* tend to put one in a holiday frame of mind. But San Diego has grown up over the past few decades, and is now the eighth largest city in the United States, with a population of almost 1.3 million in the city and more than 3 million in the county. Tijuana is the largest border crossing into the United States, and the second largest city on the West Coast of North America (only Los Angeles is bigger). More than 27 million tourists visit the area annually and more than fifteen thousand new residents move here each year. This growth has brought an even greater number and increased variety of cultural opportunities, for visitors and locals alike.

Downtown San Diego has enjoyed an unrivaled renaissance over the past several decades. I cannot overstate the transformation: A walk through the historic downtown Gaslamp Quarter would take you past tattoo parlors, adult video stores, and boarded up storefronts 20 years ago. Today in the Gaslamp the topless bars have been replaced with tapas bars, and ethnic bistros and upscale boutiques have taken residence in previously abandoned spaces. The new downtown San Diego is eclectic, beautiful, and vibrant—rivaling the most urbane cities in the world. But downtown isn't just a favorite place to play: Increasingly, couples and families are saying goodbye to suburban sprawl and congested freeway commutes and are moving to new condominium developments in downtown—many with stunning views of the harbor and all within walking distance of the action.

Tijuana has cleaned up as well, both its streets and its reputation. Since Prohibition days Californians have been crossing the border to party and seek modes of entertainment not necessarily available (or legal) in the United States. However, in the past decade the Tijuana

Tourism Board has finally acknowledged the importance of tourists to the local economy and has worked hard to make the city more appealing to a broad spectrum of foreign visitors. Officials and business people have collaborated to revitalize Avenida Revolución, the main thoroughfare downtown, and now the streets and sidewalks are cleaner, the restaurants and stores are welcoming and appealing to visitors, and illicit activity is kept mostly out of sight. In the Zona Rio neighborhood, the Tijuana Cultural Museum has become a major tourist destination and boasts one of the finest collections of Mexican cultural artifacts in the world. In addition to shopping for the ubiquitous blankets and woven baskets in the famous outdoor markets, visitors can also browse for Jimmy Choo and Prada at the Plaza Rio Tijuana Mall. And if it's a party you're looking for, you'll still find it in Tijuana, with literally hundreds of dance clubs, bars, and exotic spectator sports such as bullfighting and dog racing, all no farther than a taxi's ride from the border crossing.

I was born in San Diego, and have lived most of my life here. The sights, sounds, and tastes of San Diego and Tijuana are intimately connected with my earliest memories: I was on a boat in Mission Bay at just two weeks old, and family legend has it that by age five I begged to buy a taco from a vendor in downtown Tijuana (but my mother always said no to street food). My perspective as a long-time native informs everything that I write. In the pages that follow I'll help you discover for yourself the secrets of old-time favorites and delights of new hot spots—and I'll help you plan your days so that the geographical distance (and the concomitant traffic) doesn't become a nuisance. Once you explore it for yourself, you are sure to join the ranks of the millions of people who call this area their heart's home.

—Debbie K. Hardin

THE WAY THIS BOOK WORKS

This book is divided into 10 chapters. Chapter 1 provides historical context and chapter 2 explores transportation to and around the area. Chapters 3 through 8 divide the area into geographical regions. Entries within the regions are organized alphabetically. You can skip from chapter to chapter to suit your interests, and you can take this book along with you for handy reference in a given neighborhood or region of the city. Better yet, read the book cover to cover, and then go back and look up your favorites.

If you're searching for places to stay or to eat, I suggest you first look over the Lodging Index and Restaurant Index at the back of the book (organized by area and by price); then turn to the pages listed and read the specific entries for the places that catch your fancy. Be sure to refer to the maps throughout the book to help you become familiar with the San Diego and Tijuana area. Because it is nearly impossible to cover much ground without a car, I've included a freeway map, which ought to come in handy when negotiating the large distances that can be involved when touring the cities. Also look for the section titled "Outside the Area" in chapter 2, where I've included my favorite side trips should you wish to extend your visit beyond the San Diego and Tijuana County limits.

Some entries include specific information organized for easy reference in blocks at the head of each entry. I've included a "Handicap Access" category for lodging and restaurants, specifying "Full," "Partial," or "None" (although I've omitted this information in chapter 8, because Mexico's accessibility standards vary; be sure to call ahead if this is a concern). In the United States, full access includes such amenities as grab bars in restrooms and stalls wide enough for wheelchairs; partial access means the establishment has made an effort to accommodate visitors with handicaps. I've also included a section on "Parking" in the San Diego chapters, because this can be a limiting factor in deciding on certain locales within downtown and along most of the beaches. All details given in the information blocks—as well as all phone numbers and addresses in other parts of the book—were checked as close to publication as possible, but these details change without warning; when in doubt, please call ahead.

For the same reason, I've avoided specific prices for most entries, preferring instead to indicate a range. Lodging price codes are based on a standard (nonview) per-room rate, double occupancy, during high season (summer and holiday months). Low-season rates are likely to be as much as 40 to 50 percent less. Prices do not include taxes. Once again, it's always best to call ahead for specific rates when you make your reservations. San Diego has some of the most expensive real estate in the country, and the lodging prices reflect this reality. Most lodging will fall in the expensive to very expensive category (and note that the very expensive category can extend into thousands of dollars a night for premium rooms); but there are exceptions and a few bargains to be had.

Dining also reflects big-city prices, but there are values in this category as well. I have included many inexpensive options for budget-conscious travelers within the restaurant entries; you'll also find special sections devoted to "Taquerias"—in other words, inexpensive Mexican restaurants, which are plentiful in this area—and to "Pizza, Burgers, and Dogs," all casual restaurants that are inexpensive or moderately priced. Restaurant prices include the cost of an individual meal, including appetizer, entrée, dessert, tax, and tip but not including beverages.

Price Codes

If you're looking for surf and sand, the available neighborhoods in San Diego range from upscale, expensive oceanfront locations (e.g., Coronado, La Jolla, Del Mar) to funky and charming—and slightly less expensive—beach towns (e.g., Mission Beach, Pacific Beach, Encinitas, Carlsbad). If you're looking for a big-city experience with plenty of nightlife, you'll want to think about downtown San Diego, from the revitalized Gaslamp Quarter, the hot Little Italy section, and close-in Uptown neighborhoods such as Hillcrest and North Park. South county and the inland cities are the best bets for less expensive hotels, but the money you save on lodging may be offset by the time you lose commuting to and from attractions. In addition, independent lodging options are limited in these neighborhoods, reflecting the truth that they aren't as popular with tourists as the beaches and downtown. With San Diego currently being among the most expensive cities in the country for gasoline, you'll also need to consider fuel costs if you choose a far-flung home base.

	Lodging	Dining
Inexpensive	Up to $120	Up to $15
Moderate	$120–$200	$15–$30
Expensive	$200–$300	$30–$75
Very Expensive	More than $300	More than $75

Credit cards are abbreviated as follows:

AE—American Express	D—Discover Card	V—Visa
DC—Diner's Club	MC—MasterCard	

A Word About Coverage

There are a plethora of national chain restaurants and hotels in San Diego—some of them very fine indeed. But I've chosen to bypass most of these and instead focus on independent establishments that will be less familiar to both the traveler and to newcomers in San Diego. I made some exceptions to this rule (e.g., a Southern California taco chain, for example, that got its start in Pacific Beach and a five-star hotel chain with a landmark property in Carlsbad), but otherwise I've concentrated on those experiences you can't get outside of San Diego and Tijuana.

More Info: San Diego and Tijuana

The best sources for year-round tourist information are the **San Diego Convention and Visitors Bureau** (www.sandiego.org/nav/Visitors; 619-232-3101; 2215 India St., San Diego, CA 92101); **San Diego North Convention and Visitors Bureau** (www.sandiegonorth.com; 760-745-4741; 360 N. Escondido Blvd., Escondido, CA 92025); **Carlsbad Convention and Visitors Bureau** (www.visitcarlsbad.com; 760-434-6093; 400 Carlsbad Village Dr., Carlsbad, CA 92008); **Coronado Visitor Center** (www.coronadovisitorcenter.com; 619-437-8788; 1100 Orange Ave., Coronado, CA 92118); **Chula Vista Convention and Visitors**

Bureau (www.chulavistaconvis.com; 619-425-4444; 750 E. St., Chula Vista, CA 91910); **San Diego East Visitors Bureau** (www.visitsandiegoeast.com; 619-445-0180; 5005 Willows Rd., Ste. 208, Alpine, CA 91901); the **Tijuana Convention and Visitors Bureau** (www.tijuanaonline.org/english/logo-cotuco/cotuco.htm; 888-775-2417; Av. Paseo de los Heroes No. 9365-201, Tijuana, BC, Mexico 22320); the **Tijuana Tourist Information Center** (664-658-2210; between Third and Fourth Sts. and Av. Revolucíon); and the **Baja California State Secretariat of Tourism** (www.turismobc.gob.mx; 664-634-7330 or 664-634-6418). If you need emergency assistance while traveling, consult the **Travelers Aid Society** (www.travelersaidsandiego.org; 619-295-8393; 306 Walnut Ave., #21, San Diego, CA 92103); there is also a location in the San Diego airport (619-295-1277; San Diego International Airport, Terminal 2, San Diego, CA 92101).

The bell tower at the Mission San Diego de Alcala.
Photo courtesy of Jon Preimesberger. Used with permission.

1

HISTORY

From Missionaries to Biotech Gurus

San Diego and Tijuana have been influenced by a number of disparate cultures: Native Americans called the area home as long ago as 12,000 B.C. Nearly 14,000 years later, Spanish missionaries claimed the land—and the souls that inhabited it—as their own. But it wasn't long before Mexican revolutionaries fought for their independence from colonial Spain, only to have U.S. forces take massive tracts of territory for the pioneers who believed it was their divine right to move west. Since that time, immigrants like Chinese workers in the late 19th century, Portuguese fisherman in the early 20th century, and Vietnamese refugees in the 1970s have thronged to San Diego to pursue their own manifest destinies.

The cultural identity of San Diego and Tijuana have been enriched and enlivened with each successive wave of humanity, and this has made for a truly hospitable social climate. Citizens on both sides of the border are quick to greet visitors with a smile, and long-timers welcome newcomers—albeit grudgingly on the increasingly congested beaches and freeways. Under clear skies and unrelenting sunshine, San Diego locals congratulate each other on living in what most believe is the best place in the world.

There are a lot of locals to make this argument, because San Diego is the second most populous city in California and the eighth largest in the country. But unlike many East Coast cities that are tightly packed and have had little choice over the years but to grow upward, San Diego has sprawled outward; the county covers more than 4,000 square miles, and it takes hours to drive from one end to the other. And drive we must, because the county is actually a collection of neighborhoods strung together amid a spider web of freeways and highways. Over the past decades, developers have filled in the spaces between, and now it is nearly impossible to distinguish where one neighborhood begins and the other ends. Despite the increasing congestion, San Diegans jealously guard their quality of life—articulated by many simply as "we don't want to become another LA"—and are thankful for the buffer against blending into a megacity with Orange County/Los Angeles that the enormous Camp Pendleton marine base in the north provides.

The diverse geography around which San Diego is built ranges from miles of dramatic coastline in the west to mountains that rise up east of the city. Beyond the mountains lie vast expanses of desert that extend past the eastern border of the state. The semiarid climate that results from this proximity to the desert is world-famous for its mildness. Average precipitation is less than 10 inches per year—which translates into a serious water shortage and cyclical droughts. Because of the hilly topography punctuated with low-lying valleys, on the rare occasions when it does rain heavily, portions of the city are subject to floods and mudslides.

But as any sun worshipper knows, this mostly dry, sunny weather has its upside: The region is an outdoor sporting mecca, and the economy is fueled by tourists who want in on the action. Although the growing population and the ever-rising costs of real estate have driven out most agriculture, many parts of the county are still prime for growing flowers, strawberries, citrus, and avocados. With the natural beauty of the region, and the bounty possible with irrigation, it's no wonder why people throughout history have felt a primordial pull to settle here.

THE FIRST LOCALS

Long before Europeans "discovered" San Diego, Natives known as the San Dieguito people called the San Diego–Tijuana area home. Then came the La Jolla people, the Diegueños, and finally the Yuman and Shoshonean peoples. The latter group comprised the Luiseño, who settled in the north county, and the Kumeyaay, who settled in what is now Mission Valley and as far south as Ensenada, Mexico.

This statue in Point Loma is a replica of a sculpture of Cabrillo by Portuguese artist Alvaro de Bree.

The Natives lived in dome-shaped dwellings made from willow-branch frames covered with bark or grasses. In warm weather men generally wore no clothing at all, and women usually wore only a skirt. In colder months, both genders sported animal pelts to keep warm. The Kumeyaay were hunters and agriculturalists. They planted beans, corn, and squash and hunted bighorn sheep, deer, and rabbits. They were exceptional artisans, crafting coiled grass baskets that were of such fine quality they could hold water. They were peaceful people and initially welcomed the first colonists—although when it became apparent in later years that their lands were being overtaken, the Natives grew distinctly less cooperative.

CONQUISTADORS AND MISSIONARIES

On September 28, 1542, Portuguese explorer Juan Rodriquez Cabrillo, sailing on behalf of Spain, became the first European of record to set foot on the West Coast of the United States. He sailed his flagship the *San Salvador* into the San Diego Bay, just off the peninsula of Point Loma, in search of a trade route between Mexico and the Spice Islands in Asia. Cabrillo never found the shortcut to riches for which he was looking, but he did claim the newfound area for Spain. Cabrillo named the spot San Miguel, and then quickly moved on in search of another discovery.

In 1602, just 60 years after Cabrillo, another Spanish explorer came along: Sebastian Vizcaíno and his party celebrated the first Christian religious service in California shortly after landing to commemorate the feast day of Saint Diego. Vizcaíno renamed the city San Diego de Alcalá. This time the name stuck.

Explorers didn't come to San Diego again in significant numbers for 150 years. In the mid-18th century, however, Russian colonies started popping up in northern California, and Spain worried that Russia might threaten the Spanish settlements in southern California. So Spain decided to found its own colonies.

Father Junípero Serra, a Franciscan friar charged with establishing missions throughout California, and Gaspar de Portolá, a Spanish officer leading the accompanying military force, landed in San Diego in 1769 to begin Spanish colonization. Shortly after arriving, Father Serra chose a site on what is now Presidio Hill to build the first mission in California. Natives living near the mission were not particularly happy to see the Spaniards, but they were soon convinced to cooperate or were subdued, either through sheer force wielded by the soldiers or through the more subtle persuasion of religious conversion wielded by the friars.

A sculpture of Father Junípero Serra in the gardens at the Mission San Diego de Alcala.

Serra stayed on for the first few years to get the mission up and running. In 1771 he moved on to Mission Carmel, which served as his headquarters as he continued to oversee the missions throughout California. Father Luis Jayme succeeded Father Serra at the San Diego Mission. In 1774, when it became clear that the original site had inadequate supplies of water and poor land for farming, the friars moved 6 miles inland, near the San Diego River, where the mission stands today.

The new mission site was already a Kumeyaay village, however, and the Kumeyaay resisted the missionaries from the beginning. A little more than a year after the move, on November 5, 1775, several Kumeyaay brutally murdered Father Jayme and burned the mission structures to the ground. The Kumeyaay were soon overpowered by Spanish soldiers, and the insurrection came to a quick halt.

In the aftermath of the revolt, Father Serra returned to San Diego to oversee the rebuilding, and soon the mission was open for business again. By 1797, almost 600 souls had been baptized into the faith, and more than 1,400 converted to Christianity. The Spanish colonists were impressively successful carrying out their mission, but the natives suffered enormous losses because of the rapid spread of diseases against which they had no natural immunity. In addition to the many who died—some historians estimate that as many as half succumbed to European-spread illnesses—natives who defied the Spaniards or deserted the mission settlement were beaten, jailed, or both. Although the Kumeyaay acquired farming and ranching skills and thereby learned a more sustainable way of life, their native culture was all but wiped out within the colonies.

Through this original portal at the Mission San Luis Rey de Francia in Oceanside, guests can glimpse the first pepper tree planted in California in 1830.

In 1798, the Mission San Luis Rey de Francia was founded by Padre Fermín de Lasuén about 30 miles north of the San Diego mission, in what is now Oceanside. The Mission San Luis Rey, the 18th in a line of 21 missions in California, is much grander and larger than the first modest mission in San Diego. Although there was little physical resistance to the missionaries who moved into San Luis Rey, the Natives were again forced to relocate or to become a part of the new mission.

MEXICAN WARS RESHAPE THE BOUNDARIES

The Native Americans were not the only ones to chafe under Spanish rule. Starting in 1810, Mexico fought for independence from colonial Spain. In 1821, revolutionary troops in Mexico overthrew Spain's government. But because Spanish involvement in San Diego at the time didn't extend far beyond the missions, the political handover in the area was nonviolent and relatively anticlimactic.

At the end of the Mexican War of Independence, by Mexican law, the missions were secularized and the goal to convert Natives fell by the wayside. The settlers who'd lived in the shadows of the first mission started to move away. The settlement now known as Old Town—which was founded in 1769—became the favored place to live.

In 1845, prominent San Diegan Pio Pico became governor of California. Shortly afterward, the Mexican American War (1846–48) broke out. Before this time, Mexico's territory stretched through Texas and included all of California (divided into Alta California—or upper California—and Baja California). But U.S. settlers guided by the tenets of Manifest

Destiny moved west into California and other Mexican territories, and it wasn't long before these pioneers looked to make the land their own.

A decade earlier, in 1836, Texas settlers fought for and won independence from Mexico. However, Mexico refused to recognize the loss of Texas, and when the United States admitted Texas into the Union in 1845 (as the 28th state), Mexico fumed. President James Polk fanned the flames when he sent emissaries to Mexico in an effort to buy Alta California and New Mexico and to settle the matter of Texas once and for all. But Mexico announced its intention to take back Texas, and by mid-1846, relations between the countries deteriorated significantly. The United States declared war on Mexico in May, and U.S. forces invaded the Mexican territories.

Mexican Governor Pico and General José Castro fled from their headquarters in Los Angeles before the U.S. troops arrived, so by the time the invading forces landed, there was almost no one to fight. This nearly bloodless takeover may have given the United States false confidence, however, because the U.S. generals in charge left a skimpy occupying force. Rebel forces later attacked the remaining U.S. troops in Los Angeles and several died before the area was once again secured for the United States.

One of the most decisive battles of the war was fought in San Diego County. In 1846, General Stephen Watts Kearny's army marched from Santa Fe to San Diego, along with guide Kit Carson and more than one hundred soldiers. In response, Mexican General Andrés Pico gathered nearly double the number of men, and his forces readied to intercept the U.S. troops before they arrived in the city. On December 6, Kearny countered by attacking the Mexican army at a site near the San Pasqual Valley, about 5 miles from what is now Escondido. At least 18 U.S. soldiers were killed during the Battle of San Pasqual—the largest number of U.S. casualties in California throughout the war.

Kearny and his troops had been outwitted and outnumbered, and it wasn't long before they were surrounded and cut off from food and ammunition. Carson and another soldier managed to sneak away for help. On December 11, more than two hundred Marines and sailors from San Diego arrived to escort the remaining U.S. troops into the city. Pico's army withdrew, and within a few weeks Pico surrendered at Cahuenga Pass north of San Diego. A

What's In a Name

Place Name	English translation
Agua Hedionda (ahg-wa hed-ee-on-dah)	Stinking water
Chula Vista (chew-la vista)	Pretty view
Del Mar	Of the sea
El Cajon (el cah-hone)	The box
Encinitas (en-sa-nee-tas)	Little oak trees
Escondido (es-con-dee-doh)	Hidden, private
La Jolla (la hoy-ah)	The jewel
Leucadia (lou-cay-de-ya)	Sheltered place
Poway (pow-way)	Place where the valley ends
Solana	Sunny place
Tijuana (tee-whan-uh)	Aunt Jane (derived from Ti-wan, a Native word meaning "near the sea")

few weeks later, the Treaty of Guadalupe ended the war completely and established the current U.S. border with Mexico, which put Alta California in U.S. control. Mexicans living in Alta California and other conquered territories (which included Nevada and Utah as well as parts of New Mexico, Arizona, Colorado, and Wyoming) were given the choice to either stay and become citizens of the United States or return to Mexico.

At this time there wasn't much of a city in what is now Tijuana. Before the war, the division between Alta California and Baja California was about 20 miles farther south, near El Descanso. In the 1870s, the Mexican government built a small customs stand at the new border, and in 1889 created the Pueblo de Tijuana and promoted the area as a bathing resort, thanks to a local hot mineral springs.

Following the 1910 Mexican Revolution, a period of political and military turmoil that lasted for more than a decade, a group of Industrial Workers of the World (also known as Wobblies), led by Ricardo Magón, seized control of Tijuana for a short time. On June 22, Mexican federal troops arrived to fight the so-called Magonistas, and control was soon returned to the local government of Tijuana. This was the first time many U.S. citizens had heard of Tijuana, and it wasn't to become a major influence on San Diego for another 20 years, when the Eighteenth Amendment sent Californians south of the border looking for legal alcohol.

THE ROOTS OF "NEW TOWN"

In the aftermath of the Mexican American War, San Diego was named the seat of newly established San Diego County, and it was incorporated as a city in 1850. Businessman William Heath Davis was one of the first developers in the city, and he invested in 32 square blocks between Broadway and Market Streets (now the Gaslamp Quarter). But the citizens of San Diego were by then happily ensconced in Old Town and didn't see the point in moving the city. They watched with amusement as Davis threw up several prefabricated buildings (shipped in from a company in Maine) and began to build a wharf on the waterfront. But Davis was a man ahead of his time, and residents did not flock to his so-called New Town as he'd hoped. The failure was so complete that New Town was known as "Davis's Folly."

The William Heath Davis House is the oldest wooden structure in San Diego, and is now home to the Gaslamp Quarter Historical Society.

A few years later, in 1867, businessman Alonzo Horton came along and revived interest in New Town. He bought 800 acres of bay-front property and completed Davis's wharf. Horton and his supporters managed to move the county courthouse from Old Town (housed in the building now known as the Whaley House) to New Town, which effectively ended Old Town's reign as the seat of San Diego government. At the same time, Horton set aside 1,400 acres of the city as parkland—what would eventually become Balboa Park. The new downtown was quickly established as the heart of the city, and Old Town faded from prominence. A few years later, in 1872, a fire storm swept through Old Town and obliterated whatever was left of the settlement.

THE STINGAREE DISTRICT

The city grew quickly over the next several decades—perhaps too quickly, because downtown soon became a wild and dangerous place. By the late 1880s, there were more than 100 bordellos downtown and an estimated 350 prostitutes working in them. In addition, there were more than 70 saloons, dance halls, and gambling parlors, many of which were open all day and night. The Gaslamp Quarter at the time was called the Stingaree District, because it was said that a person could get stung as badly there as she or he could by the stingrays in the San Diego Bay.

During this period, Wyatt Earp rolled into town with his third wife, Josie. It was 1885— a few years after Earp's infamous gunfight at the OK Corral in Tombstone, Arizona—and Earp was looking to make some fast cash in the booming city of San Diego. Earp bought or leased several saloons in the Stingaree— and dropped even more cash gambling in establishments owned by others. But in 1888, the boom in population that San Diego had enjoyed finally went bust, and Earp and his wife moved on as quickly as they came. Several years later, in the first of many revitalization attempts of the area, city law enforcement swept through the Stingaree and arrested 138 prostitutes and shut down most of the bordellos and many of the bars.

One of Wyatt Earp's businesses was the Oyster Bar, located in the Louis Bank Building on Fifth Avenue.

WORLD EXPOSITIONS

In 1915, San Diego hosted a spectacular World's Fair to celebrate the completion of the Panama Canal. It was during this period that the ornate Spanish buildings in Balboa Park were built. The structures were originally intended to be temporary buildings to house exhibits, but most of them were left standing after the exposition was over. At the same time, respected nursery owner Kate Sessions was hired to plant trees and gardens throughout the park.

The Panama–California exposition was a major success and attracted the likes of Theodore Roosevelt, William Taft, and Thomas Edison. When it was all over, Harry Wegeforth, a surgeon from Baltimore who'd recently relocated to San Diego, wondered what

Artisans from Italy were brought in to Balboa Park to create the intricate flourishes and gingerbread in the plasterwork of the buildings.

would become of the animals brought into Balboa Park for the exposition. It occurred to him that the city needed a zoo, and he persuaded city leaders to help him create and fund the San Diego Zoological Society. In 1921 the park set aside 100 acres as zoo grounds, and cages were erected to house the remaining animals from the exposition. It wasn't long before the zoo started to acquire exotic species from around the world, including kangaroos and koalas from Australia—animals that most Americans had never seen before.

Because the first had been so successful, in 1935 San Diego hosted a second World's Fair, this time known as the California–Pacific Exposition. El Prado—the main thoroughfare in Balboa Park—was expanded, and more ornate Spanish buildings were erected to house an even larger collection of exhibits.

TIJUANA DURING THE 1920S: PROHIBITION

From 1920 to 1933, the U.S. government outlawed the consumption and manufacture of alcohol throughout the United States. During this period even the possession of beer and wine was illegal. But alcohol remained legal in Mexico, and not surprisingly, Americans flocked across the border to partake. Those individuals who came looking for a good time were not disappointed, because within months there were literally hundreds of bars in Tijuana where parched U.S. citizens could quench their thirst. Beyond booze, Tijuana found additional ways to satisfy the vices of its visitors. Gambling was legal and widespread, and it was during this period that prostitution first gripped the city—it hasn't let go since. When the Twenty-First Amendment repealed Prohibition, many Americans continued to visit Tijuana, in large part because of its illicit activities and, in later years, because costs were significantly less than in the United States.

But in July 1935, Mexico's then-president Lázaro Cárdenas closed the country to gambling and betting. Agua Caliente's elaborate and elegant $10 million racetrack was shut down, and for years gambling was not sanctioned in the city. In a 1947 law that still stands, the gaming industry was allowed sports and racetrack betting—and this came to include the bloody sport of cock fighting. More recently, in 2004, the Mexican Ministry of the Interior issued new regulations that opened the door to gaming machines. Although full-scale, Las Vegas-style casinos are illegal in Tijuana, Caliente and other businesses on Avenida Revolucíon downtown and some hotels in the more upscale Zona Rio have brought in gambling machines that very much *resemble* slot machines. These gaming devices seem to be legal only by virtue of a loophole in the law, however, so they may be removed in the near future.

SAN DIEGO DURING WORLD WAR II

The U.S. military looked favorably on San Diego as early as the late 19th century. By World War I, North Island in Coronado was created as a Marine base, and the Navy built a massive shipyard downtown, as well as a training station and a hospital. It wasn't until World War II, however, that the military presence in San Diego became overwhelming.

After the Japanese attack on Pearl Harbor, San Diego became a critical port for the Pacific Fleet, as well as a hub of defense contracts. The population swelled to nearly 400,000 as workers sought employment in the San Diego aircraft plants that worked 24 hours a day to meet Uncle Sam's demands. Military bases already in the city were expanded during the war, and new facilities were built throughout the county. The San Diego Bay was laced with giant netting devices intended to obstruct Japanese submarines, and the beautiful buildings in Balboa Park were converted to hospitals.

Local leaders had to scramble to keep ahead of the demand for housing and adequate water and sewer systems. Linda Vista, just east of Mission Bay, started out life as Defense Housing Project No. 4092. In the largest construction project to date, the government spent $14 million developing nearly 1,500 acres into small homes to house the burgeoning military. More than three thousand houses were built in two hundred days, all of which were immediately rented out to soldiers' families and defense plant employees. Other developments like it filled in the mesas north of downtown in the months that followed.

On February 9, 1942, President Franklin D. Roosevelt signed Executive Order 9066, which gave U.S. authorities the legal right to remove Japanese Americans living in coastal cities in the West from their homes and relocate them to inland camps (like the infamous Manzanar), where they would be forcefully detained. Proponents of the order claimed that by relocating Japanese Americans away from coastal regions, U.S. interests would be protected from possible espionage that would confound the war in the Pacific. Within weeks of the order, the Western Defense Command removed close to two thousand individuals of Japanese descent from San Diego. Most returned after the war to find their homes and property were gone.

SAN DIEGO AND TIJUANA GROW UP

The Korean and Vietnam Wars continued to fuel the San Diego economy, which was still heavily invested in the defense industry, but with urban sprawl in the late 1960s and early 1970s the city center deteriorated. Long-time businesses folded up shop and few new businesses dared to relocate in the increasingly dangerous area. The downtown became a haven for the mentally ill, sleazy businesses, and illicit activity. By the early 1980s, it wasn't safe to walk below Broadway Street—just as it wasn't safe one hundred years before, when the area was known as the Stingaree.

Thanks to the vision of a succession of local politicians, the Centre City Development Corporation, and many deep-pocket investors, downtown San Diego has undergone a remarkable revitalization in the past few decades. Starting with the opening of Seaport Village shopping mall in 1980, Horton Plaza shopping mall in 1985, and subsequent urban renewal efforts by entrepreneurs and city leaders, the downtown corridor now sparkles with fine dining, vibrant clubs, and upscale shopping. Although there are still pockets of decay throughout downtown, the Gaslamp Quarter—16 blocks that stretch from Broadway to Market between Fourth and Sixth Streets—is a stunning success. With the 2004 opening of the Petco Park baseball stadium in the East Village, once a deteriorating industrial area next to the Gaslamp, renewal is spreading. Old buildings are being renovated and new buildings are going up at an astounding rate to fill the demand for more downtown housing and office space.

The New Economy

Although the San Diego economy is still dependent on the U.S. military, as well as tourism, defense-related businesses, and commercial shipbuilding, increasingly high-tech industries are moving into the area. World-class research institutes are scattered throughout town, the most prominent among them being the University of California, San Diego; The Salk Institute; and the Scripps Research Institute. These brain trusts have spun off hundreds of research and development companies as well.

By early 2007, there were more than five hundred biomedical companies in San Diego County, accounting for nearly 39,000 jobs and an estimated $8.5 billion impact on the region. San Diego is home to 13 Nobel laureates in science, and major companies like Invitrogen and Pfizer have a significant presence in the city.

Politics and Scandal

Local politics have been rocked by scandal for years, as is well chronicled in the biting *Under the Perfect Sun: The San Diego Tourists Never See*, by Mike Davis, Kelly Mayhew, and Jim Miller. But in the past few years, the city seems to have outdone itself with spectacular political debacles.

In 2005, facing a recall election, Mayor Dick Murphy resigned in part because of public outcry over a $1.4 billion deficit of the city employees' pension account. The same year, three City Council members were accused of taking bribes in the form of campaign contributions from a strip club owner and his business partners—allegedly to pay them off for repealing the city's "no touch" laws at nude dance clubs.

Also in 2005, U.S. Congressman Randy "Duke" Cunningham was forced to resign his seat after becoming embroiled in one of the most flagrantly corrupt bribery scandals in congressional history. A U.S. District Court found Cunningham guilty of accepting bribes from defense contractors, and he was sentenced to a 100-month sentence in prison and ordered to pay $1.8 million in restitution.

Horton Plaza, opened in 1985, was one of the first grand-scale downtown revitalization efforts in the modern era.

Photo courtesy of Joanne DiBona, the San Diego Convention and Visitors Bureau. Used with permission.

Tijuana Today

Tijuana is the largest city in the Mexican state of Baja California and home to the busiest border crossing in the world. Its proximity to San Diego has meant that the city has relied on U.S. tourism for years; however, thousands of Mexicans cross into the United States daily to shop and do business in San Diego, which means that San Diego is equally dependent on Mexican tourism.

Although the Avenida Revolucíon downtown has been widened and widely sanitized in the past decade—expelling the peep shows and strip clubs off the main thoroughfare—and the city is finally getting noticed for its abundance of cultural offerings, Tijuana is still a city of spectacular vices. The sex trade is alive and well in Tijuana's red light district and beyond, and prostitutes of all ages practice throughout the city.

Tijuana and surrounding areas in Mexico are also hotbeds of illegal drug smuggling, which makes for a violent undercurrent that most tourists will never see. In recent years the city has been the site of dozens of high-profile kidnappings and murders of drug traffickers, police officers, business owners, and innocent bystanders. Mexican President Felipe Calderon has cracked down on the drug cartel throughout the country and has recently focused attention on Tijuana. In early 2007 Calderon sent in more than 3,300 federal troops to the city in an effort to combat violence related to drug cartels operating out of Tijuana and to investigate the possibility that some on the Tijuana police force might be complicit in narco-trafficking.

Maquiladoras dominate the growing manufacturing industry in Tijuana. These are foreign-owned plants that import raw materials on a tariff-free basis and then export the finished products around the world. Examples of *maquiladoras* in Tijuana include Toshiba and Zenith (Tijuana is the largest producer of television sets in the world), as well as Mattel, Fisher Price, and Hewlett-Packard. A majority of workers in these plants are women, who legally start working as young as 16—and illegally as young as 12. Working conditions are often appalling, and minimum hourly wages in these plants is a little more than a dollar an hour. Although this is shockingly low, the average minimum *daily* wage for other Mexican workers is about $5. *Maquiladoras* have brought much needed employment to Tijuana, but these plants are also responsible for increased pollution and numerous human rights violations.

The biggest question hanging over Tijuana today centers on U.S. immigration and border regulations. In the wake of the terrorist attacks on the United States in September 2001, increased security measures have been put into place along the Mexican–United States border and the U.S. Border Patrol, which falls under the jurisdiction of the Department of Homeland Security, has significantly increased its presence along the border in Tijuana. Also in response to security threats, as well as to increased pressure by some factions to address the flood of illegal immigrants coming into the country over the Mexican border, the U.S. federal government is considering actions ranging from relatively benign improvements in identification paperwork to drastic physical alterations to the border that would include a massive wall along the entire perimeter.

Whether or not the United States succeeds in making it more difficult for Mexicans to enter the United States illegally in the future, it is increasingly difficult for U.S. citizens to get back into the United States after entering Mexico. As of 2008, U.S. citizens will require a passport to visit Tijuana by land (a passport is already required to enter by air or sea), which will likely reduce the tourism traffic into the city significantly. The increased security measures and the resulting maddening congestion in crossing the border back into the United States has already discouraged many tourists from visiting Tijuana in recent years.

LOOKING TO THE FUTURE

Because of the incredible natural beauty of the region, and because of the infamous "laid-back" attitude of its inhabitants, it's easy to imagine San Diego as an idyllic city that has little to do but bask in the sun and play in the surf. But like every major municipality in the United States, we have our fair share of challenges. In the future, these will include managing natural resources, finding a site for a larger airport in San Diego, ensuring adequate and affordable housing for all San Diegans, and keeping a lid on escalating congestion.

Water, Water Everywhere

From the very beginning of San Diego's history, the region's most precious—and scarce—natural resource has been water, and it promises to continue to be so. Throughout the early missionary period and beyond, the region fell under cycles of extreme drought conditions followed by catastrophic flooding, when parched lands couldn't absorb intense rainfalls.

To provide an increased water supply for the growing population, early remedies in San Diego included major dam construction throughout the county and brokered agreements from neighboring regions to siphon off their water supplies. Despite these efforts to borrow water from other locales, city planners severely underestimated the area's need for water. When the population of San Diego exploded during World War II, President Roosevelt stepped in to authorize the building of the San Diego Aqueduct, which brought in Colorado River water that was hoped to be enough for generations. Thanks to severe droughts and a continually burgeoning population, San Diego's needs exceeded even these water rights within a decade. By 1980, the city was drawing off from the Colorado River more than four times what the original agreement allowed. The San Diego County Water Authority undertook a major public relations campaign to convince San Diegans to conserve water. (What San Diego long-timer can forget the poetic call to restrict flushing: "If it's yellow, let it mellow; if it's brown, flush it down.") In a city exploding with lush tropical vegetation and miles of parkland and golf courses, water conservation wasn't an easy sell—but the efforts did help.

By the turn of the 21st century, the city was looking for new answers to its water crisis, and within a few years civic leaders instituted yet another stop-gap measure. In 2003, the Imperial Irrigation District approved an agreement to share Colorado River water and transfer additional water rights to San Diego County—an unpopular move among Imperial Valley farmers, who were concerned about the adequacy of their own water supply in the future. The controversial agreement will supply San Diego with about a third of its water needs in the coming years. This likely still isn't enough, so the mandatory conservation efforts that have been threatened to San Diegans for decades will certainly be a reality someday.

A New Airport for San Diego

Another major problem facing the city is the inadequacy of the international airport. Lindbergh Field was built on dredged land fill from the San Diego Bay in 1928, and now sits perilously close to downtown. Jets must fly directly over crowded freeways and near high rises to approach the runways. Ours is one of the smallest metropolitan airports in the country, and direct flights into the city are hard to come by. Lindbergh long ago exceeded its intended capacity, and neighbors in pricey Mission Hills and elsewhere complain about the noise. Restrictions have been in place for decades to prevent jets from landing after 11 PM to pacify nearby residents.

City planners and business leaders are searching for new sites for a second airport, but so far nothing has been deemed satisfactory. Choices have included reclaiming military bases for the purpose, building an airport as much as 50 miles outside of the city, and even unlikely scenarios like building a floating airport in the Pacific Ocean. It will take years (and millions of dollars) to investigate each possible site, and likely decades to fund and then build a new facility. Meanwhile, the limitations of the current airport will have economic ramifications for the next generation.

Affordability and Accessibility

Another problem that won't go away is the availability of affordable housing. In 2006, San Diego was ranked as the sixth least affordable housing market in the country. The median household income in the county was calculated in 2006 as just under $65,000, but the median house price was found to be $490,000—which puts the dream of home ownership out of reach for most San Diegans. This drives many to rent or purchase homes outside of city limits, exacerbating urban sprawl and freeway congestion. Although the city is committed to increasing the number of affordable dwellings—and has strict inclusionary laws that require builders to set aside a percentage of new developments for low- and moderate-income families—the supply hasn't kept up with the demand. Although housing prices flattened in 2006 and aren't expected to rebound for a few more years, the real estate market is likely to remain inflated beyond the means of most San Diegans.

It is ironic that a city that is unaffordable for a majority of Americans continues to grow steadily, resulting in worsening congestion throughout the county. Anecdotal reports of traffic by longtime residents compare the congestion today in San Diego with traffic in Los Angeles a decade or two ago. Despite the high cost of living, San Diego just keeps growing, albeit more slowly than years past. In 2006, the city grew by approximately 27,000. A swelling population will further strain the city's natural resources, overtax the airport, and add to the pollution and freeway congestion.

A BRIGHT FUTURE

Despite these challenges, San Diego is a vibrant, exciting metropolis that has the ambiance of a much smaller city; and Tijuana has made enormous strides in diversifying its tourism and cleaning up local corruption. The area as a whole enjoys a robust economy that generally weathers national recessions, and leaders on both sides of the border are starting to pay attention to managed growth. The most valuable natural resource in the region—the diverse and optimistic group of people who call San Diego and Tijuana home—are sure to keep fighting to improve their communities for themselves and for those who choose to visit.

The Coaster commuter train takes a scenic route along the shores of Del Mar.
Photo courtesy of Jon Preimesberger. Used with permission.

2

Transportation

Getting from There to Here

Some out-of-towners believe the stereotype that Southern Californians have a love affair with our cars, but for most of us, the thrill is gone. Any lingering passion for the open road has been extinguished by increasingly oppressive traffic, particularly on freeways, and the blisteringly expensive costs of fuel (San Diego is often rated as *the* most expensive place in the nation to buy gasoline).

With that said, it is almost impossible to see much of San Diego without a car. If you arrive by other means, you'll want to rent a vehicle for your stay, if at all possible. San Diego County stretches over 4,269 square miles (roughly the size of Connecticut), and you'll find the city easier to negotiate with your own wheels, despite the traffic.

Freeways and major surface streets pile up during rush hours on weekday mornings between 6:30 and 9 AM and in the afternoons starting as early as 3:30 PM in some particularly congested areas and extending as late as 7 PM. Traffic can be heavy on both sides of a freeway, but typically, north–south freeways are most congested heading south in the mornings and north in the evenings. East–west freeways are generally more congested heading west in the morning and east in the evening. Weekend mornings offer no free rides, either, with heavy traffic coming into the south and west, toward the beaches and downtown, especially during summer months. Interstate 5 and Highway 101 (also known as the Coast Highway) at Del Mar are particular problems from mid-June through early September, when the popular county fair and the race track season create additional congestion. And on Friday and Saturday evenings, traffic picks up between the outlying suburbs and the downtown and coastal hot spots (e.g., the Gaslamp Quarter, Pacific Beach, La Jolla, and Del Mar). Even if you plan well, you are bound to find yourself spending some quality time inhaling exhaust fumes. There are really only two choices: (1) Turn up the radio and roll back the convertible top; or (2) repeat my own personal mantra, "Go early, and allow yourself extra time en route."

Parking

Once you arrive at your destination, the challenge becomes finding a place to leave your vehicle. Parking is at a premium along the beaches, especially in Pacific Beach and La Jolla, as well as throughout downtown San Diego. When it comes to the beaches, find street parking if you can, but more reliable options include paid parking lots—for example, in Pacific

Beach, try the lots at the corner of Bayard and Hornblend, from which you can easily walk to the beach, boardwalk, and Garnet Avenue shopping. In the La Jolla Cove area, most of the better restaurants offer valet parking at dinnertime. You can usually find metered parking on side streets a few blocks off Prospect Street, and at night, some office buildings open their underground parking to guests.

In downtown, it isn't unusual to snag a two-hour metered spot on the street during a weekday, but it is next to impossible in the evenings and on weekends, especially in the trendy Gaslamp Quarter. Take a tip from the locals and park in the expansive **Westfield Horton Plaza Mall** parking garage (324 Horton Plaza, between Broadway and G Sts. and First and Fourth Aves.); if you purchase even a little something in the mall, you're entitled to three free hours of parking (but be sure to get your ticket validated after purchase). Thereafter it's $6 an hour. There are also dozens of small paid lots scattered throughout downtown, and some underground office parking is available to the public in the evenings and weekends; check the Gaslamp Quarter Association's Web site at www.gaslamp.org for maps and tips on finding "hidden" parking downtown.

GETTING TO SAN DIEGO AND TIJUANA

By Air

San Diego is served by **Lindbergh Field** (619-400-2400; 3225 N. Harbor Dr., San Diego, CA 92101), an international airport that hosts more than 20 airline carriers; there are three terminals and free transportation between them via a complimentary bus system, which makes a loop between Terminals 1 and 2 and the Commuter Terminal and stops along the way every few minutes. Additional airports outside the city include the **John Wayne Airport**

Visitors flying into San Diego for the first time are often startled at the low approach over freeways and the nearby harbor.

(949-252-5200; 18601 Airport Way, Santa Ana, CA 92707) in Orange County and the **Long Beach Airport** (562-570-2600; 4100 Donald Douglas Dr., Long Beach, CA 90808) in southern Los Angeles. Although both of these are a bit far flung, you can sometimes find less expensive and more direct flights through these airports than through Lindbergh.

Tijuana is served by the **Abelardo L. Rodriguez International Airport** (TIA; 664-607-8200; Carr. Aeropuerto, Tijuana, BC, Mexico 22000), about 5 miles east of downtown Tijuana. The **Tijuana Transportation Service** (858-278-9441) runs shuttles between San Diego and TIA for a minimum of $85 for one person (and just $5 more for a second). Be sure to reserve your seat at least 24 hours in advance. Taxis from TIA are a less expensive option, but Mexican cabs won't cross the border. You'll have to get out and walk through U.S. Customs and Immigration. Don't count on finding an American cab waiting on the other side; either arrange to have a cab pick you up or plan to take the trolley from San Ysidro into downtown.

By Bus

Arrive in San Diego by bus at the **Greyhound Bus Terminal** (619-239-3266; 120 W. Broadway, San Diego, CA 92101). The terminal is within walking distance of most downtown hotels; there are generally taxicabs waiting outside the terminal as well.

By Car

Visitors arriving in San Diego in their own cars will find that freeways and surface streets are well-marked, and most parts of town are pretty easy to navigate. Freeway exits are in the far right lane, and they are generally announced well in advance. Many freeways have HOV, or high-occupancy vehicle lanes, which are well worth using if you can do so legally—you must have at least two people in the vehicle to drive in these lanes. The California Highway Patrol takes the use restrictions of the HOV lanes seriously and will look for and ticket violators.

If you arrive by other means, it's easy to rent a car. Most major rental agencies operate out of Lindbergh Field downtown; catch a shuttle from the airport to your rental car agency at the Transportation Plaza at Terminals 1 and 2. Those arriving via the Commuter Terminal should use the baggage claim transportation phones to contact the rental agencies directly. Agencies are also within walking distance of the cruise ship terminal and the Santa Fe Train Depot downtown. Be sure to reserve ahead to ensure vehicle availability, especially during holidays.

By Cruise Ship

The number of visitors arriving in San Diego via cruise ships that dock at the B Street Pier Cruise Ship Terminal has tripled since 2001, and in 2006, approximately 650,000 guests made their way to the city via a cruise ship. In addition, major carriers such as Carnival, Royal Caribbean, and Holland America initiate cruises to the Mexican Riviera (a.k.a. Cabo San Lucas, Puerto Vallerta, and Mazatlan), the Sea of Cortez, and Hawaii from the Port of San Diego. Cruise ship guests at the port are ideally situated to explore the Harbor District downtown, including the shopping mecca of Seaport Village, and are within easy walking distance of the lively downtown Gaslamp Quarter as well, which has an eclectic collection of some of the finest dining and shopping in the city.

A cruise ship in port dominates the harbor.

By Train

You can arrive in San Diego from Los Angeles by train via Amtrak's Pacific Surfliner passenger trains at the Santa Fe Depot downtown (800-872-7245; 1050 Kettner Blvd., San Diego, CA 92101). Comfortable bilevel cars make the ride along the coast a beautiful, relatively stress-free experience—especially once you're out of Los Angeles and in San Diego County!

GETTING AROUND THE AREA

Freeways and Drive Times

To save yourself headaches when you're on the roads in San Diego, try to travel on freeways during off hours, and if you are held to a timetable, be sure to leave earlier than you think you need to. Be aware of trouble spots that seem to cause backups even when everything else runs smoothly. These include the "split" when I-805 north merges with I-5 north; the Via de la Valle exit off I-5, when the freeway narrows from six lanes to four in a matter of miles; I-8 heading east from Mission Valley to La Mesa in the evening rush hour; just about anything along I-15 N during the evening rush hour from Miramar to Escondido, and I-78 west through Escondido in the mornings. Note that I-15 N is particularly bad on Friday afternoons and into the evening (and well past the San Diego County line) because this is the main route out of town toward Las Vegas.

It's possible to skirt the freeways during the worst traffic periods, especially if you're traveling north to south or vice versa, but the traffic signals and frequent stops on surface roads may be just as frustrating and time-consuming as the freeways. The best advice when traveling significant distances is to invest in a good map and have an escape plan, so that if the freeway starts looking like a parking lot, you can take the nearest exit and try to drive around it.

Before you head out, call the 24-hour hotline at the California Department of Transportation for road-closure information and trouble spots (800-427-7623) or check the CalTrans Web site for continuously updated information and real-time traffic maps (www.dot.ca.gov/dist11/d11tmc/sdmap/showmap.html).

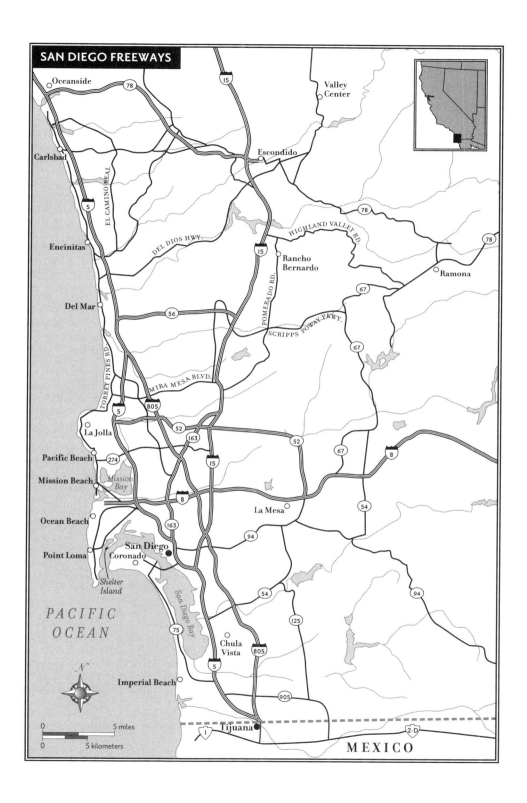

Metropolitan Transit Service

The Metropolitan Transit Service (MTS) is the overarching local body that runs most of the public transportation throughout the city, including bus lines, the Coaster train service, and the San Diego Trolley. Specifics on these options follow, but for up-to-date information on routes, schedules, and fees, check with the Information Office of the MTS at 619-233-3004 or check the Web site at www.sdcommute.com. You can also visit the **Transit Store** downtown (619-234-1060; 102 Broadway, San Diego, CA 92101) to purchase bus and trolley tokens, Day Tripper passes, and monthly passes for MTS buses, the trolley, and the Coaster. Note that public transportation runs on an abbreviated schedule on holidays, and the Coaster doesn't run at all on Sundays and major holidays.

City Buses

The MTS comprises several bus lines throughout the city proper, and routes are extensive. One-way fares are $2.25; seniors and disabled guests ride for a flat rate of $1, and there are monthly passes available. For specific information on routes and transfers, access the Web site at www.sdcommute.com.

Beyond the city limits, the North County Transit District operates a bus system called the Breeze, which serves north county coastal communities such as Del Mar, Carlsbad, and Oceanside, and northern inland communities such as Escondido, Vista, and Ramona. These buses will take you beyond the county limits as well, to San Clemente, Camp Pendleton, and Orange County. To view Breeze routes, go to the Web site at www.gonctd.com/breeze/breezes.html. Single-ride passes cost $2, or an all-day pass is available for $4. Seniors ride for $1, or $2 for an all-day pass. Children younger than five years old are free. Tickets can be purchased at NCTD bus pass outlets throughout the north county or by credit card over the phone at 760-966-6500.

Coaster

Once inside the county lines, you can take the commuter train, called the Coaster, a clean and enjoyable way to avoid the traffic that runs along the coast; it travels from Oceanside to downtown. Ticket costs range from $2 to $5.50 for one-way tickets and can be purchased at any Coaster station using easy to use automated machines. Tickets *cannot* be purchased on the train. Call 1-800-262-7837 for specific information on routes and fares. Note that the Coaster does not run on Sundays or major holidays.

As of December 2007, the NCTD will also have a commuter rail system in place called the Sprinter, starting with 22 miles running along the Highway 78 corridor from Escondido to Oceanside. For more information, call 760-599-8332.

Trolley

The bright red San Diego Trolley system has three easy-to-follow routes that cover downtown and parts of the east county. Please refer to the map on page 37 for specific routes. You can take your bike along with you on the trolley and load it at all trolley stops. Fares are based on distance, and range from $2.55 to $6. Seniors and disabled riders pay a flat $2 fee. These tickets, which can be purchased at any trolley station, are good for two hours from the time of purchase. You can also buy day passes for $5. Note that ticket machines at some stations require exact change.

Although the trolley doesn't extend beyond the border, you can take a 40-minute ride from downtown San Diego to the San Ysidro Transit Center, where you can either walk

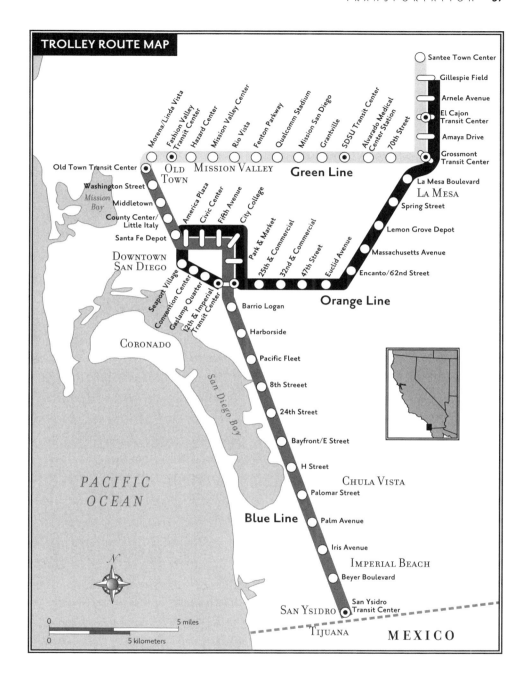

TROLLEY ROUTE MAP

through the U.S.–Mexico checkpoint to catch a Mexican cab (the area you'll want to see is more than a mile away, and the walk isn't pleasant) or catch a bus across. **Mexicoach** (619-428-9517) runs several buses throughout the day.

The San Diego Trolley in front of the Convention Center downtown.

Shuttles as an Alternative to Taxis

Shuttles from the airport are an excellent alternative to expensive taxis, especially for longer distances. **Cloud 9 Shuttle** (858-505-4900 or 800-974-8885) can be prescheduled to pick up guests at the airport or to bring them back; they are also available to charter. They have many vehicle options, from full-size motor coaches to comfortable sedans and limousines. Be sure to specify your preference when making reservations. This service is not only convenient—reliable and professional sedan and limo drivers, for example, will meet you at baggage claims and help you and your luggage to their vehicles—but it can also be cost-effective. A ride from Lindbergh Field to Carlsbad, for example, is less expensive in a Cloud 9 private sedan (about $75) than it is in a taxi (about $100), and generally much more comfortable.

You can also catch the **Mexicoach** (619-428-9517) shuttle from San Diego into Mexico; the buses run between the Border Station Parking Lot and the San Ysidro trolley station to both Tijuana and Rosarito approximately every 30 minutes, starting at 8 AM and continuing until 9 PM.

Taxis

Although you will of course find waiting taxis at the airport (on Transportation Plaza, across from Terminals 1 and 2 and the Commuter Terminal), near the cruise ship terminal when ships are in port, and outside the Greyhouse Bus Terminal, San Diego isn't a taxi-friendly city. Even in downtown it is difficult to hail a cab; better to call ahead for one or walk to the nearest large hotel, where you'll generally find several waiting. The average fare for one to four people is $2.20 per mile, plus an initial charge of $1.80. From the airport, the initial charge is $2.20, with a $2.30 per mile charge.

Taxis are easier to find in Mexico, especially waiting near the border and throughout the tourist areas of downtown and Zona Rio. Mexican cabbies will expect you to negotiate a price before you set off; expect $5 from the border crossing to downtown and another $2 from downtown to Zona Rio (more if you have more than two people in your party). Tips are included in this fare. Many taxi drivers speak excellent English and can be contracted for an hour or for the day to serve as tour guides. On hot days you'll want to verify that your intended cab has air conditioning—and make sure that the promised "air conditioning" isn't just an open window.

Tours and Organized Sightseeing

There are a number of good sightseeing tours that operate throughout San Diego. Among the most comprehensive is **City Sightseeing San Diego** (619-231-3040), which sells a ticket that is good for two days of on—off privileges aboard a narrated red double-decker tour bus. Tours depart from the cruise ship terminal and meander throughout downtown, including the Gaslamp Quarter, Balboa Park, and Petco Park, as well as Old Town State Historic Park and the Ferry Landing in Coronado. The ticket price also includes a pass for the

A bus ride out of the Mexicoach station in downtown Tijuana is the easiest way to cross back over into the United States.

ferry ride over to the island of Coronado. The price for the two-day pass is $31 for adults and $21 for children. This is an excellent option if you arrive without a vehicle or if you only have a few days to explore.

The **Old Town Trolley Tours** (619-298-8687) offers a similar on–off tour that loops throughout 10 stops around the city. You can catch the orange and green trolleys at any of the stops (including the cruise ship terminal) and ride all day, visiting Coronado, Old Town, Balboa Park, and the Gaslamp Quarter downtown. Other entertaining tour options offered by this company include a 90-minute amphibious SEAL Tour onboard a "hydra terra" vehicle that runs on city streets and then heads straight into the water for a tour of the bay.

I highly recommend taking a tour into Tijuana, especially for your first visit. Reliable operators can negotiate the roads, keep you sequestered in the best parts of town, and provide excellent suggestions for shopping and meals. Among the best are **Five Star Tours** (619-232-5049) and **Sundance Stage Lines** (619-525-1570).

CROSSING THE BORDER

Border crossings from San Diego into Tijuana (via either San Ysidro or Otay Mesa) can be nightmarish in the post–9/11 world. Note that it is much faster to get *into* Mexico than it is to get *out* of Mexico, but you are sure to encounter delays in both directions. Expect waits of up to several hours coming back to the United States on the weekends. San Ysidro is the main crossing, and is accessible from two major freeways (I-5 and I-805); truckers prefer Otay Mesa, and many people swear it is faster, but it isn't as convenient from San Diego. For up-to-date information on crossing times, call the automated border wait time report at San Ysidro (619-690-8999) or at Otay Mesa (619-671-8999).

In the past, it was a legal requirement that if one parent was traveling with a minor child, she or he must have written, notarized permission by the other parent to cross the border with the child. You may not be asked to provide such documentation, but to save yourself a headache, it is a good idea to have it on hand. In addition, minors should have some sort of identification. If children do not have passports, travel with a copy of their birth certificates. Most of the time these precautions will be unnecessary.

Most rental car agencies do not allow their cars to be driven across the border (although **Bob Baker Ford** in Mission Valley is an exception; 619-297-3106; 730 Camino del Rio North, San Diego, CA 92108, with the requirement that Mexican insurance be purchased). Better to leave the car behind: There are parking lots immediately across from the border in San Ysidro; the **Border Station Parking Lot** (619-428-1422) is monitored 24 hours a day, has an information kiosk, and is the on-loading point for the **Mexicoach** shuttles (see page 38). Or you can just walk a quarter mile to the border and cross, then catch a taxi on the other side (it is about a mile from the border crossing to the main section of town; walking from the border to downtown is not a good option). When aiming for the parking lots, be sure to look for the freeway signs that say "Last U.S. Parking" or you will inadvertently end up at the border with no place to turn around. Walking into Mexico is painless and fast; you'll pass through a series of metal turnstiles, and most of the time no one will check your ID. Look for the signs that will direct you to waiting taxis, which will be parked no more than 100 yards from the final turnstile.

I don't recommend that you try to walk over the border *back* into the United States, however. Several thousand Mexican citizens line up daily to make the crossing, and a good por-

Bargain Passes for Local Attractions

The Southern California City Pass allows visitors to buy a customized bundle of attraction passes good for six days' worth of admission (valid if used within 14 days) that includes attractions in San Diego (San Diego Zoo, San Diego Wild Animal Park, and Sea World) as well as Anaheim (Disneyland, California Adventure, and Universal Studios). Currently the passes sell for $235—what would otherwise cost $329. If you plan to visit most of these attractions, this is liable to be a big saver for you. You can purchase tickets online at www.citypass.com/city/socal.html.

Starting at $55 a day, the Go San Diego Card offers one unlimited admission for one to seven days to 45 attractions in town, including Legoland, the San Diego Zoo, a whale watching tour, a Petco Park tour, and admission to the Birch Aquarium. Purchase your Go Cards online at www.gosandiego.com.

And if you are an animal lover, you might want to consider the Three-for-One Pass. For $89 for adults and $63 for children, you'll receive unlimited admission to the San Diego Zoo, the San Diego Wild Animal Park, and Sea World over the course of five days. Tickets can be purchased at any of the participating parks.

tion of the wait time is outside on a sidewalk that runs alongside the idling cars trying to cross; you'll wait for indeterminate periods and suck in a lot of exhaust fumes this way. Better to catch a **Mexicoach Bus** from downtown Tijuana (664-685-1470; 1025 Av. Revolucíon, Tijuana, BC, Mexico 22000), which uses designated tour bus lanes that make crossing a little faster.

If you must drive on your own, and you plan to do so often over the course of several years, an alternative that will shave off as much as a few hours of time crossing the border is the SENTRI PortPass, which allows preapproved applicants to use a designated border-crossing lane, typically significantly less crowded both going into Mexico and coming out. Applicants must undergo a criminal screening and fingerprinting and provide appropriate paperwork in the form of drivers' licenses, passports, and birth certificates. Applications can be completed online at www.cbp.gov for a nonrefundable $49; fees are $80 per person (or $160 for families) for a five-year pass. For detailed application information, visit the U.S. Customs and Borders Protection Web site at www.cbp.gov.

If you do drive over the border, make sure you purchase Mexican insurance. There are a number of agencies at the San Ysidro border crossing that sell insurance for the day, including **Baja Bound Insurance Services** (619-702-4292; 888-552-2252; 750 11th Ave., Ste. 101, San Diego, CA 92101), **Baja Mex** (619-428-1616; 4575 Camino de la Plaza, San Ysidro, CA 92173), and **Instant Mexico Auto Insurance** (619-428-4714; 800-345-4701; 223 Via de San Ysidro, San Ysidro, CA 92173). Insurance can be prearranged and prepurchased via phone and fax. It will cost about $20 for liability and vehicle coverage for a car valued at $20,000, and it is well worth the investment. Even if your U.S. automobile insurance promises to cover you in foreign countries, the Mexican authorities will not recognize the coverage. If you are unfortunate enough to get into an accident while in Tijuana and you cannot pay in cash for the damages to the other cars, you will be taken to jail and held until someone can procure the funds for you. Needless to say, a Mexican jail is not where you want to be.

WHAT TO CARRY—AND *NOT* CARRY—INTO MEXICO

Make sure to carry a photo ID with you into Mexico, both for identification purposes once in Tijuana and also so that you can cross back over to the United States. If you are a U.S. citizen, through 2007 you do not need a passport going in either direction if you enter by land. If you arrive by air or ship, however, you are now required to have a valid passport. And starting in 2008, you must have a valid passport to reenter the United States from Tijuana by land as well, even if you visit only for a few hours.

If you are not a U.S. citizen, be sure to bring your passport and any other papers your individual country requires. (Check with the Mexican consulate at 619-231-8414 before you go to make sure you know the requirements for citizens of your country.) This seems to go without saying, but do not cross the border in either direction with guns, illegal drugs, or agricultural products.

Tourists are allowed to bring in only $50 worth of duty-free goods into Mexico if they arrive by bus, car, or walk over on foot. Those arriving by plane or cruise ship may bring $300 worth of goods into the country without being taxed. Note that laptop computers may be subject to duties.

PICKING A HOME BASE IN SAN DIEGO

Because of the enormity of San Diego County and its well-documented traffic, you'll want to pick your home base carefully, according to your own interests (beach vs. city, for example) and then plan day trips farther out. The closer your lodging is to what you plan to do while in town, the less time you'll spend stuck in your vehicle. If you want to split your time between the attractions downtown (e.g., the Gaslamp Quarter, Balboa Park, the Zoo) and activities that are farther afield in north county (e.g., the Wild Animal Park, Legoland, Encinitas surfing beaches), consider a midway point like La Jolla or Del Mar. If this isn't your first visit to San Diego and you're eager to broaden your horizons, or if you want a quieter, less congested experience, consider north county options in Encinitas and Carlsbad.

WHEN TO VISIT

Thanks to the mild temperatures and low precipitation, San Diego and Tijuana are year-round destinations. You can beat the heat and humidity that prevails throughout most of the rest of the United States if you visit during the summer, and you can escape the cold by coming here in winter—although ocean temperatures make it too chilly to swim without a wetsuit and on shore it can get nippy enough to require a light jacket. Spring is glorious—the normally olive-drab hills turn bright green after the winter rains and the flowers explode into color. One of the best times to visit is autumn, when the rates are lower, crowds have thinned, and the ocean water is often warmer in early October than it is in early June. In addition, the brown haze that blankets the region in the hotter months burns off, and vistas extend from the oceans to the mountains. (See chapter 9 for a guide to seasonal temperatures.)

LODGING NOTES

Rates

High-season rates generally apply in San Diego during the summer months, starting on Memorial Day weekend and continuing through the end of September. Higher rates will also apply during the holiday season running from Thanksgiving week through the first of the year and during spring break.

Minimum Stay

During high season, and at some smaller establishments all year long, it isn't unusual for hotels to insist on a minimum stay of two or even three nights for advance bookings. However, if you reserve accommodations at the last minute (which I do not recommend, because this is a recipe for disappointment), you can often bypass these requirements.

Deposit/Cancellation

You'll be expected to provide one night's security deposit, which may be charged to your account at the time of your booking or may be charged the day you are due to arrive. Most hotels will allow cancellations and rescheduling up to 72 hours in advance without penalties, but expect as much as a full night's charge if you cancel within 24 hours. Make sure you understand the hotel policies *before* you book.

Winter weather is generally mild throughout the county; here kids play on Carlsbad State Beach in December.

NEIGHBORS ALL AROUND

One of the real joys of living in or visiting San Diego is the variety of experiences available. We have oceans, mountains, deserts, and a foreign country all within an hour's drive. If you are interested in expanding your trip beyond San Diego County and Tijuana, there are some excellent options just beyond the county lines.

To the South

Rosarito Beach, Mexico

Rosarito Beach is a scenic party town about 20 miles south of Tijuana, boasting five miles of sandy shoreline, dozens of restaurants serving inexpensive and delicious Mexican seafood, and bars aplenty. In recent years it has become quite popular with college students on spring break and young people year-round as a nightlife haven. The moderately priced hotels, long stretches of beach, and abundant shopping also make Rosarito a laid-back choice for those who just want to enjoy a relatively inexpensive holiday. But don't come expecting a chi-chi resort area like Cabo or Cancun. Poverty is a tragic fact in Baja, and you're likely to be accosted by children offering to "guard" your car for a small sum, and persistent beachside peddlers. In addition, even newer establishments have a well-worn look. Nevertheless, Rosarito is where most native San Diegans go when they want a taste of Mexico.

From Tijuana, take the toll road (Mexico 1-D, which will cost about $2.50) and follow the signs to *Ensenada Cuota* (Ensenada Scenic Route) or take the Old Highway (Mexico 1) and follow the signs to *Ensenada Libre*. Both roads eventually converge onto Rosarito's main street, Boulevard Benito Juárez. If you're leaving your car north of the border, catch the **Mexicoach Rosarito Beach Express** (619-428-9517), which runs from the Border Station Parking Lot in San Ysidro every two hours (with a stop first at the Tijuana Tourist Terminal).

Eclectic shopping is available in small stores along the Boulevard Benito Juárez, as well as the large outdoor market **El Mercado de Artesianas,** which features more than 100 vendors selling hand-woven blankets, silver jewelry, leather goods, and any number of Mexican trinkets. Adventurous visitors can ride horseback on the beach via a number of concessionaires or rent a large variety of motorized water toys.

Just three miles south of Rosarito (in Popotla) is **Foxploration** (661-614-9444 or 866-369-2252; Km. 32.5 on Mexico Hwy. 1D), a movie studio complex built by Twentieth Century Fox back in 1996 when it filmed portions of the movie *Titanic* here. Guests can see the enormous saltwater tank that was constructed to hold a scale model of the ship during filming, as well as walk through recreated sets from the movie. Other blockbusters that were filmed at least in part here include *Pearl Harbor*, *The Deep Blue Sea*, and *Master and Commander: The Far Side of the World*. Admission is $12 for adults and $9 for children 3–11. Note that as of this writing, the studio is closed for tours on Mondays and Tuesdays.

In town, lodging options include the **Rosarito Beach Hotel** (800-343-8582; Blvd. Benito Juárez 31, Rosarito, BC, Mexico 22710), an elegant historic property that dates to 1926 with an expansive lobby and many oceanfront rooms that was a one-time favorite with Hollywood legends like Lana Turner and Orson Wells; and the hip and inexpensive **Hotel Festival Plaza** (661-612-2950; Blvd. Benito Juárez 1207, Rosarito, BC, Mexico 22710), a one-stop entertainment mecca that offers up onsite restaurants, dance clubs, a tequila museum (where of course the golden elixir is available for drinking as well), and a Ferris wheel.

To the North

Anaheim: Mickey's Hometown

Ninety miles north of San Diego, Anaheim is the town that Mickey Mouse built. Actually, Anaheim was home to thriving citrus groves before Walt Disney came along, but it was **Disneyland** (714-781-4400; 1313 Harbor Blvd., Anaheim, CA 92802) that put the city on the tourist map. Today more than 15 million people visit Anaheim annually, and more than 13 million of them come to Disneyland. Guests to the "Happiest Place on Earth" enter a magical theme park that offers something for every member of the family. Young children will fly through Neverland in a pirate ship with Peter Pan, float through a wonderland of singing international dolls in "It's a Small World," and battle space aliens in "Buzz Lightyear's Astro Blasters." Thrill-seekers will enjoy rollercoasters that shoot them to the stars on "Space Mountain," fly through abandoned gold mines on a runaway train on "Thunder Mountain," and dodge the abominable snow man on the "Matterhorn." Even if you aren't a big fan of amusement park rides, Disneyland is an enchanting place to visit anyhow. Main Street, a scaled-down version of an idyllic American city, offers rosy-hued nostalgia, impeccably manicured gardens, and plenty of themed shopping. Throughout the day enjoy extravagant parades, and on weekend nights and throughout the summer, don't miss the spectacular fireworks displays. For Christmas, Disney really puts on the glitz with tens of thousands of glittering decorations and a special holiday parade.

Weekends and holidays at the park can be brutally crowded; come early to avoid the worst of the congestion. And note that gates generally open as much as a half hour earlier than advertised. Once the crowds thicken, be sure to take advantage of FastPass tickets, which allow guests to bypass the standby lines. Find the FastPass machines near the front of designated rides, and insert your park ticket. You'll be issued a timed pass that allows you to come back during a given 60-minute window, at which point you present the pass and get into a significantly shorter line than you would otherwise. You can get additional FastPass tickets as soon as the designated time period of the previous ones expire.

To help draw off the crowds from the main park, Disney built **California Adventure** (714-781-4400; 1313 S. Harbor Blvd., Anaheim, CA 92802) in 2001, a Golden State-themed amusement park that features a miniaturized San Francisco cityscape, a Hollywood-themed street, Napa-esque vineyards, a beachfront-style boardwalk with carnival games, and gushing rapids that circle a mountain carved into the likeness of a growling grizzly. This park tends to be much less congested, not only because of lighter crowds but because the more modern park was built with wider walking avenues and the rides were designed to accommodate more people at one time. Inside you'll find "California Screaming," the most thrilling rollercoaster you're likely to find at any Disney property, with a bulletlike takeoff and an upside-down loop. "Tower of Terror" comes in a close second for thrills, with an "elevator" that randomly plunges 13 stories. You'll also be able to defy gravity in elevated swings on the "Orange Zinger"; glide through the air in a flying dirigible called the "Golden Zephyr"; and float above some of the most beautiful places in California in the breathtaking "Soarin' over California," which combines a giant movie screen with a gently swaying gondola ride.

Admission for either park is $63 for guests 10 and older and $53 for guests three to nine (two and under are free); for a little more ($83 for 10 and older and $73 for guests three to nine) you can purchase a Park Hopper Pass that allows you to go to both parks on the same day. There are also multiple-day passes that offer significant savings and specially priced packages for Southern California residents. Buy these at either park or online at www.disneyland.disney.go.com. Both parks are open every day of the year.

Kid-pleasing lodging options located within **Downtown Disney**—a shopping and restaurant promenade that connects the Disney properties—include the expensive **Disneyland Hotel** (714-956-6425; 1150 Magic Way, Anaheim, CA 92802), which boasts glow-in-the-dark pixie-dusted wallpaper and onsite character dining at **Goofy's Kitchen** (714-781-3463); and the even more expensive **Grand Californian** (714-956-6425; 1600 S. Disneyland Dr., Anaheim, CA 92802), a luxurious arts-and-crafts inspired Disney hotel with a massive lobby and family-friendly guest rooms with bunk beds.

Temecula: Wine Country

The Temecula wine country—just northeast of the San Diego County line in Riverside—has grown up in the past decade, and now world-class wines are being produced at many of the valley wineries. The rolling hills, granitic soils, and 1500-foot elevation provide ideal conditions for growing grapes, and vintners are finally taking advantage of this bounty.

Unfortunately, zoning laws have allowed the suburbs (and the concomitant strip malls and big box stores) to encroach on the rural feel of the valley, but the winery zone still has rolling vineyards and magnificent views of the mountains. Temecula is a 60-mile drive from downtown San Diego; most of the wineries are situated on a strip of Rancho California Road, about 6 miles east of the I-15,

Vintner Don Reha of Thornton Winery in Temecula displays recently bottled champagne.

and a handful of others are nearby on the De Portola Road loop. Although the one-lane highway gets congested on weekends, the wineries, restaurants, and resorts are still largely underappreciated by San Diegans.

There are more than 20 wineries, most of which have daily tastings (usually beginning at 10 AM and running until 4 or 5 PM), including **South Coast Winery** (951-587-9463; 34843 Rancho California Rd., Temecula, CA 92591), an elegant new property whose ruby-colored Cabernet Rosé is worth the trip to the tasting room; **Thornton Winery** (951-699-0099; 32575 Rancho California Rd., Temecula, CA 92591), an old-timer in the Valley and one of the most respected wine destinations, thanks to vintner Don Reha, who specializes in big reds and champagnes; and **Wilson Creek Winery** (951-699-9463; 35960 Rancho California Rd., Temecula, CA 92591), a family-owned facility that doesn't take itself too seriously. Owner/manager Bill Wilson jokes, "We will release no wine before its time. But when you're out of wine, it's time." Wilson Creek specializes in almond champagne and offers a respectable chocolate port.

Accommodations include the **South Coast Winery Resort and Spa** (951-587-9463; 34843 Rancho California Rd., Temecula, CA 92591), a luxurious collection of 76 private villas designed to feel like individual vacation homes; and the less pricy, slightly time-worn **Temecula Creek Inn** (800-698-9295; 44501 Rainbow Canyon Rd., Temecula, CA 92592), south of the wine country and situated on its own golf course. The finest restaurant choice in the area is **Café Champagne** (951-699-0099; 32575 Rancho California Rd., Temecula, CA 92591); don't miss superstar chef Will Greenwood's signature crab cakes.

To the East

Anza-Borrego Desert

The 600,000 acres of rolling hills and desert of the Anza-Borrego Desert State Park team with life, if you just spend a few hours looking for it. In addition to rattlesnakes, scorpions, and jackrabbits, more than 268 species of birds have been recorded in this park. In addition, the endangered Peninsular bighorn sheep calls Anza-Borrego home.

In spring (which can come as early as February), the area transforms with wildflowers that include primrose, verbena, purple nightshade, and apricot mallow. The extensiveness of the wildflowers varies widely from year to year, depending on the amount of rainfall and the ferocity of the winds. Check the wildflower hotline beforehand to ensure that you come during peak blooms and to get tips on where to find the best displays (760-767-4684 or www.anzaborrego.statepark.org).

All year long hikers will find more than 100 miles of trails winding through the lowlands, canyons, and rock formations. Be sure to stay on the paths, to preserve the ecological balance of the park and for your own safety. And come prepared—the desert is an unforgiving environment, with scorching temperatures in summer and canyons subject to flashfloods year-round. Carry plenty of water and always check weather forecasts before you head out.

If it's peace and quiet you're looking for, **Ocotillo Wells** in the eastern end of the park is *not* the place for you: This 80,000-acre recreational area is set aside for dune buggies, motorcycles, and other noisy desert toys. The interesting rock formations and the rolling dunes make for exciting and challenging off-roading.

You can pitch a tent and camp anywhere in the park without a campsite (although check with the rangers about building fires in such open areas). There is probably no better place in Southern California to observe the night sky, and during meteor showers (especially in August) you're bound to see a lot of amateur astronomers setting up camp in the hills. Cushier accommodations include the moderately priced **Palm Canyon Resort** (760-767-5341; 221 Palm Canyon Dr., Borrego Springs, CA 92004), a large property with a hotel and an RV park; and the relatively expensive **Palms at Indian Head** (760-767-7788 or 800-519-2624; 2220 Hoberg Rd., Borrego Springs, CA 92004), a smaller romantic property that is decorated with local art and southwestern furnishings.

To the West

Santa Catalina Island

A rocky, hilly island northwest of San Diego, Santa Catalina belongs to the Channel Islands chain off the coast of Long Beach. Catalina's crescent-shaped harbor has startlingly clear blue water and is perennially studded with sailboats and yachts (and sometimes cruise ships). The island has long been a favorite getaway for well-heeled Southern Californians,

A highlight of Wrigley's vision of Catalina is the round art deco casino, now the centerpiece of the Avalon harbor.

and is popular with the Hollywood glitterati (who can opt to helicopter in to save time)—and this is all thanks to a chewing gum magnate.

In 1919, William Wrigley Jr. (also one-time owner of the Chicago Cubs) purchased the island and developed it into a resort destination. Wrigley liked the serenity and pristine beauty of the place so much that he built himself a mansion in the hills, and brought the Cubs to the island for spring training for nearly 30 years. In 1975, Wrigley's heir turned over 88 percent of the island to the Catalina Island Conservancy, which now acts as steward to the wilderness reserve and runs most of the island's concessions.

To get here, take the **Catalina Express** (310-519-1212; 877-358-6363; 34675 Golden Lantern, Dana Point, CA 92629), departing from Dana Point, Long Beach, and San Pedro (Dana Point is the closest departure point from San Diego). Costs for a roundtrip ticket are $57 for adults and $44 for children, and the trip takes approximately one hour. Be prepared for a rough ride; windy conditions can make for stomach-churning swells. If you aren't prone to seasickness, the trip over can be half the fun; expect to see schools of dolphins swimming alongside the boat, especially as it nears the Catalina harbor.

Several tours are available in the city of Avalon (with concession kiosks near the offload-ing point in the harbor), including a plethora of outdoor activities, especially water sports. Exceptionally clear water and good visibility make for some of the best snorkeling and div-ing in Southern California. There are beautiful reefs nearby and some interesting ship wrecks to explore as well. You can also book kayaking trips, off-road jeep ecotours, para-sailing, glass-bottom boat tours, submarine rides, rafting, and sailing tours. Or if you pre-fer to go it alone, you can explore the harbor aboard small rented sail and paddle boats. You can also book land tours into the reserve, where you're likely to see wild buffalo (remnants of an old Hollywood western; after shooting was complete, the producers left the animals to fend for themselves). To preserve the ecosystem and to cut down on road congestion, even locals have to wait at least 10 years to obtain the right to drive a car on the island, so plan to see Catalina by foot or aboard a tour bus. You can also rent bikes and golf carts by the hour.

Lodging options include the charming boutique **Avalon Hotel** (310-510-7070; 124 Whittley Ave., Avalon, CA 90704), which is steps from the waterfront restaurants and shopping; and the **Zane Grey Pueblo Hotel** (310-510-0966; 199 Chimes Tower Rd., Avalon, CA 90704), luxurious accommodations housed in the Western writer's former home, perched high on a hill and overlooking the tranquil Avalon harbor.

Sunrise in the Harbor District downtown.

3

Old Town, Downtown, and Uptown

The Past and the Future in Dynamic Contrast

Downtown is the heart of San Diego, and includes the newly gentrified and restaurant-rich Gaslamp Quarter—16 blocks of 19th- and early 20th-century Victorian architecture restored to maintain the original character of the historic buildings—as well as the new Petco Park baseball stadium in the up and coming East Village; a wildly successful convention center on the water; stunning views and fresh seafood restaurants on the harbor; and charming Little Italy, home to new mid-rise condominiums, eclectic boutiques, and quaint bistros.

Old Town, just north of the city center, is where San Diego began. Visitors can step back in time to glimpse a charming mixture of native Kumeyaay influences, Spanish colonialism, and cowboy chic at the restaurants, shops, and museums of the Old Town State Park, and then do some serious shopping in the specialty stores of the Bazaar del Mundo and the new Plaza del Posado. Uptown, which comprises Hillcrest and tony Mission Hills, along with funky North Park and the emerging Adams Avenue district, offers kitschy shopping, plenty of comforting diners, upscale ethnic eateries, and alternative entertainment for the gay community. These cozy neighborhoods are friendly, accessible, and busy every night of the week.

LODGING

The revitalized downtown offers a number of beautifully restored historic properties and new, stylish boutique hotels that provide an intimate experience for travelers looking for something a little different. But downtown also has dozens of medium-rise hotels (the height restriction is 500 feet), many of which are off-shoots of huge national chains. In general, these large properties have predictable amenities and generic designs—and for these reasons, I've focused instead on independent properties that a visitor or newcomer to San Diego might not find on her or his own.

But with that said, there *are* several familiar franchises that have accommodations that are unique to San Diego. One of the nicest is the **Omni San Diego** (619-231-6664; 675 L St., San Diego, CA 92101), with high-rise views of the harbor, the Convention Center, and access right into Petco Park. The hotel is next door to the San Diego Padres' new home field, and there's a sky bridge that will take guests directly into the park on a game day. Scattered through-

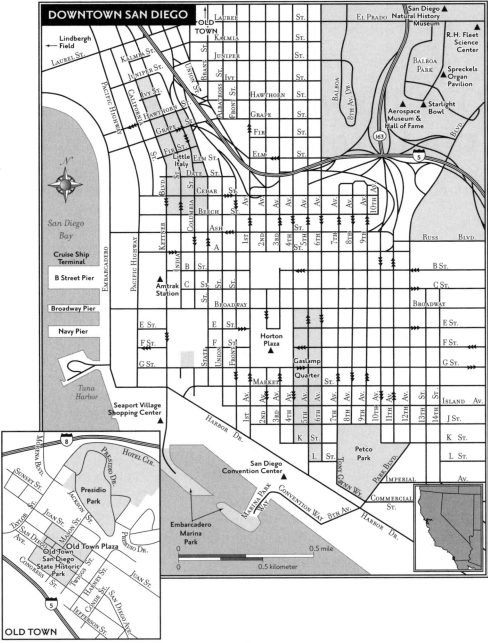

out the property are baseball artifacts such as Joe DiMaggio's spikes, worn during his 56-game hitting streak in 1941 and a rare 1850 "lemon peel" baseball, one of the first baseballs ever made.

Nearby Old Town and Uptown offer fewer accommodations in general, and they tend to be smaller, eclectic properties. Prices are generally high near the trendy Gaslamp Quarter, and therefore both Old Town and Uptown are better choices for budget travelers—but beware that the latter locations aren't as conveniently located for downtown nightlife and dining.

DOWNTOWN
THE BRISTOL

Manager: Scott D. Woods
800-662-4477; fax 619-232-0118
www.thebristolsandiego.com
1055 First Ave., San Diego, CA 92101
Price: Moderate
Credit Cards: AE, D, MC, V
Handicap Access: 2 full

The designer for the Bristol picked out the most vibrant crayons from the box to dress up the interior of this modest, modern hotel in downtown San Diego. Step into the spare lobby and you'll see oversized bright blue arm chairs and tomato-red ottomans, offset by a shiny baby grand piano and an immaculate granite floor that looks to be cut from one solid piece of stone. The playful decorations include an impressive collection of pop art from the 1960s, with pieces by Peter Max, Andy Warhol, Guy Buffet, and Roy Lichtenstein. Lines are clean and sleek, and the overall vibe is welcoming. This hotel is long on style and easy on the wallet; although prices fluctuate by season and according to room availability, given the high-style, boutique atmosphere, and the downtown location, this is an exceptional value.

HORTON GRAND HOTEL

Manager: Paula Ellis
619-544-1886; fax 619-544-0058
www.hortongrand.com
311 Island Ave, San Diego, CA 92101
Price: Expensive
Credit Cards: AE, MC, V
Handicap access: 4 partial

In the early 1980s, when the gentrification of the Gaslamp Quarter kicked off with the construction of the Horton Plaza shopping mall, two historic buildings that were in the way—the Horton Grand Hotel and Kable Saddlery—faced the wrecking ball. Enterprising preservationists bought each building for $1 and moved them board by board

The Horton Grand Hotel anticipated the remarkable revitalization of the Gaslamp Quarter, and now sits on a prime location, close to the Convention Center.

(and brick by brick) to the new, now premium location off Fourth Avenue, combining them into a gingerbread-trimmed Victorian beauty that's within easy walking distance of the best restaurants and bars downtown has to offer, and just blocks from the Convention Center. Step into the airy glass atrium and enjoy white-washed antiques and walls of historic photographs of both the original hotel and the surrounding neighborhood. You can even admire the life-size wooden horse that used to be displayed in front of Kable Saddlery. Guest rooms are individually decorated in cheerful period fabrics; count on period reproductions, a working gas fireplace in each room, and small bathrooms with classic water closets. (Look for the television hidden behind the mirror over the fireplace—many guests can't find it!) The onsite restaurant **Ida Bailey's** (619-544-1886 ext. 500) features over-the-top Victoriana and classic American food. Afternoon high tea is served at the hotel, and on the weekends jazz musicians perform in the **Palace Bar**. Next door is the long-running *Triple Espresso*, a three-man comedy performed Wednesday through Sunday at the **Horton Grand Theater** (619-234-9583). Parking is off-site valet.

HOTEL SOLAMAR

Manager: Peggy Trott
877-230-0300; fax 619-531-8742
www.hotelsolamar.com
435 Sixth Ave., San Diego, CA 92101
Price: Expensive
Credit Cards: AE, D, MC, V
Handicap Access: 12 full

A mid-sized hotel that is part of the eclectic Kimpton chain, the Hotel Solamar is near both the hot Gaslamp Quarter and the artsy East Village (home of Petco Park) in downtown San Diego. This stylish lodging option offers 235 rooms, each with ergonomic desks and work chairs, free WiFi, complimentary yoga accessories, and access to the Yoga channel via flatscreen TVs. Rooms are decorated with bold, simple patterns in deep chocolate browns and light aqua blues, with oversized headboards, funky glass lamps, and modern basin sinks in the bath-

If you fancy the furnishings in the eclectic Hotel Solamar downtown, you can buy them, courtesy of the Kimpton chain's retail catalog.

rooms. Guests are treated to zany bathrobes in zebra and leopard prints, as well as fuzzy socks to purchase if your tootsies get cold in the middle of the night. Public rooms are accented with rich wood tones and piles of silk and beaded pillows. The intimate fireplace lounge has a complimentary wine and beer reception every evening. Throughout you'll find subtle nods to the San Diego beach scene, with framed shells as artwork, tropical ceiling fans, and even a cabana in the lobby. At the water's edge of a fourth-floor rooftop pool you'll find the trendy **Jbar Lounge** (619-531-8744), accented with three fire pits and mood lighting in the evenings; the bar itself is a palm-frond affair that looks like it could have been flown in straight from Cabo San Lucas. Although the lounge packs in a young and stylish crowd of locals and visitors on the weekends, it closes down at midnight, which means guests with rooms overlooking the bar won't have to contend with noise all night long—and guests will find in general that this hotel is well-insulated and quiet, which is unusual for a downtown location. Downstairs is the surprising **JSix** restaurant (see page 77), a current favorite with locals who aren't even staying at the hotel. This is a young, fresh hotel with energetic, friendly staff who enjoy their jobs and whose enthusiasm for the property is contagious.

KEATING HOTEL

Manager: Sandra Vivas
619-814-5700; fax 619-814-5750
www.thekeating.com
432 F St., San Diego, CA 92101
Price: Very expensive
Credit Cards: AE, D, MC, V
Handicap Access: 2 full

This chic boutique hotel opened in the Gaslamp Quarter in late 2006, and its incomparable design and style are a new watermark for hip elegance in downtown.

La Pensione Hotel in Little Italy is within walking distance of fine dining and charming cafés.

The delicious cherry red lobby, with red walls, red floors, and a red ceiling, glows like a piece of jewelry. The clean lines and upscale amenities are reminiscent of what you'll find in Milan and Rome, and for good reason—the hotel was the brainchild of famed Italian design firm Pininfarina, responsible for designing the Maserati and Ferrari lines. The 35 stanzas—as suites are called—are housed in the Keating Building, an 1890s Victorian whose historic façade has been painstakingly restored. Each guest accommodation has exposed brick walls, elevated ceilings, painted concrete floors, the latest in audio equipment, plasma TVs that carry 150 channels, and gleaming espresso machines. Beds are piled thickly with six layers of goose-down feather coverings and duvets and are dressed with luxurious Frette linens. The stainless steel vanities, large rain-shower fixtures in the baths, and frosted glass panels are sleek and modern—although not as private as Americans might expect (there are no solid walls to separate the bathing area from the sleeping area). If noise bothers you, you might want to request a room that doesn't face the busy corner of Fifth and F Streets, which is usually rowdy until dawn. But don't let these caveats dissuade you: This is among the very finest independent lodging options in the Gaslamp, and for those who can afford it, well worth the investment.

LA PENSIONE HOTEL
Manager: Mark Hamel
619-236 8000; fax 619-236-8088
www.lapensionehotel.com
606 West Date St., San Diego, CA 92101
Price: Moderate
Credit Cards: AE, D, MC, V
Handicap Access: 1 full (with plans to convert more in the near future)

Tucked into an unpretentious corner of the revitalized and friendly neighborhood of Little Italy, just beyond the heart of downtown San Diego, La Pensione is a small property within steps of fine restaurants, coffee bars, and pubs, and amid some of the nicest new condo homes in San Diego. The unassuming lobby is staffed by helpful, friendly folks. The rooms themselves—also tiny—are comfortable and airily decorated, and each has its own refrigerator. You'll also find underground parking—a bonus in a neighborhood where metered spots are the norm. For a little more, spring for a room with an evening view of the downtown skyline. The location provides easy access to the city and a slightly less frenetic ambiance, and your money will stretch much further.

U. S. GRANT HOTEL

Manager: Victor Barothy-Langer
619-232-3121; fax 619-232-3626
www.usgrant.net
326 Broadway, San Diego, CA 92101
Prices: Very expensive
Credit Cards: AE, D, DC, MC, V
Handicap Access: 5 full

Built in 1910 by Ulysses Grant Jr. in memory of his father, President Grant, the luxurious U.S. Grant was one of the finest hotels in the city for decades. The hotel—and the surrounding city—went through some hard times in the 1970s and 1980s, but recently this beautiful historic property has undergone a massive renovation that has brought it back to the opulence of its heyday—and then some. The hotel was closed for almost two years, and the latest owners spent $52 million to revamp the place from the ground up. Step into the newly plush lobby, swathed in ice blue and chocolate velvets and fine hand-worked Asian rugs, and you'll find modern lines set against an art deco background. Massive crystal chandeliers (some of them dating back to the 1930s) sparkle throughout, as do the gleaming black and yellow marble floors. This 270-room hotel is just across the street from the Horton Plaza shopping mall, and a few blocks from the trendy Gaslamp Quarter—although its immediate neighborhood is still a little rough, despite the gentrification going on farther south. (Watch out

especially for a few seedy establishments just across the street on Fourth, as well as the park in front of the Horton Plaza shopping mall across the street.) Guestrooms are sumptuous, with snow-white Italian linens and down pillows on beds accented with headboards individually designed and painted by French artist Yves Clement. Each room has a flat-screen plasma TV and WiFi, and bathrooms offer high-style basin sinks, ultramodern faucets, stone counter vanities, and theatrical lighting. Indulgent (and ridiculously expensive) suites have comfortable living rooms and feature a "shower experience" in the bathrooms—a large walk-in affair with six shower heads. Onsite you'll find the clubby **Grant Grill** (619-239-6806), as well as a lobby bar. In the afternoons the **Palm Court** room offers "Tea and 'Tinis," a traditional high tea paired with a martini menu. Service is impeccable, as you would expect with these prices, and the front desk will indulge just about every whim a guest could have.

W SAN DIEGO

Manager: Roger Paull
619-231-8220; fax 619-231-5779
www.whotels.com
421 W. B St., San Diego, CA 92101
Price: Very expensive
Credit Cards: AE, D, DC, MC, V
Handicap Access: 2 full

This Starwood property, somewhat unfortunately located across the street from the county jail and a bit outside the mainstream of the action, nevertheless provides a sanctuary from the noise and traffic that can characterize downtown San Diego. Clean lines, a soothing color palette, and Asian-inspired design make for restful surroundings, both in the public places and in the calming private spaces. Modern, elegant guest rooms are swathed in sea and sky blues and clean whites, with an occasional punch of orange. To further enhance the sense of serenity, guests can indulge in in-room massages or visit the full-service onsite spa; take a dip in the beautiful heated pool; fall into the pillow-top mattress dressed in fine Egyptian cotton linens; and take the headache out of making dinner or theater arrangements by calling on the exceptionally helpful concierge service. The hotel hosts the acclaimed restaurant **Rice** (619-398-3082), where Chef A. J. Voytko conjures imaginative dishes using fresh regional ingredients. And drawing in locals and tourists alike is the popular **Beach** club (619-231-8220) on the rooftop, with real sand that is actually heated. Revelers can lounge on comfy ottomans or snuggle up around the fire pit while enjoying a cocktail or light appetizer.

WESTGATE HOTEL

Manager: George Hochfilzer
619-238-1818; fax 619-557-3737
www.westgatehotel.com
1055 Second Ave., San Diego, CA 92101
Price: Very expensive
Credit Cards: AE, D, DC, MC, V
Handicap Access: 5 full

Unless you were born into royalty, this regal, French-palatial hotel is as close as you're likely to get to staying overnight in Versailles: The lobby is decked out to impress, with museum-quality 18th-century French and European antiques, gorgeous silk fabrics, and crystal-laden chandeliers. The exceedingly polite front desk staff is helpful and well educated about San Diego. Guest rooms are among the largest in downtown, and are decorated with European imported furniture, cheerful silken fabrics in sunny yellows, corals, and spring greens; luxurious rugs; and marble-and brass-appointed bathrooms. Some rooms on higher floors have lovely views of the harbor. In total, there are 223 rooms, including a swanky Presidential Suite (a favorite of Governor and Mrs. Arnold

The refined and elegant Westgate Hotel is decked out like a presidential palace.

Swartzenegger when they visit San Diego). Onsite is the elegant, traditional **Le Fontainebleau Room** (619-557-3655), as well as the **Café Westgate** (619-557-3650). Throughout the year, a proper afternoon high tea is held in the Grand Lobby of the Westgate, including seasonal "teddy bear teas" that encourage parents to indulge their little ones in the finer things—children are served such treats as brownies, PB&J finger sandwiches, and miniature lemon tarts. This grand space really is unlike anything else in the city, and you're apt to feel more like you're in a museum in Paris or Vienna than a San Diego hotel. The popular Gaslamp Quarter is a few blocks away, and trolley stops are nearby.

Heritage Park near Old Town preserves San Diego's Victorian past.

OLD TOWN
HERITAGE PARK
BED AND BREAKFAST INN
Innkeepers: Nancy and Charles Helsper
619-299-6832; fax 619-683-4062
www.heritageparkinn.com
2470 Heritage Park Row, San Diego, CA
92110
Price: Moderate
Credit Cards: AE, D, DC, MC, V
Handicap Access: 1 partial

The Old Town Heritage Park Bed and Breakfast is located in an 8-acre reserve dedicated to preserving the Victorian heritage of
San Diego. Heritage Park is home to six
other relocated structures, which in addition to the bed–and–breakfast house a doll
shop, antique store, and law offices. This
large, heavily detailed 1889 Queen Anne
home, listed on the historical register as the
Christian House, has been lovingly restored
both inside and out, and boasts an appealing two-story corner turret and wraparound porch furnished with white wicker
rocking chairs. Guest rooms are decorated
with ornate Victorian period furnishings,
floral fabrics and lace, and heavily orna-

mented wallpapers, and some feature
carved fireplaces. High tea is served every
afternoon, complete with finger sandwiches and elegant china, and vintage films
are shared with the guests every evening in
the parlor. These pleasant accommodations
are within easy walking distance to the Old
Town restaurants and shops, and just a
short drive from downtown.

OLD TOWN INN
Manager: Beatrice Cadena
800-643-3025; fax 619-296-0524
www.oldtown-inn.com
4444 Pacific Hwy., San Diego, CA 92110
Price: Inexpensive
Credit Cards: AE, D, MC, V
Handicap Access: No

This budget lodging in historic Old Town is
just across the street from the Old Town
Transit Center and trolley station, and
within blocks of the historic attractions and
many restaurants and shopping in Old
Town. The hacienda-style exterior is
appealing, and the hotel has a heated swimming pool in a well-kept courtyard. The
large guest rooms aren't luxurious, and the

country designs are tired and worn, but the inn is kept clean. Guests enjoy a complimentary continental breakfast, and there are laundry facilities on site.

UPTOWN

BALBOA PARK INN

Manager: Edward Wilcox
619-298-0823; fax 619-294-8070
www.balboaparkinn.com
3402 Park Blvd., San Diego, CA 92103
Price: Inexpensive to moderate
Credit Cards: AE, D, DC, MC, V
Handicap Access: 1 full

This conveniently located complex of four Spanish Colonial buildings is just north of Balboa Park, within easy walking distance of the San Diego Zoo. The 26 suites feature their own décor and themes. For example, the "Jungle Nook" is decorated with animal prints, tropical greenery, and a giant brass gorilla. The small (and inexpensive) "Paris in the '30s" suite sports deep green walls, a canopy bed, and a faux fireplace. The larger, light-filled "Orient Express" features deep red fabrics and carpet, black-lacquered furniture, and a four-post Chinese wedding bed. Some rooms offer Jacuzzi tubs and upgraded shower heads. Each suite has a refrigerator, microwave, and coffeemaker, and guests will enjoy a complimentary breakfast each morning in the sunny courtyard overflowing with fuchsia bougainvillea vines. This is a great bargain, given the location. The major drawback is that there is no dedicated parking lot, but with patience you will find street parking on Upas or Park Boulevards.

BRITT SCRIPPS INN

Innkeeper: Randy Gantenbein
619-230-1991; fax 619-230-1188
www.brittscripps.com
406 Maple St., San Diego, CA 92103
Price: Very expensive
Credit Cards: AE, MC, V
Handicap Access: 1 full

Tucked into Bankers' Hill, a posh historic residential neighborhood near Balboa Park, this remarkable and lovingly restored 1887 Queen Anne Victorian mansion with a commanding turret and extensive bay windows is a showstopper. Inside you'll find jewel-like stained glass windows, fine antique furnishings, extensive original moldings, reproduction wallpapers, a doll-house perfect parlor, and an 1885 Steinway Art Case piano that will make antique lovers drool. The nine immaculately detailed guest rooms are decorated individually, with period touches like Tiffany lamps, claw-foot tubs, and Chinese Chippendale chairs. Elaborate carved beds are dressed with 1,000-thread count sheets, and the bathrooms are filled with upscale products and plush robes. This ever-so-civilized lodging option offers wine and hors d'oeuvres in the evenings, and included is a sumptuous prepared-to-order breakfast (waffles, pancakes, omelets, vegetarian options—the accommodating chef will make just about anything you want), which may be enjoyed in the darling breakfast room, outside on the porch, or in the English herb garden. Despite the old-world luxury and traditional elegance, rooms are equipped with all the modern conveniences, like high-speed Internet connections and flatscreen plasma TVs. The lavish lodgings are quite a bit more than one would normally expect from a typical bed-and-breakfast, and present an incredibly romantic option for visitors and locals looking to get away from the everyday.

KEATING HOUSE BED AND BREAKFAST

Innkeepers: Ben Baltic and Doug Scott
619-239-8585
www.inn@keatinghouse.com
2331 Second Ave., San Diego, CA 92101
Price: Moderate
Credit Cards: AE, D, MC, V
Handicap Access: No

The Keating House Bed and Breakfast offers another historic perspective in Bankers'

Hill, and it is a real value; although I've listed this bed-and-breakfast in the moderate price range, check the Web site for specials and you can sometimes find rooms in the inexpensive category. This quaint Victorian was originally built in 1886 as a private residence for George James Keating, a wealthy businessman who died in the home only a few years after it was built. (His kindly spirit is said to haunt the place.) The beautifully restored structure is designated as San Diego Historical Site #198, and it is worth a drive-by even if you aren't staying here. The inn offers nine bedrooms, including those in the main house and an adjoining cottage, all decorated in a restrained Victorian style with antiques that are not overly fussy. Main rooms include a comfortable parlor and dining room, and there is a quiet garden patio (accessible directly from some of the downstairs rooms). Daily hot breakfasts with home-made bread and fresh fruit are included in the price. Note that there is no parking lot for the Keating House; guests must find street parking, which can be challenging.

CULTURE

San Diego has long been a top destination for live theater, with the Tony-award-winning Old Globe Theatre in Balboa Park setting the standard. Balboa Park is the cultural center of downtown, boasting more than a dozen museums and several world-class gardens. The city also has its fair share of history, on display in the lovingly restored Gaslamp Quarter. And thanks to new clubs that seem to spring up overnight, downtown is *the* place to enjoy live music, sip hundreds of varieties of martini, and dance until the wee hours.

Dance

California Ballet Company (858-560-6741; 4819 Ronson Ct., San Diego, CA 92111). The CBC showcases a full season of classical and contemporary ballet in several venues downtown, including the **Civic Theater** (619-615-4000) and the **Lyceum** (619-231-3586).

City Ballet of San Diego (619-840-7353; 951 Garnet Ave., San Diego, CA 92109). For more than a decade, the City Ballet of San Diego has been staging classical and modern ballets at venues around town; spring and fall performances are staged at the beautifully restored **Spreckels Theater** (619-235-9500; 121 Broadway, San Diego, CA 92101), an elaborate movie house that dates back to 1912, as well as other venues around the city.

San Diego Ballet (619-294-7378; 2650 Truxton Rd., Ste. 102, San Diego, CA 92106). The SDB also shares venues downtown and throughout the city, performing both classical and contemporary works featuring local artists.

Galleries

Arts College International (619-231-3900; 840 G St., San Diego, CA 92101). This art school in the East Village section of downtown (near Petco Park) has a gallery space, with an annual exhibit featuring a variety of San Diego artists. The gallery also features exhibits of solo artists whose eclectic works might not be seen in commercial venues.

Four Winds Trading Company (619-692-0466; 2448 B San Diego Ave., San Diego, CA 92110). Located in Old Town, Four Winds specializes in Native American artwork from Arizona, New Mexico, and Mexico. You'll find handmade textiles and jewelry, as well as exquisite pottery.

Many Hands Craft Gallery (619-557-8303; 302 Island Ave., Ste. 101, San Diego, CA 92101). This downtown cooperative features handcrafted gifts made by more than 25 artisans from around San Diego. You'll find an eclectic mix of glass work, weaving, fine book making, jewelry, and handcrafted pottery on display and for purchase.

Spanish Village Art Center (619-233-9050; 1770 Village Pl., San Diego, CA 92101). Located in Balboa Park, near the Spreckels Organ Pavilion, this art cooperative is housed in cottages that are made to resemble an old village in Spain. Rotating gallery exhibits showcase international artists, and in the past have featured Chinese brush painting, art glass, watercolors, and print making.

Gardens

Botanical Building and Lily Pond (off El Prado, Balboa Park). The ornate wooden lath Botanical Building in the center of Balboa Park houses more than two thousand orchids and exotic palms, as well as a wide variety of herbs and rotating seasonal flowers. It makes the perfect backdrop for the much-photographed reflecting Lily Pond, which blooms in summer and is home to koi year-round. The Botanical Building is open Friday–Wednesday, 10–4. Admission is free.

Desert Garden (Park Blvd. and Village Pl., Balboa Park). Cross over Park Boulevard via a footbridge at the end of the El Prado thoroughfare in Balboa Park and you'll find a collection of more than 1,200 plants on 2.5 acres, including succulents and drought-resistant cacti. The blooming period is January through March.

Inez Grant Parker Memorial Rose Garden (south of the Park Blvd. footbridge, Balboa Park). Just south of the Desert Garden, this oasis of roses on the outskirts of Balboa Park

One of the most photographed spots in San Diego, the Lily Pond reflects the Botanical Building in Balboa Park.

has more than two hundred varieties, and is in bloom from March through December (peaking in April and May).

Japanese Friendship Garden (near the Spreckels Organ Pavilion in Balboa Park). An entertaining bamboo water fountain greets visitors to this small, serene garden, which features a bonsai exhibit and a well-stocked koi pond. Open Tuesday–Sunday, 10–4. Adults $3, seniors $2.50, children and active military $2.

Historic Places

Marston House (619-298-3142; 3525 Seventh Ave., San Diego, CA 92103). One-time home to San Diego businessman and philanthropist George Marston, the Marston House is an excellent example of the Arts and Crafts architectural movement. The home was designed by noted architects Irving Gill and William S. Hebbard, students of Frank Lloyd Wright. Most San Diegans don't even know this hidden treasure exists: That's because the restored 1905 structure really is *hidden*. Located on the northwest corner of Balboa Park, it is accessible by car only by heading north on Sixth Avenue. Although park maps and visitors' center docents locate Marston House on the corner of Upas, it is actually accessed via a right-turn-only backstreet immediately after you cross through the Upas/Balboa and Sixth Avenue intersection. Once you find the charming enclave neighborhood on which Marston House sits—and secure parking on the street—you can stroll the formal English garden and tour the period-furnished home to see Tiffany lamps, original period pottery, and a large collection of Native American baskets. Open Friday–Sunday, 10–5. Guided 45-minute tours. Adults $5, seniors and active military $4, children $2.

Old Town San Diego State Historic Park (619-220-5422; 4002 Wallace St., San Diego, CA 92110). Located on the site of one of the first European settlements on the West Coast, in the shadows of the first California mission (since relocated) and the presidio built to protect it, the restored and reconstructed buildings in Old Town make up a Westernized version of Colonial Williamsburg. With docents and shopkeepers in period costumes, historic reenactments and period demonstrations, and 37 themed buildings—some museums and some shops—that highlight the early pueblo era of 1821–72, Old Town gives visitors a chance to step into history.

Restoration of the historic area began as early as 1907, when wealthy businessman John D. Spreckels underwrote the renovation of some of the original buildings and homes in the area; during the 1930s, several new buildings were erected in Old Town to enhance the look of the Spanish village. And in 1968, Old Town San Diego officially became a state historic park. Museum exhibits today highlight the commercial and personal lives of the missionaries, Spanish colonists, wealthy Mexican families, and the native Kumeyaay Indians who lived in early San Diego. Visitors can tour the Blackhawk Livery Stables and view historic carriages; wander through the original newspaper office of the *San Diego Union*; visit the old Courthouse museum—then check out the jail next door—and stroll through the Robinson Rose Building, the one-time house and law offices of prominent attorney James W. Robinson, which currently serves as the park's visitors' center. La Casa de Estudillo, built for a former commander of the Presidio, has been preserved with period furniture and decorations. Guests today can tour the grounds and peek into the wealthy family's home kitchen, bedrooms, private chapel, and workrooms.

Concessions in the park include themed stores scattered throughout the historic area, as well as in the Plaza del Posado, which comprises stores and several period-style restaurants. Admission is free, and most buildings in the historic area are open from 10–5. Note that the park is working to improve accessibility to handicapped visitors. Call ahead to arrange accessible tours.

La Casa de Estudillo in Old Town has been restored to its 18th-century splendor.

Villa Montezuma (619-239-2211; 1925 K St., San Diego, CA 92101). An imaginative storybook Victorian house designed in 1887, the Villa Montezuma is the best example of Queen Anne architecture in San Diego. Built for Benjamin Henry Jesse Francis Shepard, who was a founder of the San Diego Theosophical Society, prominent writer, and pianist, the Villa Montezuma was acquired by the City of San Diego and the San Diego Historical Society in 1970. It underwent a massive renovation, and visitors today can admire lush Spanish cedar and redwood details, extensive stained glass windows, and gargoyles on the outside towers. The villa is closed for ongoing construction throughout 2007, so call ahead for information on the availability and hours of public tours.

Whaley House (619-297-7511; 2476 San Diego Ave., San Diego, CA 92110). Built in 1885 as the home of wealthy businessman Thomas Whaley and his family, and also used as the site of the county courthouse, the Greek-Revival-style Whaley House is carefully decorated with period furniture and accessories. But its real claim to fame comes from its long-time occupants. It is famously acknowledged by experts in such things as one of the most haunted structures in America. The Whaley House was the site of many tragedies throughout the years, and no doubt this adds to its ghostly reputation. For example, in 1885, after a scandalous divorce from her first cousin and a prolonged battle with depression, Whaley's daughter Violet committed suicide in the home by shooting herself through the heart. In addition, numerous hangings took place on the site, where gallows were erected to serve quick justice to those found guilty in the courthouse. There have been reports from visitors and museum employees of seeing the ghosts of men who were executed on the site, as well as of Violet and Mr. and Mrs. Whaley themselves. A parapsychologist even reported seeing the ghost of a spotted fox terrier, resembling the dog the Whaleys owned while living in the home. Hours are seasonal. Adults $6, seniors $5, children $4.

William Heath Davis House (619-233-4692; 410 Island Ave., San Diego, CA 92101). Headquarters of the Gaslamp Quarter Historical Foundation, this museum is housed in the oldest remaining wooden structure in San Diego, dating to 1850 (it was relocated to its present site in 1984). Davis was an early developer of downtown, and he built the home for himself with prefabricated materials shipped in from Maine. Several years later, Alonzo E. Horton—another important developer of early downtown—lived in the house with his family. A real joy of this museum is that the exhibits are not roped off. Guests can actually walk into the parlor and look closely at framed documents and photographs from the Horton family; the coal-burning stove, ice tongs, and butter churn in the kitchen; and the antique marbles, vintage quilt, and chamber pot in the children's room. Open Tuesday–Saturday, 10–6 and Sunday, 9–3. Adults $5, seniors $4, children free.

Museums

Chinese Historical Museum (619-338-9888; 404 Third Ave., San Diego, CA 92101). This nonprofit museum whose mission is to preserve and share the Chinese American experience has a library specializing in Chinese culture and rotating exhibits that include Chinese paintings, films, and photography. There is an Asian garden with a stream and fish pond on site as well. Open Tuesday–Saturday 10:30–4; Sunday noon–4. Adults $2, children free.

Junipero Serra Museum (619-297-3258; 2727 Presidio Dr., San Diego, CA 92103). Located in Presidio Park, on a hill above Old Town, the Serra Museum is housed in a beautiful white-washed Mission-style structure built in 1929 to commemorate the site where Father Junipero Serra established the first mission in California; the mission was moved a few years later to the current Mission Valley site. The museum collection includes archaeological artifacts such as pottery, furniture, tools, and a cannon from the early mission days. The onsite bookstore is a great place to find literature on San Diego and California history. Open daily, 10–4:30. Adults $5, seniors and active military $4, children $2.

Mingei International Museum (619-239-0003; 1439 El Prado, San Diego, CA 92101). A colorful sculpture by world-known artist Niki de Saint Phalle greets visitors to the Mingei International Museum in Balboa Park, alongside a giant green mosaic serpent covered in marbles, river stones, and mirrors that children are encouraged to climb. Rotating exhibits feature international art and cultural artifacts. The museum has an especially interesting gift shop (which can be accessed without a ticket) selling handmade pottery, jewelry, and imported textiles. Open Tuesday–Sunday 10–4. Adults $6, children $3.

Museum of Contemporary Art San Diego—Downtown (858-454-3541; 1100 Kettner Blvd., San Diego, CA 92101). This center-city venue of MCASD (its sister museum is in La Jolla) recently expanded into a second downtown exhibition space, located across the street in the old baggage building of the historic Santa Fe Depot, and together the two downtown locations explore national and regional trends in contemporary art, with an emphasis on works by artists from San Diego and

The Serra Museum at the top of Presidio Park in Old Town commemorates the spot where the first California mission was built.

Tijuana. Open Saturday–Tuesday 11–6, Thursday–Friday 11–9. Adults $10, seniors and active military $5, 25 years and younger free.

Museum of Photographic Arts (619-238-7559; 1649 El Prado, San Diego, CA 92101). Devoted to the photographic, film, and video arts, MOPA in Balboa Park features cameras, newsreels, and radio programs from the 1920s to the 1950s. Rotating exhibits highlight important photographers, past and current. Open daily 10–5 and until 9 on Thursday. Adults $6, children and active military $4.

Museum of San Diego History (619-232-6203; 1649 El Prado, San Diego, CA 92101). Exhibits highlight the museum's permanent collection of San Diego memorabilia and features a 30-by-30-foot map of the county that visitors can walk over. "Romp," a hands-on children's area, encourages younger visitors to make an origami animal, create a computerized timeline, and play interactive computer games. Open daily 10–4:30. Adults $6, children $2.

Reuben H. Fleet Science Center (619-238-1233; 1875 El Prado, San Diego, CA 92101). A favorite field trip destination for local schoolchildren for decades, the Reuben H. Fleet in Balboa Park offers more than one hundred fun and interactive experiments demonstrating the principles of science. The museum also hosts San Diego's only IMAX Dome Theater, which plays several regular features throughout the week (the offerings change every few months) as well as a wide variety of special after-hours shows on Friday nights. Open daily at 9:30; closing times vary. Adults $6.75, seniors $6, children $5.50. IMAX films additional.

San Diego Air and Space Museum (619-234-8291; 2001 Pan American Plaza, San Diego, CA 92101). Peer into an *Apollo* service module mockup, stroll alongside 1920s-era barnstormers, and see original fighter planes from World War II. Open daily 10–5:30; Thursdays until 11 PM. Adults $10, seniors and students $8, children $5, active military free.

San Diego Aircraft Carrier Museum (619-544-9600; 910 N. Harbor Dr., San Diego, CA 92101). The decommissioned U.S.S. *Midway*, the longest serving aircraft carrier in U.S. Navy history and, since 2004, permanently docked at the Navy Pier, provides a unique experience for civilian visitors. At 1,001 feet long, 258 feet wide, and with more than 4 acres of flight deck up top, you can literally lose yourself wandering onboard in what remain surprisingly authentic surroundings. Visit the cavernous hangar, sit in the cockpit of a Phantom fighter jet, and engage in a virtual dogfight with friends and family with networked video simulators. Let children climb aboard a Seasprite or try out an ejector seat—disconnected, of course. On the flight deck, wander among Hornets, a Sea King helicopter, and an F-14 Tomcat. My favorite is the Second Deck, where visitors can stroll the narrow (and low) corridors among the officers' staterooms and get a taste of what it must be like to live on one of these floating cities; here you can also see the laundry room, with dozens of industrial-sized washers and dryers that in the carrier's commissioned days ran 24–7; the mess and serving line (complete with rubber re-creations of Navy favorites like chipped beef and bacon and eggs; and the galley, which used to process 10 tons of food daily for the sailors onboard in a shockingly cramped space. If you are over 5 feet 5 inches, watch your head, lest you knock into the hundreds of exposed pipes and duct work. The museum entrance fee includes a free audio tour that highlights more than 40 exhibits and 21 restored aircraft. Open daily 10–5. Adults $15, seniors, active military, and children over five $10. Parking on the pier an additional $5 for an hour or $7 for up to four hours.

The flight deck of the U.S.S. Midway *Museum displays dozens of fighter jets and helicopters.*

San Diego Maritime Museum (619-234-9153; 1492 North Harbor Dr., San Diego, CA 92101). This long-time San Diego favorite located at the harbor downtown features seven sailing vessels that have been converted into museums, each with exhibits and opportunities to stroll through, including the magnificent sailing ship the *Star of India*, built in 1863 and currently the oldest active ship in the world; the *Berkeley*, an 1898 steam ferry; the HMS *Surprise*, a replica of an 18th-century Royal Navy frigate; the *Medea*, a 1914 steam yacht; and a B-39 Russian attack submarine. An unusual summertime activity hosted by the Maritime Museum is "Movies before the Mast" (in July and August), at which nautical-themed movies are projected on to the sails of the *Star of India*; the tall ship also has family sleepovers held onboard a few nights in June and July. Both are extremely popular activities, and reservations several weeks in advance are necessary. Open daily 9–8. Adults $12, seniors and active military $9, children $8.

San Diego Model Railroad Museum (619-696-0199; 1649 El Prado, San Diego, CA 92101). Located downstairs from the Museum of San Diego History in Balboa Park, you'll find more than 28,000 square feet of scale model railroad layouts, which boast amazing detail (and a slightly twisted sense of humor; look for the tiny injured human figure next to an overturned vehicle in a desert scene or the Dalmatian peeing on a fire hydrant in front of a model firehouse). Young children will go crazy for this museum, and the friendly volunteers go out of their way to make them feel welcome. Open Tuesday–Friday, 11–4. Adults $6; children free with a paying adult.

San Diego Museum of Art (619-232-7931; 1450 El Prado, San Diego, CA 92101). As the largest art museum in the county, the SDMA in Balboa Park gets world-class touring exhibits. The small permanent collection includes a few memorable pieces by William Bouguerau, Renoir, and El Greco. Open Tuesday–Sunday, 10–6. Adults $10; seniors and active military $8; children $4.

San Diego Museum of Man (619-239-2001; 1350 El Prado, San Diego, CA 92101). Although no longer as dark and creepy as it used to be, this anthropology museum still features slightly musty Egyptian mummies and sarcophagi. The Mayan icons are worth a look, as are the touring exhibits. Open daily, 10–4:30. Adults $6, seniors $5, children $3.

San Diego Natural History Museum (619-232-3821; 1788 El Prado, San Diego, CA 92101). A new exhibit on fossils opened in the summer of 2006, displaying the natural history of Southern California and Baja Mexico. Perhaps the most interesting attractions are at the front door: a Foucault pendulum and a towering slice of a petrified sequoia tree. Downstairs the museum shows big-screen science movies, free with admission. Open daily 10–5. Adults $11, seniors $9, students and active military $7, children $6.

Timken Museum of Art (619-239-5548; 1500 El Prado, San Diego, CA 92101). This tiny museum to the west of the Lily Pond in Balboa Park displays a Rembrandt and a very lovely Albert Bierstadt painting of Yosemite Falls—and a very few others. Open Tuesday–Saturday 10–4, Sunday noon–4. Admission free.

Music

Lyric Opera San Diego (619-231-5714; 2891 University Ave., San Diego, CA 92104). This relatively new musical theater is dedicated to providing an affordable theater experience to the masses. Tickets range from $30 to $50 for all performances, which are staged at the North Park Theatre. Look for revivals like *Fiddler on the Roof* and *Merry Widow*.

San Diego Opera (619-232-7636; 1200 Third Ave., San Diego, CA 92101). The longest established opera company in Southern California, with productions staged at the downtown Civic Theater, the San Diego company has been ranked by Opera America as one of the top 10 opera houses in the country. Award-winning director Ian Campbell oversees lavish productions that have featured international stars like Joan Sutherland, Luciano Pavarotti, and Beverly Sills. The San Diego Opera also has an extensive education and outreach program; their acclaimed "Operation: Opera" has introduced more than 100,000 schoolchildren in Southern California and Baja Mexico to the performing arts. Tickets for performances usually sell out several months in advance, and season ticket holders often nab the best seats, but it is possible to score last-minute cancellations.

San Diego Symphony Orchestra (619-235-0804; 750 B St., San Diego, CA 92101). The San Diego Symphony performs world-class classical and contemporary orchestral works year-round in Copley Symphony Hall downtown, in addition to the well-attended outdoor Summer Pops concert series on Friday and Saturday nights at Embarcadero Marina Park South. The symphony also sponsors family festivals and community concerts throughout the city, and in the past has played host to eclectic musicians like Aaron Neville (conducted by Marvin Hamlisch) and Woody Allen's jazz band.

Nightlife

Altitude Skybar (619-446-6088; 660 K St., San Diego, CA 92101). This rooftop beauty, 22 stories up on the top of the San Diego Marriott in the Gaslamp, overlooks the Coronado Bridge and the sparkling San Diego skyline. And if these views from up high aren't enough, you'll also find a waterfall wall, fire pit, and plenty of comfortable furniture to sink into. Drinks are imaginative and potent: Try the Del La Sol martini, a tequila, pineapple, and white cranberry juice cocktail.

belo (619-231-9200; 919 Fourth Ave., San Diego, CA 92101). Billing itself as San Diego's first (and only) "superclub," belo near the Gaslamp Quarter downtown boasts more than 20,000 square feet of space spread throughout three different rooms, each offering unique experiences (some louder than others). The hip, 1960s-inspired interior design has plenty of attitude, and you'll find VIP spaces so you can watch the other beautiful people in comfort. belo attracts internationally recognized DJs who make the most of the ultra-expensive sound system.

Bitter End (619-338-9300; 770 Fifth Ave., San Diego, CA 92101). There are three distinct levels at the Bitter End, with dancing in the Underground, billiards in the Main Room, and an upscale VIP Lounge on the top floor. This trendy bar attracts a young, upwardly mobile crowd every night of the week (from 3 PM–2 AM), with long lines forming on the weekends.

Café Sevilla (619-233-5979; 555 Fifth Ave., San Diego, CA 92101). Try the tapas upstairs for a late-night snack and then head downstairs for salsa dancing to a mix of contemporary and traditional Latin American music. Don't know how to salsa? This is one of the best places to take lessons every Tuesday and Thursday at 8 PM.

The Casbah (619-232-4355; 2501 Kettner Blvd., San Diego, CA 92101). This club is dark, loud, and cramped, but it manages to book some of the most important rock bands every night of the week (in the early days, Smashing Pumpkins and Nirvana rocked the Casbah). The doors open after 8:30 PM, and cover charge varies, but it is always reasonable.

Croce's Restaurant and Jazz Bar (619-233-4355; 802 Fifth Ave., San Diego, CA 92101). Owner Ingrid Croce (widow of the singer/songwriter Jim Croce) invested in the Gaslamp Quarter well before it was cool, and now Croce's is firmly established as a destination for sophisticated nightly live entertainment, as well as fine dining. The comfortable dining area is decorated with Croce family photographs, gold

The Gaslamp Quarter urban redevelopment has made this area one of the hottest night spots in the city. Photo courtesy of Jon Preimesberger. Used with permission.

albums, and other memorabilia. Croce's has an extensive wine list and full bar.

4th and B (619-231-4343; 345 B St., San Diego, CA 92101). One of the premier live music venues in town, this 20,000-square-foot, one thousand-seat Gaslamp Quarter facility features music from just about every genre, from hip hop, jazz, alternative rock, to country. In addition to world-class sound and lighting systems, you'll find luxurious sky boxes and private mezzanine booths.

Jimmy Love's (619-595-0123; 672 Fifth Ave., San Diego, CA 92101). Housed in the beautiful old City Hall building (and one-time city library), dating to 1887, this large Gaslamp restaurant and bar features contemporary American cuisine and live music nightly, including jazz, blues, and 1980s dance music. Enjoy the *Top Gun* aviation theme throughout, billed as "just plane fun." Open daily at 5 PM.

Joltin' Joes (619-230-1968; 379 Fourth Ave., San Diego, CA 92101). Another popular offering in the Gaslamp Quarter, this 15,000-square-foot sports bar and grill features flat-screen televisions scattered throughout the vampy red carpeted main dining room, as well as an upstairs outdoor "beach" patio, championship billiard tables, and a video arcade. All this fun, and they also serve up decent pasta and burgers.

The Shout! House (619-231-6700; 655 Fourth Ave., San Diego, CA 92101). Dueling pianos and high-energy musicians who play them are the stars at this raucous bar and grill downtown. Guests get to submit song requests with their drink orders, and then sing along to rock and roll favorites. You can also grab a simple bite here: Shout! has burgers, sandwiches, and other snackish items. Admission is $5 before 7 PM and $10 thereafter, and shows start at 6:30 PM on weekends and 6 PM during the week. Reservations are recommended and must be paid in advance by credit card. Closed Mondays.

Whiskey Girl (619-236-1616; 600 Fifth Ave., San Diego, CA 92101). This rowdy bar and grill features live bands most nights of the week, four giant screens to catch sporting events, as well as high-octane cocktails like whiskey and Red Bull. Enjoy decent pub food as well, like a six-pack of sliders (tiny White Castle-style burgers), a meatball sub, and build-your-own pizzas. Open daily.

Seasonal Events

Kick off the year with **San Diego Restaurant Week** (www.sandiegorestaurantweek.com), when more than one hundred of the best restaurants in the city offer three-course fixed-price menus for $30 or $40 per person; this is an opportunity to try the area's cutting-edge cuisine without slicing too deeply into your pocketbook, but be sure to make reservations at least a week in advance. Then catch the **Martin Luther King Jr. Day Parade and Festival** (619-264-0542) downtown, where you'll find lively marching bands and floats and a multicultural festival of food, entertainment, and art.

In February join the San Diego Chinese Center for the annual **Chinese New Year Celebration** (619-234-7844) downtown, at Third Avenue and J Street, featuring food, artisans, and entertainment. Kids can make their own Chinese lanterns and then participate in the annual lantern parade. Also this month you can join the bead-hungry revelers at the annual Mardi Gras celebration in the Gaslamp Quarter downtown (619-233-5227) on Fat Tuesday, featuring New Orleans-style food and entertainment.

In March, The Irish Congress of Southern California sponsors the annual **Saint Patrick's Day Parade** (858-268-9111), which lights up Fifth and Sixth Avenues alongside Balboa Park with bands, floats, and dancers; be sure to stick around for the **Smilin' Irishman** contest as well.

In early April join the **ArtWalk Festival** (619-615-1090); self-guided tours begin in Little Italy downtown, and highlight the visual and performing arts. Also, later in the month catch **Art Alive** (619-232-7931), a yearly exhibit of floral arrangements by some of the best designers in the city, inspired by the permanent art collection at the San Diego Museum of Art in Balboa Park, where the creations are displayed.

Cinco de Mayo is almost as important as the Fourth of July in San Diego; the **Old Town Fiesta Cinco de Mayo** (619-220-5422) is consistently one of the best parties in town, with historic recreations of the Battle of Puebla (the May 5, 1862, victory Cinco de Mayo celebrates) and plenty of food, drinks, and mariachi music to celebrate the festive and colorful holiday. If Zydeco music is more your style, head to the **Gator by the Bay** (619-234-8612) celebration in May at Spanish Landing Park, which showcases live music, dance workshops, and Louisiana-style cooking.

Starting in June, enjoy a night under the stars at the **Summer Organ Festival** (619-702-8138), a Monday night concert series at Balboa Park's outdoor Spreckels Organ Pavilion. Admission is free, and concerts run through the end of August.

A weekend-long celebration of diversity in July, the annual lesbian and gay **Pride Parade, Rally, and Festival** (619-297-7683) culminates in a parade through Hillcrest featuring more than two hundred floats, bands, and dance ensembles. Running from July through September, the **San Diego Symphony Summer Pops** (619-235-0804) provides outdoor nighttime musical entertainment in a festival atmosphere.

Celebrate Italian culture at the annual **Little Italy Precious Festa** (619-233-3898), sponsored by the Little Italy community association and the Precious Cheese Company in mid-October. Stroll through the charming 56-block community just north of downtown San Diego amid the smells of Italian sausage grilling and marinara sauce bubbling. In addition to food, food, food, you'll find displays of Italian art and culture, music, and family fun in one of the largest single-day Italian festivals in the country. And while you're here, check out four of the best teams in the nation competing for honors in the **Festa Stickball Championship.** If you're looking for something to spook up your Halloween celebrations, look into the **Ghosts and Gravestones** tour (619-298-8687) led this month by Old Town Trolley Tours and the San Diego Historical Society; you'll visit "haunted" sites throughout the city in this tongue-in-cheek historical romp.

Starting in November and running through January, strap on your ice skates and head to Horton Plaza; **The Fantasy on Ice Rink** (619-238-1596) at Horton Square downtown is a big hit with weary shoppers and children.

Usher in the holidays with **Balboa Park December Nights** (619-239-0512) on the first Friday and Saturday of December; you'll enjoy a candlelight procession beginning near the Spreckels Organ Pavilion, carolers, crafts, food, and an appearance by Santa Claus himself.

Theater

Downtown San Diego has a vibrant theater scene. Check the free *San Diego Reader* for current productions, or visit the Web site of San Diego Art + Sol at www.sandiegoartandsol.com for a complete listing of performance and visual art throughout the city.

For half-price theater tickets on the day of the performance, head to Horton Plaza's downtown **ArtTix** booth (619-238-0700; 28 Horton Plaza, San Diego, CA 92101), sponsored by the San Diego Performing Arts League. You can purchase half-price day-of tickets for dance and music events here as well. Or save yourself the wait time and go online at www.sandiegoperforms.com to see daily listings of available performances and purchase your tickets directly from the Web site.

Broadway San Diego (619-231-8995; 3666 Fourth Ave., San Diego, CA 92103). As the name suggests, this company presents touring Broadway shows like *Chicago* and *Stomp* year round at various venues, including the San Diego Civic Theatre (619-615-4000; 1100 Third Ave., San Diego, CA 92101) and the Spreckels Theater (619-235-9500; 121 Broadway, San Diego, CA 92101).

Diversionary Theatre (619-220-0097; 4545 Park Blvd., Ste. 101, San Diego, CA 92116). In University Heights in Uptown, Diversionary Theatre is one of the oldest gay and lesbian theaters in the country, and presents musicals and dramas that highlight gay, lesbian, and bisexual themes. There isn't a bad view in the 104-seat house.

Marie Hitchcock Puppet Theater (619-544-9203; 2130 Pan American Plaza, San Diego, CA 92101). Marie Hitchcock was a beloved fixture in the San Diego school district as far back as 40 years ago, traveling from classroom to classroom, introducing schoolchildren to puppetry. Today this quaint puppet theater in Balboa Park continues to enchant children with marionettes and hand puppets, in short-format plays. Open Wednesday through Sunday; hours vary. Adults $5, seniors $4, children $3.

Old Globe (619-234-5623; 1363 Old Globe Way, San Diego, CA 92101). The Tony-Award-winning Old Globe is the oldest professional theater in California, located at the center of Balboa Park; it is home to more than five hundred performances a year on its three stages, and an astonishing number of original shows have gone on to Broadway. The outdoor Lowell Davies Festival Stage features the Summer Shakespeare Festival from mid-June through the end of September. Throughout late November and into December, the Old Globe main stage presents *How the Grinch Stole Christmas*, a screenplay adaptation of Dr. Seuss's famous tale. The imaginative stage sets, costumes, and lighting are done exclusively in red, pink, and white (with the exception of the lime green Grinch himself) to mimic the pages of the Seuss book, and has become a holiday tradition for many local families, including my own.

Jay Goede as the Grinch in the Old Globe's annual production of How the Grinch Stole Christmas. Photo by Craig Schwartz. Used with permission of Craig Schwartz and The Old Globe.

San Diego Repertory Theater (619-544-1000; 79 Horton Plaza, San Diego, CA 92101). The nationally acclaimed San Diego Repertory Theater started out in 1976 as a street theater company in which one-time San Diegan Whoopi Goldberg was involved. A decade later, the Rep. partnered with the City of San Diego when it moved into the downtown Lyceum Theater at Horton Plaza and became steward to the Lyceum complex. Today the Rep. and other community organizations coproduce two thirds of the more than four hundred performances per year. Performances range from cutting-edge to traditional theater. Every Christmas season, the Rep. stages the popular Charles Dickens classic *A Christmas Carol*, and performances generally sell out.

Spreckels Organ Pavilion (619-702-8138; south of El Prado in Balboa Park). The pavilion in Balboa Park, which seats 2,400 and is also the site of community dance and music groups, houses the Spreckels Organ, the largest outdoor musical instrument in the world. The concert organ comprises 73 ranks of more than four thousand pipes, ranging in size from 32 feet long down to little more than an inch. There are free year-round concerts every Sunday from 2–3.

Starlight Theater (619-544-7827; 2005 Pan American Plaza, San Diego, CA 92101). The Starlight Bowl in Balboa Park hosts outdoor musical productions in a venue that just happens to be right in the flight path of the jets landing at Lindbergh Field. An intricate warning light system cues the actors and the orchestra to freeze during performances (often in the middle of a song!) to let especially loud aircraft pass, which is often as entertaining to watch as the revival musical productions themselves. Look for the legendary red box, a relic of show biz superstition, which has been onstage at some point for every performance at the Starlight since 1946.

RESTAURANTS AND FOOD PURVEYORS

Restaurants

There is a higher density of restaurants in this area than any other in San Diego County, and you're sure to find something to please just about every palate and pocketbook. Look for upscale dining in trendy, chic restaurants in the historic Gaslamp Quarter downtown; Mexican restaurants that offer hearty portions and plenty of libation choices in tourist-centric Old Town; and quirky ethnic eateries and comfortfood cafes throughout the Uptown area.

DOWNTOWN
BANDAR
Owner: Behrooz Farahani
619-238-0101
www.bandarrestaurant.com.
825 Fifth Ave., San Diego, CA 92101
Open: Daily
Price: Expensive
Cuisine: Persian
Serving: L, D
Credit Cards: AE, D, MC, V
Handicap Access: Yes
Reservations: Recommended
Parking: Street (limited)

The sidewalk patio with black awnings and authentic bistro tables and the quiet and elegant interior at Bandar will remind visitors of restaurants in Paris and Brussels, but the food is pure Middle Eastern. For the past several years, Bandar, located in a historic building in the Gaslamp Quarter in downtown, has been voted by local publications as the best Persian restaurant in the city. The dishes are prepared traditionally, but with an occasional nod to the Southern California influence. For example, in addition to the traditional hummus made with pureed garbanzo beans and sesame tahini, Bandar also serves hummus made with pureed avocado and accented with cilantro,

olive oil, and lemon. If you've never tried Persian food, friendly and knowledgeable wait staff will help you make choices. The shirazi salad with chopped cucumbers, tomatoes, onions, and mint is a refreshing starter using the freshest local ingredients, and for the main course you can't go wrong with the juicy and flavorful shish kebab of filet mignon, tomato, onion, and bell pepper served over saffron rice. For something more exotic, consider the *albalu polo*, an interesting combination of marinated charbroiled chicken breast, black cherries, and rice. Persian food is low in fat, so guests can keep their guilt level in check.

BLUE GINGER
Chef: Xing Ton Lin
619-888-0007
www.bluegingersd.com
715 Fourth Ave., San Diego, CA 92101
Open: Daily
Price: Expensive
Cuisine: Chinese
Serving: L, D
Credit Cards: AE, D, MC, V
Handicap access: Yes
Reservations: Recommended for dinner
Parking: Street (or park at the nearby Horton Plaza and walk over)

In the middle of the bustling Gaslamp Quarter of downtown, Blue Ginger is in anything but a tranquil setting. In fact, tables too close to the front door can be quite noisy—but nevertheless, the owners have managed to create an oasis of calm in this elegant Chinese restaurant, which sports a mural of the Yangtze River running the length of the dining room and a giant fish tank spanning the width. The bar is discretely located in a smaller room next door and fronted by a huge sculptural wall of water. Throughout, the potted palms and fresh orchids on every table, the crisp black linen tablecloths, and the calming music all add to the harmonious setting. Efficient

Café Chloe in the East Village of downtown is a welcoming bistro near Petco Park.

and opinionated servers will guide you to the best menu choices, featuring Mandarin and other regional Chinese dishes. The vegetarian pot stickers and spring rolls are nice starters, although the beautifully presented dragon ribs are bland. House specialties include the cleverly named "great wall-nut shrimp," a sizzling dish glazed with honey sauce and served on a bed of broccoli; crispy duck, stir-fried with a spicy garlic sauce; and mango chicken stir-fried with straw mushrooms, red and green bell peppers, onions, and celery and dressed with a delicate sweet and sour sauce. You'll find lots of rice and noodle dishes—the stir-fried shrimp rice is exceptional—and there is a large collection of vegetarian dishes. Everything can be prepared to your preferred level of spiciness, from mild to very hot. The full bar offers a nice selection of wines, as well as a few signature cocktails. Try the jade 'tini, a concoction of plum sake, vodka, apple liqueur, and sparkling soda.

CAFÉ CHLOE

Chef: Katie Grebow
619-232-3242
www.cafechloe.com
721 Ninth St., San Diego, CA 92101
Open: Daily
Price: Moderate
Cuisine: Continental
Serving: B, L, D
Credit Cards: AE, MC, V
Handicap Access: Yes
Reservations: Accepted for large parties only
Parking: Street

The owners of Café Chloe have managed to bring a little bit of Europe to the corner of Ninth and G Streets downtown, just blocks from Petco Park. No details were overlooked in this adorable bistro and wine bar, from the black-stained wooden floors, gleaming white demilune bar, tiny tables tucked next to floor-to-ceiling foldaway windows (some of which have views of

Petco), and a small sidewalk café. Although the brunch on Saturdays and Sundays boasts a bounty of choices, menu options for other meals are somewhat limited, but the items that are available are fresh, imaginatively prepared, and beautifully presented. Weekday breakfasts offer a *fines herbes* omelet stuffed with brie and served with duck sausage or a decadent and creamy breakfast bread pudding served with seasonal fruits. For lunch consider the mussels with saffron broth and *pommes frites*—incredible shoestring fries cooked crispy and served with a variety of dipping sauces—or the steak tartine with gorgonzola mousse and cipollini onions. For dinner, lamb chops with couscous and roasted veggies or a roast half chicken with *pommes lyonnaise* are indulgent, Francophile comfort food. Whatever meal you choose, do not miss the *affogato* for dessert—a scoop of Chloe's buttery homemade vanilla ice cream is topped with a shot of hot espresso, which softens the ice cream but doesn't turn the whole concoction into café au lait. *Divine*. Café Chloe also serves an "urban tea" in the afternoon, with upscale versions of the usual finger sandwiches and pastries, along with exotic teas like "dragon eyes," a Chinese black tea scented with longan fruit, and "white peony," a white tea with a fruity infusion. Don't like tea? Chloe offers a glass of Prosecco instead. This little treasure is slightly off the beaten path—although expanding downtown revitalization will take care of this soon enough—but it's well worth finding.

CAFÉ 222

Owner: Terryl Gavre
619-236-9902
www.cafe222.com
222 Island St., San Diego, CA 92101
Open: Daily
Price: Moderate
Cuisine: American
Serving: B, L
Credit Cards: MC, V

Handicap access: Yes
Reservations: No.
Parking: Street (limited)

Look for walls the color of an egg yolk, and you've found this quirky breakfast diner within easy walking distance of the Convention Center. Chandelier sconces are fashioned from colorful teacups, fried eggs are painted on the floors, and the friendly servers treat their customers to witty hospitality and quick service. Squeeze inside and enjoy the view of the chefs at work or spread out on the sidewalk patio and enjoy the view of the nearby midrises. Waitresses will remind you that this is a low-pressure zone, so take your time reading the entertaining breakfast menu. The café is famous for its pumpkin waffles, which are light and delicately flavored, and the amusing green eggs and spam, a scramble served with spinach and jack cheese. Another eye-opening choice is the pork tamales and eggs plate served with Mexican gravy and crispy pan-fried potatoes. My favorite, though, is the oversized peanut butter and banana stuffed French toast, which is the perfect mix of sweet and salty. Because of its diminutive interior, Café 222 is usually packed on weekend mornings, but come during the week and enjoy the peace.

CAFÉ ZUCCHERO

Pastry chef: Frank Busalacchi
619-531-1731
www.busalacchirestaurants.com
1731 India St., San Diego, CA 92101
Open: Daily
Price: Moderate
Cuisine: Italian
Serving: B, L, D daily
Credit Cards: AE, MC, V
Handicap Access: Yes
Reservations: For large parties
Parking: Street

Famed for its desserts and breakfast pastries, including plump cannoli, decadently rich flourless chocolate cake, authentic fruit gelato, and creamy tiramisu, all created onsite by Sicilian-trained pastry chef Frank Busalacchi, this Italian bistro in Little Italy is also a fine place to dine on more substantial fare. The huge outdoor patio is usually packed on weekends, although there is a better chance of snagging a table inside. The floor-to-ceiling glass windows in the front of the restaurant fold completely open on nice days, which ensures that there is little separation between inside and out anyhow, so you can still catch the cool breezes and people watch as you sip an espresso or a glass of red wine. Traditional Italian starters are reliably good and include crispy, lightly breaded calamari, and *caprese*, fresh tomatoes served with buffalo mozzarella and basil and drizzled with olive oil. For the main course don't miss the fresh *pollo alla Limone*, moist chicken breast sautéed with lemons, white wine, and capers and served over a bed of spinach. Pizzas are also a good bet; Zucchero makes their own sausages, so the meat pizzas are especially good options. Authentic pastas and homemade sauces are flavor-packed—with the exception of the *fettuccini alfredo*, which is a little bland. Don't forget that Café Zucchero has earned its stripes with an exceptional Italian bakery selection, so make sure to leave room for a pastry or three!

DICK'S LAST RESORT

Owner: Steve Shipp
619-231-9100
345 Fourth Ave., San Diego, CA 92101
Open: Daily
Price: Moderate
Cuisine: American
Serving: L, D
Credit Cards: AE, D, MC, V
Handicap Access: Yes
Reservations: Yes
Parking: Street (limited)

While some downtown restaurants take themselves and their customers too seriously, Dick's provides a fun, irreverent atmosphere where you are sure to be insulted by the wait staff and assaulted by the loud music. The indoor dining room sports wall-to-wall neon lights and an exuberant sensory overload. The huge streetside outdoor patio reminds me of cafés on the beach, but Dick's is just blocks from the Convention Center, smack in the heart of the Gaslamp. Food here is messy and hearty: Strap on your plastic bib (provided courtesy of the management) and dive into a bucket of sticky, lick-your-lips ribs or a pile of chicken-fried steak smothered in jalapeno gravy. Or play it safe and order a hearty chicken sandwich—just don't expect it to be served on a plate. Wash it all down with a "big ass glass of beer" or a Dick-tini. This is also a happening night spot, where live bands take the stage every evening after 9. As you have probably guessed by now, this is not a family-friendly place, and the atmosphere is decidedly raunchy at times. But if you're over 21, think of this as an adventure, and come ready to have a good time.

GASLAMP STRIP CLUB

Owners: Cohn family
619-231-3140
www.cohnfamilyrestaurants.com
340 Fifth Ave., San Diego, CA 92101
Open: Daily
Price: Moderate
Cuisine: Steak house
Serving: D
Credit Cards: AE, D, DC, MC, V
Handicap Access: Yes
Reservations: Accepted for large parties only
Parking: Street (limited)

You must be 21 to enter this establishment—but despite the deceptive name and the suggestive glass etchings of curvaceous women on the windows, it isn't what it sounds like.

The name refers to this restaurant's signature "strip steak," and it is also a playful homage to the Gaslamp Quarter of a few decades ago, where clothing-challenged waitresses were plentiful. The décor is dark and reminiscent of nightclubs past, and the dining room features an extensive collection of art by Alberto Vargas, who is famous for his girly pin-up posters. Diners are sure to make new friends by sharing communal grills to cook up their own steaks, chicken, kabobs, and burgers. But if you prefer to have someone else man the grill, play it simple and just order a few appetizers and a signature martini. The interactive dining and the nightclub atmosphere make this an especially good choice for late-night dining. This is a popular place with the young and hip, and can get very crowded, especially on weekends.

GREEK ISLANDS CAFÉ

Owner: Jerry G. Bishop
619-234-2407
879 W. Harbor Dr., San Diego, CA 92101
Open: Daily
Price: Moderate
Cuisine: Greek
Serving: L, D
Credit Cards: AE, D, MC, V
Handicap Access: Yes
Reservations: No
Parking: Seaport Village lots

Owned and managed by local television and radio personality Jerry G. Bishop (old-timers will remember him as the cohost of "Sun Up, San Diego"), this little take-out Greek restaurant is the best dining value in Seaport Village—and is the only eatery facing the harbor that doesn't tack on a premium for the water view. You'll order at the counter and pick up your own food; then you can decide to eat in the small blue and white dining room, decorated with Greek memorabilia and posters, or take your food to the outside picnic tables that have a mil-

lion-dollar view of the harbor. You'll find classic Greek appetizers like hummus and *tzatziki* (yogurt with cucumber); especially good *spanikopita* and *dolmades* (marinated grape leaves wrapped around seasoned rice); gyros and souvlaki; Greek salads loaded with feta, onions, and kalamata olives; and juicy Athenian chicken, served with rice, a small salad, and pita bread. The service is fast, even when there is a line (which there often is on weekends). And if you aren't familiar with Greek food, you have no farther to look than the overhead menu, which recreates the dishes in life-size plastic reproductions, so you can just point to what looks good.

HARBOR HOUSE SEAFOOD RESTAURANT AND OYSTER BAR

Manager: Debi Kaufmann
619-232-1141
www.harborhousesd.com
831 West Harbor Dr., San Diego, CA 92101
Open: Daily
Price: Very expensive
Cuisine: Seafood
Serving: L, D
Credit Cards: AE, MC, V
Handicap Access: Yes
Reservations: Recommended
Parking: Seaport Village lots

With a stellar location on the harbor in Seaport Village, just blocks from the downtown Convention Center and with some of the prettiest views in the city, the Harbor House can get away with charging more for their fresh seafood choices than other restaurants in less idyllic surroundings. A rustic, raw-wood exterior fits in with the Cape Cod-themed architecture of Seaport Village, and a plain and simple wooden interior makes for a comfortable atmosphere and somewhat unimpressive interior—until you look out the windows. Wraparound views are so close to the water that dining at the Harbor House feels like you're dining onboard a ship. To start, Harbor House offers a wide selection of the freshest oysters on the shell available; you can also get hot oysters Rockefeller, Maryland crab cakes, and messy peel-and-eat shrimp seasoned heavily with Old Bay spice. The main dining room features catch of the day entrees, as well as their famous linguini with clams, a respectable fish and chips platter, and an oyster seafood stew heavy with sherry. A beautiful raspberry chocolate cake served with raspberry coulis makes a fine ending statement. There is also an upstairs patio Oyster Bar and Pub for more casual dining, which features she-crab soup, smoked salmon and shrimp salad, and a seared ahi burger, in addition to fresh oyster choices. This isn't the place to discover the next greatest chef—or the place to come on a budget—but the atmosphere is relaxing and pure San Diego.

JSIX

Chef: Christian Graves
619-531-8744
www.jsixsandiego.com
616 J St., San Diego, CA 92101
Open: Daily
Price: Expensive
Cuisine: Californian
Serving: B, L, D
Credit Cards: AE, D, DC, MC, V
Handicap Access: Yes
Reservations: Recommended for dinner
Parking: Valet at the Hotel Solamar next door, two public lots across the street on Sixth Ave., or street (limited)

Increasingly, some of the finest new restaurants in the city are popping up at hotels. The JSix—with a glowing interior dramatically accented with eclectic glass lighting fixtures and a raised open kitchen that resembles a stage—belongs to the hip **Hotel Solamar** (see page 54,) but it draws the bulk of its crowds from locals flocking to try Chef Graves's coastal California cuisine. Graves

is dedicated to using local all-organic produce, free-range meat and chicken, and Pacific Coast fish caught by harvesters practicing sustainability. All breads, desserts, and dips are made on the premises, so everything here is fresh and healthy—and delicious. The hearty home-baked breads served with fruity black-olive tapenade would suffice as a starter, but not at the expense of "small bites" like Maine lobster risotto served with a watercress and orange salad or the rich chowder that is studded with fresh clams in the shell. "Shared bites" allow guests to split small nibbles with fellow diners, including a cheese plate with house-made lentil crackers and fresh honeycomb or the charcuterie plate with bresaeola, smoked duck proscuitto, and artisan sausage. Leave room for the signature grilled ahi tuna, served rare with Tuscan white beans and a Meyer lemon and almond chutney, or the enormous portion of wine-braised short ribs with a black truffle aioli served over a bed of rosemary-flavored potatoes and swiss chard. The rustic apple tart with a granola crust and the seasonal pumpkin cheesecake with maple-flavored cream are satisfying closers. Note that the restaurant is a few blocks up from Petco Park, and dining before or after a game at JSix is one of the best ways I can think of to avoid the baseball traffic.

LOU AND MICKEY'S

Chef: Scott Cox
619-237-4900
www.louandmickeys.com
224 Fifth Ave., San Diego, CA 92101
Open: Daily
Price: Expensive
Cuisine: Steak house
Serving: D (and L when major conventions are in town)
Credit Cards: AE, D, DC, MC, V
Handicap Access: Yes
Reservations: Recommended for dinner
Parking: Street or valet in the evenings

Conveniently located across the street from the Convention Center and near Petco Park, Lou and Mickey's is an evocative, romantic homage to East Coast steak and martini houses from the mid-century. Step inside to find dark woods, black leather chairs, moody lighting, and World War II-era tunes piped in to a clubby atmosphere. Or enjoy the extensive outdoor patio, decorated with imported palm trees and plentiful heat lamps. Although there is seafood on the menu, stick to the steaks and chops and you won't be sorry. The filet mignon is served with a tantalizing caramelized crust on the outside and rare perfection on the inside (I don't think the chef will cook one of these beautiful pieces of meat beyond medium, no matter how much a guest might beg). Other carnivore delights include top sirloin, lamb chops, rib-eyes, and extra-thick porterhouse steaks. You can pair the turf options with a lobster or crab legs as well.

Entrees arrive alone on the plate, so order up family-style sides like garlic mashed potatoes or creamed spinach to round out your meal. Desserts are traditional favorites like root beer floats, apple cobbler, and hot fudge sundaes. Don't miss the martinis here: The Coronado Cosmo blends Absolut Citron with white cranberry juice, for a mild, subtle cocktail that goes down as easily as the well-prepared food.

MASALA

Chef: Samir Gupta
619-232-4634
www.masalarestaurant.com
314 Fifth Ave., San Diego, CA 92101
Open: Daily
Price: Expensive
Cuisine: Indian
Serving: L, D
Credit Cards: AE, DC, D, MC, V

Lou and Mickey's near the Convention Center is a nostalgic, upscale dining experience.

Masala in the Gaslamp Quarter is an elegant spot for lunch or dinner.

Handicap access: Yes (but restrooms upstairs with no lift)
Reservations: Recommended for dinner
Parking: Street or valet in the evenings

Undulating curtains of mesh and beads, intricately tiled columns, and a soothing waterfall behind the full bar give this Gaslamp newcomer an elegant, exotic ambiance. Flat-screen TVs play the latest films from Bollywood, and gentle music is piped in to create a calming atmosphere. But the extensive menu immediately presents a dilemma: How to choose between the many delicacies from all corners of the subcontinent? If for no other reason than the name, consider "love story," an Indian curry hummus served with garlic *naan* bread for dipping. The king ganoush, with roasted eggplant and cilantro served with *papadum*

for dipping, is fresh and simple. For the entrees you can choose among lamb, chicken, fish, and vegetarian options, as well as tandoori specialties. *Aam murgh*, chicken with fennel seeds, ginger, green chilies, and mango from North India is heady with aromas, and the Goa fish curry prepared with Kashmiri chilies, turmeric, and tamarind is a dish you're not likely to see in other Indian restaurants in San Diego. Finish with a rose *kulfi*, an Indian ice cream made of sweetened condensed milk, or mango mousse. Attentive and friendly service combine with the beautiful interior and superior and unusual flavors to make Masala a triple threat to the many surrounding eateries.

MONSOON

Chef: Jagu Singh
619-234-5555
www.monsoonrestaurant.com
729 Fourth Ave., San Diego, CA 92101
Open: Daily
Price: Moderate
Cuisine: Indian
Serving: L, D
Credit Cards: AE, DC, D, MC, V
Handicap access: Yes
Reservations: Recommended for dinner
Parking: Street (or park at Horton Plaza and walk down)

Featuring finely prepared Northern Indian cuisine, this elegant restaurant is designed to be an oasis on bustling Fourth Avenue, just down the street from the Horton Plaza shopping mall. A vertical wall of rain running through the middle of the place—a clever allegory—drowns out the considerable noise outside, while the exotic murals, jewel-encrusted chandeliers, and comfortable high-backed chairs create an intimate dining experience. The menu is extensive, and to start you'll find favorites such as *papadum*—seasoned wheat wafers toasted in a tandoori oven—and assorted *pakoras*—

vegetable fritters served with yogurt and mint dipping sauces. Main courses offer curries in lamb, chicken, fish, and tofu; *biriyani*—rice and vegetables sautéed with your choice of protein; juicy, flavorful tandoori grilled meats; and plentiful vegetarian choices. You can choose your own level of spiciness, from mild to spicy, with the hottest being *tikhi*, which a server explained to me as meaning spicy enough for Indians (and not recommended for the faint of heart). Finish with a steaming cup of chai, spiced tea steamed with milk. For lunchtime you'll find an exceptionally good and well-priced buffet that features a wide selection of vegetarian and nonvegan dishes. There is also a full bar, with an extensive wine list.

OSETRA: THE FISH HOUSE
Chef: Jose Trinidad
619-239-1800
www.osetrafishhouse.com
904 Fifth Ave., San Diego, CA 92101
Open: Daily
Price: Very expensive
Cuisine: Seafood
Serving: D
Credit Cards: AE, D, MC, V
Handicap access: Yes
Reservations: Yes
Parking: Street (or park at nearby Horton Plaza and walk over)

This sexy, two-tiered dining room and bar has a retro feel, with subtle lighting, brightly colored post-Modernist art, and comfortable blue suede lounge chairs. Dominating the space is a glowing glass tower housing an extensive wine collection, including an impressive list of California reds. To retrieve the bottles, Osetra employs "wine angels"—attractive young women who float to the appointed shelf in the wine tower to retrieve the appropriate bottle. The bar packs in a crowd, especially on weekend nights, but first and foremost,

this is a dining destination. Do not miss the lobster three-way, a heavenly ménage à trois of creamy lobster bisque, subtle lobster salad with avocado, and lobster dynamite, a spicy and tangy custard that is bursting with lobster meat. Another sublime choice is the moist and perfectly seasoned crab cake dressed with mango salsa and served with a Russian remoulade. Or if you're really out to impress, for just under $100, you can indulge in caviar served with blini, crostini, red onion, and crème fraiche. For the entrée, consider the stuffed shrimp, grilled and presented with a stuffing of lobster, scallops, and crab meat, drizzled with a beurre blanc sauce and served with creamy asparagus risotto. The show-stopping bouillabaisse is an orgy of shellfish: a half lobster, crab legs, clams, mussels, and white fish piled into a dish and dressed with a delicate and fragrant broth flavored heavily with sherry. After the astonishing savory courses, desserts are somewhat pedestrian, with the exception of the cantaloupe sorbet that comes drizzled with a port wine reduction and, for chocolate lovers, the Godiva chocolate soufflé, which is really more like a molten cake. There is also a nice selection of specialty coffees, port wines, and sherries to finish off what is sure to be a memorable meal.

THE PRADO
Chef: Jeff Thurston
619-557-9441
www.cohnfamilyrestaurants.com
1549 El Prado, Ste. 12, San Diego, CA 92101
Open: Daily
Price: Expensive
Cuisine: Latin and Italian fusion
Serving: L daily, D Tues–Sun
Credit Cards: AE, D, DC, MC, V
Handicap Access: Yes
Reservations: Recommended
Parking: Balboa Park lots and valet for dinner

You can't find a closer restaurant to Balboa Park, because The Prado is *in* the park, located in the beautiful Spanish rococo House of Hospitality. The large space is decorated in hacienda style and accented with art glass throughout. The candlelit outdoor patio is an especially nice option on warm evenings, when you are likely to hear the calls of the peacocks from the nearby San Diego Zoo. Although the menu changes frequently, you'll usually find the black bean soup on the starter menu, featuring creamy legumes simmered with chilies and spices and served with sour cream and lime; this is substantial enough to be a meal in itself. If you can find the grilled grand shrimp on the menu, be sure to try it—large shrimp are simmered in a coconut-lime mole sauce and served with mashed sweet plantains and an avocado salad dressed with ancho chili and orange vinaigrette. The braised beef short ribs are rich and spoon-tender, served on top of a bed of mashed potatoes and doused in a biting brown sauce that has a touch of chocolate. To round off the evening, the chocolate soufflé cake is dark and decadent, and comes with the added bonus of a light orange mousse on the side—easily enough for two to share. The Prado is especially good at accommodating pre-theater diners (the Old Globe is a stone's throw away), but be sure to make reservations well in advance for this early seating.

RAMA

Owner: Alex Thao
619-501-8424
www.ramarestaurant.com
327 Fourth Ave., San Diego, CA 92101
Open: Daily
Price: Expensive
Cuisine: Thai
Serving: L, D
Credit Cards: AE, MC, V
Handicap Access: Yes
Reservations: Recommended
Parking: Street (limited)

Step into this one-time firehouse and you'll be transported to an exotic, tranquil locale. At night, the low lights and candles blur the extensive wall murals into dark and mysterious swirls. Floating orchids adorn every table, and each dining site is shrouded with a golden mesh curtain, which manages to make eating in this cavernous space an intimate experience. A stone weeping wall, which provides gentle background noise (harmonizing with an eclectic mix of piped in music), takes up the entire back of the restaurant. The food manages to be as intriguing as the interior design. Friendly servers will offer suggestions if you aren't familiar with Thai food; the menu is extensive, so it doesn't hurt to have help navigating. A favorite starter is the golden shrimp, served juicy and wrapped in noodles that are flash fried and with a slightly spicy plum dipping sauce. (These are the messiest things—the crispy noodles fly in every direction. Be ready to have them scattered across the whole table.) Also delicious is the meaty chicken satay, served with a creamy peanut sauce. If you like soup, don't miss the Tom Kha, a coconut lemon grass broth prepared with tofu, chicken, or shrimp and brought to the table steaming hot in a big family-style tureen. For the main entrée, consider the dramatically presented pineapple fried rice, a gigantic portion of which includes chicken and shrimp, served overflowing from a hollowed out whole pineapple. For beef lovers, try the "crying tiger," marinated flank steak that is grilled and served with a cold spicy dipping sauce (although to my taste it could be spicier and would be more appealing if it were served hot). Fish can be steamed, grilled, or fried and served with your choice of sauces. There are also red, yellow, and green curries, prepared with your choice of protein (including tofu). Be forewarned: The portions are ridiculously large. A serving of the fried rice alone could easily feed two or three, especially if you also order one of the hefty appetizers. Desserts, if you can fit them in, include fresh mangos in season and exotic sorbets.

REI DO GADO BRAZILIAN STEAKHOUSE

Manager: Steve Gi
619-702-8464
www.reidogado.com
939 Fourth Ave., San Diego, CA 92101
Open: Daily
Price: Expensive
Cuisine: Brazilian
Serving: L, D
Handicap Access: Yes
Credit Cards: AE, DC, MC, V
Reservations: Recommended
Parking: Street (limited)

Churrasco is a traditional Brazilian barbeque feast of mesquite-grilled meats—and plenty of them. At the elegant Rei do Gado in the Gaslamp Quarter downtown, they celebrate this Brazilian tradition by serving up skewer after skewer of tender, smoky bites in a dizzying variety. Place a green marker at your plate to indicate you're still game to try more, and servers will offer up a carnivore's orgy of succulent filet mignon wrapped in bacon, slow-cooked beef ribs, pork sausages, top sirloin, ham with fresh pineapple chunks, lamb shank, and spoon-tender beef tri-tip. For the adventurous, there are chicken hearts—although no one at Rei do Gado will be offended if you pass on these delicacies. Don't pass on the traditional Brazilian caramel-glazed flan called *pudím* or the light passion fruit mousse. Vegetarians may be turned off by the permeating smells of roasting meat, but there *is* an extensive salad bar that will sustain anyone wishing to avoid animal protein. Drinks are something special: Try the fresh and unusual cashew juice or have an iced glass of *guaraná*, a refreshing Brazilian soda. Note that the front desk service isn't as friendly as it should be.

Old Town
CAFÉ PACIFICA

Chef: Eduardo Zamarripa
619-291-6666
www.cafepacifica.com
2414 San Diego Ave., San Diego, CA 92110
Open: Daily
Price: Expensive
Cuisine: California
Serving: D
Credit Cards: AE, D, DC, MC, V
Handicap Access: Yes
Reservations: Recommended
Parking: Valet, street (very limited), or nearby lots

Located in Old Town, Café Pacifica is a decidedly upscale option in what is otherwise mostly a tourist dining mecca. Food is healthy and lovingly prepared. The restaurant specializes in fresh seafood, but there is also an eclectic menu of red meat offerings, including succulent lamb. Start with fresh oysters on the half shell; the wonton-wrapped yellow fin tuna stuffed with ginger and bell peppers and served over baby bok choy; or the New Zealand green lip mussels, impeccably fresh and steamed with fruity white wine and garlic. Daily specials are always a good bet, but it's hard to pass up the seared northern halibut, a delicate white fish stuffed with marinated ginger, coated with sesame seeds, and served with a pungent wasabi vinaigrette over rice pilaf. The sole stuffed with Dungeness crab and rock shrimp and served with fresh veggies in season is also hard to resist. A former boss of mine claims Café Pacifica has the best crème brûlée in town, but for my money I prefer the sampler dessert menu that has tastes of fresh berries in season, key lime pie with a gingersnap crust, fondue-dipped berries, *and* the famous brûlée. The restaurant has a fine wine collection, but do not miss the pomegranate margarita, one of the most distinctive cocktails in a city that prides itself on tequila-based concoctions.

CASA GUADALAJARA

Owner: Diane Powers
619-295-5111
4105 Taylor St., San Diego, CA 92110
Open: Daily
Price: Moderate
Cuisine: Mexican
Serving: B, L, D
Credit Cards: AE, D, DC, MC, V
Handicap access: Limited
Reservations: No
Parking: Lot behind the restaurant or next door, at the Bazaar del Mundo

On the outskirts of Old Town, Casa Guadalajara has an unassuming but colorful dining room and—better still—a large, breezy outdoor patio built around a big old California pepper tree and burbling water fountains. Brightly colored umbrellas shield patio diners from the sun (and shedding leaves), and on weekends and evenings, you're likely to be serenaded by a guitarist or a small strolling mariachi band. All in all, not a bad place to spend a relaxing afternoon sipping a cocktail and munching on Mexican comfort food. In addition to the traditional fare you'll find at just about any Mexican restaurant around town, Casa Guadalajara offers some unusual and tasty alternatives, such as the crab cakes picante, moist, mildly spicy cakes topped with a delicious jalapeno cream sauce, or the *pescado a la Naranja*—grilled sea bass with a sauce made from orange juice, cilantro butter, and stuffed green olives. Finish it all off with Mexican bread pudding, spiced heavily with cinnamon and served with a delicate vanilla sauce. There's also a lively cantina onsite. In addition to the ubiquitous margaritas and sangrias, try a Mexicola—a blend of Cazadores tequila, freshly squeezed lime juice, and Pepsi, served up in a salt-rimmed glass. Happy hour on Mondays through Fridays is an exceptional bargain; get $3 beers and cocktails and then help yourself to an extensive complimentary appetizer buffet.

OLD TOWN MEXICAN CAFÉ

Owners: J. D. Dahlen, Bob Estrada, and Herb Lizalde
619-297-4330
www.oldtownmexcafe.com
2489 San Diego Ave., San Diego, CA 92110
Open: Daily
Price: Moderate
Cuisine: Mexican
Serving: B, L, D
Credit Cards: AE, D, DC, MC, V
Handicap Access: Yes
Reservations: For large parties only
Parking: Street (very limited), Old Town Historic park lots

Old Town Mexican Café is a long-time favorite with locals, and because it is just outside of the park limits, has managed to escape the reinvention that chased out most of its competitors in 2005. Start with the ever-popular guacamole and chips or, for the more adventurous, try the shrimp and octopus cocktail served with cucumber and sliced avocadoes. Combinations featuring typical Mexican fare (tacos, enchiladas, burritos, fajitas) are all good choices, but for a truly authentic Mexican dish, try the chicken mole, a half bird smothered in an intricately spiced sauce that is flavored with dark chocolate. Each entree is served with rice, beans, and a salad, along with freshly made tortillas. The famous "tortilla ladies" of Old Town Mexican Café ply their trade behind a window for all to see, cranking out more than 7,000 corn and flour tortillas a day. And a restaurant in Old Town wouldn't be complete without margaritas: Try the colorful purple Cadillac, tequila blended with Chambord raspberry liquor.

BIG KITCHEN

Owner: Judy Forman
619-234-5789
3003 Grape St., San Diego, CA 92102
Open: Daily
Price: Inexpensive
Cuisine: American
Serving: B, L
Credit Cards: Cash only
Handicap Access: Yes
Reservations: No
Parking: Street

The neighborhood has been gentrified a bit since Whoopi Goldberg bussed tables and worked as a dishwasher in this Golden Hill establishment (it's safe to walk outside after dark now), but were she to return she would still recognize the homey menu—and probably some of the extremely friendly servers who are long-timers. Interior walls are plastered with photographs and posters, and there is a new trellised outdoor patio as well (although tables are hard to come by outside). This funky place attracts an eclectic clientele, who come from all around the county for the generous portions of homestyle breakfasts served up by "Judy the Beauty," the owner with a big heart and a quick smile, who looks at her eatery as a place to build community as much as it is a place to belly up to flapjacks, omelets, and really salty bacon. Try the Mexican cheese omelet, stuffed with chorizo, zucchini, cheese, and green peppers; at less than $9, it'll fill you up for the whole day. Expect long waits on weekends.

CHICKEN PIE SHOP

Owner: John Townsend
619-295-0156
2633 El Cajon Blvd., San Diego, CA 92123
Open: Daily
Price: Inexpensive
Cuisine: American
Serving: L, D
Credit Cards: Cash only
Handicap Access: Yes
Reservations: No
Parking: Street, lot in the back

This is probably the least expensive place to eat a sit-down meal in San Diego, and the very first restaurant I remember visiting with my father (likely not a coincidence!). An individual pie, with flaky crust, juicy gravy, and even a little bit of meat can be had for about $2; for a few more dollars, you can get mashed potatoes, veggies, a roll, *and* a piece of not-too-shabby apple or lemon pie. No doubt because of the prices, the Chicken Pie Shop attracts a varied and interesting crowd—from families to senior citizens to those who appear a bit down on their luck. But whatever your circumstances, the friendly servers will make you feel welcome, and you'll leave with your pocketbook intact. Old-timers will remember that the Chicken Pie Shop used to be in Hillcrest, but it was moved to the current North Park locale more than a decade ago. Never fear: The prevailing décor is still everything pertaining to chickens (with most of the poultry knick knackery donated from grateful customers).

CORVETTE DINER

Owners: Cohn Family
619-542-1476
www.cohnfamilyrestaurants.com
3946 Fifth Ave., San Diego, CA 92103
Open: Daily
Price: Inexpensive
Cuisine: American
Serving: L, D
Handicap access: Yes
Reservations: No
Parking: Metered street, small valet lot next door

I can't think of a more entertaining family dining experience outside of Orlando: Stacks of bubblegum boxes, towers of chocolate syrup cans, and miles of neon

Friendly waitresses at the Corvette Diner are half the fun of the restaurant.

greet you at the front door—along with a mint-condition vintage Corvette parked smack in the middle of the dining room. You'll soon notice the loud 1950s music and the wait staff dressed in a variety of pseudo-50s garb—anything from poodle skirts to bowling shirts to miniskirts and fishnet stockings. Once you're seated, keep your eyes open, because waitresses throw handfuls of straws and wrapped bubblegum at their unsuspecting patrons. And when you're ready to order, your waitress will pull up a chair and join you. Once an hour or so, the waitresses abandon their posts, pick up their pom poms, and dance and lip sync in a hysterical floor show that winds its way around the dining room. But the hijinks aren't the main reason to visit: Come ready to eat. As the surroundings suggest, the cuisine is mid-century comfort food, and portions are large. The signature appetizer is the spicy fried pickles, served with a ranch sauce for dipping. Other good choices are stuffed jalapeno peppers and baskets of golden brown onion rings. The daily blue plate specials feature home-cooked favorites like meatloaf and fried chicken, and there are plenty of sandwiches and burgers to choose from. But first and foremost, this is a soda fountain, so don't forget the shakes, served in tall glasses and piled high with whipped cream and cherries. You can also get monster-sized root beer floats, cherry Cokes, and authentic New York egg creams. The Corvette Diner could get away with charging a lot more, because you are getting dinner and a show here, but the prices—although not quite what they were in the 1950s—are still a real bargain.

ORTEGA'S MEXICAN BISTRO
Owners: Juan Carlos Ortega and John Haugland
619-692-4200
www.ortegasbistro.com
141 University Ave., Ste. 5, San Diego, CA 92103
Open: Daily
Price: Moderate to expensive
Cuisine: Mexican
Serving: L, D
Credit Cards: AE, D, MC, V

Handicap Access: Yes
Reservations: Yes
Parking: Very small lot in front, street
(limited)

Puerto Nuevo lobster is a treat that used to be available only south of the border: Whole Pacific lobster is boiled in oil and then sliced down the middle. The result is a tender, juicy lobster tail that is flavorful and fresh. Ortega's in Hillcrest offers the delicious shellfish with melted butter, rice, refried beans, and delicate handmade tortillas—and all without the wait at the border. At less than $25 for a pound and a quarter of the delicacy, it's a real bargain as well. Before the show-stopping crustaceans arrive, try the guacamole prepared tableside; servers mash perfectly ripe avocados with garlic, salsa, and roasted limes into a lava bowl, and the results are perfect for dipping the complimentary tortilla chips and pairing with the extraordinary salsa fresca. The thick bean and pumpkin soup dressed with more salsa fresca and cream is a nourishing starter as well—or a meal by itself. This light, large space has open-beamed ceilings; a colorful bar; and ele-

gant, restrained style; and servers are efficient and extremely friendly, owing to the fact that this is a neighborhood favorite with a lot of repeat business. It's a little out of the way in a tiny strip mall—and parking can be a headache—but it's well worth the effort.

SAIGON ON 5th
Owner: Patrick Hong Luu
619-220-8828
3900 Fifth Ave., San Diego, CA 92103
Open: Daily
Price: Moderate
Cuisine: Vietnamese
Serving: L, D
Credit Cards: AE, MC, V
Handicap Access: Yes
Reservations: Yes
Parking: Street, validated underground lot

This elegant, serene restaurant in Hillcrest is regarded as one of best Vietnamese dining options in the city, and judging by the consistent crowds, many San Diegans agree. For a real treat, order the coco-chicken soup to start: Chicken breast is simmered in a light broth and flavored with

Ortega's in Hillcrest offers some of the best Mexican food this side of the border.

green coconut milk. It is presented at the table in a whole coconut, which is enough to put me in a festive mood. The signature crunchy pan-fried dumplings are another delicious option, and come stuffed with marinated chicken and vegetables. When soft shell crabs are in season and so available fresh, don't miss them. They come in a delicate fried batter and are seasoned with just enough garlic, onion, and chili peppers. Otherwise, the lemon leaf chicken is a delicious alternative. Saigon on 5th also serves traditional pho, a classic rice noodle dish; and Vietnamese-style fried rice flavored with crab, chicken, or shrimp or pineapple fried rice with cashews, shrimp, roasted garlic, and egg. You can even prepare your own food, Vietnamese-fondue style: Try vinegar fondue beef, thin slices of filet simmered in a vinegar broth and then wrapped with veggies in rice paper; or Saigon fondue, with beef balls, tofu, or shrimp simmered in a lightly seasoned broth.

Food Purveyors

Breweries and Pubs

Dublin Square (619-239-5818; 554 Fourth St., San Diego, CA 92101). The bar made from real Irish oak is a faithful reproduction of a 19th-century bar in Kilkenny, and the interior throughout—designed by an Irish company specializing in pubs—evokes the Emerald Isle. Enjoy the ambiance while you knock back a pint and listen to authentic Irish music. In addition, you'll also find traditional pub fare like shepherd's pie and lamb stew; try the curry chips for a spicy snack.

Dublin Square Pub is a little bit of the Emerald Isle in downtown.

The Field (619-232-9840; 544 Fifth Ave., San Diego, CA 92101). This place doesn't just *look* authentic, it *is* authentic: The pub was shipped piece by piece from Ireland and then reassembled in the Gaslamp Quarter. Happy hour is 4–7 every weekday. You can also order up fish and chips, corned beef and cabbage, and beef stew simmered in Guinness.

Princess Pub & Grill (619-702-3021; 1665 India St., San Diego, CA 92101). Come in to this Little Italy establishment for a game of darts, some bangers and mash (sausage and potatoes), and indulge in a wide selection of British beers and ales. Although inside it is dark and vaguely reminiscent of a drizzly London day, the bright yellow exterior and pretty outdoor patio up front are pure San Diego sunshine.

Coffeehouses

LeStat's Coffee House (619-282-0437; 3343 Adams Ave., San Diego, CA 92116). This offbeat coffee house in Normal Heights is all about entertainment. Every Monday is open mike night for local talent, Tuesdays feature comedy nights, and there's live music the rest of the week. Open 24 hours a day.

Mrs. Burton's Tea Room (619-294-4600; 2465 Heritage Park Row, San Diego, CA 92110). This recreation of a Victorian tea house in Heritage Park in Old Town serves up high teas featuring watercress sandwiches, scones, fruit tarts, and spicy cilantro and cream cheese sandwiches on flower-patterned china and amid much lace and vintage wallpaper. So that guests may blend in properly with the turn-of-the-century surroundings, ladies will be supplied with feather boas and outrageous hats and gentlemen will be outfitted with top hats. There are also seasonal and specialty tea parties available for groups. After a relaxing hour or so with a cup of steaming Earl Grey, step outside to shoot a game of croquet with a pink-flamingo wicket, and take home a complimentary souvenir photo.

Twiggs Tea and Coffee (619-296-0616; 4590 Park Blvd., San Diego, CA 92116). A favorite with residents of the University Heights neighborhood, just northeast of downtown, Twiggs is a community gathering place. Come here to catch up with friends, sip tea or coffee, and munch on a cheese Danish or an incomparable apricot cardamom scone. Next door is the Green Room, where guests enjoy a wide variety of live entertainment, from acoustic music to poetry reading.

Urban Grind (619-299-4763; 3797 Park Blvd., San Diego, CA 92103). This Hillcrest coffee shop, part of a West Coast chain, has an expansive outdoor patio and a sleek urban interior décor. This location is a favorite community hangout, and serves up excellent muffins and pastries to go with their specialty coffees. You don't have to be an early bird to enjoy this place, because it's open until midnight.

Pizzas, Burgers, and Dogs

Bronx Pizza (619-291-3341; 111 Washington St., San Diego, CA 92103). In Hillcrest, you'll find authentic, New York-style thin crust pizzas that are hand-tossed and dressed with a treasured sauce recipe, the ingredients of which owner Matt Garden keeps highly secret.

Dobson's (619-231-6771; 956 Broadway Circle, San Diego, CA 92101). An upscale bistro near Horton Plaza downtown with a European ambiance, Dobson's serves an especially tasty—and expensive—burger to a power-lunch crowd.

Filippi's Pizza Grotto (619-232-5094; 1747 India St., San Diego, CA 92101). One of the original restaurants in Little Italy (and now with several locations throughout the city), Filippi's has been a San Diego institution since 1950. In addition to extra-cheesy meatball and pepperoni pizzas, Filippi's serves an exceptionally loaded vegetarian special, with black olives, mushrooms, bell pepper, and onions. The red-and-white vinyl table cloths and inexpensive bottles of Chianti remind you that this restaurant was a mainstay even before the neighborhood underwent a dramatic revitalization in the past decade.

Lefty's Chicago Pizzeria (619-295-1720; 3448 30th St., San Diego, CA 92104). Brendan and Lauren Hodson, an energetic young couple who hail from the Windy City, opened this North Park store in 2004, and have been winning over locals with their food ever since. Authentic Chicago-style deep-dish creations are piled high with toppings, including fresh herbs and high-quality cheeses. You can also find a stuffed crust variety, which features more than 3 pounds of cheese and takes more than an hour to cook—be sure to call ahead!

The Linkery (619-255-8778; 3382 30th St., San Diego, CA 92104). You won't find nitrates or fillers in the sausages at this North Park restaurant, because everything is made from scratch on the premises. Come here for exceptional wursts, as well as the unusual sausage tacos served with cabbage and jalapeno sauce in a corn tortilla.

Urban Mo's (619-491-0400; 308 University Ave., San Diego, CA 92103). This is a revamped version of the beloved (and now defunct) Hamburger Mary's in Hillcrest; the management is the same, but the décor is upscale, to match the increasingly gentrified neighborhood. Try the stuffed burgers for a gourmet treat, or build your own burger with their long list of fixings.

Specialty Markets

Bacchus Wine Market and Tasting Room (619-236-0005; 647 G St., San Diego, CA 92101). Located in the Gaslamp Quarter of downtown, Bacchus specializes in Italian and Californian wines. On scheduled Saturdays, they feature the popular "Drink Yourself Blind" event—this isn't as bad as it sounds. The tasting room presents 10 bottles cloaked in brown bags, and guests who can correctly identify at least five of their selections get their tasting for free; it'll cost you $10 if your palate is wrong more than half the time.

Beach City Market (619-232-2491; 3 Horton Plaza, San Diego, CA 92101). Downstairs in the Horton Plaza shopping mall downtown, this little New York-style deli sells sandwiches, smoothies, sushi, fresh juices, and coffee. You'll also find a nice selection of wines and cheeses—a perfect place to shop for a picnic at nearby Balboa Park.

Blue Water Seafood Market and Grill (619-497-0914; 3667 India St., San Diego, CA 92101). You'll find one of the best selections of fresh seafood at this market (between Little Italy and Hillcrest); you can also purchase prepared sushi to take home (as well as dine in at the grill).

Cash and Carry Market (619-232-5094; 1747 India St., San Diego, CA 92101). Despite the dubious name, this market, which fronts the famous Filipi's Pizza Grotto (see page 88), is an inspired place to find reasonably priced imported Italian sausages, cheese, canned San Marzano tomatoes, and Italian cookies and candy.

Hot Licks (619-235-4000; 865 W. Harbor Dr., Ste. C, San Diego, CA 92101). Chiliheads should not miss this tiny shop in Seaport Village, which sells more than 350 brands of hot sauce, as well as spicy-themed souvenirs.

Venissimo (619-491-0708; 754 W. Washington St., San Diego, CA 92103). Well-established and well-loved Venissimo in Mission Hills has 120 cheeses on display, with knowledgeable and helpful staff who encourage you to try before you buy. The store hosts regular wine and cheese and beer and cheese pairing events onsite and also at local restaurants.

Sweets and Treats

Bread and Cie (619-683-9322; 350 University Ave., San Diego, CA 92103). This Bohemian Hillcrest bakery sells exceptionally good breads and rolls, including delicious black olive bread, sourdough baguettes, and pumpkin walnut muffins. In addition, come for great sandwiches and picnic items. The open layout allows guests to watch the bakers at work.

Chi Chocolat (619-501-9215; 2021 India St., San Diego, CA 92101). Serious chocoholics will not want to miss this bistro in Little Italy, which features some seriously good artisan-crafted candy. Indulge in fudge fondue and chocolate-dipped ginger, or for something a little different, try a dark-chocolate raspberry peppercorn truffle or a heart-shaped bon bon filled with rosewater ganache.

Cousins Candy Shop (619-297-2000; 2711 San Diego Ave., San Diego, CA 92110). You'll find buckets full of old-time candies such as Necco wafers, Walnettos, and Bit-o-Honey at this historic-themed candy store in Old Town. You can watch salt-water taffy being pulled by machine or a bewildering variety of fudge being made by hand.

Extraordinary Desserts (619-294-7001; 1430 Union St., San Diego, CA 92101). With locations in Little Italy and Hillcrest, this sleek bistro serves up desserts that deserve the name "extraordinary." In addition to the myriad sweets, you can nosh on bruschetta, artisanal cheeses, and panini as you sip teas and coffees in-house or purchase cakes to go: Try the rich *gianduia*, heady chocolate cake soaked in Meyers' Rum and slathered with hazelnut butter cream, chocolate mousse, and berry jam; or the lighter blood orange ricotta torte with orange whipped cream and fresh berries. Owner Karen Krasne creates her confections exclusively with all-natural, organic ingredients.

Ghirardelli Soda Fountain and Chocolate Shop (619-234-2449; 643 Fifth Ave., San Diego, CA 92101). Although Ghirardelli is generally associated with San Francisco rather than Southern California, chocoholics welcome this old-fashioned soda fountain to the downtown Gaslamp District anyhow. The hot fudge sundaes, which show off the signature chocolate at its best, are pricy: A one-scoop affair in a tiny plastic cup will set you back almost $6. Spring for the large sundae, which is only about $1 more and is big enough to share (if you're so inclined).

Just Fabulous Kensington (619-584-2929; 4116 Adams Ave., San Diego, CA 92116). Pastry chef Byrl Bird highlights some of her favorite desserts (served in high-end restaurants around the city) at this Kensington bistro. The "chocolate collection" is an orgy of chocolate tortes, brûlée, dipped cookies, gelato, and various bon bons meant for two people (but share only with someone you *really* like). Another favorite is the zesty lemon tart served in an almond cookie shell.

Mariposa Homemade Ice Cream (619-284-5197; 3450 Adams Ave., San Diego, CA 92116). This Normal Heights shop is tiny (there are a very few tables inside), so get scoops of the famous homemade coconut ice cream to go; there are also shakes and sundaes available.

Solunto's (619-233-0595; 1643 India St., San Diego, CA 92101). An unassuming bakery in Little Italy, Solunto's sells fresh-baked cookies by the pound, including pignole, amaretti, and pecan-studded Mexican wedding cakes, as well as heavenly smelling fresh breads. This is also a great bargain for breakfast; enjoy a pancake for $1.50 outside on the small sidewalk patio.

Taquerias

El Cuervo Taco Shop (619-295-9713; 110 W. Washington St., San Diego, CA 92103). This storefront taco shop is a neighborhood favorite in Hillcrest serving authentic, flavorful tacos. Devotees swear the huge carne asada burrito is the best in the city. Don't miss the loaded salsa bar.

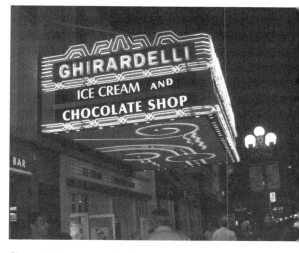

Ghirardelli lights up the Gaslamp at night.

El Indio (619-299-0333; 3695 India St., San Diego, CA 92103). To call this fast food is a disservice to the consistently high quality of El Indio, a San Diego favorite since 1940. Soft grilled chicken tacos and carnitas are among the best in town. In December, you can find sweet tamales, something normally available only in home kitchens. Located near Old Town, El Indio gives a 10 percent discount to all police, fire, and active military personnel.

Fred's Mexican Café (619-232-8226; 527 Fifth Ave., San Diego, CA 92101). Eat under palapas on the sidewalk at this energetic, loud Gaslamp Quarter Mexican joint. Celebrate "Cinco de Fred" the fifth of every month, and don't miss "Kiss My Taco" Tuesdays, when the crunchy treats sell for $2. Fred's also has locations in Old Town (619-858-8226) and Pacific Beach (858-483-8226).

Jimmy Carter's Mexican Café (619-296-6952; 807 West Washington St., San Diego, CA 92103). No, it's not *that* Jimmy Carter, but this tiny Mexican café in Mission Hills serves up food good enough for a president. Try the *carnitas*, and prepare to wait for a table on weekends.

Pokez (619-702-7160; 947 E St., San Diego, CA 92101). If you find yourself in the East Village downtown craving delicious vegetarian Mexican cuisine, Pokez (pronounced "po-keys") is the place to be. Although it isn't solely vegetarian, there are dozens of meatless and vegan options—including tasty vegetarian rolled tacos. Pokez uses lard-free beans and tortillas, and the cooking of meat and tofu are carefully segregated in the kitchen.

THEME PARKS AND ZOOS

SAN DIEGO ZOO

619-234-3153
www.sandiegozoo.org
2920 Zoo Dr., San Diego, CA 92112
Open: Daily; hours vary by season
Admission: $32 for adults; $19.75 for children 3 to 11

Although the San Diego travel industry's mantra in the past decade has been "more than just a great zoo," the fact is that the San Diego Zoo helped put this city on the tourist-destination map. The Zoo remains one of the largest and most innovative in the world, and a favorite stop with visitors and locals alike. With more than 100 acres set aside just minutes from downtown in Balboa Park, the Zoo houses more than 3,500 rare and endangered animals representing more than four hundred species, some of which no longer exist outside of zoos such as this one. In addition, the extensive botanical gardens contain more than 700,000 exotic plants, many of these endangered species as well.

What makes this zoo so special is that it is a conservation and education facility, as well as a recreational one: The Zoological Society of San Diego, the nonprofit institution that operates the Zoo and its sister in north county, the Wild Animal Park, is dedicated to the reproduction and protection of its animals—and its thousands of endangered plants—first and foremost. The Zoo was one of the first in the world to create animal habitats that do not resemble traditional animal enclosures. Animals that would normally cohabitate in the wild are housed together in so-called biomes that simulate the animals' natural habitat, in the least restrictive environment possible to ensure the safety of the animals and visitors.

Some of the most popular exhibits include the "Polar Bear Plunge," where you can watch the arctic creatures frolic in a 12-foot-deep, 130,000-gallon water tank. The Zoo has two sets of twin polar bears that are on rotating display in this exhibit; the younger twins are generally out before lunchtime, and they tend to interact with visitors, often pressing their noses right to the glass enclosure in front of a startled onlooker.

Other favorites include "Gorilla Tropics," which is considered by conservationists as one of the best gorilla exhibits in the world, and the "Koala Exhibit," which allows visitors to get close to several of the nocturnal cuties, who are generally perched high in their eucalyptus trees and—if you're visiting during the day—inactive and asleep. The "Giant Panda Research Station," which is subject to long lines for viewing, is home to three pandas, Bai Yun, Mei Sheng, and their offspring Su Lin—pandas on loan to the United States from their native Republic of China. Su Lin, which translates to "a little bit of something cute," makes the San Diego Zoo the only U.S. park to successfully breed and rear a healthy panda cub.

The newest attraction, "Monkey Trails," opened in 2006, is a series of lush pathways meandering through a tropical forest that mimics what would be found in Asia and Africa. Climb upstairs to treetop walkways that allow you to see monkeys at eye level.

The "Children's Zoo," near the front entrance, offers kids the chance to pet deer and other gentle animals; visit animal nurseries; and get an up-close view of various animals during feeding time. You'll also find shows scheduled throughout the day, including bird shows, puppet theater, and special presentations for children. Animal enrichment encounters are also available and include feeding giraffes.

For an additional charge, you can hop aboard a double-decker bus for a 35-minute guided tour of the Zoo, which will take you past Asian and African elephants, rare deer and antelope, meerkats, and spectacled bears, among others. The bus is a good way to save a little shoe leather—and because the Zoo is a big place, with uneven and hilly terrain in spots—this is sometimes a welcome alternative to hoofing it. But given the amount of time you're likely to wait to board, the bus tour is disappointing: The view of the animals isn't the best, even up top, and the bus only stops for a minute or two at each enclosure.

The ever-popular "Skyfari Aerial Tram," on the other hand, is a must see: A gondola car will carry you from the east side to the west side and back again—for the cost of an additional ticket, which can be purchased once inside the park (although it is free to members). The ride only takes a few moments, but it is well worth the time waiting in line to board. You'll cross directly over the gorilla enclosure, for premier viewing access. In addition, the view of the California Tower in Balboa Park and the nearby San Diego skyline is alone worth the extra price of the ticket. (Note that the east "Skyfari" terminal, near the entrance, is usually quite crowded. Walk to the west end of the park and board near the polar bear exhibit and you'll usually find a minimal wait.)

Visitors can save on admission costs if you plan to visit both the San Diego Zoo and the San Diego Wild Animal Park (see chapter 7). A two-park ticket will save about $6 per adult admission and $3 for children. Note that in the summer the park stays open late for Nighttime Zoo, with additional shows, live music, and animal encounters. During the entire month of October, the Zoo is free to children, which is a nice benefit if you're traveling with little ones, but the congestion increases as a result.

RECREATION: THE GREAT OUTDOORS

Even in this urban region of San Diego, the moderate temperatures and nearly constant sunshine afford abundant outdoor recreational activities, especially on and along the waterfront. In addition, downtown San Diego has the expansive Balboa Park, with venues for Frisbee golf; bocci ball; circuit training; and nice, long walks.

Canoeing, Kayaking, and Sailing

Hornblower Cruises (888-551-4855; 1066 N. Harbor Dr., San Diego, CA 92101). One of the best ways to see the skyline in San Diego is by boat. Hornblower offers nightly dinner cruises in the harbor, leaving just in time to catch the sunset and then watch the city lights start to glow. They also have champagne brunches on weekends and private charters, as well as daily one- and two-hour tours throughout the bay. Call ahead for reservations.

Next Level Sailing (800-644-3454; next to the U.S.S. *Midway* on the harbor). Next Level offers two-hour harbor cruises, charters, and sailing lessons aboard 80-foot International America's Cup Class yachts, the fastest mono-hull sailing vessels in the world. Book in advance, because excursions are limited and this company is popular.

San Diego Harbor Excursions (619-234-4111; 1050 N. Harbor Dr., San Diego, CA 92101). San Diego Harbor Excursions offers a wide variety of services, from day cruises on the harbor, nightly dinner dance cruises, guided whale watching tours, and holiday (Fourth of July and Christmas) cruises.

Hiking

Urban hiking is an enjoyable pastime in San Diego, where the weather is almost always pleasant and the terrain is relatively flat. There are wide sidewalks along the harbor, as well as many meandering pathways through Balboa Park.

If you'd like to get a bit of history with your exercise, consider taking a guided walking tour through the city. For $10 for adults, you can take a two-hour tour to learn about the city's somewhat sordid past and to hear the stories behind the beautiful façades of downtown buildings with **Gaslamp Quarter Walking Tours** (619-233-4692). You don't need to make advance reservations for these tours, sponsored by the Gaslamp Historic Society; just come to the William Heath Davis House (at the corner of Fourth Ave. and Island) on any Saturday at 11 AM and purchase tickets 10 minutes prior.

Parks

Balboa Park (619-239-0512; off Park
Blvd.). Balboa Park was built to commemorate the 1915–16 Panama–
California Exposition, and today the
El Prado pedestrian thoroughfare
running through the center of the
park appears much as it did then,
with elaborate Spanish Renaissance
architecture designed by Bertram
Goodhue, expansive subtropical gardens designed by legendary landscape architect Kate Sessions, and
several major theatrical venues. The
park is home to more than a dozen
museums (see pages 64–67); several
cultural venues, including the **Centro
Cultural de la Raza** (619-235-6135;
open Tuesday–Sunday, noon to 4;
admission $2), which is dedicated to
educating the public about Chicano,
Mexican, and Native American art
and culture; the **House of Pacific
Relations** (619-234-0739; open Sundays noon–4; admission free), a group of 20 cot-

A view of Balboa Park Tower from the Alcazar Garden.

tages representing the culture and history of 31 different nations; and plenty of park
grounds on which to picnic or just enjoy the eucalyptus and jacaranda trees spread out
over 1,200 acres. You'll even find a Frisbee golf course at the **Balboa Park Disc Golf
Course** (619-692-3607). In addition, the world-famous San Diego Zoo anchors the
north end of the park. The one hundred-bell carillon housed in the Balboa Tower
chimes every 15 minutes, but try to be outside at noon, to get the full effect. Children
will not want to miss the 1922 carousel—grab the brass ring and get a free ride.

For $5 for adults and $3 for children, the Balboa Park Visitors Center offers one-hour
audio tours, which highlight the park's history, botanical features, and architecture.
Note that most museums are free one Tuesday a month, on a rotating schedule. Check
the Web site for up-to-date schedules (www.balboapark.org). You can also buy a Balboa
Park "Passport" at the Visitors Center (located in Hospitality House), which can save as
much as 50 percent off full-price admissions. There is a free shuttle bus for all visitors
that runs every 15 minutes, with stops throughout the park.

Embarcadero Park (North and South) (off Harbor Dr. downtown). These parks surround
Seaport Village and the San Diego Convention Center, and feature walking paths with
spectacular views of the water and the pricey sailboats and yachts that call it home, picnic areas, and large expanses of grassy lawn.

Presidio Park (2727 Presidio Dr., San Diego, CA 92110). The park is anchored by the
Junipero Serra Museum (see page 64), which features archaeological treasures from
early San Diego and boasts a far-off view of the harbor (and the tangle of freeways that
fall between here and there). But most local kids prefer the steep grassy hills, which they
can roll down to their heart's content.

The New Home of Padres Baseball

Since President Jimmy Carter threw out the first pitch in 2004, **Petco Park** (619-795-5011; 100 Park Blvd., San Diego, CA 92101; www.padres.com)—the dazzling $453.4 million home of the San Diego Padres baseball team—has drawn hundreds of thousands of fans to enjoy the park-like surroundings of the new game field, as well as to enjoy the 80 baseball games, played from early April through October. Naysayers complain that ticket prices are steep at the new ballpark, but there are plenty of fun and affordable alternatives. For only $5, visitors can gain admission to the extremely popular "Park in the Park" behind center field; this is a pretty grassy area elevated enough to see into the ballpark or to watch the game on a giant video screen. Kids *love* to run the bases at the small baseball diamond. Note that the Park in the Park is open even on nongame days, and for a small fee, baseball fans can arrange for a behind-the-scenes tour of Petco any time of the year.

Shopping: Everything Under the Sun

There are a number of eclectic, entertaining shopping areas in downtown and Old Town, including **Horton Plaza**, a mainstream outdoor mall with dazzling multilevel architecture—one of the first new downtown projects (opened in 1985) and a spur to the miraculous redevelopment of the Gaslamp Quarter. Just to the north on the waterfront, you'll find charming **Seaport Village**—a 14-acre waterfront shopping district that is designed to look like a well-manicured fishing village at the turn of the century. Be sure to let little ones ride the relocated 1895 carousel, with Coney-Island-style wooden animals carved by the famous artisan Charles I. D. Looff.

In Old Town, look for the newly relocated **Bazaar del Mundo** (619-296-3161; 4133 Taylor St., San Diego, CA 92110), just a few blocks from its old site in the Old Town State Historic Park. Although it has been downsized to fit a smaller space, it is still a colorful, intriguing place with eclectic stores selling imported items you're not likely to find elsewhere. Look for the cart out front that sells bright handmade crepe-paper flowers. **Plaza del Posado** (619-297-3100), which in late 2005 took over the space occupied for decades by the Bazaar del Mundo, features three heritage restaurants that serve pseudo-period food—and a lot of contemporary margaritas. The themed area offers live music and entertainment on the weekends on an open-air stage; and small shops scattered throughout sell period souvenirs, toys, crafts, and books.

Antiques and Collectibles

Antique stores used to be plentiful in downtown, but the revitalization of the Gaslamp (and the resulting soaring rents) have chased out all but a few of the best places. Now the funky and fun neighborhood of Normal Heights, just northeast of downtown, has the greatest concentration of antiques in this region, with approximately two dozen stores on "Antique Row" on Adams Avenue, where you'll find collectibles, fine antiques, and many "shabby chic" resale stores.

Architectural Salvage San Diego (619-696-1313; 1971 India St., San Diego, CA 92101). In the Little Italy section of downtown, this jam-packed store specializes in antique stained-glass windows, salvaged doors, fireplace surrounds, and ironwork. You'll also find an amazing collection of door knobs and other vintage hardware and racks of old tin ceiling tiles. Although wares are stacked a dozen deep, whimsical touches, like a clawfoot tub filled to the brim with chandelier crystals, make this a delightful place to visit.

Artes de Mexico (619-296-3161; 4133 Taylor St., San Diego, CA 92110). Part of the newly relocated Bazaar del Mundo, this tiny store features collector-quality folk art and crafts from Mexico, including ceramic "trees of life," painted tin Christmas ornaments, and traditional and colorful imported fabrics.

India Street Antiques (619-231-3004; 2360 and 2361 India St., San Diego, CA 92101). This fun-to-browse warehouse presents another great reason to visit the Little Italy section of downtown: You'll find beautiful antique furniture, as well as vintage windows and an extensive collection of glassware.

Paper Antiquities (619-296-0656; 2608 Adams Ave., San Diego, CA 92116). Paper aficionados could spend hours digging through the wares at this specialty store in North Park. You'll find vintage magazines, newspapers, post cards, movie posters, greeting cards, and even old menus.

The shops at Seaport Village are meant to evoke a New England fishing town.

Books and Music

Adams Avenue Bookstore (619-281-3330; 3502 Adams Ave., San Diego, CA 92116). With more than 90,000 used books in more than one hundred subject categories—including philosophy, Shakespearean studies, and mysteries as well as German and French literature in the original language, book lovers can browse happily for hours.

Blue Stocking Books (619-296-1424; 3817 Fifth Ave., San Diego, CA 92103). This small, welcoming store in Hillcrest sells new and used books, and carries a selection of journals, magazines, and gift items. The store hosts informal poetry readings the first Monday of every month.

Folk Art Rare Records (619-282-7833; 2881 Adams Ave., San Diego, CA 92116). This store has been a San Diego fixture for 40 years, and specializes in folk, blues, and jazz music. You'll find an extensive collection of 78 RPM records here, and knowledgeable staff will help you locate just about whatever you want.

Obelisk (619-297-4171; 1029 University Ave., San Diego, CA 92103). This bookstore in Hillcrest specializes in gay and lesbian books, magazines, and newspapers, and carries cards and small gift items as well.

Off the Record (619-298-4755; 2912 University Ave., San Diego, CA 92104). Now located in North Park (Off the Record was in Hillcrest for years), this store draws a young, colorful crowd shopping for eclectic music, especially alternative and punk rock. You'll even find actual *records* here, in addition to stacks and stacks of CDs.

Upstart Crow (619-232-4855; 835 W. Harbor Dr., Ste. C, San Diego, CA 92101). The original San Diego coffee shop/bookstore, the Upstart Crow in Seaport Village nestles tables among the stacks. You'll find a good children's book collection here, as well as games and puzzles. They also make a pretty good cup of joe.

Wahrenbrock's Book House (619-232-0132; 726 Broadway, San Diego, CA 92101). The oldest continually operating bookstore in San Diego, Wahrenbrock's in downtown specializes in antiquarian illustrated and color-plate books, Western Americana, and offers many autographed and first-edition copies for sale.

The slightly downsized Bazaar del Mundo relocated to its present site in 2006.

Clothing

Buffalo Exchange (619-298-4411; 3862 Fifth Ave., San Diego, CA 92103). Racks and more racks of retro clothing will greet you on entering this entertaining Hillcrest store, which employs friendly sales staff and items priced to move.

Carol Gardyne (619-233-8066; 1840 Columbia St., San Diego, CA 92101). Gorgeous handmade leather purses from France, hand-painted silk scarves, and locally crafted jewelry in this Little Italy boutique provide a varied selection of fashion accessories you won't find anywhere else in the city.

Kurios (619-236-8790; 935 Fifth Ave., San Diego, CA 92101). This spacious, high-ceilinged store in the Gaslamp Quarter sells tailored, upscale clothing for young fashionistas in a sophisticated, chic setting.

Mango (619-237-1344; 230 Fifth Ave., San Diego, CA 92101). This high-style boutique catering to stylish young urbanites often has sales racks with items for $10 and $16, and pretty window displays that will give even fashion-impaired browsers ideas.

Western Hat Works (619-234-0457; 433 E. St., San Diego, CA 92101). Western Hat Works has been selling Stetsons and fedoras downtown since 1922, and given the revitalization that has transformed the area in the past decade, this is no mean feat.

Home Goods

Avitatt (619-338-8245; 232 Fifth Ave., San Diego, CA 92101). European urban furnishings are paired with bold accessories like ethnic-inspired sculptures and art glass in this pretty showroom near the Convention Center downtown. (There is another store in Fashion Valley as well.)

Bella Stanza (619-239-2929; 1501 India St., #120, San Diego, CA 92101). Appropriately located in Little Italy, Bella Stanza has a large collection of imported Tuscan Majolica and Umbrian pottery, Murano glass, and Venetian carnival masks. The sunny collection is a joy to browse, although it is hard to walk out of this small store without making a purchase.

Boomerang for Modern (619-239-2040; 2040 India St., San Diego, CA 92101). The vintage collection turns over quickly, but look for pieces by Charles and Ray Eames and other high-style mid-century designers. Boomerang is an authorized dealer for Herman Miller and Vitra.

Disegno Italiano (619-515-0191; 1605 India St., San Diego, CA 92101). Come here for Italian-made, Italian-designed house wares, including chic table settings, sleek espresso machines, space-age bottle openers, and colanders beautiful enough to be backlit. Sometimes you'll even find a vintage Vespa for sale!

Pomegranate Home (619-220-0225; 1037 University Ave., San Diego, CA 92103). Luxurious pillows, sculptural vases, chic home furnishings, fine linens, and unusual accessories pack this elegant showroom in Hillcrest. This is also a great place to find distinctive, eclectic chandeliers and lamps.

Just for Fun

Hilo Hattie's (619-546-7289; 301 Fifth Ave., San Diego, CA 92101). This Hawaiian franchise is even larger than the store *in* Hilo; you'll find a large collection of quality Aloha shirts, macadamia nuts flown in from the islands, fresh orchid leis, Kona coffee, and an extensive collection of black pearl jewelry.

Kite Flite (619-234-5483; 849 W. Harbor Dr., San Diego, CA 92101). Friendly salespeople will help children of all ages explore the huge collection of kites at this little store in Seaport Village; you'll find beautiful hand-painted kites in the shape of butterflies and surfboards, windsocks, and Frisbees that come equipped with their own built-in headlights.

Bella Stanza imports Italian pottery in sunny yellows and sky blues.

Le Travel Store (619-544-0005; 745 Fourth Ave., San Diego, CA 92101). Travel buffs will not want to miss this store, which in addition to an extensive collection of durable and versatile luggage, wrinkle-resistant clothing, and miniaturized personal care essentials boasts one of the best travel book collections in the city.

Presenting the Soap Opera (619-230-1300; 817 W. Harbor Dr., Ste. B, San Diego, CA 92101). You'll find a treasure trove of imported soaps, bath products, bath beads, and the full line of Burt's Bees products in this pretty smelling store in Seaport Village.

San Diego City Store (619-234-2489; 803 W. Harbor Dr., San Diego, CA 92101). Love San Diego and wish you could take a little bit of it home? This Seaport Village Store is the place to choose from a collection of city artifacts, including actual street signs from the city, t-shirts from the San Diego Firefighters Association, and lots of postcards.

So Good (619-238-3599; 450 Fifth Ave., San Diego, CA 92101). This brightly lighted store glitters with hundreds of thousands of faux jewels, in the largest collection of costume jewelry I've ever seen. Look for sparkling necklaces, bracelets, dangling earrings, and hair adornments, most for under $20.

Street Machine (619-687-0270; 924 Fifth Ave., San Diego, CA 92101). This very popular Gaslamp shop offers the latest in skateboarding gear, including cutting-edge boards, clothing, and shoes. Helpful sales staff will guide you in purchases, should this seem like a foreign world to you.

Unusual rock formations off the coast in La Jolla are habitats for a variety of wildlife.

4

LA JOLLA AND
NEARBY BEACH TOWNS

Coastal Jewels

Few places have the cachet of La Jolla. In addition to miles of some of the loveliest (and costliest) shoreline in the country, arguably the most important contemporary art museum in California, and multi-million dollar homes, La Jolla offers hot new restaurants and clubs, cutting-edge boutique hotels and elegant historic properties, and shopping along Prospect Street that rivals Rodeo Drive in Beverly Hills. La Jolla has been home to the likes of Gregory Peck, Raquel Welch, and Dr. Seuss (a.k.a. Theodor Geisel), and hosts world-class scientific research centers like the Scripps Institute of Oceanography, the Salk Institute, and the University of California, San Diego. The art scene is vibrant, thanks to the famed La Jolla Playhouse, which has sent dozens of plays to Broadway, and to a plethora of galleries featuring internationally recognized artists. La Jolla is the Riviera of California, and attracts a cosmopolitan, upscale crowd that keeps the manicured streets humming every night of the week.

Inland La Jolla encompasses the Golden Triangle, an area bordered by I-5 on the west, I-805 on the east, and CA 52 in the south. This area centers on the Westfield University Towne Center shopping mall (known as UTC by locals) and includes a number of financial and scientific research institutions, as well as several large-scale chain hotels and a wide selection of fine dining opportunities. Northern La Jolla includes the neighborhood that revolves around the Torrey Pines State Reserve, and includes the adjacent beach, the Torrey Pines Glider Port (2800 Torrey Pines Scenic Dr.), and the internationally recognized Torrey Pines Golf Course.

Just to the south, Pacific Beach is a densely packed blend of hip new design and beach-cottage chic; increasingly you'll find sleek restaurants and bars in "PB," but this is still surfer central, and bare feet on the boardwalk are as common as little black dresses. This vaguely retro neighborhood is the place to find live music, Bohemian boutiques, and bikini shops. Merging nearly seamlessly into PB from the south is youth-centric, party-hearty Mission Beach, a community that revels in sun, surf, and suds. You'll find board shops and funky bars here, along with a vintage rollercoaster just off the most populated shoreline in the city. To the east is Mission Bay, which is vacation central for folks visiting San Diego: You'll find miles of walkways for strolling hand in hand or for a leisurely bike ride, all the while surrounded by tall palm trees, calm waters, and a relaxed atmosphere. You can rent all manner of water toys or just pull up a hammock and soak in the sun.

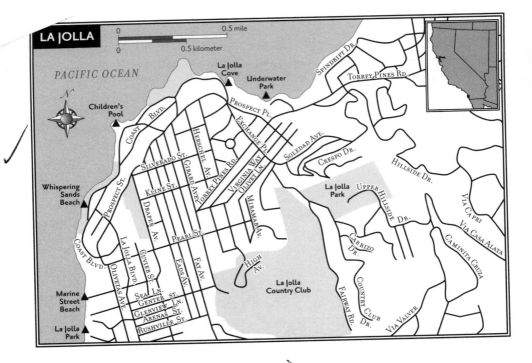

LODGING

These are the most popular beaches in San Diego County, and there are plentiful hotel options on the water. You'll find that in general the prices edge up as you move northward along the coast, with La Jolla being significantly more expensive than Mission Beach and Mission Bay.

LA JOLLA
BED AND BREAKFAST INN AT LA JOLLA

Innkeeper: Gayle Wildowsky
858-456-2066; fax 858-456-1510
www.innlajolla.com
7773 Draper St., La Jolla, CA 92037
Price: Expensive
Credit Cards: AE, D, MC, V
Handicap Access: 1 partial

Famous local architect Irving Gill, who worked with Frank Lloyd Wright, built this charming bed-and-breakfast as a private residence in 1913. The lush gardens were planned by Kate Sessions, who landscaped much of Balboa Park, and the house was once home to John Philip Sousa, the legendary conductor. The charming residential location, with 15 guest rooms, offers ocean and garden views, and is elegantly decorated with fine antiques and art in a restrained Victorian style. Many rooms feature fireplaces and clawfoot tubs, and the enormous beds are piled high with fine linens. Guests enjoy a complimentary full breakfast in the mornings (including the inn's homemade granola as well as delicious baked-apple pancakes) and a wine and cheese reception in the afternoons.

THE GRANDE COLONIAL

Manager: Terry Underwood
858-454-2181 or 888-530-5766; fax 858-454-5679
www.thegrandecolonial.com
910 Prospect St., La Jolla, CA 92037
Price: Expensive
Credit Cards: AE, D, MC, V
Handicap Access: 4 full

The immaculately restored Grande Colonial is the oldest hotel in La Jolla, dating to 1913. This tranquil inn offers graceful service and understated luxury, with 75 guest rooms, many featuring stunning ocean views. The comfortable lobby is decorated in elegant fabrics, and the deep couches and bergère chairs are perfect for flipping through the inn's collection of coffee table books or just warming up by the inviting fireplace. But I would be happy to sequester myself in an idyllic guest room, decked out with butter yellow walls, lustrous original moldings, and pale floral upholstery. Bathrooms are small, but make up for their size with Aveda products and thick robes. Beds are invitingly plush and piled with down pillows. Large windows—and lots of them—actually open to let in fresh ocean breezes. The small round pool tucked into a cozy courtyard is heated to a comfortable 82 degrees year-round. The Grande Colonial is located to allow nearly instant access to La Jolla Cove, upscale shopping, and fine dining, but guests needn't stray off property to experience exquisite California cuisine: **Nine-Ten** (see pages 116) onsite is one of the most highly regarded restaurants in the city.

And it gets even better: In 2007, the hotel completed a $3.5 million renovation of the eight-room **Little Hotel by the Sea** next door and the adjacent ten-room **Garden Terraces.** Both of these jewel-box hotels maintain separate identities, but they are managed by the Grande Colonial, thus increasing the variety of accommodations the inn is able to offer.

HOTEL PARISI

Manager: Virginie Berron
858-454-1511; fax 858-454-1531
www.hotelparisi.com
1111 Prospect St., La Jolla, CA 92037

The Grande Colonial's façade has been restored to its early 20th-century splendor.

Price: Very expensive
Credit Cards: AE, D, DC, MC, V
Handicap Access: 1 full

Imagine a European castle designed according to Chinese Feng Shui principles, decorated in warm chocolate tones, and heavily perfumed with essential oils: This is the Hotel Parisi, which aims to provide its guests with the gift of peace and well-being, wrapped in a contemporary Zen-inspired package. To avoid starting off your stay in a frustrated state, be sure to climb the winding staircase to the right of the front door and look for the small table floating slightly off-center, which is the obscured registration desk. From here you'll be directed to a clean-lined, contemporary guest room with dark woods, snow-white linens, organic prints, and flat-screen TVs. Bathrooms are generously proportioned and have deep tubs and upscale bath products. Amenities include an onsite yoga instructor, an acupuncturist, and a massage therapist. A beautifully presented continental breakfast, with fresh fruit and French pastries, is included. The hotel also has eight apartments for short-term rent, located across the street on Herschel.

LA JOLLA BEACH AND TENNIS CLUB
Manager: John Campbell
800-624-2582; fax 858-456-3805
www.ljbtc.com
2000 Spindrift Dr., La Jolla, CA 92037
Price: Very expensive
Credit Cards: AE, D, DC, MC, V
Handicap Access: 2 full

An elite gathering place for locals who come for the 12 championship tennis courts and the landmark **Marine Room** restaurant (see pages 114–115), the distinctly upscale La Jolla Beach and Tennis Club directly on La Jolla Shores is an exclusive enclave for the well-heeled. The property offers 90 guest rooms and suites, including recently remodeled one- to three-bedroom beach-

The large pool at La Jolla Beach and Tennis Club is an inviting oasis on hot summer days.

front accommodations that are big enough for families. Public spaces show off gleaming wood and clubby accents, and private interiors are decorated with soft fabrics in beach-inspired colors. Although the hotel claims to have a "private" beach, in fact it is just somewhat secluded—all San Diego beaches are open to the public. If you aren't up for sand between your toes, pull up a comfortably padded chaise lounge by the uncrowded pool, or try your luck at the three-par nine-hole golf course onsite. In the evening, indulge in a sophisticated barbeque on the beach, where you'll dine on fine china at tables set with fresh linens. The views never stop, because even after the sun goes down, tiki torches and floodlights continue to illuminate the waves.

LA JOLLA COVE SUITES
Manager: Krista Baroudi
888-525-6552; fax 858-551-3405
www.lajollacove.com
1155 Coast Blvd., La Jolla, CA 92037

Price: Moderate
Credit Cards: AE, D, V, MC
Handicap Access: 2 full suites (ocean view)

I recommend this hotel to budget-minded out-of-town friends who want to stay on the water—although I caution them that the La Jolla Cove Suites isn't at all luxurious or trendy. In fact, some locals marvel that the place hasn't been torn down by now. Located in a hundred-million-dollar site just across the street from La Jolla Cove and within easy walking distance of some of the finest restaurants in San Diego, this time-worn hotel has one *huge* redeeming feature: It is built above a storybook beach, with a grassy park nearby and a mile of ocean-view sidewalk to stroll. The suites feature commodious seating areas, full kitchens, and expansive balconies—and those that face the ocean have incomparable views over La Jolla Cove (better views, in my opinion, than the extremely pricey La Valencia just down the street). Alas, the place isn't in the best repair, despite a recent renovation to replace some of the shabby furniture: Carpets are dingy and fabrics are tired. But despite rate increases over the years, this is still a bargain for otherwise ultra-expensive La Jolla. Compare the rates with any lodging in the immediate vicinity and it can even be called a budget option. The property has a small pool and spa in the back, and the views from the rooftop deck where daily breakfast is served will take your breath away. Book this place with your eyes wide open to its limitations and you'll appreciate that location, location, location is everything.

LA VALENCIA

Manager: Michael Ullman
858-454-0771; fax 858-456-3921
www.lavalencia.com
1132 Prospect St., La Jolla, CA 92037
Price: Very expensive
Credit Cards: AE, D, DC, MC, V
Handicap Access: 2 full

Since 1926, the much-lauded Spanish Colonial "pink lady" has lured the rich and famous, like old-time Hollywood luminaries Groucho Marx, Mary Pickford, and Greta Garbo, who were frequent guests. The La Valencia offers impeccable service and boasts one of the most spectacular lobbies in the world, decorated like a grand hacienda that just happens to have a drop-dead gorgeous view of the Pacific. You can plant yourself in one of the intimate seating arrangements, listen to live piano music nightly, and sip cocktails until the wee hours, all without leaving the rarified air of this regal hotel. Or step into the clubby onsite **Whaling Bar** (see page 111) and rub elbows with gentrified locals; this is also a good place for a power lunch. There are three restaurants onsite, including the **Mediterranean Room** (858-551-3765), a sunny display of yellow and blue painted tiles that offers up another killer view. A state-of-the-art fitness center will let guests work off their fine dining, and a sparkling rooftop pool overlooks lovely La Jolla Cove. Thanks to an impressive reputation, the La Valencia commands blisteringly expensive rates, but note that the standard guest rooms (which can be priced at close to $400 in season *without* an ocean view) are tiny, as are the bathrooms. Suites are roomier—and pricier—and if money is no object, the ocean villas offer stepped up interior designs, private butler service, wet bars, unparalleled views of the ocean, and most have fireplaces. This is a La Jolla institution, but understand before you book that you are paying for its prestige. There are larger, prettier rooms and better views to be had elsewhere in the neighborhood—although they won't garner the same respect as the La Valencia.

SEA LODGE

Manager: John Campbell
800-237-5211; fax 858-456-9346
www.sealodge.com

With one of the grandest lobbies in the city, La Valencia is cozy despite its size.

8110 Camino del Oro, La Jolla, CA 92037
Price: Expensive to very expensive
Credit Cards: AE, D, DC, MC, V
Handicap Access: 2 full

The Sea Lodge is directly on the sands of La Jolla Shores, the most swimmable and family-friendly beach in San Diego, extremely popular with divers and kayakers. This premier location and the billion-dollar views from the guest rooms, make the Sea Lodge an obvious choice for vacationers looking for a relaxing seaside retreat. The lodge offers a small heated pool and a tiny spa, as well as a spacious courtyard that reminds me more of Hawaii than San Diego, thanks to extensive palms and ferns. But the real appeal is the view: Oceanside accommodations have balconies or patios looking toward the sea, just a few dozen yards from the water's edge. The interiors are decorated with lustrous Italian wood furniture and warm fabrics. You'll also find lots of greenery and lamps that are bright enough to read by (a rarity in hotels these days). The bathrooms aren't as luxurious as one might expect for these prices, and the architectural design screams 1970s, but the overall vibe is understated elegance. Many of the 128 rooms have kitchenettes, and the pricey La Jolla Suite has a full kitchen, dining room, and large living area—perfect for long stays (for those travelers with deep pockets).

MISSION BEACH AND MISSION BAY
BAHIA RESORT

Manager: Jim Green
800-576-4229; fax 858-488-7055
www.bahiahotel.com
998 W. Mission Bay Dr., San Diego, CA 92109
Price: Moderate
Credit Cards: AE, D, MC, V
Handicap Access: 6 full

A Mission Bay fixture for 50 years, the Bahia is surrounded by water—which means good views are nearly a sure bet. The landscaping is tropical, with meandering water features and palm trees throughout. Although the exterior shows its age, the public rooms have been rejuvenated with thematic Moroccan style. There are two lighted tennis courts, and professional lessons and clinics are available by appointment. The resort is family-friendly, with an active kids' club throughout the year and a "Mad Science" camp for the 5- to 12-year-old set in the summer. Children will also enjoy the seal pond, where the Bahia has license to keep three seals on the property. My favorite feature of this resort is the *Bahia Belle*, an immaculate Mississippi sternwheeler that departs from the hotel's dock and cruises the calm waters of the bay every evening. The *Bahia Belle* is free to guests (and only $6 for nonguests), and sails for a little less than an hour. The first cruises of the evening are appropriate for families; later cruises feature cocktails, music, and dancing.

THE DANA
Manager: Kevin Konopasek
619-222-6440; fax 619-222-5916
www.thedana.net
1710 W. Mission Bay Dr., San Diego, CA 92109
Price: Moderate to expensive
Credit Cards: AE, D, DC, MC, V
Handicap Access: 10 full

The Dana, a low-rise property that doesn't obstruct the natural beauty of Mission Bay, is a hidden treasure tucked into a southwest peninsula. The self-contained resort has its own marina and is surrounded by water. Guest rooms are decorated with clean lines, Asian-inspired colors, and restrained tropical fabrics; many offer private balconies. Secure a pool-view room in the Marina Cove section of the hotel during the summer and you'll enjoy outstanding views of nearby Sea World's seasonal fireworks. The hotel offers its guests two pools: one a lush, tropical oasis with Mexican-style palapas and the other an infinity pool that seems to melt into Mission Bay. There is almost nothing within easy walking distance of the resort, although excellent beaches, downtown dining, and La Jolla shopping are all easy car rides away. Note the recently remodeled hotel is 100 percent nonsmoking.

PARADISE POINT RESORT AND SPA
Manager: Geoff Young
858-274-4630 or 800-344-2626; fax 858-581-5919
www.paradisepoint.com
1404 Vacation Rd., San Diego, CA 92109
Price: Very expensive
Credit Cards: AE, D, DC, MC, V
Handicap Access: 11 full

This self-contained 44-acre island in Mission Bay has more than a mile of sandy beaches; expansive, lush gardens; an 18-hole putting course; five pools, one of them with a spectacular tropical waterfall; championship tennis courts; a full-service marina to rent a wide variety of boats and water toys; two onsite restaurants; and an exotic spa. **SpaTerre** (858-490-6350) offers Balinese treatments and Thai body rituals like the "sacred stone body massage" performed with warmed volcanic rocks. Or to satisfy the true hedonists in the crowd, the "chocolate ice cream pedicure" includes a chocolate sugar scrub, a marshmallow foot mask, and chocolate body lotion; afterward guests will be treated to a bowl of Ben and Jerry's chocolate ice cream. There's almost no reason to leave the property, especially after the recent $9 million renovation, which included a new "Bali Modern" interior design. Each room has a private lanai with comfy furniture and tropical views, and the interiors are decorated in beach-cottage style, with plenty of wicker and

The Crystal Pier Hotel cottages in Pacific Beach offer a unique vantage point to enjoy the seaside in accommodations that rest over the water.

bright colors. Check the Web site for good values on hotel and spa packages.

PACIFIC BEACH
CRYSTAL PIER HOTEL
Manager: Randy Williams
800-748-5894; fax 858-483-6811
www.crystalpier.com
4500 Ocean Blvd., San Diego, CA 92109
Price: Expensive
Credit Cards: D, MC, V
Handicap Access: 2 full

This unique lodging option offers the opportunity to sleep *over* the water, in 29 individual Cape Code-style cottages built directly on the historic Crystal Pier in Pacific Beach. The quaint white and blue structures have window boxes overflowing with flowers and a nearby parking space right on the pier. Inside you'll find hardwood floors, simple furniture, and kitchenettes. The cottages have been around since the late 1920s—although they've been remodeled several times over. Thanks to the relentless sun and saltwater exposure, they're a little rough around the edges, but the management keeps them clean and in good working condition. If you're looking for privacy and peace, this might not be the place for you: The pier is open to the public during daytime hours, when locals head to the far end to fish or people watch—and hardly a person passes without trying to steal a peek inside. At night the waves below will drown out the worst noise from the PB revelers. Secure a north-facing cottage and watch the surfers shred the waves just feet from the pier pilings. Demand is high, and the manager suggests booking at least six months in advance for summer and holiday stays.

PACIFIC TERRACE HOTEL
Manager: Robert Kingery
858-581-3500; fax 858-274-2534
www.pacificterrace.com
610 Diamond St., San Diego, CA 92109
Price: Expensive to very expensive
Credit Cards: AE, DC, MC, V
Handicap access: 3 full

This chocolate-colored hotel is all angles and edges, allowing it to wedge into the available space between ramshackle apartments, a public restroom facility, and a budget hotel across the street. Despite the dubious neighbors, the location is still prime: right on lively Pacific Beach, just north of the Crystal Pier, and within easy walking distance of numerous restaurants and bars. Each guest room has a spacious private balcony and floor-to-ceiling windows to make the most of the scenery. Guest rooms are decorated with deeply colored tropical fabrics, vibrant artwork, and richly carved Colonial-style wood furniture. The hotel has a small pool overlooking the ocean, and full-service spa amenities, including poolside massages. The lobby is spare and utilitarian, but the front desk staff is friendly and efficient, and there are concierge services onsite. Guests enjoy a daily continental breakfast and a nightly wine reception.

TOWER 23

Manager: Eric Rimmele
858-270-2323; fax 858-274-2333
www.t23hotel.com
723 Felspar St., San Diego, CA 92109

Price: Expensive
Credit Cards: AE, D, DC, MC, V
Handicap access: 2 full

Tower 23 is a high-style, elegant lodging option in a neighborhood otherwise ruled by surfer bars and Hawaiian-themed eateries. Named after the nearby lifeguard tower of the same number, this ultra hip hotel (opened in 2005) sports minimalist design created in glass, concrete, and steel. Forty-four guest rooms have flat-screen TVs, equally minimalist interior design, and feature walk-in rain showers and aromatherapy baths. The upscale hotel is within easy walking distance to the Crystal Pier, numerous restaurants, and the rowdy nightlife that makes Pacific Beach a perennial favorite with 20-somethings. But you don't have to go offsite for a great cocktail lounge. The chic onsite restaurant, **Jrdn** (858-270-5736), boasts a sleek interior and a large outdoor patio just off the boardwalk, with a sushi bar, a fireside patio, and a casual fire pit. Relax, catch the sunset, and sip a delicious tangerine martini.

CULTURE

La Jolla is imminently civilized, and there is no better place to browse fine art galleries than Prospect Street; add to the mix the famed contemporary art museum and the La Jolla Playhouse, and La Jolla comes in second only to downtown as San Diego's premier spot for high-brow culture. But if you're looking for a more casual atmosphere and just want to have fun, head south to Pacific and Mission Beaches, where the streets are thick with funky bars.

Galleries

Images of Nature (858-551-9553; 7916 Girard Ave., La Jolla, CA 92037). This inviting gallery exclusively carries Thomas D. Mangelson's luminous nature photography. Prices for limited-edition originals are surprisingly reasonable, and the gallery also carries affordable posters, calendars, and note cards. An interesting historical note: Gregory Peck's father used to own a pharmacy on this site.

Morrison Hotel Gallery (858-551-0835; 1230 Prospect St., La Jolla, CA 92037). This unusual gallery sells limited-edition, signed photography of famous musicians, predominately rock and rollers.

Obernier Gallery (858-459-5004; 7979 Ivanhoe, #150, La Jolla, CA 92037). A beautiful, museum-like gallery space, the Obernier specializes in contemporary sculptures and paintings.

Wentworth Gallery (858-551-7071; 1025 Prospect St., La Jolla, CA 92037). This gallery carries more than three hundred different artists from around the world, including Peter Max, Picasso, and Miro. Friendly, well-educated staff help even art neophytes to feel comfortable.

Museums

Museum of Contemporary Art San Diego (858-454-3541; www.mcasd.org; 700 Prospect St., La Jolla, CA 92037). This internationally known museum has a permanent collection of more than three thousand works representing myriad art genres from the past half century and includes paintings, sculpture, photography, video, and multimedia works. The expansive museum also attracts arguably the most important touring exhibits of contemporary art in Southern California. Visitors will also find outside sculptures that were crafted specifically for this site, including a sculpture made from a cluster of small boats and surfboards, which seems to explode from the upper floor of the museum. The beautiful structure, which was designed by famous architect Irving Gill in 1916, is spectacularly located on the La Jolla cliffs overlooking the ocean. There's a nice café in the front, and an eclectic bookstore that also sells high-style jewelry and decorating accessories. Open Monday–Tuesday, Friday–Sunday, 11 AM–5 PM; Thursday 11 AM–7 PM. General admission $6, students and seniors $2, individuals 25 and younger free. Note that there is now also a downtown venue for exhibits (see chapter 3).

Music

La Jolla Music Society (858-459-3724; 7946 Ivanhoe Ave., Ste. 309, La Jolla, CA 92037). This beloved music society showcases visiting orchestras, ensembles, and soloists in several series during the season, which generally runs from October through May but also includes a summer music festival. More than 40 performances a year are held in various venues around town. Look for chamber music, piano series, and a "discovery series" that focuses on young performers.

Nightlife

Canes (858-488-1780; 3105 Ocean Front Walk, San Diego, CA 92109). Canes in Mission Beach claims to be closer to the ocean than any other music bar in town, and it features rock, hip-hop, and reggae. While you're here, enjoy a casual meal on the rooftop patio. Admission varies; tickets can be purchased at the door or through TicketMaster (www.ticketmaster.com).

Comedy Store La Jolla (858-454-9176; 916 Pearl St., La Jolla, CA 92037). Some of the best comedy acts in the country have made their way to the stage at the famous Comedy Store. In its heyday during the 1980s, Robin Williams used to show up unannounced and unbilled, and Whoopi Goldberg got her start here. Today the names are usually less recognizable, but the laughs are still plentiful. Wednesday is open mike night. Cover charge varies.

Moondoggies (858-483-6550; 832 Garnet Ave., San Diego, CA 92109). With a laidback atmosphere and dozens of screens playing surfing videos (as well as major sporting events), Gidget would feel right at home at this casual beach bar and grill in Pacific

Beach. Come on a Monday evening and enjoy all-night happy hour specials with amusing names like The Grateful Dog and Surf Wax shots.

Whaling Bar (858-531-3764; 1132 Prospect St., La Jolla, CA 92037). Within the hallowed halls of the exclusive La Valencia Hotel, the Whaling Bar is a clubby, old-fashioned lounge with mahogany tables, retro décor, and scrimshaw collections. Come for a subdued evening of cocktails and quiet discussions.

Seasonal Events

The **Buick Invitational Golf Tournament** (800-888-2842), one of the biggest golf events in the country, is held at the Torrey Pines Municipal Golf Course in La Jolla in January. The event includes Pro-Am and practice rounds as well and plays to a sell-out crowd.

In early April, catch the **San Diego Crew Classic** (619-225-0300) at Crown Point Shores Park in Mission Bay. The annual regatta features more than three thousand collegiate, masters, and high school rowers. Arrive early (races begin at 7 AM) with a beach chair and picnic.

Get a peek into some of the most beautiful residential gardens in the city in May with the **Secret Garden Tour** (858-459-5335), sponsored by the La Jolla Historical Society.

Starting in June and continuing through Labor Day, come to La Jolla Cove on Sunday afternoons for the free **La Jolla Concerts by the Sea** (www.ljconcertsbythesea.org) series, with musical offerings ranging from rock and roll oldies to big band and swing groups.

It doesn't get bigger (or rowdier) than the **World Championship Over-the-Line Tournament** (619-688-0817) on Fiesta Island in Mission Bay, held over two weekends in

Site of the annual Rough Water Swim in September, the La Jolla Cove is a favorite with sports enthusiasts and families.

July, where more than 1,200 three-member teams compete in a softball-like tourney that inevitably devolves into good-humored debauchery.

August ushers in the La Jolla Music Society's **SummerFest** (858-459-3724), featuring more than a dozen performances of classical and new compositions performed by ensembles and world-class artists in venues throughout the city.

Be ready for some noise—and high-speed excitement—at the **Thunderboat Regatta** (619-225-9160) in September, where you can watch hydroplanes roar through Mission Bay. Another exhilarating event on the water, catch the largest swim competition of its kind in the United States at the **La Jolla Rough Water Swim** (www.ljrws.com), which starts off at the La Jolla Cove in September as well.

In October, get your polka on at the annual **Polish Festival** (858-272-7655) in Pacific Beach, sponsored by the Polish Mission St. Maximilian Kolbe parish in Pacific Beach. You'll enjoy traditional music, dancing, and plenty of food, as well as activities for the children. Also this month, enjoy an only-in-Southern-California event at the annual **Underwater Pumpkin Carving Contest** (858-565-6054) off La Jolla Shores, where scuba divers compete to carve the best jack-o'-lanterns while submerged. Sponsored by a local dive shop, proceeds from the event, which includes a barbeque, are donated to local charities.

Bring your holiday cheer to La Jolla for the annual **La Jolla Christmas Parade** held in early December, starting on Silverado Road and featuring local marching bands, scout groups, floats, and classic cars. The day ends with the traditional lighting of the community Christmas tree.

Theater

La Jolla Playhouse (858-550-1070; P.O. Box 12039, La Jolla, CA 92039). Considered one of the finest regional theaters in the country, the La Jolla Playhouse has premiered more than 30 productions that have gone on to Broadway, including the Tony Award-winning *Jersey Boys* in 2004, Matthew Broderick's *How to Succeed in Business Without Really Trying*, and Lee Blessings's *A Walk in the Woods*. The theater was founded in 1947 by La Jolla native Gregory Peck, along with Hollywood pals Mel Ferrer and Dorothy McGuire. Today the theater performs in three venues, all located on the University of California, San Diego, campus in La Jolla. Artistic director and local legend Des McAnuff oversees six main-stage productions each season. The theater is open May through November.

RESTAURANTS AND FOOD PURVEYORS

Proximity to the ocean, cool breezes that come on shore during even the hottest summer days, and a prevailing vacation spirit make these coastal communities a popular choice for a romantic meal or a quick and casual bite. Plentiful outdoor dining makes every day feel like a holiday.

Restaurants

La Jolla

APOLLONIA
Owner: Tony Farah
858-455-1535
8650 Genesee Ave., San Diego, CA 92122
Open: Daily
Price: Moderate
Cuisine: Greek
Serving: L, D
Credit Cards: D, MC, V

Apollonia can accommodate large groups as well as offer intimate dining spaces to enjoy a quiet conversation.

Handicap Access: Yes
Reservations: Recommended for dinner
Parking: Lot

Tucked into the Costa Verde Shopping Center in the Golden Triangle area, this expansive, warm taverna, formerly called Aesop's Tables, has been serving locals and visitors for years. Check out the huge atlas hanging near the front door; guests are encouraged to add pushpins to indicate their hometowns, and judging from the sea of pins that cover the continents, Apollonia draws an impressively international crowd. The homey interior is decorated with touches of the old country, and the tables allow for quiet conversations (if the restaurant is not too packed). The *spanikopita*, a tasty blend of spinach and feta cheese wrapped in phyllo dough, and the *tyropita*, a similar pastry minus the spinach, are crispy, satisfying starters, especially when paired with a side of yogurt and cucumber dipping sauce.

The *keftedes*, meatballs made of ground beef and spices and served in a spicy tomato sauce, and the *pastitsio*, a creamy casserole of ground lamb and macaroni topped with béchamel sauce, are generously portioned and prepared traditionally. And to finish, try the sticky, chewy *baklava*, a confection made from honey, nuts, and phyllo pastry.

CODY'S

Chef: Joe Baraco
858-459-0040
www.codys.com
8030 Girard Ave., La Jolla, CA 92037
Open: Daily
Price: Moderate
Cuisine: Californian
Serving, B, L, D
Credit cards: AE, MC, V
Handicap Access: Yes
Reservations: Recommended
Parking: Street (very limited)

Housed in a charming yellow cottage surrounded by a white picket fence, Cody's is a comfortable place to enjoy a casual breakfast on the patio while looking out over La Jolla Cove. The classic eggs Benedict are served over your choice of a crispy bed of oniony home fries or a mound of grits. The "millionaire" buttermilk pancakes with blueberries are also great eye-openers. Or for an intimate dinner, dine inside in the bistro-style dining room, which has an open kitchen and is decorated with vintage rock posters. Start with the duck confit quesadilla with jalapenos and red onions or the crostini with brie, pear–jalapeno jam, and fig compote. For an unusual entrée, try the pumpkin seed- and coriander-crusted tuna served rare with white bean and garlic puree. Desserts are comfortingly homey, and include apple pie à la mode, southern red velvet cake, and a decadent flourless chocolate cake.

JACK'S LA JOLLA
Chef: Tony DiSalvo
858-456-8111
www.jackslajolla.com
7863 Girard Ave., La Jolla, CA 92037
Open: Daily
Price: Moderate to very expensive (depending on venue)
Cuisine: Californian
Serving: L, D (depending on venue)
Credit Cards: AE, D, DC, MC, V
Handicap Access: Yes
Reservations: Recommended
Parking: Valet and street (limited)

Jack's is a collection of posh restaurants and bars spread across multi-levels in an indoor/outdoor, quintessentially La Jolla establishment—and it's one of the best places for the young and beautiful to see and be seen. The separate spaces flow into each other and manage to be intimate and at the same time open and expansive. **Jack's Grille**, a casual and moderately priced restaurant downstairs, serves pastas, salads, and other light meals. The cozy seating area clusters around a fire pit, and the tables glow with romantic candlelight in the evening. The **Ocean Room and Oyster Bar** upstairs is all about seafood. For ultimate privacy, pull gauzy drapes around a tableside cabana to shut out the rest of the world, or plop down in comfortable communal sofas near the colorful tiled fireplace. **Jack's Dining Room** at the midlevel offers an unforgettable fine-dining experience: Dramatic lighting, richly upholstered banquettes scattered with velvet throw pillows, and two-story ceilings flowing with crisp canvas drapes are almost as impressive as Tony DiSalvo's jaw-dropping food. Fish selections melt in your mouth—and are stunningly presented—but it is the beef tenderloin that should not be missed. Presented with short ribs and a puree of celery root, this is among the best meals I've ever enjoyed. For dessert, the passion fruit crème brûlée topped at the table with melted Valrhona chocolate is nothing short of transporting. San Diego magazine readers voted this the best new restaurant in the city, and it has certainly been well-received by locals and visitors alike. On weeknights the place is packed by 7 PM; on weekends, when the bars open for lunch, there are nonstop crowds, and you're unlikely to get a table without reservations well in advance.

THE MARINE ROOM
Chef: Bernard Guillas
858-459-7222
www.marineroom.com
2000 Spindrift Dr., La Jolla, CA 92037
Open: Daily
Price: Very Expensive
Cuisine: French
Serving: D
Credit Cards: AE, D, DC, MC, V
Handicap Access: Yes
Reservations: Yes
Parking: Valet

This La Jolla landmark is considered by many locals to be the most romantic place to dine in San Diego. The restaurant juts out over the sand, and during high tide the waves sometimes crash against the expansive windows. The white, nondescript dining room is a clean canvas to allow the mesmerizing views of La Jolla Shores to come into full focus, and waiters are so reverential of these vistas that they will pause their service to let diners watch the sunset. This venerable institution hardly needs more to recommend it, but in addition to being a feast for the eyes, come here for a *true* feast: Exotic ingredients, inventive recipes, and superbly prepared dishes are brought to the table with formality and panache. The signature appetizer, a delicately flavored blue crab cake served with duck confit hash and butternut squash is true to its East Coast origins. The sweet corn and mascarpone brûleé is subtle and rich, presented with lightly dressed organic greens and fig jam. And for the entrée, consider Chef Guillas's fennel-pollen scented Maine lobster tail served with a perfumy fruit polenta and Lemoncello butter. Another guest favorite is the game trilogy, a presentation of elk, antelope, and venison served with a trio of chutneys and white asparagus. The daily specials allow the chef's full creative range

to take wing, and these will not disappoint. For dessert, the cobblestone pie piles ice cream studded with nuts and white chocolate on a chocolate crust, and the dessert trilogy offers up tiny portions of blueberry zinfandel brûlée, rich chocolate fondant, and spicy chai gelato. The Marine Room has an impressive wine list, and a helpful sommelier will guide you if you need him. This is a splurge, for sure, but dining at the Marine Room is an experience you will not soon forget.

MISS CHINA

Owner: Kitty Tow
858-454-2311
2240 Avenida de la Playa, La Jolla, CA 92037
Open: Tues–Sun
Price: Inexpensive
Cuisine: Chinese
Serving: L, D
Credit Cards: No
Handicap Access: Yes
Reservations: No
Parking: Street

This small restaurant, owned by Hong Kong native and local Chinese gourmet cooking instructor Kitty Tow, has been a fixture at La Jolla Shores for more than 30 years. There are only a handful of tables inside the homey interior, where colorful paper parasols and lanterns hang upside down from the ceiling to enliven the atmosphere, and a few more tables outside on the patio. In addition to offering the usual Americanized favorites such as kung pao chicken, beef with broccoli, and shrimp with lobster sauce, Miss China also has unique gourmet specials, such as spring chicken filet in rainbow sauce and pine nut chicken. A half-dozen vegetarian dishes are also available. This is one of the few casual dining options in La Jolla, and it's reliably good and always affordable, especially for lunch, when specials are about $7.

A perfect crab cake from the Marine Room is accented with a sprig of lavender.

NINE-TEN

Chef: Jason Knibb
858-964-5400
www.nine-ten.com
910 Prospect St., La Jolla, CA 92037
Open: Daily
Price: Expensive
Cuisine: California
Serving: B, L, D
Credit Cards: AE, D, DC, MC, V
Handicap Access: Yes
Reservations: Yes
Parking: Valet or street (very limited)

This intimate restaurant in the Grande Colonial Hotel receives its fair share of professional accolades, but it is often overlooked by locals, no doubt because La Jolla offers up an embarrassment of riches when it comes to cutting-edge food. But don't pass it by, because Chef Jason Knibb's "evolving California cuisine" is some of the most innovative in the county. The intimate dining room has an unobtrusive, clean design—all the better to showcase the artistry coming out of the kitchen. Menus change regularly, to reflect what's in season, but look for first courses like the baby beet salad served with roasted carrots, toasted walnuts, baby fennel, and arugula and the marinated black mission figs with white truffle oil, both exquisitely plated. Second courses can include spicy marinated shrimp with feta cheese and melon salad or the spoon-tender, port wine-braised short ribs drizzled with potato froth, which come to the table looking like three perfect bon bons. Final courses might include Hudson Valley duck breast with black rice, Valencia oranges, red currants, and candied juniper; perfectly moist *sous vide* halibut; and slightly spicy flat iron steak and onions. Desserts also change with the seasons, but count on the half-baked chocolate cake served with caramel sauce, which is like a hot brownie soup. For $90, you can put yourself at the "Mercy of the Chef" for an unforgettable five-course menu dreamed up by Chef Knibb and paired with wines (or $60 without wines). Friendly and knowledgeable sommelier Dan Pilkey will steer you in the right direction, even if you're just looking to order a single glass.

ROPPONGI

Chef: Stephen Window
858-551-5252
www.roppongiusa.com
875 Prospect St., La Jolla, CA 92037
Open: Daily
Price: Expensive
Cuisine: Californian, Asian
Serving: L, D
Credit Cards: AE, D, MC, V
Handicap Access: Yes
Reservations: Recommended
Parking: Valet and underground lot for dinner; street (very limited) for lunch

Look for the tiki torches and *crowds* on Prospect Street and you've found Roppongi, one of the hottest restaurants and bars in La Jolla. This popular weekday happy hour destination has a lively sidewalk patio, as well as a large indoor dining room, a full bar, and a small sushi bar. Creamy natural materials and Asian artwork in the neutral interior would produce a soothing atmosphere if this wasn't such a noisy place. The Asian *tapas* menu is more extensive than the entrée menu, and diners could easily make a meal on a few of these generously proportioned appetizers. Roppongi is known for its high-quality sushi, and in addition to the traditional offerings such as California rolls and a variety of sashimi, Roppongi has a few unusual selections, like the beautiful spicy scallop sushi rolls with cucumber and Tobiko caviar and the spicy albacore jalapeno roll with sesame seeds. The signature starter is the Polynesian crab stack, a gorgeously engineered tower of crab meat, avocado, mango, red onions, and pea shoots served with an oil-free ginger sauce,

Roppongi's Asian-inspired interior design is especially serene before diners pack the popular restaurant.

which servers are inexplicably hell-bent on smashing up the minute it arrives. If you're up for a main course, consider the Mongolian grilled shrimp, served with a fruity barbeque sauce and mango salsa and arranged artistically on a square of perfect pineapple-and-egg fried rice. There is also crispy striped whole bass, pan-seared mahi mahi, and a few chicken and beef options. Desserts are enormous, but worth the calories, especially the Tahitian bananas served over vanilla gelato and topped with paperthin almond brittle. Be sure to ask for a table well away from the front desk, which tends to overflow with guests waiting to be seated.

ROY'S

Owner: Roy Yamaguchi
858-455-1616
www.roysrestaurant.com
8670 Genesee Ave., San Diego, CA 92122
Open: Daily
Price: Expensive

Cuisine: Hawaiian Fusion
Serving: D
Credit Cards: AE, D, MC, V
Handicap Access: Yes
Reservations: Recommended
Parking: Adjacent lot and valet

Celebrity chef Roy Yamaguchi has imported the taste of Hawaii to this unassuming location in the Costa Verde Shopping Center, in the Golden Triangle area. Yamaguchi opened the first Roy's in Honolulu to great acclaim; now this master chef has several dozen Roy's around the world. Roy's menu marries the fresh flavors of Hawaii with French-inspired sauces and Asian spices. Start with lobster pot stickers, fried crunchy dumplings filled with tender, buttery lobster; or pork and shrimp lumpia, a crispy Philipino eggroll. If you crave seafood, you'll be delighted to discover a sushi bar, hidden behind a jungle of bamboo poles at the back of the restaurant. Or if you prefer your fish cooked, consider the signature entrée, a macadamia-encrusted mahi mahi, smothered in brown butter sauce that is infused with a hint of island fruit. Other choices include the blackened island Ahi, seared to rare perfection, or the wood-grilled, Szechwan-spiced baby-back pork ribs that are tender enough to eat with a spoon. For dessert indulge in the melting hot chocolate soufflé: dip your spoon in and hot fudge oozes out like magma from a volcano. The friendly folks at Roy's try hard to bring home the Hawaiian spirit, and the servers are impeccably trained and polite.

THE SHORES
Chef: Augie Saucedo
858-456-0600
www.theshores.restaurant.com
8110 Camino del Oro, La Jolla, CA 92037
Open: Daily
Price: Expensive
Cuisine: Steak and seafood
Serving: B, L, D
Credit Cards: AE, D, DC, MC, V
Handicap Access: Yes
Reservations: Recommended
Parking: Validated underground lot at the Sea Lodge hotel (access from Camino del Oro)

Just steps from the sand, on the south end of La Jolla Shores, this restaurant in the Sea Lodge hotel is a comfortable, family-friendly place to enjoy an upscale meal along with a killer view. The creamy monotone décor is dimly lighted, all the better to enjoy sunsets through the numerous Palladian windows without distraction. To start, don't miss the Portobello mushroom stuffed with Kobe beef short ribs and served with a rich sauce over greens, or the mild Louisiana blue crab cake laced with andouille sausage and sweet potatoes. Chef Augie Saucedo knows his way around both surf and turf, so you won't go wrong with the five-spice ono—pan roasted and moist, served with pomegranate butter—or the filet mignon accompanied by three sauces (a cabernet

reduction, classic béarnaise, and a mustard aioli), served with a family-style bowl of creamy cheddar mashed potatoes and crisp green beans almandine. Desserts put a creative spin on classic dishes: The blueberry vanilla crème brûlée has a light, mousse-like texture, and the mud pie concocted out of coffee-flavored ice cream and chocolate cookies is accented with exotic fruit purees. If you arrive early enough (5–6:30), you can create your own surf and turf platter, which comes with an appetizer and dessert, for only $30. Service is friendly and efficient, although poor dining room acoustics make it noisier than expected.

TAPENADE
Chef and Owner: Jean-Michel Diot
858-551-7500
www.tapenaderestaurant.com
7612 Fay Ave., La Jolla, CA 92037
Open: Daily
Price: Expensive
Cuisine: French
Serving: L, D
Credit Cards: AE, D, DC, MC, V
Handicap Access: Yes
Reservations: Yes
Parking: Street (very limited) or nearby paid lot

A few blocks off pricey Prospect Street in La Jolla, Tapenade's charming façade opens up to an expansive, elegant dining room and bar, with intimate lighting and comfortable black leather booths. There is also sidewalk dining available, although Chef Diot's classic French food deserves more reverence than the noisy street allows. Once you are seated, you'll want to eat every morsel of the crusty bread served with creamy homemade tapenade—the poor man's caviar (Ossetra caviar is available with potato blinis for those with deeper pockets)—but save room enough for the generously sized dishes. Helpful wait staff recommend the tasting menu, a five-course meal that changes regularly, but I prefer to pick my own favorites, so I don't miss any of the intriguing starters. Lobster medallions are served on top of a chopped mango relish and floated with a frothy coconut milk emulsion that compliments the sweetness of the lobster. A generous portion of rich, homemade raviolis stuffed with wild mushrooms are presented in a port wine reduction and finished with white truffle oil. Tapenade also offers fragrant *escargot*, served with herbed butter and plenty of garlic. For the main course, consider the Maine diver scallops, lightly seared and served with tangy baby cheese ravioli in a chardonnay emulsion. Another option, the classic *steak au poivre* is fork tender and the accompanying *pommes frites* are crisp and tasty. Pastry chef Jerome Maure presents an assortment of inventive final choices, including a traditional cheese plate accented with dried fruits and walnut bread; a trio of tiny crème brûlées, my favorite of which is flavored with lemon and thyme; a pear poached in Muscat wine and vanilla; and luscious poached black figs served on a delicate French toast round with balsamic sorbet (which I don't recommended unless you *love* balsamic vinegar). There is an extensive wine list and live jazz on Thursday nights.

TRATTORIA ACQUA

Chef: Damaso Lee
858-454-0709
www.trattoriaacqua.com
1298 Prospect St., La Jolla, CA 92037
Open: Daily
Price: Expensive
Cuisine: Italian
Serving: B, D: Sat.–Sun., L, D: Mon.–Fri.
Credit Cards: AE, D, MC, V
Handicap Access: Yes
Reservations: Yes
Parking: Validated underground garage, street (very limited)

Outdoor terraces, cozy patios, and a gazebo room provide several choices for intimate dining at Trattoria Acqua, located just above La Jolla Cove, with breathtaking views of the calm waters. The extensive menu offers the best in seafood and pastas. Start out with the *katafi al gamberi*, jumbo shrimp wrapped in phyllo pastry and served with creamy avocado and a tangerine and orange *vin cotto* or the *carpaccio di tonno*, paper-thin ahi served with shaved fennel, arugula, watermelon, and lemon-horseradish vinaigrette. The lobster bisque is served in a generous tureen and topped with a pillow of puffed pastry; the soup is loaded with large chunks of lobster, although the lemongrass in this recipe overwhelms the delicate flavors of the seafood. For the main course try the *sarago con mandorle*, juicy Mahi Mahi crusted with almonds served over whipped potatoes and accented with a spinach–chive beurre blanc sauce or the succulent lobster pot pie, made with a half pound of Maine lobster tail and accompanied by herbed French fries. On weekends brunch is served, and in addition to the lunch menu choices you can enjoy creamy eggs Benedict served with crab cakes. The dessert menu presents you with an impossible choice: Will it be the Meyer lemon tart with fresh berries, the warm blueberry bread pudding served with blueberry gelato, or the fried bananas with chocolate and caramel dipping sauce? If you can't decide, split the *il piatto di dolci acqua*, a sampler plate with a little taste of everything.

PACIFIC BEACH
GREEN FLASH

Owner: Armando Gemora
858-270-7715
www.greenflashrestaurant.com
701 Thomas Ave., San Diego, CA 92109
Open: Daily
Price: Moderate to expensive
Cuisine: California
Serving: B, L, D
Credit Cards: AE, D, DC, MC, V
Handicap Access: Yes

Reservations: No
Parking: Street (very limited)

Relax on the large outdoor patio and watch the parade of characters stroll down the Pacific Beach boardwalk or dine inside and take advantage of the large windows looking toward the water. A favorite place to watch the sun go down (the place is named after the green flash of light that can sometimes be seen the moment the sun sets into the ocean), the view of the sea and beach are quintessentially San Diego no matter what time of the day you visit. For dinner, start with seafood favorites like oyster shooters, shrimp cocktail, and calamari strips. Entrée choices include fresh seafood—especially good are the seafood kabobs, with shrimp and scallops—and beef filets. If you can't decide between surf and turf, get a pricey combination of both. Or try the chicken tomatillo, juicy breast meat accented with a spicy, lemony green tomato sauce. Don't miss the signature cocktail, the Green Flash: lemon-lime Bacardi, pineapple and orange juices, and melon liqueur. A few of these will have you seeing green flashes long after the sun sets.

KONO'S CAFÉ

Owner: Steve Bettles
858-483-1669
704 Garnet Ave., San Diego, CA 92109
Open: Daily
Price: Inexpensive
Cuisine: American
Serving: B, L
Credit Cards: Cash only
Handicap Access: Yes
Reservations: No
Parking: Street (very limited)

Just behind the famous Crystal Pier, this Hawaiian-themed diner in Pacific Beach is a local favorite, serving up huge portions of good food at an exceptional value (the average cost of a meal is about $5). This place is *busy*, and on weekends there is sure to be a line around the corner, although it moves pretty quickly, and you'll have great views of the ocean while you wait. Once you squeeze in, order one of their famous hamburgers, or consider the breakfast items, which are served all day long. The super-sized egg burritos are a typical San Diego treat, or go for a hearty veggie sandwich. If you're not staying in Pacific Beach, plan to make a morning of it when you come to Kono's, because you'll struggle long and hard to find a parking spot; stroll out to the end of the Crystal Pier to see what the fisherman are hauling in or strap on your rollerblades and cruise the boardwalk.

WORLD FAMOUS

Owner: Dieter May
858-272-3100
711 Pacific Beach Dr., San Diego, CA 92109
Open: Daily
Price: Moderate
Cuisine: American
Serving: B, L, D
Credit Cards: AE, D, MC, V
Handicap Access: Yes
Reservations: No
Parking: Street (very limited)

World Famous serves fresh seafood and California coastal cuisine in a relaxed, comfortable atmosphere. Eat in or, better yet, soak up the sun on the outdoor sidewalk patio. Breakfast options are creative and reflect San Diego's eclectic ethnic heritage. Try the kalua pork hash, eggs scrambled with Hawaiian-style slow-cooked shredded pork; the banana macadamia nut pancakes; or the inventive *carne asada* eggs Benedict, served with avocado and traditional Hollandaise sauce. For dinner, start with the crunchy nut-crusted brie or the shrimp and crab martini. The entrée menu includes the unusual blackened mako shark crusted with pistachio nuts and avocado and served with a mango beurre blanc sauce. Dishes are presented artistically, and the food is creative and well prepared.

Food Purveyors

Breweries and Pubs

Australian Pub (858-273-9921; 1014 Grand Ave., San Diego, CA 92109). Expect to be greeted with a friendly "G'day" at this Aussie pub in Pacific Beach, which offers up delights like sausage rolls and meat pies. Knock back a pint on the sunny outdoor patio or play darts or shoot pool in the dim interior. Although the connection to the land down under isn't clear, this is fan central for the Green Bay Packers; you'll find memorabilia everywhere, and on game days, don't even think about watching anything else on the pub's TVs.

La Jolla Brewhouse (858-456-6279; 7536 Fay Ave., La Jolla, CA 92037). One of the most unassuming establishments in upscale La Jolla, this paneling-clad bar decorated with surf boards and fishing trophies attracts an eclectic clientele, from long-time neighborhood devotees to college students, and offers a rotating menu of beers brewed onsite.

Rock Bottom (858-450-9277; 8980 Villa La Jolla Dr., La Jolla, CA 92037). Across the street from the UCSD medical school campus, this outpost of the established chain of microbreweries claims to be "serious about food, crazy about beer," although the menu suggests it's the other way around. The interior sparkles with shiny brass brewing vessels and back-lighted bottles at the two bars, and patio seating is available if you want to get away from the crowds that pack in on weekends.

Coffeehouses

Goldfish Point Café (858-459-7407; 1255 Coast Blvd., La Jolla, CA 92037). This tiny café, just across from the Sunny Jim Cave in La Jolla, has the best views of any coffeehouse I know. Grab a sidewalk table overlooking the Cove and enjoy a buttery croissant or a blueberry muffin as you watch the waves roll in.

Harry's Coffee Shop (858-454-7381; 7545 Girard Ave., La Jolla, CA 92037). A local hangout and breakfast favorite since 1960, this friendly coffee shop is open daily 6 AM to 3 PM. Don't miss the corned beef hash and eggs and the incredible raisin walnut French toast.

Javanican Coffee House (858-483-8035; 4338 Cass St., San Diego, CA 92109). This funky Goth (or is it strictly heavy metal?) coffee house in Pacific Beach serves up vegetarian treats in addition to exclusively organic coffees. Javanican offers live music on select evenings, and through the years has attracted big-name performers.

The Living Room Coffeehouse (858-459-1187; 1010 Prospect St., La Jolla, CA 92037). Look for the big black awning on Prospect and you've found the La Jolla branch of the Living Room chain. Despite the Rodeo Drive-esque digs, the place manages to exude a homey feel, especially on the sunny sidewalk café. Expect to find La Jolla matrons sipping cappuccinos alongside UCSD students. If you're looking for a treat, try the snow-white Monte Bianco cake infused with framboise and brandy.

The Mission Coffee Cup (858-454-2819; 1111 Wall St., La Jolla, CA 92037). This coffee joint and diner doesn't fit the vibe of upscale La Jolla, and the fact that it is a little rough around the edges makes it all the more appealing. The open kitchen and stainless steel-quilted walls are vaguely retro, and the tiny sidewalk café is peaceful on all but weekend mornings, when the traffic can be noisy. Come for the blueberry cornmeal pancakes topped with fresh berries.

Zanzibar Coffee Bar and Gallery (858-272-4762; 976 Garnet Ave., San Diego, CA 92109). This welcoming, artsy coffee bar in Pacific Beach has live music a couple of nights a week (call for a schedule). Enjoy the pretty sidewalk dining area, a great spot to people watch.

Pizzas, Burgers, and Dogs

BJ's Chicago Style Pizza (858-455-0662; 8873 Villa La Jolla Dr., La Jolla, CA 92037). You'll find chewy, crispy deep-dish pizza piled with toppings in this pizzeria in the Golden Triangle area, part of a chain that has restaurants in several other Western cities. The buffalo chicken pizza is covered in grilled chicken breast and spicy buffalo sauce, drizzled with ranch dressing; and the great white is topped with alfredo sauce, mushrooms, garlic, and chunks of chicken breast. You'll also find traditional pepperoni and sausage pies. But the pizookie® could be the best pizza of all: A hot cookie, baked medium rare in a tiny pizza pan and topped with vanilla ice cream. Don't be tempted to share one; it will disappear faster than you think!

Chicago on a Bun (858-622-0222; 8935 Towne Center Dr., La Jolla, CA 92122). Located near the University Towne Center in Golden Triangle, this little slice of the Windy City displays Cubs memorabilia as décor and serves up Vienna-brand all-beef dogs with the obligatory plethora of toppings. You can also buy a freshly fried order of potato chips, juicy cheeseburgers, and Italian sandwiches.

Rocky's Crown Pub (858-273-9140; 3786 Ingraham St., San Diego, CA 92019). Large, juicy burgers, a side of greasy fries, and beer on tap at this unassuming joint in Pacific Beach: What more could you want? A friend claims that "this is what heaven must taste like."

The Spot (858-459-0800; 1005 Prospect St., La Jolla, CA 92037). When you think of Chicago pizza, you probably think of deep dish. But folks from Chicago love their crispy crusts almost as much. The Spot, a La Jolla institution for decades (and one of the only affordable bars/restaurants on pricey Prospect Street) serves up thin-crust pies that native Chicagoans swear by.

Specialty Markets

Girard Gourmet (858-454-3321; 7837 Girard Ave., La Jolla, CA 92037). This popular neighborhood bakery and deli offers European specialties like croissants, Greek salads, traditional quiches, and potato pancakes served with sour cream. Owner Francois Goedhuys creates decadent desserts as well, including adorable cookies for sale by the pound (shaped and decorated, among other things, like surfboards and popular pet breeds), homemade rugulach, and the deepest dark chocolate cakes imaginable. There is a tiny space inside to dine, but most locals buy their treats and take them to go. Girard Gourmet opens at 7 AM, a good hour earlier than most restaurants in the area, which makes this a perfect breakfast option for early birds.

Jonathan's Market (858-459-2677; 7611 Fay Ave., La Jolla, CA 92037). In addition to a wide selection of European jams, international candies, condiments and spices from around the globe, and a bewildering selection of potato chips, this upscale grocery store sells a variety of prepared foods, which makes it an ideal choice to shop for an elegant picnic at the nearby La Jolla Cove.

Sweets and Treats

Banana Cabana (619-275-7920; 1775 E. Mission Bay Dr., San Diego, CA 92122). After a hike or bike along the paths that rim Mission Bay, stop by the Banana Cabana (across from the Hilton boat rental pavilion) for a refreshing mango, raspberry, chocolate, or cappuccino smoothie. At $6 for a large glass, the prices reflect the fact that this is the only game in town on this well-traveled route (not counting vending machines). Open from Memorial Day to Labor Day only.

Belgian Frie (858-270-9900; 4614 Mission Blvd., San Diego, CA 92019). Although neither the waffles nor the fries are authentically Belgian—much to my disappointment—the fries are exceptionally good, and the waffles are better than average. If you've already secured a parking space in Pacific Beach, then by all means, stop by for a snack!

Forever Fondue (858-551-4509; 909 Prospect St., La Jolla, CA 92037). Enjoy made-at-your-table cheese fondue served with fruits and vegetables or indulge in chocolate fondue concoctions, served with strawberries, pineapple, peanut-covered marshmallows, and chunks of cheesecake.

French Pastry Shop (858-454-9094; 909 Prospect St., La Jolla, CA 92037). A long-time favorite with locals, this pastry shop in the Birdrock neighborhood of La Jolla features authentic French pastries and breads. Pick up a traditional *bûche de Noël* during the winter holidays or a chocolate croissant any old day. This is also a full-service restaurant, with bistro cuisine for breakfast and lunch.

Gelateria Frizzanie (858-454-5798; 1025 Prospect St., La Jolla, CA 92037). A tiny shop decorated with photographs of Italy, this gelateria serves up intensely flavored treats like passion fruit sorbet, tiramisu gelato, and chocolate and hazelnut frozen yogurt. You can also pick up a panini for lunch.

Lana's Bake Shoppe (858-581-2367; 4150 Mission Blvd., #107, San Diego, CA 92109). This little bakery hidden in the Promenade Mall in Pacific Beach is worth searching out: In addition to freshly made breads and pies—including a luscious variety of Granny Smith apple covered in caramel—try the *piroshkies*, sweet yeast dough pastries filled with cream cheese and cranberries or savory and filled with meat and rice.

Taquerias

Los Panchos Taco Shop (858-272-0567; 1775 Garnett Ave., San Diego, CA 92109). Pacific Beach has no shortage of inexpensive Mexican joints, but the authenticity of Los Panchos makes it stand out from the crowd. Try the crispy carnitas tacos and burritos.

Porkyland (858-459-1708; 1030 Torrey Pines Rd., La Jolla, CA 92037). Quality Mexican takeout reaches its zenith at Porkyland in La Jolla (and their second location at 2196 Logan Ave. in San Diego). Try the succulent pork loin tacos or my favorite, the *carne asada* tacos made with marinated flank steak.

Rubio's (858-272-2801; 4504 East Mission Bay Dr., San Diego, CA 92109). This walk-up taco stand is the original location of a beloved local chain of Mexican grills that can now be found throughout Southern California. Brainchild of Ralph Rubio, a San Diegan who fell in love with the food in the surfing town of Ensenada, Mexico, during his college years, Ralph started this first small taco shop in the early 1980s to bring Baja cuisine home. It was here that locals were first introduced to the Baja-style fish taco, now unofficially recognized as *the* signature dish of San Diego. Rubio's wraps a piece of lightly breaded white fish in a corn tortilla, adds a little white sauce made from yogurt and mayonnaise and a little more sauce

Rubio's Pesky Combo is the quintessential San Diego plate: Two fish tacos, beans, and chips.

The Giant Dipper rollercoaster in Mission Beach opened in 1925; the creaky wooden coaster reaches a top speed of 43 miles an hour and traverses 13 plunges and more than 2,600 feet of track. Photo courtesy of Belmont Park/ Wave House. Used with permission.

made from smoky chilies, and then tops it all with a mound of shredded cabbage. The tacos are served with limes to squeeze on top, and there is a salsa bar on the premises. Often the restaurants feature $1 fish (or shrimp) tacos on a given weekday. You'll find Rubio's throughout the county, but this location is my favorite because you never forget your first love.

Taco Surf Taco Shop (858-272-3877; 4657 Mission Blvd., San Diego, CA 92109). A popular surfer hangout a few blocks from the shores in Pacific Beach, the fast service and modest surroundings (decorated with some old-time boards) complement the huge portions at modest prices. Try the monster burrito to get the biggest bang for your buck.

THEME PARKS AND ZOOS

BELMONT PARK
858-488-1549
3190 Mission Blvd., San Diego, CA 92109

Drive into Mission Beach and you can't miss the white-washed wooden rollercoaster called the Giant Dipper, which has been rattling riders for eight decades—a holdover from the days when there was a full-scale amusement park on the site. You'll also find the newer Beach Blaster, a giant arm ride, and the FlowRider, a simulated wave maker. The small park opens at 11 AM during the summer, and guests can purchase individual rides from $2 to $4 or an unlimited-ride wristband for $20 for adults and $14 for children 50 inches or shorter. (Height seems like a strange way to calculate admission prices, but this reflects the restrictions on the Giant Dipper; anyone shorter than 50 inches cannot ride.) The coaster closes down for several weeks in the winter for routine repairs, and then reopens on Thursday–Sunday until late May. Call ahead for updated hours.

BIRCH AQUARIUM AT SCRIPPS
858-534-3474
www.aquarium.ucsd.edu
2300 Expedition Wy., La Jolla, CA 92037
Open: Daily 9:00 AM to 5:00 PM
Admission: Adults $11, seniors $9, children $7.50

A compact aquarium that is part of the public outreach program at the Scripps Institution of Oceanography at the University of California, San Diego, the Birch sits atop a cliff overlooking one of the most spectacular ocean views in the city. Enjoy these vistas at the extensive outdoor tide pool exhibit, where visitors can touch creatures such as starfish and sea cucumbers and watch local garibaldi fish swim through humanmade ponds. More exotic specimens are available inside the aquarium, including ethereal jellyfish, leafy sea dragons that look like something out of a Dr. Seuss book, and various varieties of small sharks. In the summer the Birch hosts its Green Flash Concert series on the outdoor patio, an intimate venue where you can watch the sunset as you listen to live music from local artists, as well as enjoy the aquarium after hours, when crowds are small.

Famous mascot of Sea World, 9,000-pound Shamu and friend star in Believe, *the park's newest killer whale attraction.* Copyright Sea World. Used with permission.

SEA WORLD

800-257-4268
www.seaworld.com
500 Sea World Dr., San Diego, CA 92109
Open: Daily; hours vary by season
Admission: $54 for adults and children 10 and older; $44 for children three to nine, $10 for parking

Second only to the San Diego Zoo in fame, this marine zoological park on south Mission Bay is a must-see attraction in San Diego. Part aquarium, part amusement park, and part botanical garden, Sea World is deservedly world-famous, and its feature killer whale Shamu has been San Diego's unofficial mascot for decades.

Animal shows are the heart of Sea World, so be sure to get a map and show schedule at the front entrance when you arrive so you can plan your day accordingly. During off-peak season, there are only two Shamu shows a day. On busy days plan to arrive about 30 to 45 minutes prior to show time to get a good seat. And note that sometimes a "good" seat means a dry one. Watch for the marked bleachers in the first dozen or so rows, which indicate the "soak zone," where it's almost certain that you'll get drenched with 50-degree saltwater that smells of fish. If you see nothing else, plan your visit around "Believe," which features Shamu and other killer whales in an inspirational video-and-music choreographed extravaganza, staged in a state-of-the-art tank that holds more than six million gallons of water. Another crowd pleaser is "Dolphin Discovery," which features flying, leaping, and diving bottlenose dolphins, lots of music, and humorous audience participation. "Clyde and Seamore's Risky Rescue" stars noisy sea lions, and is the silliest of the shows—and sure to be a big hit with young children.

If you visited Sea World a decade or so ago and haven't been back lately, you'll be surprised to find several water-themed thrill rides on the property, including the newest "Journey to Atlantis," an exciting, fast-paced water rollercoaster ride that plunges 60 feet while riders listen to a soundtrack of dolphin calls; "Shipwreck Rapids," a whitewater raft adventure through waterfalls and spouting water jets that is guaranteed to leave you drenched; and "Wild Arctic," a convincing simulator ride that will take you onboard a helicopter to see polar bears and caribou as you ride out an avalanche. Two original, tamer rides require additional tickets: "Skyride," a six-minute gondola ride across Mission Bay affords lovely views of the water; and the emblematic "Skytower," a 265-feet-tall tower with a gently revolving compartment shows off views up to 100 miles away.

The real fun of Sea World is getting personally involved with the attractions. Pet a California bat ray at "Forbidden Reef"; watch the antics of the tuxedoed darlings at the indoor "Penguin Encounter"; stroll through a 57-foot acrylic tube as sand tiger and bonnethead sharks swim over your head at the 280,000-gallon "Shark Encounter"; or visit the classic "Tide Pool" exhibit, where you can pick up a starfish or pet a sea cucumber.

For an additional investment—and advance reservations—you can dine tankside with Shamu; attend beer school with the Anheuser Busch Company, which owns the park; be a trainer for a day and swim alongside dolphins; or children can attend overnight and week-long Adventure Camps (Sea World has its own camp accommodations). Rest assured that even if the marine attractions aren't your cup of tea, Sea World is one of the most beautiful places in San Diego to spend an afternoon, thanks to acres of lovingly maintained gardens that showcase native and tropical flowers, trees, and shrubs. Even on crowded days, you can find quiet pathways along the bay to enjoy the water, gardens, and plentiful birds.

RECREATION: THE GREAT OUTDOORS

This strip of coastline offers up some of the best outdoor activities in the state. Beaches range from pristine seaside oases to sand-lot party spots; visitors can bare it all and bask in the sun, grab a water toy and dive into the waves, or just kick back and enjoy the show.

Beaches

Black's Beach (from Torrey Pines Rd., follow the signs to the Glider Port; park in the dirt lot and hike down the cliff pathways; or walk in past the Scripps Pier from La Jolla Shores). Between 1974 and 1977, Black's Beach, just north of La Jolla Shores, was officially designated as a swimsuit-optional beach. Because nudity was (and still is) banned at all other San Diego-area beaches, uninhibited people were attracted in droves to Black's. Although Black's lost its official designation as a nude beach decades ago, the tradition continues at the northern end.

Children's Pool (off Coast Blvd., south of La Jolla Cove). Don't let the name fool you; this crescent-shaped beach just south of La Jolla Cove is not overrun with children but rather with seals. The shallow cove is protected by a seawall (it's fun to walk to the end of the curving concrete walkway, with waves crashing all around), and it would have made for a protected, calm place for youngsters to swim—if the noisy seals hadn't claimed it decades ago. Although the city has made attempts to take back the beach for the children for whom it was intended, environmentalists have balked—and federally protected seals are likely to rule the shore for years to come. You are not allowed to approach the wildlife, and thus the beach itself isn't accessible, but you can watch the amusing creatures bask on the sand from the walkway above. The smell is appalling, so you'll want to stay downwind.

La Jolla Cove (off Coast Blvd., west of Prospect St.). This is by far my favorite place to enjoy the sea in San Diego; unfortunately, there are many others who share my enthusiasm for this tiny beach, which is protected on three sides by the C-shaped cliffs. Finding parking here would test Job's patience. As always, come early and be prepared to hike in if you can't find something close. The waters are calm enough for snorkeling (and thanks to the San Diego–La Jolla Underwater Ecological Reserve, you have a decent chance of spotting sea life, especially the bright orange garibaldis that call Southern California home). You might even find yourself swimming alongside a seal (but note that it is illegal to harass them in any way, so keep your distance—for your safety and theirs). If you come early in the morning you'll see a dedicated band of rough water swimmers head out in even the coldest weather. If you're not up for the sand between your toes, try the Ellen Browning Scripps Park, an expansive grassy park at the top of the Cove stairs, or stroll around the sidewalk that rings the Cove and heads south to **Children's Pool.** This is an excellent place for tide pooling and is especially family friendly.

La Jolla Shores (off Vallecitos St.). Crystal blue waters, white sand beaches, and countless oiled bodies baking in the sun define La Jolla Shores, which has some of the loveliest views, calmest waves, and widest strips of sand in the city. This is a great place to kayak, thanks to the gentle waves, and it's a popular place to take surf lessons as well. From the parking lot walk north past the Scripps Pier and you'll get away from the crowds—although be careful not to get stranded during high tide (and too far north will take you into the clothing-optional zone of **Black's**). Traffic into and out of the area can become so snarled on weekends (and even weekdays during hot summer days) that it can take hours to drive just a few miles. Take public transportation; park a distance away and hike in; or come very early and plan to stay very late.

Mission Beach (south off Mission Blvd.). There are two miles of sand from the north entrance of Mission Beach to Pacific Beach, and these two miles are packed body to body on weekends and all through the summer, making this one of the most popular—and crowded—beaches in the city. The wide boardwalk is immensely popular with

Spectators enjoy watching seals sun themselves at Children's Pool in La Jolla.

A seldom seen view of La Jolla Shores from the Scripps Pier, which is generally closed to the public.

rollerbladers, runners, and bikers—although it is possible for pedestrians to stroll the boardwalk safely if you keep your wits about you! Families will feel more comfortable staying on the southern portion of the beach—you can catch a beach volleyball game at Cohasset Court on the south end as well; the northern end tends to attract a rougher crowd. And in general, this beach, although beautiful, is a high-crime area, despite the horse and bike patrols the San Diego Police instituted a decade ago to cut down on rowdy behavior. Watch your wallets and do not forget to lock your car.

Pacific Beach (north off Mission Blvd.). Pacific Beach officially runs from the north end of Mission Beach, where the boardwalk terminates and becomes a sidewalk, north to the Crystal Pier. This can also be a raucous scene, and not necessarily the best for families— but it *is* one of the best places to people watch—and what a lot of beautiful people there are! This beach is popular with surfers as well. Restroom facilities, showers, and fire rings are plentiful, even if parking is not. As always, your best bet is to arrive early, before 10 AM (before the morning haze burns off), and be patient.

Torrey Pines State Beach and Reserve (858-755-2063; off of Highway 101, north of La Jolla). This is a quiet, relatively uncrowded beach on all but the hottest summer week- ends. And even when it does get crowded, just walk a few minutes north or south from the beach parking lot and you're likely to find secluded spots along the cliffs. You can also access the shores via the many trails coming down off the cliffs (although be care- ful, because these can be unstable). This is one of the best family beaches in the city, and very popular with longtime locals. You'll find a less frenetic atmosphere here than at most beaches to the south.

Tourmaline Surfing Park (at the west end of Tourmaline St.). No swimming is allowed on this beach; it is open only for surfers and sail boarders. And note: The wave riders are territorial here, so unless you are extremely skilled, better leave your board at home and just enjoy watching the locals.

Windansea (off Nautilus St.). An offshore reef makes for huge waves (when the conditions are right), making this south La Jolla beach a world-class surfing destination. This is a popular beach for sunbathing as well, even though the shoreline is rocky; the extra effort to hike in helps seclude the beach.

Camping

Campland on the Bay (800-422-9386; 2211 Pacific Beach Dr., San Diego, CA 92109). You'll find an array of amenities at this campground resort on Mission Bay, including a private beach where you can rent small sail boats, wave runners, and water tricycles; a huge children's playground and a separate dog park; an onsite restaurant and store; pedicab and bicycle rentals; and a "central park" that is the site of nighttime concerts, luaus, and other entertainment just for campers. In addition, the campground overlooks the Kendall Frost Wildlife Preserve, which means you have an excellent chance of spotting egrets and herons, and if you're really lucky you might even see the endangered least terns that make their home here. Note that although there *are* tent sites available, this is really better suited to RVs that can shut out the noise on rowdy weekend nights.

Canoeing, Kayaking, and Sailing

Bahia Belle (858-488-0551; 998 W. Mission Bay Dr., San Diego, CA 92109). For only $6, you can board this Mississippi riverboat sternwheeler and cruise Mission Bay, all the while dancing and enjoying cocktails (for an additional charge). Purchase boarding tickets at the Bahia Resort (or if you're staying at the Bahia, ride for free!). Early cruises are family-friendly, and children can board for only $3. Note that there are no cruises offered in December.

La Jolla Kayak (858-459-1114; 2199 Avenida de la Playa, La Jolla, CA 92037). La Jolla Kayak rents kayaks to experienced paddlers, and for novices offers one and a half hour guided tours through the La Jolla caves, including a special sunset tour. Be sure to make an advance reservation for both tours and rentals.

Mission Bay Aquatic Center (858-488-1000; 1001 Santa Clara Pt., San Diego, CA 92109). The Mission Bay Aquatic Center claims to be the largest waterfront instructional facility in the world, offering classes in sailing, kayaking, rowing, windsurfing, and wakeboarding; it also has myriad equipment rentals. In cooperation with the California Depart-

---

Sunny Jim Cave

Kayakers in La Jolla Cove can explore six different ocean caves, carved through the years by the relentless waves. The most interesting of these is probably the Sunny Jim Cave, named by Frank Baum (author of *The Wizard of Oz*) after a 1920s cartoon character the opening of the cave is said to resemble. The cavity of the cave displays colorful mineral deposits from iron oxide and iodine from kelp. The cave is also accessible via a humanmade tunnel and network of 145 steps (which can be slippery) through the **Cave Store** (858-459-0746; 1325 Cave St., La Jolla, CA 92037). Entrance fees are $4 for adults and $3 for children.

Kayakers paddle out just before sunset at La Jolla Shores.

ment of Boating and Waterways, the Center offers a certification course on seamanship and boat handling. During the summer the Center provides a Youth Water Sports Camp, where children can learn boating skills; they also offer a Marine Science camp in conjunction with Sea World and Scripp's Birch Aquarium.

Seaforth Boat Rental (619-223-1681; 1641 Quivira Rd., San Diego, CA 92109). Located on Mission Bay (as well as Coronado and the harbor downtown), this company rents out sail boats, jet skis, and speed boats. They also provide crewed sunset sail cruises and charter fishing expeditions.

Diving and Snorkeling

Two favorite dive spots in this area are the La Jolla kelp forests and Wreck Alley, an artificial reef made up of sunken vessels, including an old weather station that blew over during a storm 20 years ago; a retired kelp cutter; a 160-foot Coast Guard cutter; a 366-foot Canadian destroyer; a sports fishing boat; two submarines; and a World War II bomber. Dive shops and charter boats will take you out to the wrecks, which are thriving with marine life.

The **San Diego–La Jolla Underwater Park Ecological Preserve**, just off the coast of La Jolla Cove and running north to Torrey Pines State Preserve, is a 6,000 acre marine habitat—the first coastal underwater preserve on the U.S. West Coast. The visibility is generally good and the waters are relatively calm, which makes for some of the best diving and snorkeling on the coast. In addition to the state fish, the golden garibaldi (bright orange, with fluorescent blue markings in young fish), you are likely to see giant lobsters, sculpin, and harmless leopard sharks.

The San Diego City Lifeguard Service provides updated recorded diving information (619-231-8824). Note that spear fishing requires a license (available at most dive stores), although it is illegal year-round to take any sea life from the San Diego–La Jolla Underwater Park Ecological Preserve. Local dive shops include **Diving Locker** (858-272-1120; 6167 Balboa Ave., San Diego, CA 92109) and **Scuba San Diego** (619-260-1880; 1775 E. Mission Bay Dr., San Diego, CA 92109).

Fishing
As noted earlier, all fishing is prohibited along the marine reserve that runs from La Jolla Cove north to Torrey Pines.

Deep-Sea Fishing
Mission Bay has several launch points for deep-sea fishing, including **Islandia Sportfishing** (619-222-1164; 1551 W. Mission Bay Dr., San Diego, CA 92109) and **Seaforth Landing** (619-224-3383; 1717 Quivira Rd., San Diego, CA 92109), which offer daytrips to the Point Loma kelp beds and multiple-day trips aboard the long-range fleet.

Pier and Surf Fishing
Crystal Pier (at the west end of Garnet Ave.) is a remnant of San Diego past; located in Pacific Beach, you'll find a small crowd of anglers casting from this 80-year-old structure, along with nonfishermen enjoying the peaceful atmosphere and the people watching. You won't need a fishing license here or for any other pier in San Diego.

Lagoons and Bays
San Diego County has an embarrassment of riches when it comes to the calm bay waters and abundant lagoons, and fishing is allowed in all but a few places that are otherwise reserved for swimming. **Mission Bay** has more than 4,000 acres to fish; check out **Quivira**

Grunion Hunting
If someone invites you to a midnight "grunion hunt" at the beach, you might suspect fishy business. Have no fear: Grunion hunting is an actual Southern California phenomenon. From March until August, schools of grunions (cousins of smelts) swim as far inland as possible during high tide at night to lay and then fertilize eggs. Grunion romance takes only a few seconds, and afterward they aim to swim back out to sea with a retreating wave. But the 6-inch silver fish often get stranded on the beach for several minutes. Opportunistic grunion hunters scoop them up as they swim up the beach or when they are flailing on the sand awaiting the next wave. The largest runs are on the second through fifth nights following a new or full moon, and the heaviest part of any given run is about an hour into the run (which can last up to three hours). The best beaches in San Diego to hunt grunion are the Strand on Coronado, Mission Beach near the jetty, Torrey Pines Beach north of La Jolla, and Del Mar Beach. Flashlight and firelight disturb the fish and minimize the number of grunion spawning. Hunters 12 years and older must have a valid fishing license, and nets and digging holes to trap the grunions are prohibited. April and May are closed season, so that the fish may replenish themselves.

And what do you do with your catch after a nighttime foray? Scale the fish, coat them in corn meal or flour, and fry them up whole. They aren't bad to eat, but they aren't good, either! A better use is probably as bait. To check expected grunion runs for the season, visit the Web site of the California Department of Fish and Game at www.dfg.ca.gov/mrd/gruschd.

On clear days, expect the trails at Torrey Pines Reserve to be crowded as soon as the sun comes up.

Basin, in the southwest end of the Bay; a public bait barge is located nearby, and the ubiquitous spills of anchovies attracts a huge number of fish. You'll want to practice catch-and-release here, because the waters are not as clean as we wish they were. Fishing licenses are required for anglers 12 and older.

Golfing

Mission Bay Golf Course (858-581-7880; 2702 N. Mission Bay Dr., San Diego, CA 92109). The only night-lighted public golf course in San Diego, you'll find a par 58 executive course with 18 holes. Green fee: $19–$23.

Torrey Pines Golf Course (800-985-4653; 11480 N. Torrey Pines Rd., La Jolla, CA 92037). One of the nation's premier municipal golf facilities, with 36 holes, a driving range, and equipment rentals, this PGA-sanctioned course is extremely popular with serious local golfers. Deep canyons and dense vegetation make the course feel farther away from civilization than it really is. Almost every hole has a view of the ocean. The South Course is extremely difficult, and has challenged the best players in the world during the Buick Invitational played here every January—and it is also more expensive. The North Course is a little less challenging, but it is perhaps the more scenic of the two. Torrey Pines is set to host the prestigious U.S. Open in June 2008. Green fee $140–205.

Hiking

La Jolla Cove Walkway (starting just above La Jolla Cove). An extremely easy half-mile sidewalk stroll packs in the ocean scenery: Traveling north to south, you'll pass La Jolla Cove, Shell Beach, Seal Rock—look for the seals basking in the sun—and Children's Pool. If you missed the seals at Seal Rock, you're likely to see them in abundance on the sands between the cliffs and the breakers. Along this route you'll also see cormorants drying their feathers, pelicans dive-bombing for snacks, enough seagulls to populate an Alfred Hitchcock thriller, and overfed and overdomisticated ground squirrels.

Torrey Pines State Reserve (858-755-2063; off Highway 101, north of La Jolla). A number of well-worn trails wind through the native scrub brush and indigenous (and rare) Torrey Pines and along cliffs that lead to pristine ocean vistas—and these trails are heavily trafficked, especially on weekends. Once you pass through the ranger station entrance, drive up to the top of the mountain to access the trails. Or if you're looking for a serious workout, park at the beach and walk up (but watch out for cars—there are no sidewalks). Parking $8.

Parks

Kate Sessions Memorial Park (in Pacific Beach, take Lamont St. north). Named after the legendary landscape designer of Balboa Park, this hilltop green space has a sweeping view of the ocean and bay and beautiful city lights after dark (that's probably why so many teenagers come here to park in the evenings), as well as a large expanse of lawn for picnicking or a game of Frisbee or football. You'll find 79 acres of mature trees and plants, crisscrossed with dirt hiking trails.

Mission Bay Park (off Mission Bay Dr.). This picturesque humanmade park encompasses more than 4,000 acres. Created more than 60 years ago when the city dredged the natural tidelands area, it offers numerous recreational activities and is extremely popular with families and fitness buffs. The paved and nearly flat bike path that runs from De Anza Cove on the northeast side of the park (accessed off the Mission Bay Dr. exit from I-5) through a 2.5 mile arc passes several children's playgrounds, acres of lush grass lawn, and follows the waterline to the Mission Bay Parkway bridge. This route is extremely popular with joggers and inline skaters as well, and on summer weekends (especially holidays) the pathway can get congested.

If you want to be even closer to the water, you can rent sailboats, jet skis, powerboats, and aquatic bicycles at several junctions or you can bring your own watercraft and use one of several public boat launches. Although there are always a few children splashing in the calm waters of Mission Bay, and some die-hard swimmers, the pollution levels thanks to the powerboats and the fact that the bay is the terminus point for local drains makes this a fairly bad idea. Better to use this park for picnics, sports, and kite-flying (there is usually a nice breeze and always plenty of open space to run). You'll find fire rings, picnic tables, and large covered pavilions (most of the latter require a permit if you want to reserve them).

Fiesta Island, little more than a dirt mound in the middle of the eastern portion of the bay, is the site of the raunchy, boozy Over-the-Line Tournament every summer; the rest of the year it reigns as party-central. You can drive over to the island via the Fiesta Island Drive bridge and park your vehicle right on the beach. The waters surrounding the island allow power boating, so it is a good place to launch wave runners and ski boats, and thus it tends to be noisy, especially on the weekends.

Sea World is sited along the southern perimeter, and just north is the tiny Vacation Isle, accessed via Ingraham Street (going north from Mission Bay Dr.), where you'll find a model yacht pond and many quiet picnic spots. Sail Bay dominates the northwest portion.

The park is a birders' paradise; throughout the year you'll see blue herons, black-necked stilts, osprey, and mallards. During the winter months, at least 10,000 water birds make their home in Mission Bay, including the northern pintail, bufflehead, cinnamon teal, and California brown pelicans. During April through August, the endangered California least tern nests in the area, and you are apt to come across fenced off areas on north Fiesta Island, Mariner's Point, Stoney Point, and a small area called Government Island to protect the least tern nests from natural predators. Dogs should be leashed year-round at the park, but especially during least tern season, because their numbers are so few that the loss of even one chick represents an environmental tragedy.

Unlike many waterfront parks in San Diego, the parking is plentiful at Mission Bay, both in the many lots along the eastern portion and streetside along Mission Bay Drive. You'll find every facility you could hope for, including regularly spaced (and relatively clean) public restrooms, boat launches, RV pump-out stations, and boat pump-out stations. For more information on Mission Bay, drop by the Visitor Information Center (619-276-8200; 2688 Mission Bay Dr., San Diego, CA 92109).

Mount Soledad Park (north of Mt. Soledad Rd. in La Jolla). The 43-foot cross on the top of Mount Soledad has been a source of controversy over the years, and there is a possibility it will be removed in the future. The park still provides panoramic views of La Jolla and, on really clear days, south to Mexico and north to the Channel Islands.

Torrey Pines State Reserve (868-755-2063; off of Highway 101, north of La Jolla). This is probably the best place to get a glimpse of what coastal San Diego must have looked like before massive human settlement. At Torrey Pines Reserve you'll find 2,000 pristine acres of sandstone mesas and canyons, marshes, and eight miles of trails. Visitors will see native plants (including the rare Torrey pine tree) and animals, spectacular red and white wind-carved cliffs, and miles of unobstructed sea views. A visitors' center that dates to 1922 made from adobe bricks hosts free guided naturalist tours every weekend to a point overlooking Peñasquitos Lagoon and the ocean beyond. The center also has a small theater showing a 10-minute video on the park, as well as a bookstore and tiny museum. At the foot of the mountain is the Torrey Pines State Beach, which can be accessed for free if you are lucky enough to nab one of the unmetered parking spaces along Highway 101.

No place in the world can boast a larger collection of rare Torrey pines than the Torrey Pine Reserve.

Surfers practice patience while waiting for a wave, just north of the Crystal Pier in Pacific Beach.

Surfing

You'll find some of the best surfing in this region, including the shores at Mission Beach, especially near the jetty off Mission Boulevard, Pacific Beach, Tourmaline Surfing Park, La Jolla Shores, Scripps Pier, and Black's Beach. You'll also find some of the most territorial locals here, especially at the beaches in La Jolla. If you're going to surf these beaches, make sure you know what you're doing, and mind your surfing etiquette.

If you're a beginner, surf lessons will get you up on a board in no time, although it takes years of practice and innate athletic ability to really be good. Reliable surf schools include **Menehune Surf** (858-663-7299; 8070 La Jolla Shores Dr., #478, La Jolla, CA 92037), **Mission Bay Aquatic Center** (858-488-1000; 1001 Santa Clara Pt., San Diego, CA 92109), and the women's-only **Surf Diva** (858-454-8273; 2160 Avenida de la Playa, La Jolla, CA 92037).

If the waves are flat at the beach, check out the **Wave House Athletic Club** (858-228-9300; 3115 Ocean Front Walk, San Diego, CA 92109), where you can ride one of three wave-generating devices that promise the perfect swell every time.

Shopping: Everything Under the Sun

University Towne Center, in the Golden Triangle area, is an expansive outdoor mall with fine department stores and many smaller stores, but head to La Jolla's Prospect Street and Pacific Beach's Garnet Avenue to find one-of-a-kind boutiques.

Antiques and Collectibles

D.D. Allen Antiques (858-454-8708; 7728 Fay Ave., La Jolla, CA 92037). Owners of many of the finest homes in the county find museum-quality antiques from around the world, china, fine oil paintings, crystal, silver, and one-of-a-kind finishing touches at this elegant, impeccably staged store. Note that hours are somewhat limited (11–5 Mon.–Sat.; 11–3 Sun.) and subject to change.

Glass Reveries (858-454-5277; 8008 Girard Ave., La Jolla, CA 92037). This little shop features blown art glass from Poland, sculptural appliquéd glass from Azerbaijan, and pressed glass pendants and bracelets. Given the high rent in this area, the prices are remarkably reasonable.

Pangaea Outpost (858-581-0555; 909 Garnet Ave., San Diego, CA 92109). This unusual warehouse space hosts 70 international vendors under the same Pacific Beach roof. Browse through Mexican folk art, including a large collection of Day of the Dead pieces; carved wooden tiki masks from Indonesia; beaded cocktail purses; handcrafted jewelry; and beach clothing and shoes.

Parkers' Posters (858-270-0274; 4010 Morena Blvd., Ste. 105, San Diego, CA 92117). Although the hours are limited, a serious collector can make an appointment to check out Parkers' eclectic international collection of vintage posters, which come in a wide range of prices.

Books and Music

D.G. Wills (858-456-1800; 7461 Girard Ave., La Jolla, CA 92037). A stuffed-to-the-rafters old-fashioned bookstore that specializes in new and used scholarly books as well as rare collector's items, D.G. Wills hosts regular readings by an eclectic mix of authors, poets, and journalists. The owner and staff are knowledgeable and extremely helpful.

Open Door Books (858-270-8642; 4761 Cass St., San Diego, CA 92109). Tucked into a residential neighborhood of Pacific Beach, Open Door is just the kind of bookstore you'd expect to find near the shore: Casual and welcoming. The inventory is wide-ranging, including a good children's book collection and an extensive selection of spiritual titles.

University of California, San Diego, Bookstore (858-534-3149; 9500 Gilman Dr., La Jolla, CA 92093). This multilevel store located in the Price Center on campus carries, of course, textbooks for UCSD's students; you'll also find a good collection of literary fiction and lots of Dr. Seuss memorabilia (reflecting the school's generous endowment by the famous author's estate).

Warwicks (858-454-0347; 7812 Girard Ave., La Jolla, CA 92037). This beloved independent bookstore manages to survive a market flooded with discount bookstores by offering unwaveringly good service and regular book signings by big-name authors. They also carry high-end gift papers and stationery.

Clothing

Anna Brazil (858-273-3032; 954 Garnet Ave., San Diego, CA 92109). In addition to some of the smallest slivers of fabric you'll ever see masquerading as bikinis, Anna (who really is from Brazil) sells sarongs, lingerie, and sportswear with an international flair.

Encore of La Jolla (858-454-7540; 7655 Girard Ave., La Jolla, CA 92037). Upscale resale at its best, Encore sells previously owned designer fashions for men and women for pennies on the dollar of original prices, including labels like Prada, Hermes, Gucci, Vera Wang, Chanel, and Louis Vuitton. This store will even help you with alterations for your new wardrobe.

JEP Boutique (858-551-0600; 7501 La Jolla Blvd., La Jolla, CA 92037). Upscale women's and men's fashion is featured in this La Jolla shop in the Birdrock neighborhood, which carries jewelry, accessories, and perfumes as well.

Nicole Miller (858-454-3434; 1275 Prospect St., La Jolla, CA 92037). Manhattan-based designer Nicole Miller's La Jolla boutique sells evening wear, wedding gowns, fine sports wear, and a wide selection of accessories. If you are a serious shopper, call ahead and arrange for a private showing.

Pout (858-456-7088; 935 Silverado Ave., La Jolla, CA 92037). This upscale children's fashion boutique carries the kinds of precious items doting grandmas and aunties love to buy for their little darlings.

Sigi's Boutique (858-454-7244; 7888 Girard Ave., La Jolla, CA 92037). European designer fashions and accessories are the stars in this extremely high-end salon; plop down in an elegant chair in front and browse the fashion mags, and then head back to peruse the elegant evening gowns or the gorgeous leather jackets from Italy.

Home Furnishings

Bo Danica (858-454-6107; 7722 Girard Ave., La Jolla, CA 92037). Come here when you're looking for a special piece to enliven the holiday table or an elegant dinner party; you'll find large, festive serving platters, fine linens, and elegant china, as well as a collection of fragrant candles.

My Own Space (858-459-0099; 7840 Girard Ave., La Jolla, CA 92037). As gloriously staged as a modern art museum, this sleek store featuring cutting-edge furnishing and accessory designs by Kartell Allessi and Herman Miller, among others, is a marvel. Just browsing through the suspended Aarnio bubble chairs, Charles Ghost Lucite stools, and the Nelson "marshmallow" sofas will raise your sophistication quotient.

Underground Furniture (858-581-0229; 1345 Garnet Ave., San Diego, CA 92109). Shop this boutique in Pacific Beach for designer 1950s and 1960s sofas, tables, and accessories.

Just for Fun

Bob's Mission Surf Shop (858-483-8837; 4320 Mission Blvd., San Diego, CA 92019). In addition to board sales and rentals, you can also get repairs in this one-stop shop, which sells its own brand of surf boards alongside a wide variety of designer brands.

City Lights Christmas Store (619-275-1006; 1212 Knoxville St., San Diego, CA 92110). This is reported to be the largest Christmas store in Southern California, with more than 27,000 square feet of display space. Browse through the holiday spirit all year round, or shop for collectibles and fine ornaments, including Christopher Radko ornaments, Slavic Treasures, Steinbach nutcrackers, Hummel figurines, and Thomas Kinkade exclusive designs.

Great News! (858-270-1582; 1788 Garnet Ave., San Diego, CA 92109). Tucked into a strip mall in Pacific Beach, this discount cookware store sells name brands of cookware for bargain prices, and also offers reasonably priced onsite cooking classes.

La Mano (858-454-7732; 1298 Prospect St., La Jolla, CA 92037). Going to Carnival this year? Head to La Mano (located off the street, just above the Cove) first to choose from a wide selection of finely crafted Venetian masks. The shop also rents authentic period costumes.

Muttropolis (858-459-9663; 7755 Girard Ave., La Jolla, CA 92037). Appropriately located in dog-friendly La Jolla, Muttropolis offers exquisite food and water bowls, couture dog wear, and pet beds to complement the nicest interior designs. Canine companions are welcome.

Water and wind have eroded the cliffs in Point Loma into spectacular shapes.

5

SOUTH COUNTY

A Blending of Cultures

South County comprises those neighborhoods that fall south of downtown, including Chula Vista, Coronado, Imperial Beach, Point Loma, and Shelter Island. I've also included Ocean Beach into this category, because although it stretches northwest of downtown, its isolated location at the end of a peninsula makes it distinct from the beaches covered in the previous chapter. These disparate communities couldn't be more different, with wildly varying socioeconomic and cultural influences.

Chula Vista, an established suburb southeast of downtown with a strong Hispanic influence, is a close-knit community that blends long-time blue-collar neighborhoods with newer, upscale planned communities. This is an inexpensive place to get a great meal, and it's a special favorite with golfers and nature lovers. Just south of downtown and connected to San Diego via the beautiful curving Coronado Bay Bridge, Coronado "island" (really, a peninsula) is the town that time forgot. The ultra-expensive enclave is part relaxing beach resort and part U.S. military base, dominated on one end by North Island and subject to spectacular jet fly-bys and military helicopters. The homeness of this "small town" community belies its upscale underpinnings, and it feels a lot like Mayberry by the Sea. Visitors can stroll along the exceptionally wide, dune-riddled beach that fronts the famous Hotel del Coronado, browse the independent shops along Orange Avenue (the main street through town), or relax with a cup of coffee at any number of sidewalk bistros.

Just northwest of downtown, Ocean Beach (affectionately known to locals as "OB") is an insular neighborhood that is home to iconoclasts of all sorts, and popular with vegans and surfers; OB is the epitome of "laid back," with a strong community spirit and a welcoming vibe. To the south, Point Loma juts out to the southernmost point of the county, insulated on a natural peninsula that was the first bit of land to be discovered by Europeans. This area, with panoramic views of the ocean, is home to a training center for the U.S. Navy, which draws its fair share of strip clubs and fast food joints along main corridors into town, but it also has a beautiful old residential district. And Shelter Island, which is technically part of Point Loma, a little humanmade offshoot, is *the* place to come if you're in the market for a yacht: There are dozens of brokers in this small area, as well as a stunning waterfront park with premier vantage points to watch other people's sailboats or just enjoy a relaxing picnic.

LODGING

You'll find some of the most expensive lodging in the south county (in Coronado) and some of the least (in Chula Vista), and the luxury level is generally commensurate with price. This area is conveniently located near downtown and the Mexican border, but it is a little far flung if you're interested in exploring farther north than La Jolla.

CHULA VISTA
EL PRIMERO HOTEL

Manager: Solorpie Roque
619-425-4486; 619-425-3938
www.elprimerohotel.com
416 Third Ave., Chula Vista, CA 91910
Price: Inexpensive
Credit Cards: MC, V
Handicap Access: 1 full

This tiny historic hotel in downtown Chula Vista has only 20 rooms, and thanks to the cozy size, guests will be reminded of a bed-and-breakfast. The butter yellow art deco exterior shows off the revitalization of this 1930s structure, built as the first "modern" hotel in Chula Vista, with such amenities as hot and cold running water and steam heat. The small but comfortable lobby resembles someone's living room, and the rooms are crisp and clean, dressed with white linens and dark wood. There is a cheerful, sunny outdoor patio to enjoy a morning cup of coffee. All rooms are nonsmoking and come with a hot breakfast that includes dishes such as frittatas, freshly baked banana bread, and a large selection of fruit in season.

GOOD NITE INN

Innkeeper: Maria Nunez
619-425-8200
www.good-night.com/southbay
225 Bay Blvd., Chula Vista, CA 91910
Price: Inexpensive
Credit Cards: AE, D, MC, V
Handicap Access: 8 full

This motel, across the street from the Chula Vista Nature Center, is part of a statewide chain of budget lodging. The location is quiet and slightly out of the way—although it is within walking distance of a few chain restaurants, as well as the south bay **Anthony's Fish Grotto** (619-425-4200)—and close to the San Diego Trolley stop. The accommodations are nothing fancy. Furnishings are modest, and the bedding and drapes are dated but clean. There is a small pool and a game room, and free coffee is provided every morning.

CORONADO
EL CORDOVA HOTEL

Manager: Josh Murphy
800-229-2032; fax 619-435-0632
www.elcordovahotel.com
1351 Orange Ave., Coronado, CA 92118
Prices: Moderate
Credit Cards: AE, D, DC, MC, V
Handicap Access: 2 full

This friendly boutique hotel was originally built as a mansion in 1902 for Elisha Babcock, one of the masterminds behind the Hotel del Coronado, which sits across the street. The historic property has been renovated several times throughout the past century, but still retains its turn-of-the-century elegance and glamour. Prices are more accessible than the luxurious Hotel del, and although the views and the ambiance cannot compare with its grand neighbor, guests of the El Cordova can still avail themselves of the expansive Coronado Beach nearby. The Mediterranean décor carries throughout the property, and the lush open courtyard features tiled barbeques and pretty picnic seating. There are a wide variety of accommodations available, and interior designs vary, but expect to find comfortable Mexican-style carved wooden armchairs, authentic Spanish tiles in the bathrooms, and a hacienda feel throughout. Many rooms feature kitchenettes and patios, and the romantic honeymoon suite has its own circular porch. There is also a relatively new pool and spa on site. And you won't have far to go for excellent Mexican food: **Miguel's Cocina** (see page 156) is on the ground floor.

GLORIETTA BAY INN
Manager: Holly Shumate
619-435-3101; fax 619-435-6182
www.gloriettabayinn.com
1630 Glorietta Blvd., Coronado, CA 92118
Prices: Moderate
Credit Cards: AE, D, MC, V
Handicap Access: 2 full

This beautiful historic property was built in 1906 as the dream home for John Spreckels, a major investor and booster of early San Diego. At one time Spreckels owned a good chunk of Coronado as well as downtown San Diego, including the Hotel del Coronado. The old mansion is on Glorietta Bay, which today has jaw-dropping views of the downtown San Diego skyline Spreckels helped make possible. A few decades back the mansion was lovingly restored to its original grandeur, and many period fixtures are original. The elegant Italian Renaissance architecture features rich details like ornate moldings, carved pillars, and a dramatic marble staircase accented with gleaming brass. There are 11 suites in the old Spreckels mansion, as well as 89 contemporary rooms available next door. Guests will be treated to milk and cookies at bedtime, a continental breakfast, and an afternoon snack. In the summer, a kids' program offers craft projects and ice cream socials, and little ones can dial up a reading of *Goodnight Moon* from their rooms all year round. The hotel offers a variety of special packages and Internet specials worth watching for. The "babymoon" package, billed as a last hurrah before the blessed event, includes a luxurious mansion room, a picnic breakfast delivered to your door, a one-hour pregnancy massage, and a jar of pickles and a certificate that can be redeemed for ice cream.

HOTEL DEL CORONADO
Manager: Todd Shallan
619-435-6611; fax 619-522-8262
www.hoteldel.com
1500 Orange Ave., Coronado, CA 92118
Price: Very expensive
Credit Cards: AE, D, MC, V
Handicap Access: 19 full

Built in 1888 by businessmen Elisha Babcock and H. L. Story, who were inspired by a Norman castle, this beautiful old resort hotel is listed as a National Historic Landmark and is considered by many as one of the top destination hotels in the country. The sprawling white-washed complex accented with bright red-roofed conical towers is sited on a sugary white sand beach that is exceptionally wide by California standards. Landscaping throughout the large resort is manicured, with fuchsia bougainvillea climbing romantic gazebos and exotic palms lining perfect emerald green lawns. The public rooms are rich in carved mahogany wood details, plush rugs, and extravagant Victorian furnishings. The luxurious Hotel del Coronado may seem familiar to those who've never been here, because in 1958, the hotel was the backdrop for the Hollywood comedy *Some Like It Hot*, starring Marilyn Monroe, Tony Curtis, and Jack Lemmon.

Guest accommodations are sited in three distinct locations: The original and historic Victorian Building, the Towers and Cabana, and the brand new Beach Village featuring condo properties for purchase and for rent. (Note that as this book went to press, construction was ongoing; expect dust and noise through 2007.) All three feature gleaming carved wood beds, exquisite linens, and plump terry cloth robes. The newer guest accommodations in the Towers and the Beach Village are more spacious—

the Victorian rooms can have astonishingly low ceilings—but if you have a choice, opt for the older period rooms, to fully experience the ambiance of this classic beauty. From either of the sites you can choose from stunning ocean views (many rooms feature small balconies) or tranquil garden views.

This is a full-service resort, with a large sparkling pool and new state-of-the-art spa featuring hydrotherapy, steam rooms, and a full complement of treatments; numerous boutiques, including upscale clothing stores and fine jewelry stores; kids' and teens' activities in the summer; and several onsite bars and restaurants. Visit **Babcock and Story** for cocktails with a view of the ocean in a setting that is straight out of the 19th century (the carved wooden bar belongs in a museum). The new **1500 Ocean** restaurant offers contemporary California coastal cuisine with impeccable views. And the historic **Crown Room** (see page 153) has long been voted the best Sunday brunch in San Diego by local newspapers and magazines. You can also indulge in a Victorian high tea on Sunday afternoons (or every day during the month of December, when the Del is decked out to the nines in holiday decorations).

THE VILLAGE INN
619-435-9318
www.coronadovillageinn.com
1017 Park Pl., Coronado, CA 92118
Price: Moderate
Credit Cards: AE, MC, V
Handicap Access: No

This small bed-and-breakfast (with 15 rooms) is housed in a historic 1926 building just off the main thoroughfare of Orange Avenue (and about a block from the beach). Tiny guest rooms are individually decorated, and some have Jacuzzi tubs. A self-serve breakfast of fresh fruit, muffins and pastries, and coffee and tea is served daily. Guests can also make use of the full kitchen to prepare their own meals, if they are so inclined, and can also borrow from the well-stocked mystery library.

Ocean Beach
THE ELSBREE HOUSE
Innkeepers: Katie and Phil Elsbree
619-226-4133
www.BBinOB.com

The Hotel del Coronado is one of the most recognized landmarks in the city and regarded as one of the finest historic resorts in the world.

5054 Narragansett Ave., San Diego, CA
92017
Prices: Moderate
Credit Cards: V, MC
Handicap Access: No

This tiny bed-and-breakfast in a funky
Ocean Beach neighborhood just minutes
from the ocean and close to the pier has
only six rooms, each with their own private
bath and each decorated with homey
touches like fresh flowers and lace doilies.
The charming green clapboard cottage is
bordered with a white picket fence and
English-style flower gardens, and public
rooms have fireplaces. Guests will be
treated to granola, yogurt, and fruit for
breakfast, along with fresh bread, muffins,
and good coffee. This place really feels like
someone's home—and in fact, it is: The
Elsbbrees live on the property.

OCEAN BEACH HOTEL
Manager: Larry Clark
619-223-7191; fax 619-222-1455
www.obhotel.com
5080 Newport Ave., San Diego, CA 92017
Price: Moderate
Credit Cards: AE, D, MC, V
Handicap Access: 2 full

If you're looking for moderately priced
accommodations on the water and inexpensive dining options, the Ocean Beach Hotel
in a Bohemian neighborhood right on the
sand could be a good choice. The hotel is
near the almost 2,000-foot-long pier and
south of Dog Beach, where San Diego pets
run wild. The ocean views are as beautiful
here as they are anywhere else in the city,
and the beach is well used, despite especially strong rip currents in front of the
hotel. Nearby is the antique district of
Ocean Beach, located on Newport Avenue,
as well as numerous bars, inexpensive
restaurants, and board shops. The 60 small,
worn rooms at the Ocean Beach Hotel have
showers only.

BAY CLUB HOTEL AND MARINA
Manager: Michael Ardelt
619-224-8888; fax 619-225-1604
www.bayclubhotel.com
2131 Shelter Island Dr., San Diego, CA
92106
Price: Moderate
Credit Cards: AE, D, DC, MC, V
Handicap Access: 5 full

Shelter Island is a humanmade peninsula
just off Point Loma, 6 miles from downtown
and right on the water. Staying here offers
both proximity to the nightlife of the hot
Gaslamp Quarter and the beauty of waterfront San Diego. The entirely nonsmoking
hotel is Polynesian-themed, and the South
Pacific décor features bamboo and rattan
furniture and neutral-toned batik print
fabrics. Rates include a varied and extensive full breakfast buffet, complimentary
shuttle to and from the airport and the
Amtrak station, and a small heated pool and
spa. Jumbo jet traffic crosses near the hotel
from 6 AM until 11 PM (the latest flights that
are allowed to land in San Diego), and this
makes for loud outdoor patios and balconies and might be an issue indoors for
light sleepers or those otherwise sensitive
to sound.

HUMPHREY'S HALF MOON INN
Manager: Sergio Davies
619-224-3411; fax 619-224-3478
www.halfmooninn.com
2303 Shelter Island Dr., San Diego, CA
92106
Price: Expensive
Credit Cards: AE, D, DC, M, V
Handicap Access: 3 full rooms plus 1 suite

The entrance of this hotel on Shelter Island
looks like the prow of an old ship. The sea-
faring motif is particularly appropriate,
because the nearby San Diego Bay is chock
full of sailboats and yachts. The grounds are
thick with tropical palms, brightly colored

flowers bloom year-round, and the lushly landscaped pool could well be in the South Pacific. Guest rooms are a mix of airy Polynesian exotica and contemporary Mediterranean style, with light woods, brightly patterned fabrics, and large windows, almost all of which have a view of the bay and the skyline beyond or the lovely tropical gardens. Bathrooms feature stone vanity tops and dramatic lighting. The inn hosts the Humphrey's Outdoor Concerts by the Bay (see page 149), a series popular with locals that runs from May through October and features jazz, comedy acts, blues, and international music. Check the Web site for excellent values on package deals that include concert tickets as well as passes to local attractions.

THE INN AT SUNSET CLIFFS
Manager: Crystal Peterson
619-222-7901; fax 619-222-4201
www.innatsunsetcliffs.com
1370 Sunset Cliffs Blvd., Point Loma, CA 92017
Prices: Moderate
Credit Cards: AE, D, MC, V
Handicap Access: 1 partial

This 24-room inn right on the ocean boasts a panoramic two-tiered Pacific-view deck with picnic tables and lounge chairs. The 1950s-era, two-story hotel is well-kept and clean. All of the rooms have undergone a recent refurbishing, making them light and airy—although extensive use of pickled woods and pastel fabrics in many rooms already date the design. One- and two-bedroom suites are available with full kitchens and separate living rooms, and a new presidential suite offers a giant Jacuzzi spa tub and stellar views of the ocean. All accommodations have a refrigerator and WiFi.

The Old Point Loma Lighthouse operated for only a few decades, before a new—more effective—lighthouse was built closer to the water's edge.

Off the Bayside Trail, the tide pools in Point Loma are home to exotic seaside creatures like periwinkles and wooly sculpins.

Culture

Being close to the border means most south bay neighborhoods enjoy a blending of cultures and a rich historical backdrop. And it doesn't get older and more historic than Point Loma, where the Spanish first landed in the 16th century.

Historic Places

Cabrillo National Monument and Old Point Loma Lighthouse (619-557-5450; 1800 Cabrillo Memorial Dr., San Diego, CA 92106). Juan Rodriguez Cabrillo, said to be the first European to set foot on the West Coast of what is now the United States, sailed into the San Diego harbor on September 28, 1542, on his way to search for a shortcut from Central America to Asia. He never found this route, but he did claim San Diego (he named it San Miguel) for Spain. The Cabrillo National Monument at the very tip of the Point Loma peninsula memorializes his accomplishments with a sculpture of the famous conquistador, which looks out onto one of the greatest views in the city. From this vantage point you can view the San Diego skyline, the graceful Coronado Bridge and the island it connects, and beyond to the mountains of Mexico. Onsite is a small museum that displays Cabrillo artifacts, including navigational tools like a quadrant and an astrolabe, and a scale model of Cabrillo's flag ship, the *San Salvadore*. There's also a book store that sells prints and posters.

Whale Watching

Gray whales pass by the San Diego coastline every year during their 10,000-mile roundtrip migration from the frigid Arctic Sea to the warm and shallow lagoons of Baja Mexico to mate and have their babies, starting in late December and through the end of March. About 200 whales pass by San Diego in a day during the peak migration period (late January and through February). To get a closer look, check out the whale-watching tours sponsored jointly by the **Birch Aquarium at Scripps Institution of Oceanography** (858-534-3474; 2300 Expedition Way, La Jolla, CA 92037) and **San Diego Harbor Excursion** (619-234-4111; 1050 N. Harbor Dr., San Diego, CA, 92101). As ships embark on three-hour tours to deep waters off San Diego, onboard Birch naturalists highlight biological and historical facts about gray whales. You really can't go wrong with these tours, because the San Diego Harbor Excursion promises that if you don't spot a whale, you can come back for a second tour at no additional cost. There are also longer whale-watching trips leaving from San Diego heading to Baja, starting in mid-February. These extended tours last between three and five days, and guests will visit Ojo de Liebre (Scammon's Lagoon) and secluded Bahia de San Ignacio, where the whales have their offspring. It isn't uncommon to see the whales in these locations from extremely close range; mother whales swim beneath the boats, and Crystal De Sota, Education Specialist at the Birch Aquarium, says the baby whales show off for the tourists, behaving "a lot like puppies trying to get attention."

If you and your stomach are not up for a boat tour, try watching for whales from atop the hills at the Cabrillo National Monument in Point Loma or inside its partially glassed-in observatory, which is just a short walk from the Old Point Loma Lighthouse. Look about a mile offshore for water spouts 8 to 15 feet tall, the byproduct of whales breathing through their blowholes. Generally the whales blow four or five spouts, then sound (dive down) for about five minutes. You're apt to see the head or the tail surfacing shortly after a spout, and if you're really lucky, you'll see a whale breach.

Also onsite is the picturesque Old Point Loma Lighthouse, which dates back to 1854. Visitors can peek into recreated rooms that show how the light keeper Robert Israel and his family lived for 30-plus years, including a cozy parlor decorated with shell crafts made by Mrs. Israel, a kitchen that has breathtaking views of the ocean out both windows, and—up a very narrow spiral staircase—the sleeping quarters of the couple and their children. Further up, a ladder leads to the lighthouse lens (although guests are permitted to the very top only two days a year).

Because Point Loma juts out into the sea, this is an excellent place to watch gray whales, which migrate from the Arctic Sea down to Baja Mexico, starting in late December and through March. Hike past the lighthouse and you'll find a short trail that loops to the Whale Overlook, a glass-enclosed structure that has educational displays on the whales.

In 1974, President Gerald Ford increased the size of the park by adding the protected coastline, which includes a small, rocky beach and some of the best tide pools in the city. Hike down native scrub landscape via the Bayside Trail (2 miles roundtrip, descending about 300 feet) or drive down to access the tide pools (look for the sign on the west side of the road going into the park and you'll see the turnoff). At low tide, you are likely to discover anemones, shore crabs, dead man's fingers, bat stars, and sea hares. Note that the sandstone cliffs that surround the tide pools, although hauntingly beautiful, are unstable and extremely dangerous, especially anywhere near the edges, where they can give way without warning. Stay on established pathways, wear appropriate shoe wear (the tide pools themselves are slippery), and use caution. Open daily 9–5. $5 per vehicle.

Nightlife

Humphrey's (619-224-3577; 2241 Shelter Island Dr., San Diego, CA 92106). This gorgeous outdoor waterfront venue in Shelter Island (at **Humphrey's Half Moon Inn** by the yacht club) allows you to sit waterfront under the stars and enjoy live entertainment from May through October. In the past several years, top artists such as India Arie, George Benson, Jimmy Buffett, Aretha Franklin, Jewel, and Brad Paisley have played to sellout crowds.

The Manhattan (619-422-6641; 400 Broadway St., Chula Vista, CA 91910). A popular neighborhood bar, the Manhattan in downtown Chula Vista features karaoke Sunday through Thursday starting at 9 PM.

Over the Border (619-427-5889; 3008 Main St., Chula Vista 91910). This club is one of the hottest Latin rock music destinations for patrons on either side of the border. Dance to live music on the weekends. Cover charge varies.

Sunshine Company Saloon (619-222-0722; 5028 Newport Ave., San Diego, CA 92107). A spacious open-air bar in Ocean Beach, the aptly named Sunshine Company offers up half-price pitchers from 5 to 6 PM daily in a relaxed, friendly atmosphere.

Seasonal Events

Ring in the new year—literally—with the Buddhist Temple of San Diego (619-239-0896) at the annual **New Year's Eve Bell-Ringing Ceremony** at Shelter Island's Friendship Bell, a gift from San Diego's sister city, Yokohama, Japan. The giant bronze bell is rung 108 times, symbolizing a fresh start to the new year.

Don't miss the **Kiwanis Ocean Beach Kite Festival** (619-531-1527) in March, which features contests for making and flying kites, as well as free food for participants, entertainment, and a craft show. The event culminates in a parade to the beach, where the new creations are launched on the winds.

The annual **Festival Cinco de Mayo** (619-422-1982) sponsored by the Chula Vista Chamber of Commerce, is actually held the weekend before the big day (unless the holiday happens to fall on a weekend) on Third Avenue, between G and E Streets. In addition to more than 250 vendors selling food and handcrafted items, there is also live entertainment on three stages, Mexican Folklorico dancers and mariachis, and a fun zone for kids.

You'll find an old-fashioned Fourth of July celebration at the **Coronado Independence Day** bash (619-437-8788), with a flag-waving parade, demonstrations by the U.S. Navy (including exhilarating Navy flybys), and fireworks over Glorietta Bay, with the San Diego skyline as a backdrop. Also this month, the **U.S. Open Sandcastle Competition** (http://members.cox.net/usopensandcastle), held at Imperial Beach every summer, brings together professional sand sculptors, amateurs, and kids of all ages for one of the largest sandcastle-building competitions in the United States.

In early August, pucker up for the **Lemon Festival** (619-422-1982), held in downtown Chula Vista to celebrate what was once the lemon capital of the world. You'll find entertainment, vendors selling crafts and homemade fare, and of course lemon-flavored treats of all kinds. In mid-August, head to the California Yacht Marina in Chula Vista for the annual **Little Race for Little People** (619-432-1982), a wacky and wet inflatable boat race that bills itself as the "biggest water fight on the West Coast"—even the fire department gets in

Revelers ring in the new year at the Friendship Bell on Shelter Island. Photo courtesy of Joyce Teague. Used with permission.

on the act and turns its hoses on racers. Spectators and participants raise money to benefit the Neonatal Intensive Care Unit of Children's Hospital in San Diego.

In September check out the **Cabrillo Festival** (619-557-5450) at the Cabrillo National Monument in Point Loma, which commemorates Juan Cabrillo's explorations with a week-long celebration that includes a historical reenactment. The **Ocean Beach Jazz Festival** (619-224-4906), sponsored by a local jazz radio station and the Ocean Beach Mainstreet Association, features dozens of musicians from around the country at this annual event, held at the Ocean Beach Pier. **YachtFest** (www.yachtfest.com) in mid-September at Shelter Island celebrates the Port of San Diego, which is said to attract more yachts than any other harbor in the Pacific Rim. Even if you don't have your own vessel, this is a chance to tour some beautiful boats and dream a little.

In December, prepare to celebrate Christmas in pure San Diego fashion at the **San Diego Bay Parade of Lights** (619-224-2240); watch the harbor overflow with lighted and holiday-themed boats that sail in a procession beginning at Shelter Island and ending at the Coronado Ferry Landing; the evenings' festivities are capped off by a rousing fireworks show. And throughout the month, enjoy afternoon ice skating (call for hours) with a view of the ocean at the **Hotel del Coronado** (619-435-6611), which puts up a temporary rink on the beach every December.

Theater

Lamb's Players Theater (619-437-0600; 1142 Orange Ave., Coronado, CA 92118). Close to the Hotel del Coronado and located inside a historic art-deco bank building, the Lamb's Players have a resident ensemble of actors and singers. For the winter holidays they stage a Festival of Christmas, featuring traditional carols and lavish costumes.

RESTAURANTS AND FOOD PURVEYORS

Restaurants

Because the south county encompasses a wide variety of socioeconomic and ethnic backgrounds, the neighborhood eateries offer myriad possibilities, from a high-end, high-priced meal in Coronado overlooking the ever-expanding downtown San Diego skyline to incomparably fresh fish on the docks in Point Loma to a laid-back burger shack in Ocean Beach.

CHULA VISTA
AUNT EMMA'S PANCAKES
Owner: Nick Gelastopoulos
619-427-2722
700 E St., Chula Vista, CA 91902
Open: Daily
Price: Inexpensive
Cuisine: American
Serving: B and L
Credit Cards: AE, D, MC, V
Handicap Access: No
Reservations: No
Parking: Small lot on the premises or street parking

This old-fashioned diner hasn't changed much since the place opened in 1959. The noisy, popular neighborhood hangout specializes in pancakes of every imaginable variety: They have buckwheat pancakes, banana nut pancakes, mango pancakes, strawberry crepes, and chocolate-hazelnut crepes. You can also get just about any other breakfast item you want, including biscuits and gravy, cheesy Monte Cristo sandwiches, Mexican specialties like *chilachiles* and *huevos con chorizo*, and omelets made to order. If you aren't in the mood for breakfast, there are a few sandwich and burger options as well. The quality is superior, the service is friendly and efficient, and the prices are phenomenal: For $3.49, you can get a breakfast special that includes two eggs, two pancakes, and two slices of bacon or sausage. Weekend mornings are crowded, but if there is a line, put your name in with the front desk, and you probably won't wait more than a half hour. It will be time well spent.

CORONADO
BEACH DINER
Owner: David Spatafore
619-437-6087
www.nadolife.com

1015 Orange Ave., Coronado, 92118
Open: Daily
Price: Inexpensive
Cuisine: American
Serving, B, L, D
Credit Cards: AE, MC, V
Handicap Access: Partial
Reservations: No
Parking: Metered street

This art-deco diner sports a shimmery tin ceiling, vintage surfboards suspended overhead, and framed beach posters on the walls. The tables look like your grandma's kitchen set, with sparkling blue and silver vinyl chairs and lots of chrome trim. You'll also find an extensive outdoor patio that looks out onto the heart of downtown Coronado. Breakfasts are especially popular, and portions are large: Check out the pile of homemade waffles or any entrée that comes with the fresh hash browns. For lunch and dinner, start with chili cheese fries piled high with melting cheddar or a plate of three sliders, served with grilled onions and pickles, both of which are a bargain at about $7 (and both of which could be a meal by themselves). "Yo Mama's Meatloaf" is a perennial favorite, made with beef and pork and slathered with mushroom gravy. Or try the enormous portion of Cincinnati chili, served over spaghetti, smothered in melted cheese, and then doused in sour cream. The soda fountain selections are worth a try, too, and include traditional New York egg creams, purple cows (vanilla ice cream and grape soda), and root beer floats. The food is a bargain, especially considering the large portions, but be prepared to wait: The place is often crowded and the service is astonishingly slow.

CHEZ LOMA FRENCH BISTRO

Owner: Ken Irvine
619-435-0661
www.chezloma.com
1132 Loma Ave., Coronado 92118

Chez Loma in Coronado is a romantic spot for traditional French fare.

Open: Daily
Price: Moderate to Expensive
Cuisine: French
Serving: D; brunch on weekends
Credit Cards: AE, MC, V
Handicap Access: Yes
Reservations: Yes
Parking: Street

This cozy, romantic restaurant near the Hotel del Coronado (and just off Orange Avenue) is housed in the Carey Hizar House, a historic landmark in Coronado that dates to 1889. Intimate dining spaces, crisp white linens, and fine art on the walls offer a cozy atmosphere in which to dine on hearty traditional French fare—no tiny portions or sauces for sauces' sake here. Start with the creamy duck liver *pâté* served with cornichons, olives, and grainy mustard; or the decadent *crêpe de homard*, a paper-thin pancake stuffed with Maine lobster, rich mascarpone cheese, and finished with a delicate white truffle and carrot juice emulsion. For entrees, Chez Loma offers familiar favorites like filet mignon, roasted duck, and rack of lamb, as well as fortifying *cassoulets* of black mussels, sea scallops, salmon sausage, and white beans in a luscious lobster sauce. No French meal is complete without dessert—the spicy, aromatic ginger bread is drenched with a light caramel sauce, and the unusual chocolate bread pudding is served warm with cherries and creamy vanilla ice cream. Although à la carte dishes can be pricey, for as little as $25, you can order a fixed-price menu that includes an appetizer, entrée, and dessert—a nice way to splurge without blowing the budget.

CROWN ROOM

Chef: John Shelton
619-435-6611
www.hoteldel.com/dining
1500 Orange Ave., Coronado, CA 92118
Open: Sunday
Price: Expensive
Cuisine: American
Serving: Brunch
Credit Cards: AE, DC, MC, V
Handicap Access: Yes
Reservations: Yes
Parking: Lot or limited street

The glowing wood interior of this barrel-vaulted, high-ceiling beauty within the historic Hotel del Coronado speaks to an earlier era, when dining at a fine resort like this one was gracious, unrushed, and eminently civilized. Legend has it that the crown-shaped chandeliers were designed by Frank L. Baum, author of *The Wizard of Oz*. Despite the unbeatable location of the "Hotel del" on one of the most beautiful beaches in San Diego, the views are limited, but the refined atmosphere instead fosters intimate discussions and a less distracted setting. Sunday brunch (for which reservations are advised at least two weeks in advance) is nothing short of sublime. A bottomless glass of champagne is paired with a staggering selection of buffet items, which include glorious eggs Benedict, smoked

salmon and bagels, shrimp, crab legs, sushi, a waffle station, an omelet station, exotic fruits, and a mouth-watering collection of pastries and chocolate-covered morsels. There is also a kids-only section that offers cereals, pancakes, and finger sausages. Do not miss the chocolate buffet, which features luscious truffles and hand-dipped strawberries.

PEOHE'S

Manager: Jim Gorzelanski
619-437-4474
www.landrys.com
1201 First St., Coronado, CA 92118
Open: Daily
Price: Expensive
Cuisine: Asian, Polynesian
Serving: L, D; brunch on Sundays
Credit Cards: AE, D, DC, MC, V
Handicap Access: Yes
Reservations: Yes
Parking: Lot (or if you come by boat, a private dock)

Located in the Ferry Landing Marketplace in Coronado, Peohe's has been a local favorite for special occasions for several decades. Be warned that the price of a meal at this Island-inspired restaurant—decorated somewhat excessively with a lava "cave" and indoor waterfall—includes a tariff on the fabulous views, which look over the water and face downtown—but thanks to the building boom in the past several years, the San Diego skyline just keeps getting better. Naturally enough, seafood predominates on the menu, and the quality and freshness are impeccable. Plate presentations are as stunning as the outside views: Start with the huge Pacific fire shrimp, a spicy appetizer prepared with garlic, butter, and island spices; or the oversized crispy Maui-style onion rings, served with Peohe's homemade chipotle catsup. For the main course, consider the crab-stuffed tilapia, a delicate white fish coated with bread crumbs and stuffed with lump crab meat and finished with a light caper and butter sauce; or the seared Maine scallops, prepared with fresh ginger and lemongrass and topped with a sesame oil vinaigrette. Carnivores needn't despair, because there are plenty of red-meat offerings as well: A perfectly prepared 12-ounce prime rib is offered with buttery mashed potatoes or you can order up a New York steak with mushrooms in a rich Merlot sauce. For dessert don't miss the hot chocolate lava cake, a gooey, warm Godiva chocolate cake with a liquid chocolate center. You'll also find a full-service sushi bar on site. On sunny days, grab a table outside on the dockside courtyard for lunch or Sunday brunch.

RHINOCEROS CAFÉ

Owner: Scott Hanlon
619-435-2121
www.rhinocafe.com
1166 Orange Ave., Coronado, CA 92118
Open: Daily
Price: Expensive
Cuisine: American
Serving: L and D
Credit Cards: AE, D, DC, MC, V
Handicap Access: Yes
Reservations: For dinner
Parking: Metered street

This sleek, crisply decorated bistro in Coronado attracts tourists and locals, who find it conveniently located near the Lamb's Players Theater in the heart of downtown Coronado. Dine inside and enjoy the vibrant art on the walls or soak up the sun on the tiny sidewalk dining area. Start with the Thai chicken salad tossed with Asian noodles and a Thai dressing or the refreshing Rhinoceros summer salad with fresh pears, dried cranberries, blueberries, and walnuts tossed with a light pomegranate vinaigrette. Seafood specials include New Zealand green lip mussels steamed in white wine and tangy lemon scampi served over

spaghetti with tomatoes and mushrooms. Flavorful charbroiled pork chops are marinated in Italian spices, and the cowboy rib eye is served with savory chipotle butter. You'll find daily dessert specials, and there is an extensive wine list, along with knowledgeable servers who will suggest pairings.

POINT LOMA AND SHELTER ISLAND

POINT LOMA SEAFOODS

Owner: Christianson family
619-223-1109
www.plsf.com
2805 Emerson St., Pt. Loma, CA 92106
Open: Daily
Price: Inexpensive to moderate
Cuisine: Seafood
Serving: L, D (closes at 6:30 PM)
Credit Cards: No
Handicap Access: Yes
Reservations: No
Parking: Free adjacent lot (30-minute limit); paid lot nearby

In addition to being one of the best places in town to buy fresh fish—both because of the variety and because of the quality—Point Loma Seafoods is also a no-frills café that sells takeout prepared foods. There's generally a chaotic line waiting to order, but push yourself to the front—just know what you want or the busy wait staff won't be happy. Take a number and then grab a picnic table outside to enjoy the view of the boats at the marina next door. You'll wait for a bit, but you'll be rewarded for your patience with the immaculately fresh fish at bargain prices. Try the cold crab sandwich; the seared ahi salad; and the simply named fish combo plate, with catch of the day prepared to your specifications and served with slaw and fries. Crab cakes are thin and a little overly browned, but they are served in generous proportions with creamy homemade tartar sauce. Watch out for the seagulls outside; they've been known to steal a whole sandwich from the plate of an unsuspecting diner.

Food Purveyors

Breweries and Pubs

Coronado Brewing Company (619-437-4452; 170 Orange Ave., Coronado, CA 92118).
Coronado Brewing makes small batches of handcrafted beers onsite that range from the
pale, crisp "golden ale" to the black, malty "outlet stout." You'll also find seasonal
favorites like cranberry wheat for Thanksgiving and Independence Day ale in July. Enjoy
a pint inside by the fireplace or outside on the large heated patio. You can also buy
wood-fired pizzas, steaks, and other grill staples for lunch and dinner; on Tuesday
nights children under 12 eat for free.

McP's Pub (619-435-5280; 1107 Orange Ave., Coronado, CA 92118). This friendly Irish pub
and restaurant on the main drag in Coronado serves lunch and dinner daily, as well as a
late-night menu; nightly live music draws a loyal local crowd. There are 10 brews on tap, including Wyder's Pear Cider and Guinness Stout, as well as fine wines, frozen drinks, and a collection of premium whiskeys.

McP's Pub in Coronado.

Coffeehouses

Clayton's Coffee Shop (619-435-5425, 979 Orange Ave., Coronado, CA 92118). This long-time neighborhood hangout in Coronado is frequently crowded, thanks both to the diminutive interior—an authentic mid-century diner with a horseshoe-shaped counter—and to the home-style cooking and generous portions.

Living Room Coffeehouse (619-222-6852; 1018 Rosecrans St., San Diego, CA 92106). This Point Loma location is the newest venue for the local Living Room chain, and like the others scattered around the city, it is meant to be as comfortable as your own living room. This outlet is housed in the historic Jennings House, a two-story home with an expansive front porch. Look for the delicious walnut cinnamon cookies.

Pizzas, Burgers, and Dogs

Hodads (619-224-4623; 5010 Newport Ave., Ocean Beach, CA 92107). Watch for the giant
wave mural outside, and you've found Hodads, a surfer joint with a hippy vibe. Open for
lunch and dinner daily, this place has served up some of the best, biggest burgers in the
city for almost 40 years. Check out the halved VW bus inside and the numerous license
plates that decorate the walls.

Pizza Nova (619-226-0268; 5050 N. Harbor Dr., San Diego, CA 92106). You don't normally
expect to dine on the waterfront when you nosh pizza, but prepare to be dazzled by the
harbor views at Pizza Nova, as well as by the crispy, smoky wood-fired pies. There are
less scenic Pizza Nova locations in Hillcrest (619-296-6682) and Solana Beach (858-259-0666) as well.

Venetian (619-223-8197; 3663 Voltaire St., San Diego, CA 92106). Vince Giacalone started this restaurant in 1965, and now his sons Joey and Frank (and their children) continue to turn out exceptional, traditional pizzas; they still use the same recipes and even the same pizza ovens, and still top their pies with sausages they make on the premises.

Specialty Markets

Boney's Bayside Market (619-435-0776; 155 Orange Ave., Coronado, CA 92118). Near the Ferry Landing, this market sells organic and whole foods, as well as a nice selection of prepared dishes, perfect for picnics on the beach. The store opens at 8:30 AM, but if you can't wait you can pick up coffee and pastries as early as 6 from the early-bird window.

People's Market (619-224-1387; 4765 Voltaire St., San Diego, CA 92107). This Ocean Beach gem across from Sunset Cliffs is the county's only community-owned grocery store, specializing in organic meats, grains, and produce. They also offer classes and workshops on organic living and even live acoustic music nights.

Sweets and Treats

Con Pane Rustic Breads and Café (619-224-4344; 1110 Rosecrans St., San Diego, CA 92106). A full-service bakery in Point Loma that specializes in breads, scones, and cinnamon rolls, you can also get sandwiches to go or to eat at sidewalk tables. The view of busy Rosecrans isn't particularly scenic, but the patio is appealing.

Hans and Harry's Bakery (619-475-2253; 5080 Bonita Rd., Bonita, CA 91902). This bakery just northeast of Chula Vista serves up a wide variety of muffins and breakfast pastries, as well as specialty cakes, fruit tarts, and dozens of varieties of mouth-watering cookies.

La Concha Bakery (619-427-7147; 334 E. St., Chula Vista, CA 91910). This is *the* place to find Mexican sweets in San Diego County, with a wide selection of freshly prepared traditional pastries that are typically less sugary and more colorful than their U.S. counterparts. Don't miss the fruit *empanadas*, small turnovers filled with apple, cherries, or pineapple. An added bonus is that they stay open into the evening, so you can get your fix even after breakfast hours.

MooTime Creamery (619-435-2422; 1025 Orange Ave., Coronado, CA 92118). Look for the life-size statue of a spotted cow standing next to Elvis, and you've found MooTime in Coronado. (There is a second location on the island as well, downstairs in the Hotel del Coronado.) In addition to traditional flavored ice creams, try their creamy toasted coconut, brownie batter, or cinnamon varieties.

Taquerias

Lolita's Taco Shop (619-585-0232; 413 Telegraph Canyon Rd., Chula Vista, CA 91910). In business in the south bay for 20 years, this original Lolita's (which has three other shops nearby) has exceptional rolled tacos served with a pile of guacamole, home-style carnitas, and gigantic chorizo burritos.

Miguel's Cocina (619-437-4237; 1351 Orange Ave., Coronado, CA 92118). Across the street from the Hotel del Coronado, this Miguel's (there are two others—one in Point Loma and another in Chula Vista) is a sit-down restaurant on the ground floor of the **El Cordova Hotel** (see pages 142–143) that offers authentic carne asada burritos and tacos, along with interesting entrees like calamari rellenos and jalapeno shrimp.

MooTime Creamery is a favorite with beachgoers in Coronado—and the King likes it, too.

Tamales Ancira (619-424-3416; 2260 Main St., Chula Vista, CA 91910). Tamales to die for—including my favorite sweet tamales with pineapple or nuts and raisins, as well as *chichirron tamales* made with pork cracklings and tomatillo sauce and tamales with spicy cheese and jalapenos—can be enjoyed in the restaurant, picked up to go, or shipped in bulk throughout the United States. If you're an adventurous cook, you can even buy the prepared masa and assemble your own.

RECREATION: THE GREAT OUTDOORS

Miles of waterfront property, expansive nature reserves, and some of the best saltwater fishing in the world draw outdoors people to the south bay from around the country. Surfers and divers especially love this region, although as noted below, water quality is a concern.

Beaches

Water pollution has been a problem at south bay beaches (especially near the border) for years, and it continues to worsen—and to move northward—thanks to persistent pollution from the Tijuana River, which crosses into the United States and dumps into the ocean in San Diego. Although waters in Coronado and Sunset Cliffs are acceptable, you'll want to think twice about swimming or surfing any farther south. Never ignore the closed-beach flags, and shower off even when the beach is open for business.

Coronado Beach (take the bridge to Coronado, follow the signs from Orange Ave.). Parking can be a headache anywhere in Coronado, especially if you're looking to walk to the beach. Come early to enjoy this picturesque strip of shoreline, with the widest expanse of sand of all San Diego beaches. With the Hotel del Coronado as a backdrop, you'll have a chance to get in touch with your inner Marilyn Monroe (parts of the 1950s film *Some Like It Hot*, starring Monroe, were filmed on this stretch of beach). Unfortunately, as noted earlier, pollution from Tijuana sometimes drifts up to the waters, and swimming is occasionally prohibited as a result. (An interesting tidbit: Kite flying is prohibited north of the rock jetty, because kites interfere with the nearby North Island's military radar.)

Silver Strand State Beach (take the bridge to Coronado, follow the signs from Orange Ave.). This is the best beach in the area to find seashells; head out at dawn with a pail and be prepared to keep your eyes peeled on the powdery sand to find the morning's treasures. It's also a gentle swimming beach for children, because the water gets deep very gradually.

Imperial Beach (westernmost point of Palm Ave.). The wide sandy shore and high surf attracts crowds despite the consistently polluted waters (thanks to sewage overflows from nearby Tijuana). South of Imperial Beach you'll find **Border Field State Beach** (west on Monument Rd. South), the southernmost beach in San Diego. Swimming is prohibited, but you'll find plentiful parking and fire rings.

Ocean Beach (south of the channel entrance to Mission Bay, off Abbott St.). This beach is popular with surfers (and street people, especially on the south end of the pier). You'll also find a dog beach at the north end. Parking is extremely limited, and swimmers should beware: The rip currents can be uncommonly strong.

Sunset Cliffs (west on Sunset Cliffs Blvd.; staircases lead to beach access). A remote beach that is popular with locals and surfers, you'll find more seclusion on the sands here than just about any other beach in town. Go toward the south near Cabrillo Point (also accessible from the Cabrillo Monument) and find great tide pooling; in the north you'll find bigger waves and more surfers. Note that there are no facilities here, and water pollution is sometimes an issue. Check water conditions before venturing in.

Canoeing, Kayaking, and Sailing

Action Sports (619-424-4466; 4000 Coronado Bay, Coronado, CA 92118). At the Loews Coronado Bay Resort, this aquatic rental store offers jet skis, kayaks, wake boards, motorboats, and sailboats. And if you are a landlubber, Action Sports will hook you up with lessons.

Gondola Company (619-429-6317; 4000 Coronado Bay Rd., Coronado, 92118). Imagine a gondolier in a straw hat plying the waters of a canal, traditional Italian music plays softly in the background, as you sit back and sip a beverage of your choice. A romantic outing in Venice, you say? No! Coronado has its very own Gondola Company, with vessels imported from Italy (as well as replicas made in the United States). For about $90 an hour, two guests enjoy a scenic cruise through the canals of the Coronado Cays; included in the price is a dessert or appetizer plate, and ice buckets and glasses are provided to chill whatever libation you choose to bring along. For a bit more money they'll throw in a three-course dinner at a restaurant on the water and live mandolin or violin music.

Seaforth Coronado Boat Rental (619-437-1514; 1715 Strand Wy., Coronado, CA 92118). Skiff rentals are just under $50 for a half day and $70 for a full day. This organization also offers sailing classes and rents speedboats, water skis, and kayaks.

Diving and Snorkeling

The Point Loma kelp beds are a popular diving destination in south county, and can be accessed from a number of companies, including **Aqua Tech Dive Center** (619-237-1800; 1800 Logan Ave., San Diego, CA 92113), located in the south bay, and a number of dive shops in Mission Bay, Mission Beach, and La Jolla (see chapter 4).

Although the water quality is sometimes poor, Imperial Beach has one of the best diving attractions in Southern California: a sunken submarine known as *S-37*. The wreck's bow is buried in the sand, at a depth of about 30 feet. The World War II-era sub saw action in Japan, but was decommissioned in 1945 and was to be used as a target for aerial bombing. However, as she was being towed out for positioning, the line broke, the sub sank, and the Navy left her to rest on the ocean floor, originally positioned much farther from the beach. A private salvage company tried to rescue the submarine in the late 1970s; it was floated toward the beach, but it buried its nose in the sand, and remains in this stuck position, with the conning tower sometimes visible from the shore at low tide. Only experienced divers should enter the vessel, and all divers should use caution. The 219-foot hull is only 20 feet wide, lists to the port side, and is extremely cramped.

Fishing

San Diego County is known as one of the best fishing destinations in the world, and south bay is the hub for deep-sea fishing. Check the *San Diego Union Tribune* fishing report at www.signonsandiego.com/sports/outdoors/index, updated weekly. Note that nearly 650 acres off Point Loma are protected as the Point Loma Ecological Reserve.

Fresh-Water Fishing

Chollas Lake (6350 College Grove Dr., San Diego, CA 92115). Actually a tiny 16-acre pond, Chollas Lake is where new fishermen and women are spawned: Chollas Lake is available

Sailboats clog the San Diego Bay on a busy weekend.

for fishing only for children 15 and younger. Throughout the year there are day camps and fishing clinics offered to children, who will delight in catching bluegill and trout.

Lower Otay Reservoir (take Telegraph Canyon Rd. to Wueste Rd.). Just east of the newly sprawling Chula Vista suburbs of Eastlake, Lower Otay is a bass tournament lake that attracts serious anglers. The smaller **Upper Otay Reservoir** is a catch-and-release only lake, with catfish and bluegill. (Barbless hooks are required.)

Deep-Sea Fishing

The San Diego and Baja coastlines are among the best places in the world for deep-sea fishing. You'll find yellowtail, albacore, skipjack, and several species of tuna, and the deeper out you go, the bigger the fish you're likely to land. In 1977, a 388-pound yellowfin tuna was caught off the shores of San Diego, a record-setting weight that stands to this day—although the average caught tuna weighs closer to 15 or 20 pounds.

Popular six-hour day trips are available from a number of sports-fishing tour operators, which will take you out to the Point Loma kelp beds and along the coastline of Imperial Beach. Nine- and ten-hour trips go out deeper, as well as down the Baja coast. Overnight trips are available during winter months to fish the 60 Mile Bank or 43 Fathom, where you'll fish for more than 50 varieties of rock cod and bottom fish. If you're hankering for an old-man-and-the-sea experience, check out the multiple-day options (three to twenty-eight days in length) aboard San Diego's famous long-range fleet, huge platform ships with accommodations akin to cruise ships. In summer and fall you can board five-day trips to the offshore Baja islands to fish for dorado, tuna, and yellowtail. Longer trips will travel up to 1,000 miles south of San Diego to places like Alijos Rocks and Thetis Bank, where you'll fish for bluefin tuna and wahoo, and to the more distant islands of Revilla Gigedos-Clarian and Socorro, where it isn't unusual to catch 300-pound yellowtail and wahoo up to 100 pounds.

Prices vary, but figure an average of $200–$300 per day on multiday trips (meals and accommodations onboard included). Day trips range from $125–$300. Most trips of any length include rods and other equipment in the overall price, and when fishing in Mexican waters, sport fishing trips generally include the price of the required Mexican fishing license. If you want to bring your own gear, make sure you have a minimum 20-pound tackle—or you won't be reeling in the really big ones. Sport-fishing boats leaving from Point Loma in San Diego Bay include **Fisherman's Landing** (619-224-1421; 2838 Garrison St., San Diego, CA 92106); **H&M Landing** (619-222-1144; 2803 Emerson St., San Diego, CA 92106); and **Point Loma Sportfishing** (619-223-1627; 1403 Scott St., San Diego, CA 92106).

Pier and Surf Fishing

Smaller fish live in the shallows, and there are plenty of them to be had along San Diego's piers and beaches. If you're casting in waters up to six feet deep, expect to catch croaker, corbina, and perch; from 6 to 20 feet, expect to haul in halibut, mackerel, and even bonito. Fishing licenses are not required at any of the San Diego piers, but anyone 12 or older will need a license to surf fish. Catch limits apply.

Ocean Beach Pier (at the end of Niagara St.) is a favorite with locals, and offers a fully stocked bait and tackle shop. The Ocean Beach Pier is nearly 2,000 feet long—the longest pier on the West Coast. The **Imperial Beach Pier** (at Seacoast Dr.) is also picturesque and extends out into water at least 20 feet deep—but don't even think about eating the fish here, because the waters are just too polluted. Another good spot for the small ones is **Coronado**

Pier (at the foot of Orange Ave.). Try **Ocean Beach** or the **Silver Strand Beach** in Coronado for surf fishing.

Golfing

Coronado Municipal Golf Course (619-435-3121; 2000 Visalia Row, San Diego 92118). A relatively hidden gem with some of the best views of San Diego Bay and the Coronado bridge you'll find in the city, a well-maintained and challenging course, and green fees for only $25 makes this one of the best golf values in California. Local golfers rate this as among their favorite courses in the city. Avoid the crowds and reserve a tee time. Green fee: $25.

Eastlake Country Club (619-482-5757; 2375 Clubhouse Dr., Chula Vista, CA 91915). A good course for all levels, this par-72 course in Chula Vista has 18 holes and a driving range, with challenging water hazards and a beautiful open-air pavilion—and is another great golfing value. Green fee: $60–$80.

Salt Creek Golf Course (619-482-4666; 525 Hunte Pkwy., Chula Vista, CA 91914). For-merly known as the Auld Course, this Scottish-links style course is bordered on the north by a state park and in all other directions by protected habitats, so the natural serenity of the area is ensured. Generous fairways and flat bunkering promise an approachable course for golfers of most levels. Green fee: $75–$95.

Hiking

Bayside Trail (follow signs off Cabrillo Memorial Dr.). This 3-mile out-and-back gravel trail near the Cabrillo Lighthouse in Point Loma offers stunning views of San Diego Bay and beyond to Tijuana. The U-shaped trail, which used to be a military patrol road, winds down a 300-foot descent along the cliffs through native wildflowers and scrub bushes; in the winter, you might even see migrating gray whales from this vantage point. $5 fee for parking.

Tijuana River National Estuarian Research Reserve (301 Caspian Wy., Imperial Beach, CA 91932). Access the north and south McCoy Trails (open daily) from the visitors' cen-ter at the Tijuana Estuary Reserve; both trails pass through prime bird-watching habitat at the mouth of the Tijuana River. Included in this reserve is the Tijuana Slough National Wildlife Refuge, more than 1,000 acres of wetlands where the Tijuana River runs into the Pacific. More than 370 species have been recorded here, including the Belding's

---

United States Olympic Training Center

(619-656-1500; 2800 Olympic Pkwy., Chula Vista, CA 91915)

U.S. Olympic Training Centers are dedicated to developing U.S. Olympic and Paralympic athletes in myriad sports, including archery, field hockey, softball, swimming, track and field, and various Para-lympic sports. The OTC in Chula Vista is one of three official Olympic training centers in the country, and the first training facility to be master-planned from the ground up. Visitors can stroll along desig-nated pathways through the beautiful 155 acres that make up the sports facility and actually watch the athletes in training. The campus includes onsite housing to accommodate the short- and long-term resident athletes who train here (although these areas are off-limits to visitors). The sprawling com-plex is picturesquely situated at the foot of the mountains and next to Lower Otay Lake—in a serene environment sure to bring out the best in any athlete. Free guided tours are offered daily.

From the Chula Vista Nature Center trails, guests can get a pristine view of the San Diego Bay and sometimes the Coronado Bay Bridge in the distance.

Savannah sparrow, the American peregrine falcon, and the northern harrier, as well as the endangered California least tern. The western snowy plover, which is a threatened species, nests on the beaches of the refuge and makes its home here year-round.

Parks

Chula Vista Bayside Park (off Bayside Pkwy.). Panoramic views of the Coronado Bridge, the skyline of San Diego, and even the mountains of Mexico (on a clear day) are visible from this beautiful waterside 6-acre recreational area (also called J Street Marina). The park features picnic tables, game tables with checkerboard inlays, a circuit-training course, biking and jogging paths, and killer views of the open water and the marina. You can also fish from the pier and then clean your catch at the fish-cleaning stations. Look for a public sculpture display called *Konoids*, by the renown artist Kenneth Capps.

Chula Vista Nature Center (619-409-5900; 1000 Gunpowder Point Dr., Chula Vista, CA 91910). Located in the middle of the Sweetwater Marsh National Wildlife Refuge on San Diego Bay, the Nature Center showcases animals and plants native to this San Diego wetland habitat. The facility's numerous exhibits include sea creatures in more than 50 aquariums; the Shark and Ray experience, where visitors can pet small bat stingrays and observe tiger and sand sharks; and bird enclosures with burrowing owls, bald eagles, and red-tailed hawks. Best of all, head out on the 1.5 miles of walking trails to enjoy the beautiful views of the Coronado bridge, downtown San Diego, and the bay, as well as to watch the more than 200 species of birds that pass through the Sweetwater Marsh throughout the year. You'll see the footings of a kelp-processing plant that was on the site in the early 20th century, which manufactured smokeless gun powder for Britain during World War I. To access the center, park in the lot near the train tracks and wait for a free shuttle to carry you inside; shuttles run every 15 minutes. Adults $6, seniors $5, children $3.

Shoreline Park (off Shelter Island Dr.). Situated directly on the bay, there are picnic tables, grassy areas, a public fishing pier, and a boat launch at this little park on Shelter Island. This is usually a quiet spot on the weekends to watch the many sailboats breeze by. Look for sea lions, as well as seabirds like auklets and murres.

Surfing

Imperial Beach, Sunset Cliffs, and Ocean Beach are laid-back surfing communities popular with many old timers in San Diego. The shores are beautiful, as all beaches along the California coast are, but years of shoddy watershed management in Tijuana (and, frankly, lax enforcement of dumping restraints on this side of the border as well) have contributed to an appalling environmental state for these south county beaches. Imperial Beach is considered by most authorities to be the most polluted beach in California. During the winter season of 2004–05, border beaches were closed a whopping 90 percent of the time. Although there are diehards who hit the waves (some even risking their health and surfing when the warning flags are up), it is a foolhardy endeavor.

THEME PARKS AND ZOOS

KNOTT'S SOAK CITY

www.knotts.com/soakcity/sd
619-661-7373
2052 Entertainment Circle, Chula Vista, CA 91911
Open: Memorial Day weekend through early fall; hours vary
Admission: Adults $27, children and seniors $15

Set amid the otherwise dry hills of southern Chula Vista, the 32 colorful acres of water park at Knott's Soak City San Diego remind visitors of the San Diego long-board surfing scene in the 1950s. As soon as you approach the park, you'll see the giant fuschia and yellow striped "Pacific Spin," a 132-foot spiral ride that terminates in a six-story funnel. Among the other 22 attractions, you'll find the "La Jolla Falls," which offers up a quartet of high-speed, fast-action tube slides, and "Palisades Plunge," which features a triplet of wild and steep inner tube slides. For somewhat tamer fun, try the "Coronado Express," a family raft ride that plunges down milder dips, or the "Sunset River," lazy river rapids where you can sit back, float, and catch some rays. Kids will also love the "Balboa Bay," an 800,000-gallon wave pool that generates swells suitable for body surfing. The "Gremmie Lagoon," a themed section designed for toddlers and young children, has its own paddling pool and kinder, gentler water slides. There are locker rentals onsite, as well as plenty of casual dining options. Come early to secure a beach chair—or if you're willing to plunk down some extra cash, you can rent a private cabana.

SHOPPING: EVERYTHING UNDER THE SUN

Plaza Bonita (619-267-2850; 3030 Plaza Bonita Rd., National City, CA 91950) near Chula Vista is the largest retail mall in the area. In Coronado, head to the outdoor **Ferry**

Landing (619-435-8895; 1201 First St., Coronado, CA 92118) for tourist shops and gorgeous views of the downtown skyline across the water.

Antiques and Collectibles

The Ocean Beach Antique District on the 4,800 block of Newport Avenue has one of the most concentrated areas for antique and collectible dealers in the city. You can find estate furniture, vintage jewelry, mid-century modern furniture, Depression glass, and toys from the 1920s.

The Attic (619-435-5432; 1011 Orange Ave., Coronado, CA 92118). This nicely staged, sun-bleached store on the main drag in Coronado carries beach cottage accessories and white-washed furniture, vintage clothing, and interesting street signs, perfect for decorating a weekend home on the shores.

Cottage Antiques (619-222-1967; 4896 Newport Ave., San Diego, CA 92107). Located in the heart of the Ocean Beach antique district, this store specializes in fine English china, French furniture, and vintage quilts.

Ocean Beach Antique Center (619-223-6170; 4926 Newport Ave., San Diego, CA 92107). A huge antique mall that draws crowds on the weekends; there's almost nothing you can't find here, from estate jewelry to vintage toys to fine furniture.

Books and Music

Bay Books (619-435-0070; 1029 Orange Ave., Coronado, CA 92118). An outdoor coffee bar, a good children's section, and an extensive collection of international magazines and newspapers makes this large, open store a relaxing stop for the afternoon. This is the best place to find picture and history books on Coronado.

Moctezuma Books (619-426-1283; 289 Third Ave., Chula Vista, CA 91910). Located in downtown Chula Vista, Lisa Moctezuma's friendly bookstore carries exclusively Spanish volumes.

Orange Avenue in Coronado is home to eclectic boutiques, like the quaint and beachy The Attic.

Just for Fun

Andy Montana's Surfside Fly Fishing (619-435-9992; 957 Orange Ave., Coronado, CA 92118). On the main thoroughfare of Coronado, this place has an extensive collection of saltwater rods, reels, and a display of bright and shiny lures in the back that resembles a jewelry counter. You'll also find hiking equipment and clothing.

Seaside Papery (619-435-5565; 1162 Orange Ave., Coronado, CA 92118). In addition to exquisite stationery, invitations, and unique gift cards, you'll also find interesting trinkets like seashell nightlights and blown-glass paperweights.

Spirit Store (619-656-1500; 2800 Olympic Parkway, Chula Vista, CA 91915). Located inside the visitor's center of the U.S. Olympic Training Center in Chula Vista (see page 161), this large store sells official Olympic gear, including t-shirts, sweatshirts, caps, pins, posters, equipment emblazoned with the Olympic symbol, and pricey signed photographs and sports memorabilia. This is a fun place to shop for unusual items, and you might even recognize a famous Olympic athlete or two browsing the racks with you. Note that the store only accepts Visa—and cash, of course.

*Del Mar Beach as seen from lovely
Sea Grove Park.*

6

Coastal North County

From Ranchos to Real Estate Mecca

A drive through parts of north county 20-some years ago would take you through stretches of open area, a few agricultural fields, and alongside the remains of some of the county's largest remaining *ranchos*—large cattle ranches that blanketed Southern California one hundred years ago. Although today you'll still pass by small patches of strawberry and flower fields in Carlsbad and Encinitas, anything else resembling farmland has been replaced with upscale tract homes and the infrastructure that goes along with them. This is now one of the fastest growing residential areas in the county, and new suburbs seem to appear overnight.

Visitors will find great variety in coastal north county (which runs along the coastline from Del Mar through Oceanside), from upscale, tony residential neighborhoods to laid-back beach towns with plenty of cafés and boutique shopping. In general these areas are much less congested than their coastal counterparts to the south—although the freeways required to reach them have among the worst traffic in the city.

Expansive Carlsbad has two distinct regions: Southern Carlsbad is home to several internationally known spas and golf courses, set alongside pricey suburbs and the lovely Batiquitos Lagoon; northern Carlsbad offers small-town appeal in its resortlike downtown and family-friendly destinations like Legoland and the Museum of Making Music. Del Mar and its tiny neighbor just to the north, Solana Beach, are expensive beach towns, with the Del Mar Racetrack at the heart of the neighborhood and fine dining and extraordinary shopping in upscale malls in Del Mar and in the Cedros Avenue design center in Solana Beach. Encinitas (which incorporates Cardiff-by-the-Sea and Leucadia) is the capital of surf culture, with popular beaches, numerous friendly cafés, and board shops everywhere. Tiny Leucadia is an artsy, casual neighborhood, famous for funky Mexican cafés and for quirky, bargain shopping. Charming Cardiff is another small surfing enclave and home to the ecological reserve at the San Elijo Lagoon. Downtown Encinitas offers fine dining at pretty cafés, with plenty of small stores to explore and a pedestrian-friendly layout.

Finally, to the far north, Oceanside has the feel of a small fishing community on the harbor; although once known primarily as a military town (Camp Pendleton is next door), Oceanside is another favorite with surfers and with suburbanites looking to beat the real estate inflation to the south.

LODGING

Lodging options in coastal north county tend toward small, no-frills motels and expensive upscale resorts—there isn't much middle ground, with the exception of northern Carlsbad, which has a handful of larger, moderately priced hotels, and a few small bed-and-breakfasts scattered along the coast. Be aware, when choosing any neighborhood in north county, that the north—south freeway corridors are the most congested in the city, and if you plan to spend most of your time in downtown San Diego, these options will probably not be the best choice for you. However, if you're looking to enjoy all of San Diego County, or if you want to concentrate on the northern beaches, you'll find friendly folks and a little more breathing room in this area.

CARLSBAD
BEACH TERRACE INN
Manager: Rick Smock
760-729-5951 or 800-433-5414; fax 760-729-9078
www.beachterraceinn.com
2775 Ocean St., Carlsbad, CA 92008
Price: Moderate
Credit Cards: AE, D, DC, M, V
Handicap Access: None

At the Beach Terrace Inn, you're never more than a few steps from having the sand between your toes. This is one of the few moderately priced hotels in Carlsbad that is located directly on the beach. With only 49 guest rooms, the Inn can't offer the amenities of many larger inns (no room service, no luxurious fixtures in the bathrooms), but it does boast a spacious ocean-view pool and Jacuzzi. The property is located in downtown Carlsbad, within a few miles of Legoland and minutes from the quaint downtown restaurants and shops. Most of the rooms have large balconies, although guest rooms themselves are small.

CARLSBAD INN
Manager: Randy Chapin
760-434-7020; fax 760-729-4853
www.carlsbadinn.com
3075 Carlsbad Blvd., Carlsbad, CA 92008
Price: Expensive
Credit Cards: AE, D, DC, MC, V
Handicap Access: 3 full

You'll find old-fashioned European charm at the Carlsbad Inn, which is located right on the beach—literally steps from the ocean and close to several fine dining options and the charming downtown Carlsbad shopping district. The exterior of the hotel fits in with the Scandinavian-themed architecture throughout downtown Carlsbad, and the gardens and landscaping enhance the privacy of the resort, despite its centrality. The 198 guest rooms and condominiums encircle an expansive grass lawn—the site of numerous weddings in the spring—that leads guests directly to the sand. There is a small pool and spa that overlook the ocean, and a full health club facility. Accommodations vary, from standard rooms—some with kitchenettes, fireplaces, and private spas—to more luxurious ocean-view rooms and condominiums. The quaint interiors are decorated with dark-wood furniture, floral-print fabrics, and lace curtains. The rooms are compact, and bathrooms are even smaller, but there is plenty of closet space. Lower rooms can be noisy, so if stairs

The Carlsbad Inn is within easy walking distance to fine dining and shopping.

are not a problem, consider a top-floor option.

FOUR SEASONS AVIARA

Manager: Vincent Parotta
760-603-6800; fax 760-603-6801
www.fourseasons.com/aviara
7100 Four Seasons Pt., Carlsbad, CA 92011
Price: Very Expensive
Credit Cards: AE, D, M, V
Handicap Access: 12 full

A gorgeous property perched on a hill over-looking its own golf course, the Batiquitos Lagoon (a protected wildlife sanctuary), and the Pacific Ocean, the Four Seasons Aviara is a masterpiece in understated elegance. The creamy wood tones and rich fabrics in the public rooms are the epitome of Southern California design, and the expansive windows and sprawling flower- and citrus-filled gardens suggest a stately mansion by the sea. The resort opened in 1997 and has become one of the premier destination resorts in the San Diego area. Built in the Spanish Colonial architectural style and featuring hand-painted trompe l'oeil ceilings and walls, the resort has 331 commodious guest rooms, each with a private balcony or landscaped terrace. For a truly indulgent experience, book the ultra-expensive Couples Spa Suite, with its own private, full-size pool. The five-star resort features an incomparable spa that offers more than 20 kinds of massages, facials, and body scrubs. Golfers will fall for the Arnold Palmer-designed course, which is one of the most challenging—and stunning—in a city of top-notch golf courses. There is also a tennis center with lighted clay- and hard-courts, outstanding onsite restaurants, and a complimentary children's program. The luxurious pools are large enough to let you choose between a quiet, shady cabana or a sunny beach chair in the middle of the action. All you need to do is lift your little finger and a cocktail server will be at your side to bring you your choice of beverage or a light snack. The Lobby Lounge offers afternoon high tea for a moderate price. Starched-white linen tablecloths are strewn generously with fresh rose petals, and an unobtrusive pianist provides subtle background ambiance. The resort is located in the exclusive residential area of south Carlsbad known as Aviara, where the smallest homes start at $1 million. The 200-acre resort is meant to be a self-contained entity—and not many people would complain if they never left the grounds. However, if you do want to venture out, the main north—south freeway (I-5) is only miles away, and the restaurants and shops of downtown Carlsbad and Encinitas are also nearby.

GRAND PACIFIC PALISADES

Manager: Michael Flickinger
760-827-3200; fax 760-827-3210
www.grandpacificpalisades.com
5805 Armada Dr., Carlsbad, CA 92008
Price: Expensive
Credit Cards: AE, D, M, V
Handicap Access: 2 full

A family resort located close to Legoland (the hotel offers a private entrance to the park), the Grand Pacific Palisades overlooks the Carlsbad Flower Fields, an explosion of rainbow-colored ranunculas during the blooming months of March and April. This large property, also offering ridge-top views of the Pacific, has everything to make a family comfortable, including a spacious pool, outdoor playground area, and even a mini water park for young children. This hotel does more than cater to the little ones, however: The **Karl Strauss Brewery** (760-431-BREW) and restaurant is onsite, offering a lively happy hour and eight different microbrews from which to choose. The resort has planned activities for its guests throughout the week, including ping pong tournaments, jazz nights, and wine tastings.

The guest rooms are bright and spacious, and the décor features light woods and citrus-colored fabrics. Also on property are longer-stay condominiums.

LA COSTA RESORT AND SPA

Manager: April Shute
760-438-9111; fax: 760-633-3696
www.lacosta.com
2100 Costa Del Mar Rd., Carlsbad, CA 92009
Price: Very Expensive
Credit Cards: AE, D, M, V
Handicap Access: 4 full

This venerable resort is internationally known as a premier spa and the site of several important golfing and tennis events throughout the year. Guests can enjoy four sparkling pools (one with a waterslide worthy of a theme park), world-class golf on two PGA 18-hole courses, innovative spa treatments, four-star restaurants, and boutique shopping. A few years ago the resort started to look a little tired, but new ownership in 2001 invested more than $140 million in revamping the property, which included rebuilding the spa from scratch. The reworked bright-white stucco buildings topped with red Spanish roof tiles and adorned with delicate curling wrought iron, as well as the overflowing flower gardens, blooming vines, and millions of dollars worth of imported Canary Island palm trees have given this aging beauty a successful facelift. Note, however, that as this book went to press construction is still underway to add additional guest rooms and facilities, and noise and dust could be a factor for a few years to come.

Guest rooms are richly appointed, with ample use of butter-soft leather and dark woods, evocative of the Spanish influence in décor throughout the resort. In addition to the usual amenities, La Costa provides its guests with its signature brand of bath care products, flatscreen TVs, and a Nintendo Game Cube. The spa includes a thunderous Roman waterfall and 15,000-square-foot

La Costa Resort and Spa is one of the most respected and well-known spas in the world.

outdoor patio. Visitors can indulge in deep-tissue massages, skin-revitalizing facials, and full-body salt scrubs. All spa guests are treated to the complimentary "Agua de la Vida" (a refreshing water treatment and body scrub), a bathing ritual designed to relax the body and soothe the mind. And on Thursday evenings, don't miss the Spa under the Stars, where guests can enjoy live music and champagne while they indulge in their treatments. In addition, the resort is home to the **Chopra Center for Well Being**, founded by famed Deepak Chopra, which promotes health of the total person: mind, body, and spirit. You needn't stray off the property to eat in exceptional restaurants, including the **Legends California Bistro** and the **BlueFire Grill**. If you travel with little ones, you'll love the new Kid's Club at La Costa, with a 7-foot treehouse, a 600-gallon saltwater aquarium, computer and video games, and a teen lounge call **Vibz**, which offers music and dancing; billiards, and an X-Box™ gaming lounge.

TAMARACK BEACH RESORT
Manager: Tony Nieblas
760-729-3500; fax: 760-434-5942
www.tamarakresort.com
3200 Carlsbad Blvd., Carlsbad, CA 92008
Price: Expensive
Credit Cards: AE, MC, V
Handicap Access: 1 full

Across the street from the beach and the wide sidewalk promenade that runs along the ocean, the Tamarack Beach Resort's greatest assets are its well-positioned north county location and a friendly and helpful front desk staff. Amenities include a small pool and spa inside a palm tree-decked courtyard, game room and billiards, an outdoor patio with barbeque grills and dining tables, and a library of movies on DVD that may be borrowed for free by guests. Commodious rooms have private balconies, and many of the rooms on the top floor have excellent ocean views. Rooms are equipped with refrigerators, and guests will enjoy in-room coffee service, daily newspaper, and a continental breakfast. There are also fully furnished one- and two-bedroom condominiums available for either daily or weekly rentals; these condos are spacious, clean, and a particularly good option for families. The lobby and other public rooms are a bit dated, with an overabundance of faux marble and leatherette furniture—not to mention the many taxidermied sport fish that adorn the walls. Although this property doesn't look as expensive as it is, the beach access mostly makes up for the lack of luxury.

DEL MAR AND SOLANA BEACH
DEL MAR MOTEL
Manager: Mikki Ellis
858-755-1534
ww.delmarmotelonthebeach.com
1702 Coast Blvd., Del Mar, CA 92014
Price: Expensive
Credit Cards: AE, D, MC, V
Handicap Access: 1 full

This small motel property on the cliffs above Del Mar has exceptional views of the ocean and beach below and has easy beach access—in fact, it is the only beachfront hotel in Del Mar. Outdoor public spaces come with picnic tables, lounge chairs, barbeque grills, and an outdoor beach shower. The small rooms are simply decorated and bright; the basic rooms are furnished with a small desk, table and chairs, and a coffeemaker. All rooms open to the outside on wrap-around-porches, which are equipped with patio furniture. Guests can borrow beach chairs and boogie boards at no cost from the front desk. Although I've listed this hotel as expensive based on their high-season rates, note that in winter months, rooms fall into the inexpensive to moderate range, depending on views. If there is availability at this time, you can get a real bargain in one of the priciest beach areas in San Diego.

THE GRAND DEL MAR

Manager: Vikram Sood
858-350-7600; fax 858-720-0025
www.thegranddelmar.com
5200 Grand Del Mar Way, San Diego, CA 92130
Price: Very expensive
Credit Cards: AE, D, MC, V
Handicap Access: Yes

This landmark property in north county debuted its five-star accommodations in late 2007. Although it offers club membership and has 39 exclusive "ownership" suites, the Grand Del Mar also offers 249 guest rooms and 19 suites available for rent. The luxurious resort combines Spanish, Portuguese, Moroccan, and Venetian design elements, all of which reflect the indigenous architecture of San Diego. There is even a private chapel onsite, a thoughtful addition for those visitors who plan to stay on property for most of their vacation. Guest rooms are spacious, elegant, and intended to pamper. The resort offers a kid's club and a fun teen lounge, so that busy parents can indulge their offspring while they visit the spa or get in a round of golf at the on-site, 18-hole Tom Fazio-designed course. The hotel restaurant **Addison** (858-314-1900) is making waves, thanks to renowned Chef William Bradley's Mediterranean interpretation of fresh, local ingredients. Note that the resort isn't due for completion until 2007, so expect some dust and noise in the meantime.

L'AUBERGE DEL MAR RESORT AND SPA

Manager: Michael Slosser
858-259-1515; fax 858-755-4940
www.laubergedelmar.com
1540 Camino Del Mar, Del Mar, CA 92014
Price: Very expensive
Credit Cards: AE, D, MC, V
Handicap Access: 4 full

This luxurious resort and full-service spa in the heart of downtown Del Mar, set across the street from the beach (with the upscale Del Mar Plaza boutiques and restaurants nearby) will pamper you with superior service and immaculate attention to detail. The Tudor-inspired exterior is somewhat incongruously accented with an abundance of tropical palm trees and towering fuchsia bougainvillea vines. The richly appointed lobby has a clubby feeling, thanks to beamed ceilings, elegant chairs and sofas, and a wall of French doors that open to ocean views. The guest rooms are bright and light, decorated with cottage-style furnishings in sunny colors, and some include fireplaces. The hotel has two lighted tennis courts and a professional on staff for private or group instructions; there is also a pool, an outdoor hot tub, and a lap pool. The tranquil onsite spa welcomes guests with thick robes and slippers provided by oh-so-elegant attendees. Patrons can then indulge in a full array of massages, facial treatments, and body purification treatments, including the signature chardonnay body scrub, a "vinotherapy" scrub made with sugar crystals and chardonnay grapes imported from France. Onsight dining is at the romantic **J. Taylor's** (858-793-6460), featuring Chef Paul McCabe's inspirational contemporary American cuisine. The delightful outdoor patio opens to a musical waterfall and an herb garden, and is a perfect place to enjoy a glass of wine or sip an espresso.

WINNER'S CIRCLE RESORT

Manager: Gail Hall
858-755-6666; fax 858-481-3706
www.winnerscircleresort.com
550 Via de la Valle, Solana Beach, CA 92075
Price: Moderate
Credit Cards: AE, D, DC, MC, V
Handicap Access: 5 full

You really can't find accommodations any closer to the races than this resort, which is across the street and within easy walking distance of the Del Mar Racetrack—a bonus for track aficionados who would prefer to skip the pricey parking fees and the congestion during the summer season. It's equally convenient to the San Diego County Fair, which is held earlier in the summer on the grounds as well. Although the resort is not on the beach, it is just a mile away from the Del Mar shores. The 94 suites come equipped with a furnished kitchenette, a separate seating area, dining area, and a patio or balcony. The recently renovated studio and one- and two-bedroom suites are comfortably decorated in monochromatic color schemes. Outside you'll find towering palm trees, four lighted tennis courts, and a kidney-shaped pool and spa in a minimalist Mediterranean-style courtyard. The expansive club house is currently under renovation throughout 2007, and is set to include a state-of-the-art sound and lighting system, a home theater system, and children's activities.

ENCINITAS, INCLUDING CARDIFF-BY-THE-SEA AND LEUCADIA

CARDIFF BY THE SEA LODGE

Innkeeper: Jeanette Statser
760-944-6474; fax 760-944-6841
www.cardifflodge.com
142 Chesterfield St., Cardiff-by-the-Sea, CA 92007
Price: Expensive
Credit Cards: AE, D, M, V
Handicap Access: 1 full

This romantic bed-and-breakfast is centrally located in Cardiff-by-the-Sea, a charming village that time seems to have forgotten. The cedar clapboard siding and stone walkways suggest a Tudor influence to the otherwise neo-Spanish Colonial building, which looks as if it's been here since the 1900s. This isn't a historical property, but the stately structure near the sea suggests an era of bygone elegance. The Sea Lodge is surrounded by lush gardens, and each of the 17 guest rooms are furnished

individually, with styles ranging from serene contemporary to over-the-top Victorian. Breakfasts feature fresh fruit and locally prepared pastries.

MOONLIGHT BEACH MOTEL

Manager: Yingqian Liao
760-753-0623; fax 760-944-9827
www.moonlightbeachmotel.com
233 Second St., Encinitas, CA 92024
Price: Inexpensive
Credit Cards: AE, M, V
Handicap Access: None

With only 24 rooms, this small motel has a premium location just three blocks away from Moonlight Beach in Encinitas. (Some rooms have ocean views.) This is a family-oriented motel, and each unit comes with a kitchenette as well as a full-size balcony. A lighted tennis court is accessible to guests. Week-long and month-long rates are available. These aren't luxury accommodations, and the inexpensive prices reflect the bare-bones quality, but the location in north county is central, rooms are clean and comfortable, and you won't feel guilty if your little ones drag back some of the beach in their shoes.

PORTOFINO BEACH INN

Innkeeper: Illa Yoshi
760-944-0301; fax: 760-944-0642
www.portofinobeachinn.com
186 N. Coast Hwy., Encinitas, CA 92024
Price: Moderate
Credit Cards: AE, M, V
Handicap Access: None

The newly remodeled Portofino Beach Inn is a small hotel located on historic Highway 101, just steps away from the many bistros and boutiques in downtown Encinitas. The location is unbeatable, because so much of the area can be explored on foot. Rooms are spacious and well-lighted, but the décor is lackluster. Some guest rooms have partial ocean views, but this isn't the kind of place you'll want to stay if you plan to spend a lot of time indoors. Choose it, instead, because of the prime location in north county, near the action and within easy access to other coastal communities. The 45 rooms come with a hearty complimentary breakfast and a good cup of coffee.

CULTURE

North county isn't just for surfers. Laid-back Leucadia, for example, has long attracted artists; and charming Encinitas is a mecca for gourmets. Carlsbad has expansive flower fields that rival those in Holland. And the Cedros Avenue design district in Solana Beach offers some of the best furniture and accessory designs in the county.

Galleries

101 Artists Colony (760-632-9074; 90C North Coast Hwy., Encinitas, CA 92024). This co-op of artists supports and showcases the vibrant visual arts community in north county. The gallery features a rotating collection by various artists, which changes every three weeks. On Fridays the gallery sponsors an interactive experience called "Journey of the Arts," and on Sunday afternoons there is a "Meet the Artist" open house.

Galerie D'Art International (858-793-0316; 320 S. Cedros Ave., Ste. 500, Solana Beach, CA 92075). A part of the community since 1973, this respected gallery specializes in contemporary oil paintings, sculptures, prints, and photographs by internationally recognized artists. The light and airy museum-like space is in the heart of the Cedros Design Center, and also offers an opera concert series and hosts numerous benefit galas throughout the year.

Michael Seewald Gallery (760-633-1351; 835 N. Vulcan Ave., Encinitas, CA 92024). Landscape photographer Michael Seewald's work is showcased in this small gallery, which features studies from Russia, Iceland, India, and other countries around the world. Call ahead to confirm hours.

Gardens

Flower Fields of Carlsbad (760-431-0352; corner of Palomar Airport Rd. and Paseo del Norte). In the spring these 50 acres become a dazzling mosaic of brilliantly colored flowers, planted in rainbow ribbons and laid out into the shape of a giant U.S. flag. This spectacular field grows more than 8 million Tecolote Giant™ ranunculas, mainly to harvest for bulbs. For a price, starting in March and through early May, visitors can stroll through the fields, take photographs, and enjoy other garden-related attractions, including a sweet pea maze and activities for children. The fields overlook the ocean and a decorative windmill, which together give the feeling of being someplace altogether different than north county. Entrance fees go up regularly, so call ahead for prices and hours.

Quail Botanical Gardens (760-436-3036; 230 Quail Gardens Dr., Encinitas, CA 92024). The 35 acres of exhibits at this beautiful botanical garden include a bamboo orchard, a Mediterranean landscapes garden, and a subtropical fruit garden. The miles of trails that crisscross the property wind by a gingerbread-style gazebo that is a child magnet. You'll also find a lily pond (that blooms most prodigiously in August) and a peaceful, secluded waterfall. A small onsite nursery sells exotic plant specimens you will encounter on your visit to the garden. $8 for adults, $5 for seniors and active military, $3 for children 12 and younger.

Self-Realization Fellowship Temple and Ashram Center (760-753-2888; 215 K St., Encinitas, CA 92024). You cannot miss the Temple driving along the Coast Highway in Encinitas; the large cream-colored structure is topped with several gold-leafed onion domes, and the temple itself is surrounded by a high stucco wall. Along the side entrance on K Street, you can access the small meditation gardens, which are open to the public Tuesday through Saturday 9 AM to 5 PM and Sunday 11 AM to 5 PM. Stroll through a well-manicured shade garden and enjoy a koi pond and small waterfall. At the summit of the garden there is a panoramic view of the ocean and several benches to contemplate the beauty of the surroundings. Admission is free.

Historic Places

Mission San Luis Rey de Francia (760-757-3651; 4050 Mission Ave., Oceanside, CA 92057). Known as the King of the Missions, the Mission San Luis Rey was founded in 1798 by Padre Fermín de Lasuén as the 18th in a line of 21 Spanish missions established in California. This is the largest of all the missions, and there is quite a lot to explore. The museum displays mission-era artifacts like Native American hand-woven baskets and pottery, Roman Catholic vestments and liturgical vessels from the 18th century, and 3-foot-tall psalm books printed on sheepskin. Visitors can stroll through re-creations of mission living quarters, including the kitchen, a padre's bedchamber, and workshops for weaving and handicrafts. Visitors can also explore a small garden courtyard before stepping into the large church, which has hand-painted ceilings and walls (the original paint has been gone over a number of times), a bright cupola highlighted with skylights,

The "King of the Missions," San Luis Rey in Oceanside.

and carved and painted wooden religious statues. An audio tour narrates continually during visiting hours. Outside visitors can hike through trails that explore the Lavandaria—the Native American laundry and site of the sunken gardens (which these days aren't much to look at, frankly, and are very loud because of the nearby highway traffic). To the west of the mission, look for California's first pepper tree, grown from seeds brought back from Peruvian sailors in 1830. Note that this is a working church, and the grounds and onsite accommodations are used for religious retreats, as well as by the Franciscan monks who still live and work here. Open daily 9:30 AM to 4:30 PM. Adults $5, students $3, children under 7 free.

Museums

California Surf Museum (760-721-6876; 223 N. Coast Hwy., Oceanside, CA 92054). This museum, dedicated to all things that pertain to the surfing lifestyle, sponsors a new exhibit each year highlighting surfing equipment, sports photography, or a surfing legend. You'll also find a small gift shop featuring surfing books, DVDs, and an amusing collection of bumper stickers (GOT SURF?). Open daily, 10–4. Admission is free.

Museum of Making Music (760-438-5996; 5790 Armada Dr., Carlsbad, CA 92008).You'll find more than five hundred instruments on display, as well as traveling exhibits at this small museum near Legoland. You can see the inner workings of a grand piano, the casing of which is made of Lucite; pick and then listen to selections on a Victrola; or examine a replica of Ringo Starr's drum set. The fun really begins in the "Hands on the Future Exhibit," where patrons get in on the act by playing an electronic drum set; testing their version of "Stairway to Heaven" on a Daisy Rock bass guitar; or creating a virtual band with Apple software's latest music-making product. Guests can also arrange for private tours of the museum, and the facility is available to rent out for special events in the evenings. Open: 10–5; closed Monday and holidays. Adults $5, seniors, active military, students $3.

Nightlife

Coastal north county has a relaxed, hip vibe that you won't find downtown or farther inland. The proximity to the ocean (and the resultant higher rents) attracts upscale and often expensive businesses, although there are plenty of funky surf dives sprinkled in for flavor. Look for casual neighborhood bars, swanky beachside bistros, and larger venues that offer world-class live music.

The Bellyup Tavern (858-481-8140; 143 S. Cedros Ave., Solana Beach, CA 92075). Locals have been rocking at the Bellyup since 1974, and it is still the premier nightclub for live music in the city. The warehouse space has enough room for a huge bar, a handful of billiards tables, and a cavernous dance floor. The Bellyup features eclectic live music from local bands as well as nationally recognized artists. There are regular theme nights, with dance instruction to match. The Bellyup claims to have patrons ranging in age from 21 to 81—and this probably isn't an exaggeration. The senior crowd rules the dance floor during weekday nostalgia nights, and their grandchildren take over on the rowdier weekend evenings. Closed Monday; cover charge varies.

Blanca (858-792-0072; 437 S. Hwy. 101, Solano Beach, CA 92075). The chic, tone-on-tone minimalist design of this upscale restaurant and bar befits its proximity to the elegant Cedros Avenue design district. The chef serves up beautifully presented seafood entrees like butter-poached Maine lobster and merlot-braised short ribs, but while you're here for the food, don't miss some of the best martinis in the city, sorted on the cocktail menu by color. Try "blue," a blend of currant-flavored vodka and blue Curacao, or "pink," a potent concoction of rum, amaretto, and whiskey served in a sugar-rimmed glass.

Crazy Burro (760-438-3373; 6996 El Camino Real, Carlsbad, CA 92009). A few blocks up the street from the La Costa Resort and Spa, the Crazy Burro is a passable (albeit slightly expensive) Mexican restaurant adorned with heavy wrought-iron chandeliers, brightly painted walls, and enormous picture windows that look out over the La Costa Resort's north golf course (although the view is now partially blocked by a new apartment complex). The large bar is hopping every night of the week with 30- and 40-somethings looking to hook up, and a large outdoor patio in the front offers full dining and karaoke on select nights.

Gaffney's Wine Bar (760-633-1011; 897 S. Coast Hwy. 101, Encinitas, CA 92024). Located in the strip mall known as the Lumberyard in Encinitas, Gaffney's is a casual and friendly establishment that specializes in small-production wines from around the world. The list changes daily, and they host regular "meet the wine makers" events in which vintners come and personally share their favorites. Gaffney's offers the option of buying wine by the half-glass, which is a perfect way to sample without too much commitment. To accompany your picks, you can order up cheese and light appetizers or munch on fine Venezuelan chocolates. Open 5–10 or 11; closed Monday.

Jimmy O's Sports Bar and Restaurant (858-350-3735; 225 W. 15th St., Del Mar, CA 92014). A sports bar and restaurant with a lively night life, Jimmy O's is lined with TVs, so you won't miss a minute of sports action. The kitchen is open until midnight, and has a nice variety of salads, pastas, and respectable steaks. Happy hour specials include discounted drinks (from 4–6 and then again from 10–midnight) and an abbreviated appetizer and sandwich menu for only $6.

Squid Joes (760-729-4996; 850 Tamarack Ave., Carlsbad, CA 92008). This is one of the best places in north county to see local talent; Squid Joe's features eclectic live music, including reggae, rock, blues, and hip hop. In addition to the small stage and wooden dance floor, you'll find pool tables, dart boards, TVs, and basic bar food as well as burgers and sandwiches.

Seasonal Events

The **San Diego Marathon** in Carlsbad kicks off the year's events in north county. The marathon starts at the Westfield Mall on Plaza Camino Real on the first Saturday of January. Entry fees apply for participants, but admission to the accompanying events is free.

February is prime whale watching season; catch a two-hour tour with **Helgren's Sportfishing** (760-722-2133), and for about $25 head out into the migration path as the California gray whales make their way from Alaska to the warmer waters of Baja lagoons to mate and have their babies.

Starting in early March and running through mid-May, ranunculas in Carlsbad's famous **Flower Fields** in **Carlsbad Ranch** (760-431-0352) are blooming, and for a fee you can wander around the 50 acres of colorful blossoms. If your favorite color is green, check out the **St. Patrick's Day Parade and Festival** (760-931-8400) held in Carlsbad Village on March 17 and beginning at Roosevelt Street and Walnut Avenue, with food and live music.

Quail Botanical Gardens (760-436-3036) in Encinitas hosts the **Flower by the Sea Show** the first weekend in April, showcasing professional horticulturalists and floral designers. Admission to the show is free with entry into the Gardens.

The San Diego County Fair midway is choked with rides and food stands. Photo courtesy of Jon Preimesberger. Used with permission.

The **Carlsbad Village Street Faire** (760-931-8400) is held the first Sunday in May, and is the largest single-day street fair in California. You'll find the festivities along the whole of Grand Avenue, one block north of Carlsbad Village Drive.

The first weekend in the month of June, the city of Solana Beach hosts the annual **Fiesta del Sol** (858-755-4889) with live music, arts and crafts for children, and international food tastings. Camp Pendleton in Oceanside hosts a full-event **Rodeo** (760-725-4111) throughout the month of June, from 1 PM each Saturday and Sunday. Admission is $12. And starting in mid-June and stretching through the Fourth of July is the **San Diego County Fair** (858-755-4111), formerly known as the Del Mar Fair, held on the **Del Mar Fairgrounds and Racetrack.** This expansive event comprises 4-H animal displays, cooking contests, arts and crafts displays, hundreds of entertaining exhibitors hawking their gadgets, a midway with more than 50 thrill rides and nearly one hundred games, and food booths that specialize in anything fried on a stick. Special events and displays are scheduled throughout the run of the fair, and include dance demonstrations by local troupes, cattle roping, and big-name entertainment (well—the names were big *once*; most of the headliners enjoyed popularity in past decades). Weekends are flooded with people; come early if you want a spot in the $13 parking lot. Admission is $11 for adults, $6 for children (although youth exhibitors receive free admittance on the day of their contest).

Jazz in the Parks is a free outdoor event in Carlsbad held every Friday evening throughout the month of July and rotates between **Stagecoach Park** (3420 Camino de los Coches) and **Calavera Hills Park** (2997 Glasgow Drive) in Carlsbad. Beginning the last week of the month, the **La Costa Spa and Resort** (760-438-9111) in Carlsbad hosts the **Acura Classic**, a week-long U.S. Open women's tennis event that attracts sell-out crowds.

In August, head to the Oceanside Pier and Beach to watch the **World Body Surfing Championships** (www.worldbodysurfing.org), where more than two hundred of the world's best body surfers battle it out.

Oktoberfest (760-931-8400) is celebrated the first weekend in October at **Holiday Park** at the corner of Chestnut Street and Pio Pico in Carlsbad. The festivities feature music, dancing, crafts, German food, and—of course—beer.

November brings the **Fall Village Fair** (760-931-8400) in Carlsbad, near Grand Avenue and Carlsbad Boulevard, where you can shop for handcrafted holiday gifts, listen to live music, and stroll through an organic farmer's market. In late November, and running through the end of the year, enjoy the **Holiday of Lights at Del Mar** (858-755-1161), when the Del Mar Race Track is transformed with more than 350 brilliant holiday light displays that guests can view from their car while driving the infield racetrack (an interesting experience even without the festive lights).

The poinsettia plant was first bred commercially in Encinitas by the Ecke family nurseries, and this heritage is celebrated throughout December at the **Carlsbad Ranch** (760-431-0352), where poinsettias of every shade are shown off in a blaze of holiday color. And on the first Saturday of the month, Encinitas holds its annual evening **Holiday Parade** (760-633-2740) down historic Highway 101, starting at E Street and continuing south to Swami's Beach, with floats and bands from around the city vying to outdo each other with lights and glitz.

Theater

North Coast Repertory Theater (858-481-2155; 987 Lomas Santa Fe Dr., Solana Beach, CA 92075). With year-round performances in an intimate two-hundred-seat theater, the North Coast Repertory Theater is one of the best small theaters in San Diego. The NCRT is known for the diversity of performances it presents, from the classics to contemporary theater. The NCRT also functions as a community outreach venue, hosting eight-week theater schools for local students that teach performance skills, which are then showcased in productions at the end of each class cycle.

RESTAURANTS AND FOOD PURVEYORS

Restaurants

Along the north coast of San Diego, you'll find numerous upscale restaurants overlooking the Pacific, as well as plenty of mom and pop cafes and a few dives—perfect places to get a traditional Mexican plate or one of the innumerable variations of fish tacos you'll find throughout the county. Although Del Mar can be pricey, especially if your table has a water view, fine dining is generally a little less expensive in north county than in downtown (chapter 3) and in La Jolla (chapter 4).

CARLSBAD
FISH HOUSE VERA CRUZ
Owner: Rex Butler
760-434-6777
417 Carlsbad Village Dr., Carlsbad, CA 92008
Open: Daily
Price: Moderate
Cuisine: Seafood
Serving: L, D
Credit Cards: AE, MC, V
Handicap Access: Yes
Reservations: Recommended
Parking: Small lot and street parking

You know the fish is going to be fresh here the minute you walk in the door and see the seafood counter at the front of the restaurant, where they also sell fish to take home. But why bother to cook when everything is prepared so well here? The menu changes daily, based on the catch of the day, but count on mahi mahi, salmon, and halibut straight off the boat. All fish is mesquite grilled, which gives it a smoky, light flavor that highlights the delicate textures. Start out with the oysters Rockefeller or a bowl of the Boston clam chowder. Each meal comes with a crisp salad and two generously proportioned sides (the cheddar mashed potatoes are decadent). You'll also be served a loaf of piping hot sour dough bread, which would suffice as a meal. The portions are really too big to allow for dessert, but if you're looking to be a hero, the pecan apple cheesecake or the rocky road cake are among the many gut-busting options. The food is a relative bargain for seafood, but the restaurant's large size makes for a noisy dining experience, and the service is a little too efficient: On weekends, especially, it seems as if the servers rush from course to course, in order to free up another table more quickly.

FIDEL'S NORTE

Owners: Montanez Family
760-729-0903
3003 Carlsbad Blvd., Carlsbad, CA 92008
Open: Daily
Price: Moderate
Cuisine: Mexican
Serving: L, D
Credit Cards: M, V
Handicap Access: Yes
Reservations: Recommended for large parties
Parking: Small lot in front, underground lot on the corner of Ocean St. and Carlsbad Village Blvd., street (limited)

Fidel Montanez started out in 1960 with a barbershop in Solana Beach, where his wife Martha served beer and tacos to hungry customers; soon enough the barbershop became a restaurant. The original location is still operating in a somewhat out of the way locale (607 Valley Ave., Solana Beach); and in the 1970s, Fidel opened this second restaurant in the more accessible tourist destination of Carlsbad Village. Within minutes of being seated, you'll be given a complimentary bowl of tortilla chips and very spicy salsa. If that isn't enough appetizer for you, consider the soups—*albondigas*, a spicy meatball soup, or for the more adventurous, *menudo*, a tripe and hominy soup (an acquired taste, for sure). Entrees include *carne asada*, a buttery, thinly sliced flank steak served with onions and peppers; *pescado ranchero*, grilled mahi mahi smothered in a mild red sauce; or *nopales*, cactus cooked in a spicy tomato and serrano chili sauce and topped with cheese. All entrees are served with huge portions of rice and refried beans. If you somehow manage to have room for dessert, try the *buñuelos*, a deep-fried flour tortilla covered with sugar and cinnamon, along with a cup of Mexican hot chocolate flavored with cinnamon. The restaurant interior is bland (except for an obstructed view of the ocean, visible from only a few tables), so if the weather permits, request seating in the large outdoor patio beneath colorful umbrellas. But inside or out, the friendly wait staff is slow and sometimes befuddled, seemingly overloaded even when the crowds are thin.

LA PASSAGE FRENCH BISTRO

Owner: Michelle Rocca
760-729-7097
www.lapassagefrenchbistro.com
2961 State St., Carlsbad, CA 92008
Open: Tuesday–Sunday
Price: Expensive
Cuisine: French
Serving: L, Tues–Friday; D, Tues–Sunday
Credit Cards: AE, D, M, V

Handicap Access: No
Reservations: Recommended
Parking: Street parking

Every table in the tiny dining room of La
Passage French Bistro has a vista into the
equally tiny open kitchen, which is a good
thing because aside from faux-painted
stones on the walls, there is nothing else to
see—but La Passage's artful meals will provide views enough. Start with the light (and
inexpensive) Nicoise and Picholine olives,
which are marinated in sherry vinegar and
mustard seeds. If you're feeling more
adventurous, there is *escargots* served in
garlic butter with a puff pastry round or
black mussels steamed in white wine and
served with an herbed cream sauce. For the
main course, wild mushroom ravioli
dressed in a brown butter sauce is a comforting and filling choice. But if you're ready
to throw caution—and cholesterol—to the
wind, try the grilled filet mignon smothered
in melted Roquefort cheese sauce and
served with potatoes dauphine. For dessert
there are apples poached in white wine and
served with vanilla ice cream and caramel
sauce or a dense and rich chocolate cake
served with in-season berries.

WEST STEAK AND SEAFOOD
Chef: Eugenio Martignago
760-930-9100
www.weststeakandseafood.com
4980 Avenida Encinas, Carlsbad, CA 92009
Open: Daily
Price: Expensive
Cuisine: Steakhouse
Serving: D (from 3:30 PM)
Credit Cards: AE, D, MC, V
Handicap Access: Yes
Reservations: Suggested
Parking: Adjacent lot

One of the hottest new restaurants to come
on the scene in north county in years, this
upscale steakhouse, opened in late 2005,
flaunts the huge investments made to this

*West Steak and Seafood in Carlsbad has an aura of
nostalgia.*

property. West is decorated nostalgically,
with sink-down comfortable leather booths
and highly polished tables. The style is pur-
ported to be new-Californian, and there is
an unmistakable Western influence: Everything at West is done on a bigger-than-life
scale, with prices to match. Specialties
include, of course, prime filet steaks and
comfort-food sides such as mashed potatoes, creamed spinach, and potatoes au
gratin. The silky lobster bisque is notable,
served in a generous seashell-shaped bowl
with tomato and brie broiled on top. There
are also seared Colorado lamb chops,
grilled pork chops dredged in fresh rosemary, and grilled fish served with a luscious
lobster-tarragon sauce. If you have room
after the enormous entrees, don't miss the
mousse-like bread pudding, served hot,
studded with cherries, figs, and raisins and
topped with a Tahitian vanilla ice cream.

Del Mar and Solana Beach
ARTERRA
Chef: Brian Pekarcik
858-369-6032
www.arterrarestaurant.com
11966 El Camino Real, Carmel Valley, CA
92130
Open: Daily
Price: Expensive to Very Expensive
Cuisine: American
Serving: B, L, D

Credit cards: AE, D, MC, V
Reservations: Recommended for dinner
Parking: Hotel parking lot or valet

Arterra, which stands for "art of the earth," specializes in contemporary cuisine that highlights the freshest, best quality regional food available. Chef Brian Pekarcik's imaginative menu changes according to the availability of produce and meats—and with the seasons and the chef's moods—so you never know what to expect. But look for starters that feature Chino Farms produce, which consistently provides the best the county has to offer. In season, heirloom tomatoes are served with a cucumber sorbet and a light balsamic vinaigrette and pepper soup is accented with shrimp and curry croutons. Main courses include Kobe beef, locally caught seafood along with the best imported fish, and tantalizing vegetarian options. There is also an extensive sushi menu. There is no better way to celebrate a special occasion—or a really good day at the nearby Del Mar Racetrack—than to indulge in Arterra's seven-course chef-inspired "grand tasting," which highlights the best of the best. Chef Pekarcik jokes that he doesn't try to "make the dishes levitate off the plate," but even so, each of the offerings is elegantly and artfully presented. Wine director Ted Glennon will walk you through the extensive wine list; his enthusiasm and energy are contagious, and you're likely to learn quite a lot from him about choosing wines. Finish up with a dessert from pastry chef James Foran, whose chocolate soufflé with a liquid chocolate center is the stuff of my dreams.

EPAZOTE

Chef: Anthony De Luca
858-259-9966
www.epazotedelmar.com
1555 Camino del Mar, Ste. 322, Del Mar, CA 92014
Open: Daily

Price: Expensive
Cuisine: Steak house, contemporary American
Serving: L, D, brunch on Sundays
Credit Cards: AE, D, MC, V
Handicap Access: Yes
Reservations: Recommended for dinner
Parking: Validated underground parking at the mall or street (limited)

An expansive outdoor dining patio makes the most of the second floor location in trendy Del Mar Plaza; diners can enjoy views of the ocean across the street or watch the hundreds of people parading down Highway 101 below. Weekend lunches are relaxing, and a good opportunity to enjoy traditional dishes with a unique twist. The lobster BLT, for example, is served up on toasted brioche, with diced tomatoes, crispy applewood-smoked bacon, and a delicate poached lobster salad. When the sun sets and the heat lamps are lighted, the chic clientele come for the food and the inventive bar—don't miss the espresso martini, which pairs vanilla vodka with cold espresso and Kahlua liqueur. For dinner, first, choose your favorite cut of premium Midwestern, corn-fed beef (or chicken and pork); then pair it with your favorite rub or glaze. Delicious options include the signature Epazote rub, with smoky chipotle chilies and ancho and pasilla powders; the peppered blue brûlée, with blue cheese, cracked black pepper, and a shallot marmalade; or the orange-honey cumin glaze with freshly grated citrus zest, honey, and plenty of cumin and pepper. To finish, indulge in the hot banana bread pudding made with buttery croissants and finished with a caramel sauce or the deep, dark, decadent chocolate cake served with gelato and fresh berries. The restaurant offers the best children's menu I've seen in San Diego—instead of the usual mac and cheese and chicken fingers, "future fine diners" can order small portions of perfectly grilled filet mignon served with appealingly presented veggies, grilled tiger shrimp with dipping sauce, or grilled salmon with brown rice and lemon butter—all for $10.

JAKE'S DEL MAR
Owner: Sandy Saxten
858-755-2002
www.hulapie.com
1660 Coast Blvd., Del Mar, CA 92014
Open: Daily
Price: Expensive
Cuisine: Seafood
Serving: L and D Tues–Sat; S brunch
Credit Cards: AE, MC, V
Handicap: Yes
Reservations: Recommended
Parking: Valet, street (limited)

Jake's is right on the beach, and the views are no less than breathtaking. The relaxed atmosphere and friendly service attract crowds of all ages, and the food manages to live up to the beautiful surroundings. Calamari is ubiquitous in Southern California, but Jake's signature appetizer manages to make something special out of squid by crusting it in macadamias and finishing it with a tart glaze that cuts through the richness of the nuts. The roasted beet salad is also a winner, served with arugula, endive, and smoky bacon in champagne vinaigrette. Fresh fish is always featured on the daily specials, and Jake's will prepare it however you like. My favorites on the regular menu include mahi mahi, a firm white fish, prepared with a mirin glaze; and the rare wok-seared ahi prepared with a tomato ginger sauce. Or for a special treat, order the two oven-roasted Maine lobster tails served with cognac butter. Jake's bar packs them in at sunset, so even if you don't have an appetite, grab a cocktail and enjoy the ocean view.

POSEIDON'S
Chef: Timothy Guttman
858-755-9345
www.poseidonrestaurant.com
1670 Coast Blvd., Del Mar, CA 92014
Open: Daily
Price: Expensive
Cuisine: Seafood
Serving: L and D; B on weekends
Credit Cards: AE, D, DC, MC, V
Handicap Access: Yes
Reservations: Recommended
Parking: Valet, street (limited)

This restaurant, with an extensive bar inside, is all about the views; located right on the sand, Poseidon's has a large outdoor dining patio with billion-dollar views of the surf and sunsets, and is extremely popular with locals, especially on weekend evenings. An eclectic menu specializes in seafood, but you can also get a good steak here, and there are a few vegetarian options. The chefs have supersized the perennial shrimp cocktail—it arrives at your table looking like a martini glass full of small lobsters—and as a California twist it is served with avocado. Other starters include the ceviche, made from halibut, bay shrimp, lemon and lime juices, and lots of onions, and the sake-steamed black mussels served in coconut milk and accented with pickled ginger and shaved fennel. The catch of the day generally includes oven-roasted sea bass served with couscous, spinach, and wild mushrooms in a sweet balsamic reduction and tender grilled swordfish served with a mango salsa. If you're not ready to tear yourself away from the ocean views after your meal, treat yourself to a slice of mud pie—mocha gelato on a dark chocolate cookie crust and topped with whipped cream, fudge sauce, and nuts—or the bananas foster, gooey warm bananas served with roasted banana gelato and Meyers' rum.

SBICCA

Chef: Susan Sbicca
858-481-1001
www.sbiccabistro.com
215 15th St., Del Mar, CA 92024
Open: Daily
Price: Expensive
Cuisine: Contemporary American
Serving: L, C
Credit Cards: AE, D, DC, MC, V
Handicap Access: Yes
Reservations: Recommended
Parking: Street (limited)

Honored as 2006 Chef of the Year by the California Restaurant Association, Susan Sbicca has attracted a lot of attention to her Del Mar restaurant. The site has an expansive patio that takes full advantage of the Pacific Ocean views, and Sbicca's menu takes full advantage of the bounty of fresh ingredients available in San Diego. The restaurant offers a wide selection of wines, and servers are knowledgeable and helpful in suggesting pairings. As sumptuous as the entrees are, I would be perfectly happy to make a meal on just appetizers. Shitake-blue crab egg rolls are a sweet, salty fusion of delicate crab, pecans, sweet onions, and Asian dipping sauce. And the grilled portobello mushroom served with creamy blue cheese, crunchy walnuts, and chewy dried currants successfully balances the seemingly disparate textures and flavors. Inventive entrees include the prosciutto-wrapped sea scallops served with chard and truffle aioli; the hearty grilled lamb loin served with a rich, creamy butternut risotto with a hazelnut glaze; and the maple-roasted pork prime rib served with sweet potatoes, a spicy pecan butter, and a bourbon chantilly sauce. To finish consider the apricot-almond cake soaked with brandy and served with fresh strawberries and cream or a cup of Mexican coffee, a strong brew blended with tequila, Kahlua, and whipped cream—perfect for chasing the chill away on the outdoor patio after the sun sets.

TASTE OF THAI

Owner: Thai Villa
858-793-9695
www.tasteofthaidelmar.com
15770 San Andreas Dr., Del Mar, CA 92014
Open: Daily
Price: Moderate
Cuisine: Thai
Serving: L, D
Credit Cards: AE, M, V
Handicap: Yes
Reservations: Recommended for dinner
Parking: Lot

Located in the east end of Flower Hill Mall, just off I-5 and conveniently located near the Del Mar Race Track, Taste of Thai serves up flavor-packed meals that you can customize on a spiciness scale of 1–10. To start, try the beef or chicken satay skewers with rich peanut sauce or the shrimp sa-rong, wrapped with egg noodles and fried up golden and crispy. You can build your own entrees by picking a protein (beef, chicken, pork, shrimp, scallops, or tofu) and pairing it with a selection of complexly spiced sauces. You'll also find creamy Thai curries perfumed with coconut milk and a wide selection of noodle dishes, including the ever-popular pad thai—rice noodles with dried shrimp, bean sprouts, scallions, eggs, and ground nuts. Finish up with the Thai custard, a not-overly-sweet bright orange concoction made with pumpkin. The interior is exotic, with deep burgundy, green, and gold walls and ceilings, and there are plenty of comfortable tables to accommodate the post-races crowd—although something about the acoustics makes conversations carry and amplify. A second location in Hillcrest (619-291-7525; 527 University Ave., San Diego, CA 92103) is no quieter, and it's much harder to secure a table there, especially at lunchtime.

TONY'S JACAL

Owners: Gonzales Family
858-755-2274
621 Valley Ave., Solana Beach, CA 92075
Open: Wednesday–Monday
Price: Moderate
Cuisine: Homestyle Mexican
Serving: L Monday, Wednesday–Saturday; D Monday, Wednesday–Sunday (hours increase during Del Mar Race season)
Credit Cards: AE, D, MC, V
Handicap Access: Yes
Reservations: No
Parking: Small lot in front, large lot across the street

This San Diego institution, located in a residential neighborhood of Solana Beach, has been serving homestyle Mexican food to locals since 1947, when Tony and Catalina Gonzalez opened the Jacal (loosely translated as "shack") out of the front of what was the family's home. The restaurant has grown in size considerably in the past 60 years, and the menu has expanded. But current managers and wait staff are still Gonzalez family members—and a very gracious, welcoming bunch. An intimate, quiet patio provides outdoor seating, and the centerpiece water pond is surrounded by myriad blooming flowers. There is also a roomy interior dining room, with pine-paneled walls and stained-glass windows. Fresh ingredients have brought customers back for generations. *Chiles rellenos*—a mild poblano chile that is stuffed with tangy *antijo* cheese, lightly breaded and fried in a fluffy egg batter, and then covered in a mild red sauce—is a specialty. Their extensive menu of combinations lets you try a little bit of just about anything—although note that the enchiladas can be lackluster. A trip to Tony's is not complete without an order of *sopapillas* for dessert, a fried pillow of pastry, the hollow center of which is perfect for filling with honey.

ENCINITAS, INCLUDING CARDIFF-BY-THE-SEA AND LEUCADIA

CHARLIE'S BY THE SEA

Chef: Miguel Moreno
760-942-1300
www.charliesbythesea.com
2526 S. Hwy. 101, Cardiff-by-the-Sea, CA 92007
Open: Daily

The view facing south from Charlie's by the Sea in Cardiff.

Price: Expensive
Cuisine: Seafood
Serving: L, D; Sunday Brunch
Credit Cards: AE, D, DC, MC, V
Handicap Access: Yes
Reservations: Recommended
Parking: Valet

For its stunning location just feet from the surf, Charlie's is well worth a visit. The interior is disappointing; in fact, the main dining room looks to be furnished with indoor–outdoor furniture. But the 180-degree views of the Pacific and the shores are among the best in north county. Sit at a waterview table (and most of them *are* waterview tables) and watch the surfers and dolphins play in the waves. If the breeze isn't too overpowering, a table on the small outdoor patio is a nicer choice. The New England-style clam chowder, creamy and loaded with clams and smoky bacon, is a bargain at $3 a cup. Other notable appetizers include crab cakes served in an ancho chili and lime remoulade, and sautéed calamari filet, which is served with an herb-flavored parmesan crust and a lemon- flavored beurre blanc sauce. The seafood entrees are as fresh as you would expect from the seaside location, although the sides are less interesting. The grilled day boat scallops, coated in soy sauce and served with a golden sear atop a browned butter sauce flavored with Thai chilies, are cooked to perfection. Shrimp can be a little overdone, but the seaside scampi, prepared with mushrooms, tomatoes, lemon vodka cream, and plenty of garlic, is fragrant and hearty. Unlike many restaurants whose huge portions have you crying "uncle" before you've made a dent, the portions here are small enough to allow room for a dessert. Consider Charlie's aloha pie, made with macadamia nut ice cream on a chocolate-cookie crust and topped with whipped cream and caramel sauce, or the chocolate fudge cake, with three layers of fudge topped with whipped cream and chocolate sauce.

EL CALLEJON

Owners: Robert and Bernard Vourdain
760-758-5651
345 S. Coast Hwy. 101, Encinitas, CA 92024
Open: Daily
Price: Moderate
Cuisine: Mexican
Serving: L, D
Credit Cards: AE, D, M, V
Handicap Access: Yes
Reservations: Recommended for large parties
Parking: Small lot in front and street (very limited)

This colorful patio restaurant tucked in front of the train tracks and near Moonlight Beach has an added bonus: The bar boasts a a selection of more than 750 kinds of tequila, and the bartenders make a mean margarita. The guacamole is made fresh daily, and the cream of black bean soup served with bacon and tortillas is a good bet to start. You'll find the usual combination plates, but consider instead the *medallones al cilantro*, filet mignon medallions served with melted cheese and topped with a piquant cilantro sauce, or *ceviche valentin*, raw red snapper marinated in lemon juice and spices and served with crackers. For lighter meals try the *tortas*, Mexican sandwiches made on a crispy roll, or choose from a wide variety of quesadillas (quesadillas with *rajas*—strips of poblano chilies in a cheese and cream sauce—is a tasty vegetarian option). Desserts are unremarkable, and the enormous portions probably won't leave room anyhow. This is a popular choice for young families, and tends to be noisy in the early evenings.

SWAMI'S CAFÉ

Owner: Jaime Osuna
760-944-0612
1163 S. Coast Hwy. 101, Encinitas, CA 92024
Open: Daily
Price: Inexpensive
Cuisine: Vegetarian and whole foods

Serving: B, L, D
Credit Cards: MC, V
Handicap Access: No
Reservations: No
Parking: Street

Catering to the health-conscious surfing crowd and to other long-time Encinitas residents, Swami's Café (across from Swami's Beach) features fresh whole foods and vegetarian offerings. Hearty breakfast options include the black egg burrito, a concoction of scrambled eggs, black beans, avocado, and cheddar wrapped in a wheat tortilla and served with home-style potatoes (ingeniously mixed with zucchini); organic multigrain pancakes served with your choice of soy or real bacon; and a wide variety of made-to-order omelets. For lunch and dinner choose from salads, whole-wheat wraps, and sandwiches. Smoothies are something special: Nirvana Nectar blends apple juice, bananas, strawberries, raspberries, boysenberries, ginseng, protein powder, vitamin C, and bee pollen. Want a real pick-me-up? Try the Iron Horse, a combination of carrot and beet juice. Expect a wait to order and another wait for your food to be delivered; weekend mornings are insanely busy. The outdoor seating in front of the café is tight and a little noisy from Highway 101 just steps away, but the shady little side patio with a soothing (sound-drowning) water fountain offers a more relaxing choice.

WHEN IN ROME

Chefs/Owners: Joe and Rosemary Ragone
760-944-1771
1108 S. Coast Hwy. 101, Encinitas, CA 92024
Open: Tuesday–Sunday
Price: Expensive
Cuisine: Italian
Serving: D (lunch served in the summer)
Credit Cards: AE, D, DC, MC, V
Handicap Access: Yes
Parking: Street

The delicious aromas wafting out the door of this family-owned restaurant just north of Swami's Beach foreshadow the lovingly prepared dishes and the elegant and relaxing atmosphere inside. The main dining space is designed as a garden room, with brick floors and a canopy "roof" that rolls back on warm days, and it is flanked by two more intimate dining rooms, separated by French doors and lighted subtly by ornate chandeliers and candlelight. A baby grand near the front door provides live music. Owners and chefs Joe and Rosemary Ragone serve up a mix of traditional and contemporary Italian meals, all made with the finest ingredients—to ensure the best, they even grow their own vegetables and herbs and make their pastas from scratch. Portions are quite large, so consider sharing an antipasto dish to start: The *caprese*, made with buffalo mozzarella and the choicest tomatoes and fragrant basil drizzled with olive oil, is too beautiful to eat. Or try the *insalata di mele*, a salad made from red apples, mixed baby greens, goat cheese, and grapes tossed in a vinigerette. The fresh pasta is almost as good as anything you'd find in Italy. *Fettucine con gamberi aglio e olio*, large juicy shrimps sautéed with slivers of garlic are served over pasta dressed with fruity olive oil, and the *ravioli alla panna con salvia*, spinach and cheese stuffed ravioli dressed with a creamy sauce with sage and parmesan, are cooked to perfection. Other specialties of the house include *linguini al granchio*, fettuccine with a tomato and crab cream sauce; *tortiglioni alla Mediterraneo*, pasta served with spicy Italian sausage in a tomato, olives, and mushroom sauce; and *lombata all Zingara*, a veal chop grilled with olive oil, garlic, and lemon. On Sunday nights, the restaurant offers a small plates special—petite portions of antipasto and pasta—and a "bottomless" glass of wine (choose among four options) for only $30. Even though the service is a little slow, the wait staff is helpful and courteous.

Oceanside
BEACH BREAK CAFÉ
Owner: Gary and Zelda Dewelly
760-439-6355
1902 S. Coast Hwy, Oceanside, CA 92054
Open: Daily
Price: Inexpensive
Cuisine: American
Serving: B, L
Credit cards: MC, V
Handicap Access: Yes
Reservations: No
Parking: Lot

If a friend hadn't taken me to this tiny neighborhood favorite tucked next to a Laundromat, I would never have tried it—or probably even noticed it; I'm grateful she did. North county surfers swear by this place, and the walls are a shrine to the surfing culture, with hundreds of signed photographs of famous surfers and other memorabilia, including a half-dozen surfboards hanging from the rafters. There aren't many tables inside, so be prepared to wait on weekends. Put your name in, grab a cup of coffee from the honor bar outside, and relax: Service is *fast*, so you won't have to wait as long as you might think—and portions are huge. The spicy and delicious Santa Fe omelet comes bursting with chorizo sausage, cheese, onions, and fresh slices of avocado and it's topped with a mountain of sour cream. Sides include your choice of a monster portion of homemade hash browns or home fries and tortillas or a yummy hunk of glazed coffee cake. Banana crunch French toast is crispy and sweet and topped with whipped cream and sliced bananas, along with turkey sausage. Breakfast is served until closing (2 PM), but there is also a lunch menu with the usual selection of sandwiches and burgers. This is a true value, and the unpretentious atmosphere attracts its fair share of local surf and skate celebrities—so it's not a bad place to people watch, either.

ROBIN'S NEST CAFÉ
Owner: Carmen and Jose Barrazza
760-722-7837
www.robinsnestcafe.com
280 South Harbor Dr., Oceanside, CA 92054
Open: Daily
Price: Moderate to expensive
Cuisine: Californian
Serving: B, L, D
Credit Cards: AE, D, DC, MC, V
Handicap Access: Yes
Reservations: Yes
Parking: Lot behind the marina

The marina in Oceanside is a quaint walking-only collection of shops and restaurants, frequented by local fishermen who moor their boats here, U.S. Marines from nearby Camp Pendleton, and families (although the area is less child-friendly in the evenings, when rowdiness from the bars often spills outside). This small café on the water offers an expansive outdoor patio to view the lovely marina, and is an especially good place to enjoy a quiet breakfast or lunch. As you would imagine when surrounded by sport fishing boats, seafood prevails here, and breakfast specials include items like lobster eggs Benedict and a seafood omelet made with snow crab, bay shrimp, and cheddar cheese. Robin's Nest also has a nice selection of Mexican breakfasts. (You shouldn't leave San Diego without trying *huevos rancheros*—corn tortillas topped with eggs cooked any style and served with beans and salsa.) For lunch, look for the blackened mahi mahi salad with organic baby greens or "the world's best chili dog," a grilled wiener smothered in homemade chili, two kinds of cheeses, and lots of chopped onions. Dinner specialties include the Pacific northwest cioppino made with shrimp, mahi mahi, and baby clams; Alaskan halibut stuffed with snow crab and cream cheese; and the pepper-roasted prime rib, served with creamy garlic mashed potatoes and homemade soup or salad. Weekend mornings pack them in, so if you want to sit outside and enjoy the view, be sure to make a reservation or come early.

Food Purveyors

Breweries and Pubs

Hennessey's Tavern (760-729-6951; 2777 Roosevelt St., Carlsbad, CA 92008). An Irish pub serving breakfast, lunch, and dinner, Hennessey's is better known as a nightspot that sometimes hosts live music. Although the Tavern isn't likely to get big names, there is never a shortage of amplitude.

Karl Strauss Brewery (760-431-2739; 5801 Armada Dr., Carlsbad, CA 92008). This chain of microbreweries started right here in San Diego, and there are several outlets in town (including downtown and La Jolla). Although the restaurant fare is pedestrian, the bar is hopping, especially on weekends. All brews are on tap, and you can buy sampler glasses to get the full range of beers. Try a pint of the easy-going Red Trolley Ale, brewed with caramel malts, or the rich, nutty Black's Beach Extra Dark lager.

Pizza Port and Brewery (858-481-7332; 135 N. Hwy. 101, Solana Beach, CA 92075). With an additional location in Carlsbad (and one in San Clemente, in Orange County), you'd think this pizza and beer pub wouldn't get so crowded—but expect lines out the door with folks angling to get a cold, wet Sharkbite Red or seasonal specialties like Blonde Bombshell Barleywine and McHale's Irish Stout. The pizza is pretty tasty, too; you'll need plenty of brew to wash down the fiery Pizza Vallarta, with Canadian bacon, olives, onions, and jalapenos.

Karl Strauss in Carlsbad is just off the I-5 and near Legoland and the Carlsbad Company Stores outlet mall.

Coffeehouses

E Street Café (760-230-2038; 130 West E St., Encinitas, CA 92024). E Street specializes in fair-trade organic coffees, and also offers a huge selection of teas and vegetarian snacks and sweets. The comfortable and eclectically decorated café has free high-speed Internet access, and there are regular poetry readings and occasional live music.

Pannikin Coffee and Tea (760-436-0033; 510 N. Hwy. 101, Encinitas, CA 92024). Drive up to what looks like a big yellow house with white picket railing (actually it's a converted 19th-century train station), and it'll feel like you're visiting a favorite auntie's place. You'll be welcomed with comfortable surroundings, friendly people, and on-the-premises freshly baked cookies, muffins, breads, pies, and quiches, as well as a fine collection of gourmet coffees and teas. The small Pannikin chain has been a San Diego institution since 1968 (there are locations in La Jolla and Del Mar), well before the idea of coffeehouses became chic, and they have a loyal local clientele.

Surfdogs Java Hut (760-634-2326; 1126 S. Coast Hwy., Encinitas, CA 92024). This laid-back surfer café—that looks a little like a grass shack—specializes in organic, gourmet coffee and wholesome smoothies. The baristas can whip up a mean soy latte *and* point you to the best breaks.

Vinaka Café (760-720-7890; 300 Carlsbad Village Dr., Carlsbad, CA 92008). Upstairs in downtown Carlsbad's Village Faire, Vinaka is a welcoming, homey coffeehouse with overstuffed sofas and chairs, stacks of board games, a pretty outdoor patio, and free WiFi. While you're here try one of the dozen flavors of homemade ice cream.

Pizza, Burgers, and Dogs

Allen's New York Pizza (760-918-9999; 6943 El Camino Real, Carlsbad, CA 92008). You know you're getting the real deal in this La Costa neighborhood gem in south Carlsbad when you hear Allen's New York accent: It's a dead giveaway. Thin, crunchy crust is lightly sauced and heavily topped with the finest quality mozzarella; pepperoni is always a safe bet, but the vegetarian and sausage pizzas also deliver the goods.

Daily News Café (760-729-1023; 3001-A Carlsbad Blvd., Carlsbad, CA 92008). Serving breakfast and lunch only, the Daily News in downtown Carlsbad has a good selection of omelets and salads—but the *piece de résistance* is the popular Belly Bomber Burger. As the name suggests, this isn't for petite appetites.

Knock Out Burgers (760-729-8478; 2971 Carlsbad Blvd., Carlsbad, CA 92008). Don't let the crowd of teenage surfers and skaters dissuade you from trying this hole in the wall. For about $3.50 you can get a made-while-you-wait 1/4 pound cheese burger that is as

Sammy's enormous "messy sundae" lives up to its name.

good as a burger has a right to be. You can also buy a bag of tasty mini burgers by the dozen or half dozen.

Leucadia Pizzeria (760-942-2222; 315 S. Coast Hwy. 101, Encinitas, CA 92024). Just across from Moonlight Beach, this pizzeria (which also has locations in Rancho Santa Fe and La Jolla) features traditional pies, including a generously loaded pepperoni, and "gourmet" pies, such as shrimp pesto pizza and Greek pizza with feta cheese. In addition, they have some of the hottest hot wings I've ever had in my life.

Manhattan Pizza (760-632-0107; 143 West D St., Encinitas, CA 92024). Why be content to be just good when you can be good *and* giant? Manhattan Pizza sells by the pie or the slice, and produces the largest pizza in town: a supersized 28-inch round that will feed up to 12 people.

Sammy's Woodfired Pizza (760-438-1212; 5970 Avenida Encinas, Carlsbad, CA 92008). Sami Ladeki opened the first Sammy's Woodfired Pizza in north county nearly 20 years ago, and locals liked the smoky flavors and crisp crust so much that it wasn't long before Sammy's expanded to locations throughout San Diego. The LaDou's Barbeque Chicken Pizza is a signature dish featuring sweet barbeque sauce topped with chunks of chicken breast, smoked Gouda, red onion, and fresh cilantro. But the real star of the show is Sammy's famous dessert, the trademarked Messy Sundae®—vanilla ice cream served in an enormous wine glass and literally overflowing with caramel sauce, walnuts, fudge, and whipped cream.

Specialty Markets

Aniata Cheese Company (858-847-9616; 2710 Via de la Valle, B-138, Del Mar, CA 92014). In the Flower Hill Mall, just off I-5, this store is a favorite with local foodies and carries a wide variety of artisanal cheeses. Although their stock varies based on availability from small suppliers, expect pungent Camembert from France, buttery Kasseri from Greece, nutty Asiago from Italy, creamy Gouda from the Netherlands, and delicious offerings from California dairies, such as sheep's milk ricotta and goat cheese.

La Costa Farms (corner of La Costa Blvd. and Saxony Rd., Encinitas, CA, 92024). This open-air farm stand tucked between the cliffs of Encinitas and the Batiquitos Lagoon is a favorite with locals, where you can find farm-fresh fruits and vegetables and buy made-to-order flower arrangements. You'll also find the city's *best* chipotle salsa for sale, as well as bags of homemade tortilla chips.

Tip Top Meats (760-438-2620; 6118 Paseo del Norte, Carlsbad, CA 92009). "Big John" Heidrich started out with a butcher store in 1967, and Tip Top is still one of the best places in town to find high-quality sausages and specialty cuts. In addition, the store features a wide selection of gourmet items, including an extensive offering of European candy and jams. If you can't find what you're looking for, just ask: John is happy to fill special requests. Out back you'll find a small diner, specializing in breakfasts heavy on the meat.

Sweets and Treats

Bubby's (760-436-3563; 937 S. Hwy. 101, Encinitas, CA 92024). There are some foods that just don't translate outside of their places of origin: Croissants outside of France or bagels outside of New York, for example, are just never as good. And gelato outside of Italy? Thanks to Bubby's, a shop in the Lumberyard Mall in Encinitas, you don't have to go to Europe to get this rich, creamy, frozen treat. Bubby's has an intriguing rotating

La Costa Farms sells local produce and the freshest imports from throughout the West Coast.

menu with intriguing flavors, such as vanilla rosewater and lemon cheesecake. Just like in Italy, it is pricier than ice cream and served in tiny portions, but the flavors are so concentrated that a little goes a long way.

Carlsbad Danish Bakery (760-729-6186; 2805 Roosevelt St., Carlsbad, CA 92008). This bakery's authentic Danish pastries are about as good as you'll get outside of Copenhagen; don't miss the cinnamon custard bun or the lemon-filled pastry. You'll also find an array of crusty home-baked breads. Sadly, the bakery is closed on Sundays.

Champagne French Bakery and Café (858-792-2222; 12955 El Camino Real, San Diego, CA 92130). This Parisian-style bakery east of Del Mar serves fragrant pastries like chocolate croissants, cinnamon elephant ears, and deep, dark chocolate tortes.

Chuao (760-753-1350; 1935 Calle Barcelona, Carlsbad, CA 92008). Named *Chuao* after the Venezuelan region that grows some of the finest cacao beans (and coincidently pronounced "chew-wow"), this sweets boutique specializes in fine chocolate candies and desserts made with no artificial preservatives or flavorings. Each artisan-crafted morsel is displayed behind glass and lighted like a piece of costly jewelry—and the candy is well worth the dramatic presentation (and the hefty prices). The "Chevre" bon bon features goat cheese butter cream and black pepper (which goes surprising well with chocolate) and "Zen" is flavored with green tea and ginger.

Hillstreet Donuts (760-439-7741; 1926 S. Coast Hwy. 101, Oceanside, CA 92054). On Highway 101, just as you cross into Oceanside from Carlsbad, you'll find Hillstreet, an old-fashioned donut shop with tables to dine in. In addition to a wide selection of fresh, homemade donuts, Hillstreet also offers made-to-order smoothies.

St. Tropez Bakery and Bistro (760-633-0084; 947 S. Coast Highway 101, Encinitas, CA 92024). This cozy bakery and bistro is decorated in the bright yellows and blues of Provence, and murals of French scenes remind visitors of a sidewalk café almost anywhere in France. Croissants are lackluster and too soft to be authentic; stick with the numerous dessert pastries, such as the tiny raspberry and chocolate tarts or the crème brûlée. This is a wildly popular place on weekends, and it is a nice atmosphere to while away an hour with a passable café au lait or cappuccino.

Taquerias

La Especial Norte (760-942-1040; 664 N. Coast Hwy. 101, Leucadia, CA 92024). This long-time local favorite offers little curb appeal, but don't let the bars on the windows scare you away. The pleasant interior is almost always full at dinnertime, and the Mexican food is authentic and fresh. Rolled chicken tacos are crispy and flavorful, and the *molcajete*—strips of beef and cactus served with a piquant sauce inside a boiling hot stone bowl—is something you won't find most places. Their Mexican-style chicken soup, full of chicken breast chunks, rice, tomatoes, avocadoes, and sprigs of fresh cilantro is fortifying and delicious.

Los Olas (760-942-1860; 2655 S. Coast Hwy. 101, Cardiff-by-the-Sea, CA 92007). Just south of Chestfield Avenue, near the San Elijo Lagoon, Los Olas is a funky, always crowded, and usually noisy Mexican joint that serves up great fish tacos, as well as a pile of nachos at their artery-clogging best. They also feature Puerto Nuevo-style lobster (although not at Puerto Nuevo-style prices). The otherwise moderately priced food and full bar attract a young happy hour crowd. Parking is in a dirt lot next door. There is also a more family-friendly Los Olas in downtown Carlsbad (760-434-5850), although the large bar there gets rowdy in the evenings as well.

Roberto's (760 634-2909; 1900 Coast Hwy. 101, Leucadia, CA 92024). Roberto's in Leucadia, just south of the Carlsbad State Beach, cranks out hundreds of inexpensive, authentic tacos a day, made with thick, crispy corn tortillas and stuffed generously with shredded beef or chicken. (You'll want to pass on the fish tacos here.) This local chain has been serving addictive, slightly greasy food to surfers and others for years. The lines can be long during mealtime rush, but for $5 or less, it's worth the wait.

Roberto's taco stand in Leucadia is a favorite with surfers.

THEME PARKS AND ZOOS

LEGOLAND

760-918-5346
www.lego.com/legoland
1 Legoland Dr., Carlsbad, CA 92008
Open: Thursday–Monday (September–May) and daily from June–August; opens 10 AM;
closing varies seasonally
Admission: $44 for children under 13; $57 for adults

Sprawling across 128 acres in south Carlsbad, Legoland California is a triumph of engineering. Once you pass through the entrance gates (themselves designed to look like giant Legos), you enter a world of impressive building on a tiny scale. The park is divided into several zones, including Dino Island, Fun Town, Explore Village, Knights Kingdom, and Imagination Zone, each with attractions to match. At the heart of the park is Miniland USA, featuring scale models of a dozen U.S. cities. More than 20 million Legos were used to design Minitown alone, and no detail is left out to convey the flavor of the cities. The New York City scale model includes the 25-foot-tall Freedom Tower, anticipating the monument to be built on the site of Ground Zero in the real city someday. There is also a miniature New Orleans featuring a Mardi Gras parade and buxom Lego women shouting, "Mister, throw me some beads"; and a miniature Washington, D.C., displays a changing of the Honor Guard in front of a model of the U.S. Capitol and pink-blooming bonsai trees standing in for cherry blossoms around the model of the Tidal Basin.

The new water-themed pirate ride at Legoland promises to be a wet adventure for kids of all ages.

In addition to a staggering display of Lego building, the park boasts more than 50 rides and attractions, many of which are kid-powered via rope pulling, pedal pushing, and water squirting. You'll also find Wild Woods Golf, a Lego-themed miniature golf course (a round is an additional cost), and a huge playground featuring rope ladders and elaborate slides. In summer 2006, the park opened a major new attraction called "Pirate Shores," which features water slides, a pirate ship boat ride, and a playground structure dominated by a huge bucket that periodically dumps 600 gallons of water on anyone in the vicinity. More expansion is planned in the future. The park is landscaped beautifully, and looks as if it were established much earlier than 1999, thanks to the addition of full-size trees and palms. The lines are manageable throughout most of the year—with the exception of summer and holiday weekends, when the waits can build up later in the afternoon. The park always seems to have at least one attraction closed due to maintenance problems, however, and some of the rides are already showing wear in this relatively new park (e.g., the Lego characters in the "Fairytale Brook" ride could use a good scrubbing, and many of the brightly colored Lego displays throughout the park are starting to fade). Children past 10–12 will probably not be excited by the park, unless they are huge Lego fans. And adults will find little to occupy themselves if they are not accompanied by children, although Minitown is an impressive sight for just about anyone. Beware of height restrictions, which range from 34 to 48 inches for even the tamest rides. Waiting in a hot line only to be told your little one is *too* little could be the trigger for a memorable tantrum.

THE WAVE WATERPARK

www.thewavewaterpark.com
760-940-9283
101 Wave Dr., Vista, CA 92084
Open: Daily 10:30–5 (from the end of May through mid-September)
Admission: $14 for adults; $10.50 for children; $7 for spectators

A small family aquatic park in Vista, just east of Carlsbad, The Wave is a favorite summer destination for the under-16 crowd (and their parents). Cool off on the "Salsa Twist," a 35-foot tube slide; the "Slam Dunk," an enclosed waterslide that will plummet you three stories; or test your surfing skills on the "Flow-Rider," a simulator that promises the perfect wave every time. If you're looking to relax, try floating on an inner tube down the "Rio Loco," a lazy river that rings the perimeter of the park—but note that the river gets congested by lunchtime, so you might want to visit this attraction first. You aren't allowed to bring food into the park, but there is a decent onsite grill where you can buy pizza, chicken nuggets, and the like. Lockers are available for an additional price.

RECREATION: THE GREAT OUTDOORS

Beaches

Carlsbad State Beach (off Hwy. 101, north of La Costa Blvd.). **South Carlsbad Beach,** known to locals as Ponto Beach, has a paid parking lot ($8 for a weekend day, with seasonal passes available) and a long expanse of free street parking (although this can be hard to find, especially in the early morning hours, when surfers arrive before dawn). To get a truly expansive view of the ocean here, climb the well-maintained concrete stair-

Carlsbad State Beach attracts families and surfers.

case to the south of the parking lot, from the top of which you can see as far south as La Jolla on clear days. The crowds are generally manageable, and the beach is popular with families and local surfers alike.

Del Mar City Beach (accessed most easily from 15th St. and Coast Blvd.). Del Mar City Beach is one of the loveliest stretches of sand in Southern California, with bottle-glass green waves backed by ragged red cliffs and blanketed with miles of uninterrupted sand. Except during high tides, visitors can walk all the way down the coast from the northernmost stretch to Torrey Pines State Beach to the south. Several reefs off the coast make for good surf breaks, especially at 15th Street and 11th Street (the "neighborhoods" within the beach are named for the numbered streets that run perpendicular to the shoreline). Note that the everyday congestion here reaches nightmarish proportions during racetrack season in July and August, when your best bet is to arrive as early as possible (likely before the sun breaks through the summertime coastal haze) and plan to stay late, past the afternoon rush hour. From October through May, dogs are allowed to run at Rivermouth, the northernmost beach.

Moonlight State Beach (off Encinitas Blvd.). This beach lives up to its romantic name and is an excellent spot to watch the sunset (and wait for the moonlight). The waves can be huge here, and so this is quite popular with surfers and those who like to watch them. There are fire rings and volleyball courts just beneath the elevated parking lot.

Swami's Beach (off Hwy. 101, just south of the Self-Realization and Fellowship Center). Swami's has a tiny off-street parking lot that fills up quickly, but roadside parking is generally available if you aren't shy about walking. You'll need good legs anyhow to tackle the *very* steep staircase that leads from the top of the cliffs down to the shores, but your aerobic undertaking will be rewarded with a quiet beach, interesting cliff caves (a byproduct of coastal erosion), and good tide pooling (especially in January and February, when the tides are at their lowest). You're sure to see anemones, starfish, sea cucumbers, mollusks of all sorts, and—if you're patient—you might even seen tiny octopi. This is also a favorite of local surfers, who seem to defy gravity even before they hit the water, as they balance their cumbersome boards and navigate down the precarious staircase. During winter, when the swells are at their biggest, this is one of the best surfing beaches in the country, and a prime spot for watching the experts.

Oceanside City Beach (off N. Coast Hwy.). Just north of the Oceanside pier, behind the harbor, Oceanside City Beach has a nice covered picnic area, with a dozen tables. The beach is wide and long, and waves are good—this is the site of several surfing champi-onships throughout the year. But the water is frequently polluted, and the sands aren't as clean as you'll find to the south. If you're willing to walk a bit beyond the parking, this is a good place to find a little seclusion.

Canoeing, Kayaking, and Sailing

California Watersports (760-434-3089; 4215 Harrison St., Carlsbad, CA 92008). Rent aqua cycles, paddle boats, kayaks, and wave runners at this water center on the secluded Carlsbad Lagoon, a quiet, beautiful body of water just off the I-5. This is also home to the Snug Harbor Wake Boarding School, which offers group and private instruction as well as equipment rentals.

Diving and Snorkeling

North County Scuba Center (760-753-0036; 122 Encinitas Blvd., Encinitas, CA 92024). This organization has monthly boat trips to prime dive spots such as Wreck Alley, the Coronado Islands, and the La Jolla kelp beds. Instruction is available, from beginning certification to a refresher academic course.

Moonlight State Beach is popular with beach volleyball players, and attracts folks at night as well as during the day.

Visitors can rent boats and other watercraft at the picturesque Oceanside harbor.

USA Dive Shop Oceanside (760-722-7826; 225 Brooks St., Oceanside, CA 92054). Purchase dive equipment, or take scuba classes, from beginning certification to master diver programs. Also onsite is an adaptive scuba course for individuals with physical disabilities.

Fishing

The pretty Oceanside marina is the starting point for deep-sea fishing in the north county. Although there are fewer trips heading out than from Point Loma in the south county, it's often easier to book trips from here at the last minute. You'll also find several peaceful, protected lagoons in the north coastal region that allow fishing in limited areas.

Deep-Sea Fishing

Catch deep-sea fishing trips from Oceanside Harbor via **Helgren's Oceanside Sportfishing** (760-722-2133; 315 Harbor Dr. S., Oceanside, CA 92054), which offers daytrips to local kelp beds up to three miles out and multiple-day trips (up to six days) to Guadalupe and islands off the coast of Mexico, depending on where the fish are running.

Pier and Surf Fishing

Oceanside Pier (off Pier View Way) is the longest municipal wooden pier on the U.S. West Coast—so long that a golf cart is used to take visitors to the end! This is a popular spot for fishing, as well as a picturesque place to spend an afternoon. The crowds are generally smaller here than at piers to the south. As with all piers in San Diego, you won't need a fishing license, but catch limits are enforced.

Lagoons and Bays

The calm waters of **Agua Hedionda Lagoon** (north of Cannon Rd.), which translates to "stinking waters" (it was once a trash dump for Native Americans—but never fear; the bad smell is gone now) is a beautiful 400-acre saltwater lagoon that is popular for fishing croaker, halibut, and sea bass. Fishing is only allowed in the 50-acre passive-use portion of the lagoon, in the southeast section. **Batiquitos Lagoon** (off Batiquitos Dr.) can only be fished from the rock jetties at the mouth of the lagoon and from the rocks under I-5 (east or west of the freeway, but only on the north side). Avoid the marsh areas to protect waterfowl nesting sites. Fishing licenses are required at both lagoons.

Golfing

Arrowood Golf Course (760-967-8400; 5201A Village Dr., Oceanside, CA 92057). This relatively new course designed by Ted Robinson Jr. is located next to a protected wildlife refuge, which makes Arrowood a serene experience. The open course will please golfers with a range of skill levels. Green fee: $57–$100.

Encinitas Ranch Golf Course (760-944-1936; 1275 Quail Gardens Dr., Encinitas, CA 92024). With 18 championship holes carved into the bluffs of Encinitas, overlooking the ocean, Encinitas Ranch provides a scenic golfing experience on a par 72 course. The first nine holes are relatively straightforward, but the back nine provide a greater challenge. Green fee: $63–$95.

Four Seasons Aviara Golf Club (760-603-6900; 7447 Batiquitos Dr., Carlsbad, CA 92009). This pricey, gorgeous 18 hole course in the suburbs of south Carlsbad was designed by Arnold Palmer to take advantage of the lovely views of the adjacent Batiquitos Lagoon. The course has great variety and some especially difficult holes. Carts, included in the cost of the green fee, come with GPS systems that will pinpoint the exact distance from your cart to the pin. Green fee: $195–225.

Hiking

Batiquitos Lagoon Trail (trailhead is off Gabbiano Ln.; parking lot at trailhead). A flat three-mile out-and-back trail takes you along the waterline through coastal salt marshes and mudflats—one of the few remaining tidal wetlands in southern California. You'll see native scrub, abundant water birds, and plenty of locals getting some exercise. Information panels flank the trail, and benches are placed along the way so you can stop and enjoy the lagoon views. The **Batiquitos Lagoon Foundation** (760-91-0800) maintains a nature center at the west end of the hike, which offers guided walks.

San Elijo Lagoon (off La Orvilla). An ecological preserve, the lagoon and surrounding marshland is a birder's paradise: You'll likely see herons, egrets, and sandpipers. The trail is a flat four miles out and back, with water views most of the way. No biking is allowed, but you may share the trail with a few horses.

Parks

Leo Carrillo Park (760-476-1042; 6200 Flying LC Lane, Carlsbad, CA 92009). This 2004 addition to the Carlsbad city park system gives visitors a taste of old San Diego, with an expansive ranch and restored original adobe buildings. Leo Carrillo, a one-time

"Where the Turf Meets the Surf"

Hollywood legend Bing Crosby, along with pals Pat O'Brien, Jimmy Durante, and other tinsel town luminaries, founded Del Mar Thoroughbred racing in 1937, in what was then a sleepy seaside community, so that they could while away the summer hours betting on horses in a casual, relaxed atmosphere. Thanks to the cool seaside breezes and the charm of the Spanish Colonial architecture at what is now called the **Del Mar Racetrack and Fairgrounds** (858-755-1161; 2260 Jimmy Durante Blvd., Del Mar, CA 92014), Del Mar quickly became the place to be in August. In the early days it wasn't uncommon to see Lucille Ball and Desi Arnaz (who incidentally spent his final days living in the area), W. C. Fields, Ava Gardner, Bob Hope, Dorothy Lamour, and other stars of the golden era of cinema.

Hollywood glitterati still make the Del Mar race scene, and in recent years Rod Stewart, Leonardo DiCaprio, and Jessica Simpson, among others, have dropped by. But it isn't a casual affair anymore. These days it has grown into one of the best racing venues in the world and one of the biggest parties on the West Coast. Del Mar consistently posts record-breaking pari-mutuel exchanges (an average of $2.5 million a day), and track attendance has grown consistently over the past several decades. Races run six days a week (the track is closed on Tuesdays) in August through early September, with post times generally at 2 PM. Del Mar is home to the Pacific Classic, a Grade I event that draws the nation's top thoroughbreds and the season's largest crowds.

But Del Mar is about more than just racing and betting; it is a place to see and be seen. Opening day is "Hat Day," where ladies can show off outlandish chapeaus; family days are featured on the weekends, with activities, crafts, and special programs for children; and throughout the season live concerts are held after the Friday races, featuring nationally known artists.

reporter for Randolph Hearst, and—later in his life—an actor, best known for his role as Pancho in the 1950s *Cisco Kid* series, bought the ranch in 1937. He restored the 1800s-era buildings himself, which were originally built as the *Rancho de los Kiotes*. Carrillo renamed the ranch the Flying LC Ranch. The city acquired the land in 1977 from Carrillo's daughter, and undertook a second restoration of the farm and adobe dwellings at considerable cost, most of which was required to make the old mud buildings comply to current earthquake standards.

Visitors can stroll the trails, on the weekends take an informative and entertaining guided tour through the buildings (including a family living area that boasts a lavish sunken tub, an art studio that belonged to Leo's wife, and extensive stables), and observe native vegetation in the extensive gardens. Carrillo liked to entertain his Hollywood friends here (it's said that Clark Gable and Carole Lombard visited often), and he built an impressive outdoor kitchen with an open fireplace and extensive barbeque area alongside an in-ground pool. He even imported sand from the local beaches to surround the pool. Throughout the gardens are species of native cacti that are well over one hundred years old, and the pathways are lined with abundantly productive citrus trees, aloe vera plants, and a hybrid of the ubiquitous Southern California prickly pear—bred so that it is completely without thorns. Throughout the year there are community festivals that feature native crafts and demonstrations of how life on the old rancho might have been.

A unique feature of the park are the wild peacocks, descended from a flock Carrillo kept, that roam the grounds—including one rare all-white peacock. The grounds keepers feed them and discourage visiting children from chasing them, but otherwise leave them undisturbed. Visitors are apt to find shed specimens of the showy feathers on their hikes; but if you don't find one on your own, the docent's office at the front of the park will provide you with a feather in exchange for a small donation. This park hasn't truly been discovered yet, and except for an occasional group of children on a field trip, you're unlikely to see more than a handful of other people here. This is good news, because the hiking trails around the property are serene and provide an oasis in an otherwise bustling suburb. Open 10–5; closed Monday. Admission: Free.

Surfing

Surfing and pristine waves put coastal north county on the map, and even though the beach communities have grown and evolved, at the heart of many young and old residents alike is the search for perfect waves—and lots of them. Swami's is a world-famous surfing beach in Encinitas, chosen by *Surfing* magazine as one of the 10 best surfing cities in the country— only one of four in California and the *only* one chosen in San Diego County. Also check out 15th Street beach in Del Mar and Cardiff Reef, and farther north Leucadia State Beach, Ponto Beach (a.k.a. Carlsbad State Beach), and Tamarack Surf Beach in Carlsbad. Ocean-side Beach at the Strand and 6th St. are also popular. Diehard locals can be territorial, but the waves are open to anyone who dares.

Good surf schools include **Kahuna Bob's Surf School** (760-721-7700; 2526 Woodland Wy., Oceanside, CA 92054) and **Surfin' Fire** (760-473-2281; 6714 Lemon Leaf Dr., Carlsbad, CA 92011), which is run by local fire fighters.

A proud peacock at the Leo Carrillo Ranch park. Photo courtesy of Jon Preimesberger. Used with permission.

SHOPPING: EVERYTHING UNDER THE SUN

In addition to **Carlsbad Mall** (2525 El Camino Real, Carlsbad, CA 92008), a fairly generic retail center, there are some fun shopping options in the north coastal county. Cedros Design Center in Solana Beach has become the place for designers and decorating divas to find unusual furniture and accessories. **The Carlsbad Company Stores** (5600 Paseo del Norte, Carlsbad, CA 92009) is an upscale outlet mall featuring bargains on such name brands as Waterford, Coach, and Wedgewood. And the small and refined **Del Mar Plaza** (1555 Camino del Mar, Del Mar, CA 92014) has eclectic boutiques in a storybook outdoor setting.

The upscale Del Mar Plaza features eclectic boutiques and fine dining.

Antiques and Collectibles

Bellini's Antique Italia (858-509-9399; 118 S. Cedros Ave., Solana Beach, CA 92075). Located in the Cedros Design Center, Bellini's is an upscale shopping experience where the Italian wares are beautifully staged. You'll find primarily vintage Tuscan and Tuscan-inspired furniture here, as well as garden art, including glorious (and blisteringly expensive) antique olive oil jugs, patinaed statuary, and imposing fountains.

Bon Bon (858-792-1668; 301 Coast Hwy., Solana Beach, CA 92075). This Solana Beach antique store literally overflows with tempting items from Europe; the owners specialize in British and French wares, and the collection is always eclectic and fun. You'll find one-of-a-kind chandeliers, salvaged wrought-iron gates, and smaller accessories to give your home and garden a Continental flair.

Carlsbad Village Art and Antique Mall (760-730-9494; 2742 and 2752 State St., Carlsbad, CA 92008). With more than 15,000 square feet of display space and one hundred dealers, this is the best one-stop antique shopping experience for every budget and taste. Featured are displays of fine European antique furniture, American vintage "kitsch" from the 1940s and 1950s, and a large collection of U.S. Depression glass and flow blue pottery from England. You'll also find vintage surf art and Californiana here. It is an overwhelming space, as most antique warehouses can be, but it is well-organized, and friendly salespersons will go out of their way to help you find what you need.

White Lion (760-635-3668; 7750 El Camino Real, Ste. E, Carlsbad, CA 92008). A tiny consignment shop tucked into an almost unnoticeable strip mall in the tony La Costa neighborhood of Carlsbad, the White Lion has an eclectic collection of fine furniture, inexpensive and tasteful home decorating items, and vintage jewelry. The owner has arranged the pieces to perfection—down to an imitation cake on an antique Waterford crystal dessert stand. Even though the saleswomen can be less than hospitable and the location makes it out of the way for antique hunters, this relatively new shop is worth a look.

Books and Music

Blessings Christian Books and Gifts (760-434-8755; 540 Carlsbad Village Dr., Carlsbad, CA 92008). A small bookstore and gift shop, Blessings carries Christian books, music, magazines, greeting cards, and software. There is also a small gift section featuring costume jewelry and children's items.

Lou's Records (760-753-1382; 434 N. Coast Hwy 101, Encinitas, CA 92024). This independent music store draws people from throughout California, thanks to an impressive collection of new and used records, CDs, tapes, DVDs, and laserdiscs, representing almost any music genre you can imagine, including a large selection of local artists. The staff is friendly and knowledgeable, and if you can't find what you're looking for, chances are Lou's can order it for you.

Spin Records (760-434-0807; 370 Grand Ave., Carlsbad, CA 92008). If you can't make it to Lou's, come to Spin Records instead. This store also carries tough to find CDs (and records) and carries just about every genre.

Clothing

Barbarella (760-944-6754; 570 S. Coast Hwy., Encinitas, CA 92024). Sun worshipers will fall to their knees in this store, which features Brazilian and designer swimwear for women. Their fashions have been featured on some of the world's most beautiful bodies in the annual *Sports Illustrated* swimsuit edition.

Madison Leather & Luggage (760-434-1140, 2940 State St., Carlsbad, CA 92008). Accessorize to your heart's delight; this store features yummy designer handbags, shoes, and unusual scarves. You can also find fine leather totes and sunglasses.

Ooh La La (858-1896; 1555 Camino del Mar, Del Mar, CA 92014). In Del Mar Plaza, among an impressive collection of interesting and unique stores, this boutique stands out. You'll find a beautiful collection of glittering cocktail dresses and special-occasion accessories, including creamy leather handbags and hand-painted scarves.

Home Goods

Fiesta Imports (760-942-8842; 7720 El Camino Real, Carlsbad, CA 92009). The unusual decorative items in this artisan's market in south Carlsbad, near the La Costa Spa, reflect the cultural diversity of Southern California. All wares are imported from Latin America, including items from Peru, El Salvador, and Ecuador.

Gardenology (760-753-5500; 587 South Coast Hwy., Encinitas, CA 92024). In the heart of downtown Encinitas, this quaint store is a great place for gardeners—and design fans— to browse. Look for upscale outdoor furniture and accessories, with especially lovely European urns and whimsical garden statuary.

Leaping Lotus (858-720-8283; 240 S. Cedros Ave., Solana Beach, CA 92075). This rambling department store in the Cedros Design Center sells just about everything, from handmade clothing and dramatic costume jewelry to eclectic designs for the home. Look for charming accent pieces for the patio and garden, one-of-a-kind tableware, and fine small furnishings.

The Poached Pear (760-730-9050; 2946 State St., Carlsbad, CA 92008). In this downtown Carlsbad store you'll find Emile Henry cookware, hundreds of kitchen gadgets, fine table linens, and unusual serving pieces displayed in catalog-perfect arrangements.

Wall-to-wall yarn at the Black Sheep in Encinitas.

Just for Fun

The Black Sheep (760-436-9973; 1060 S. Coast Hwy. 101, Encinitas, CA 92024). This shop is nirvana for knitters and crocheters; you'll find fine yarns here that you won't find anyplace else, and even if you aren't crafty, it is worth a stop into this artistically displayed store to see examples of free-form crocheting, fanciful "junkyard fairies" created with yarn and beads, and the colorful walls lined with specialty yarns. And if the collection of samples inspires you, you can sign up for a number of workshops and learn to make the creations yourself.

Just Pretend (858-259-9079; 1555 Camino Del Mar, Ste. 106, Del Mar, CA 92014). After rubbing elbows with the stylish and beautiful people of Del Mar, you might find yourself feeling short on bling—and cash. Get yourself to Just Pretend in the trendy Del Mar Plaza Mall, where you can buy exceptionally convincing knock-offs of designer jewelry, including cubic zirconium set in 14-karat white and yellow gold that is almost prettier than the real thing.

Longboard Grotto (760-634-1920; 978 N. Coast Hwy. 101, Encinitas, CA 92024). The Longboard Grotto's motto is "not quite a museum but more than a surf shop," which speaks to its extensive collective of vintage boards on display. You can buy new and used boards here as well.

Maukilo (760-730-3633; 2835 Roosevelt St., Carlsbad, CA 92008). Nestled in the Carlsbad Village Mall, Maukilo features unique and hard-to-find European toys that are durable creations heavy on imagination and light on plastic.

Paint and Clay (760-632-5124; 7740 El Camino Real, Ste. C, Carlsbad, CA 92009). Pick out a piece of unpainted stoneware, choose your glazes, and then sit down at a worktable to create your own food-safe masterpieces. The store will add a clear glaze and then fire the piece, which you can retrieve a few days later. Pieces range in price from $5 to $50; the $6 studio fee covers the cost of your paints, and you can stay as long as you like.

Dixon Lake in Escondido is popular with fishermen and is a serene spot for picnics.

7

EAST COUNTY

Life East of I-5

A bumper sticker popular with surfers and other coastal residents a few years back proclaimed that "There Is No Life East of I-5." But visitors and residents now have plenty of evidence to dispute this rather unfriendly sentiment. Once home to ranches and dairy farms—and still one of the few areas in the county where you'll see horses (and ostriches and llamas!), east county is also home to beautiful estates, new home communities, and plenty of open space. This is where you'll find rambling outdoor shopping malls, plenty of golf courses, Las Vegas-style casinos, and a wide range of dining options.

The east county covers a lot of terrain and comprises a wide variety of socioeconomic strata. The upscale residential neighborhood Rancho Santa Fe just east of Solana Beach was ranked in 2005 by *Forbes* magazine as the second most expensive zip code in the country. The contrast couldn't be greater with little Ramona, east of Escondido, a tiny rural community at the foot of the Cuyamaca Mountains that features nostalgic mom and pop cafes and kitschy antique shopping.

Even farther up into the mountains, Julian is a quaint local tourist destination famous for its apple pies and *the* place where winter-deprived locals drive to see the occasional snow shower. Another community with a small-town feel, La Mesa, east of downtown, offers eclectic antique shopping and inexpensive and moderate restaurant options.

Closer to the heart of the action, Mission Valley, just northeast of downtown, was a dairy farm 50 years ago; now it is a shopping mecca, with Mission Valley Mall, Fashion Valley Mall, countless strip malls, dozens of budget-minded chain hotels and motels, and innumerable townhomes wedged among them. As the name indicates, this is also home to the Mission San Diego de Alcala, where San Diego began, and site of the Qualcomm Stadium, the current home to the San Diego Chargers football team.

East of Encinitas, Rancho Bernardo long had the reputation as a sleepy retirement community, but relatively affordable housing has attracted many young families to the area in recent decades, and golf carts are making way for tricycles on the local streets. And finally, San Marcos and Escondido lie east of Carlsbad, and are rich with freshwater lakes and prime sports fishing, and San Marcos's Old California Restaurant Row provides a collection of moderately priced dining establishments housed in an old-West-themed area.

LODGING

Lodging in many of the neighborhoods in east county tends to moderately priced large chains and inexpensive motels. These accommodations live up (or down) to the parent company's reputations, and it's easy enough for you to search the Internet for your favorite megahotel in this neighborhood if this is an appealing option to you (or if you have hotel points you need to use!). If you are looking to save a little money, this wide-ranging region might be a good choice. Mission Valley especially—just south of downtown, near the beaches, and surrounded by freeways for easy access—has dozens of fine chain lodging options in a variety of price ranges (e.g., Hilton, Sheraton, Marriott, Doubletree, Holiday Inn, Comfort Inn, Travelodge), and all are likely to be up to 25 to 50 percent less expensive in the Valley than their beach or downtown counterparts. But if you want to experience the local flavor and stay in an independent hotel in the east county, I've included a few of the best options below.

MISSION VALLEY
HANALEI HOTEL

Manager: Richard Donovan
619-297-1101; fax 619-297-6049
www.hanaleihotel.com
2270 Hotel Circle North, San Diego, CA 92108
Price: Inexpensive to Moderate
Credit Cards: AE, D, MC, V
Handicap Access: 4 full

This recently remodeled Polynesian-themed hotel has been a mainstay in Mission Valley for decades, and although it is now part of the Red Lion chain, it maintains a unique identity that is faithful to the Hanalei's history in the community. The renovated lobby is light and bright, with pale marble floors, wicker furniture, and a restrained smattering of tropical plants. The exterior is full-tilt Hawaiian, with lush tropical landscaping and a dramatic waterfall that terminates in a large, well-stocked koi pond. The Polynesian theme is more subdued in the spacious guest rooms, which feature traditional light-wood furniture, elegant patterned fabrics, and either a private balcony or veranda. The pool is surrounded by mature palm trees; there is also a large spa, a small fitness center, and a barber shop on site. The **Peacock Restaurant** serves casual California cuisine and the **Islands Sushi and PuPu Bar** offers a full-service sushi bar and Polynesian appetizers. The hotel includes a complimentary shuttle to and from Old Town, the nearby Fashion Valley shopping mall, and the Metro transit center (a hub for the bus and trolley system).

TOWN AND COUNTRY RESORT

Manager: Duke Sovek
619-202-4372; 619-291-3584
www.towncountry.com
500 Hotel Circle North, San Diego, CA 92108
Price: Inexpensive
Credit Cards: AE, D, DC, MC, V
Handicap Access: 20 full

Another San Diego perennial in the "hotel circle" in Mission Valley, the Town and Country Resort is a family-friendly destination priced to please. Guests can stay in the towers or in garden bungalows. The traditionally decorated hotel's most appealing feature is the mature, lush landscaping: The Town and Country claims to have more than 2,500 palm trees (most of them towering specimens), hundreds of species of ferns, and more than two thousand rose bushes on the large property. *Don't* come here if you're looking for luxury or opulence, despite what the fancy name implies. Guest rooms are spacious enough, but the accommodations are worn. Proximity to a freeway (and 40-year-old sound insulation) means that many of the rooms are noisy. *Do* come here if you are looking for an inexpensive hotel that is close to the action.

RANCHO BERNARDO AND RANCHO SANTA FE
THE INN AT RANCHO SANTA FE
Manager: Kerman Beriker
858-756-1131; 858-759-1604
www.theinnatrsf.com
5951 Linea Del Cielo, Rancho Santa Fe, CA 92067
Price: Expensive
Credit Cards: AE, D, DC, MC, V
Handicap Access: 2 full

Built on the former Rancho San Dieguito, a nearly 9,000-acre land grant ranch owned by Juan Maria Osuna in the 19th century (the restored original adobe structure still stands) is the prestigious, expansive Inn at Rancho Santa Fe. The original lodging was built as La Morada in 1924, designed by famed architect Lilian Rice. Guest cottages and suites are built to be part of a rambling hacienda set amid lush gardens, and each accommodation is unique. All have wood-burning fireplaces, flat-screen TVs, fine Italian linens, bright interiors, and huge bathrooms, many of which have spa tubs and multihead showers. There is a full-service spa onsite, with its signature eucalyptus scrub followed by a warm citrus oil massage. For an upscale property such as this one, the spa rates are reasonable, with massages averaging $100 an hour. Guests will enjoy tennis, golf, and lawn croquet, as well as onsite dining at the **Dining Room,** featuring "Rancho-inspired cuisine," and **Inn Fusion,** an Asian-inspired bistro.

RANCHO BERNARDO INN
Manager: John Gates
858-675-8500; fax 858-675-8501
www.ranchobernardoinn.com
17555 Bernardo Oaks Rd., San Diego, CA 92128

The Rancho Bernardo Inn is full of cozy sitting areas that make the large property feel intimate.

Price: Expensive
Credit Cards: AE, D, MC, V
Handicap Access: 4 full

The somewhat sleepy community of Rancho Bernardo is a favorite with golfers, who won't be disappointed with the Inn's 18-hole championship course, once the site of PGA events. The elegant hotel looks like a beautiful old hacienda, with antiqued plaster walls, ironwork embellishments, rich Spanish rugs, and cozy public spaces. The 287 spacious guest rooms are decorated with custom furniture in warm colors and dark wood. The well-dressed beds offer quality linens, and each room displays original artwork. Views include the lovely and somewhat rural golf course or the manicured grounds and gardens. Standard rooms offer a separate seating area, and all come with a patio or balcony. All bathrooms have deep soaking tubs, thick bath towels, and complimentary imported bath products. This is a full-service resort hotel, so after a long day on the links, indulge in a massage or facial treatment in the beautiful **Buena Vista Spa** or take a dip in one of the two sparkling pools. The Inn also offers six lighted tennis courts, although at the time this book went to print all but two of these were inaccessible because of construction. Note that the entire Inn enjoyed a $20 million update in early 2007, which includes a new 2,500 square foot lap pool and a hydrotherapy spa. You'll also find award-winning dining onsite (don't miss the exceptional **El Bizcocho**, see page 219) and several lounges where you can unwind with a cocktail or a cup of tea. Although the location is a bit remote, the Rancho Bernardo Inn offers a relaxing setting and impeccable service for those who don't mind commuting to the San Diego hot spots.

THE FAR EAST: JULIAN AND RAMONA
JULIAN HOTEL
Innkeepers: Steve and Gig Ballinger
760-765-0201; 800-734-5854

www.julianhotel.com
2032 Main St., Julian, CA 92036
Prices: Moderate
Credit Cards: AE, MC, V
Handicap Access: No

This tidy, appealing historic hotel was built in 1887 by Albert Robinson, a former slave from Missouri. It is thought to be the oldest continually operating hotel in the county, and its vintage façade commands attention on a prominent corner of Main Street. Step inside to a country Victorian gem, with leather-cushioned rocking chairs, brightly patterned red carpets, and curio cabinets stacked with books. Tables in the parlor, which doubles as the breakfast room, are strewn with wooden puzzles and old-fashioned games. The standard rooms are miniscule—with barely enough space to house a full-size bed, a tiny dresser, and a chair—but they all come with their own private bathrooms, albeit little ones. Iron beds are dressed with quilts, the walls are adorned with flowery wallpaper and borders, and the chandeliers look like vintage gas fixtures. Also available is the patio cottage, which has its own fireplace and a private veranda, and the honeymoon house that features a canopy bed, cast-iron fireplace, and a large antique clawfoot tub. You won't find televisions or even telephones in the rooms, and guests are discouraged from

The Julian Hotel is the oldest continually operating hotel in the county.

using their own cell phones in public areas. A complimentary afternoon tea and hot apple cider are served with homemade cakes, and in the morning expect a full hot breakfast featuring **Dudley's** (see pages 225–226) famous nut and raisin bread and the hotel's special blend of granola. Note that the hotel does not have its own parking; during the week, the streets empty by 4 PM and this is not a problem, but on weekends, expect to fight for a spot.

PINE HILLS LODGE

Owner: Terry Sheldon
760-765-1100; fax 760-765-1121
www.pinehillslodge.com
2960 La Posada Wy., Julian, CA 92036
Prices: Moderate
Credit Cards: AE, D, MC, V
Handicap Access: 1 full lodge room; no cabins

Just minutes from picturesque downtown Julian, Pine Hills Lodge is a rambling, bucolic property surrounded by trees. Guests can choose from cozy rooms in the historic main lodge or rustic, private cabins spread throughout the property. The six lodge rooms feature quilts, extensive wood trim, and—gulp—shared bathroom facilities. For about the same price, consider a cabin; although most share common walls, the wooded setting makes them private and romantic. The larger cabins have balconies, and the smaller ones have a pretty communal porch complete with Adirondack chairs. Interiors are bright and clean, with comfortable beds and plenty of pillows for snuggling. Each cabin has its own bathroom, some with clawfoot tubs. The "Pinecone" cabins have separate living rooms, and the "North Star" cabin is a separate building with a sitting room, wood-burning fireplace, and screened in porch. There's an inviting pub on the premises (although it is open only sporadically), where you can plunk down by a roaring fire and play board games or sip especially good martinis; sometimes you'll even find live entertainment. The lodge used to have regular dinner theater, but, sadly, management has discontinued this tradition. This lodge is a great choice if you want to get away from the congestion and parking nightmare of Main Street Julian on a weekend—and yet it's still close enough to pop in for dinner or a slice of pie.

CULTURE

It doesn't get more historic than the hills above Mission Valley, where the first European settlement was built around the Mission San Diego de Alcala; the east county is also home to several ranchos that preserve the legacy of early California. But if you're looking to enjoy the here and now, you'll find enormous casinos, boot-stomping dance halls, and even a mystery theater that will bring out your inner Agatha Christie.

Casinos

San Diego County has the largest concentration of Native American tribes (18) in the United States. Approximately 5,000 tribe members in the county live on tribal land, which accounts for nearly 130,000 acres. Of these, several local tribes run gaming casinos that feature Las Vegas-style gambling, entertainment, and world-class restaurants and accommodations, spas, and golf and host big-name live entertainment. Most of these are within 30 to 45 minutes from downtown. Among the largest are **Barona Casino** (619-443-2300, 888-7-BARONA; 1932 Wildcat Canyon Rd., Lakeside, CA 92040), **Harrah's Rincon Casino and Resort** (760-751-3100, 877-777-2457; 3375 Valley Center Rd., Valley Center, CA

92082), **Sycuan Resort and Casino** (619-445-6002, 800-2-SYCUAN; 5469 Dehesa Rd., El Cajon, CA 92019), and **Viejas** (619-445-5400, 800-847-6537; 5000 Willows Rd., Alpine, CA 91901).

Gardens

Summers Past Farm (619-390-1523; 15602 Olde Hwy. 80, Flinn Springs, CA 92021). This 4-acre beauty in east county is both a retail nursery and an exhibit space, featuring a secret walled garden, a children's garden, and an extensive collection of herbs. Admission is free, and the facility is closed Mondays and Tuesdays. There is also a coffee bar onsite and a gift shop.

The Water Conservation Garden (619-660-0614; 12122 Cuyamaca College Dr. W., El Cajon, CA 92019). Although San Diego looks like a lush tropical paradise, especially along the coastline, the habitat is actually a semiarid desert. The 4.5-acre Water Conservation Garden at the Cuyamaca College in Rancho San Diego is dedicated to teaching local gardeners about xeriscaping, a waterwise approach to landscaping that promotes the use of native plants and plants that are indigenous to other arid climates. The garden is open seven days a week 9–5, and admission is free, as are the docent-led tours every Saturday.

Historic Places

Mission Basilica San Diego de Alcala (619-281-8449; 10818 San Diego Mission Rd., San Diego, CA 92108). Padre Junípero Serra, along with explorer Gaspar de Portolá, arrived in San Diego in 1769 to establish this first of 21 Spanish missions in California. The San Diego mission was originally located on Presidio Hill, site of the current Serra Museum,

Behind the façade of the Mission San Diego de Alcala, visitors can see excavations of the original settlement.

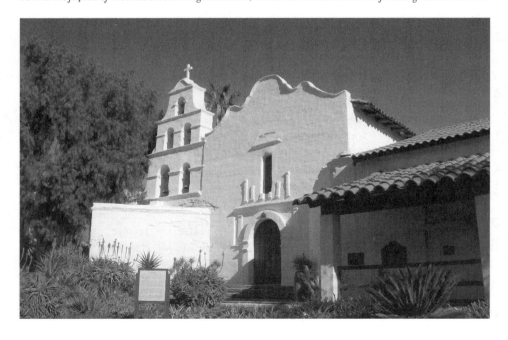

but the fathers moved it 6 miles inland in 1774 for better farmland and a more reliable source of water. The mission was built and rebuilt many times after it was destroyed by fires, and what is displayed today dates to 1931, when the mission was rebuilt to look like the church in 1813. Self-guided tours take visitors through Father Serra's apartment, which is sparsely furnished with a bed and a table. The small, dark chapel features a few nice statues, including an armless depiction of Christ that was purchased in Rome, and a Madonna and Child. The *campanario*, or bell tower, is nearly 50 feet tall. Most bells are not historic, with the exception of the bell on the lower right, which has been named Ave Maria Purisima; it was cast in 1802 and hung at the mission in 1931. Also onsite is the Padre Luis Jayme Mission Museum, which displays artifacts from the mission era, including religious vestments and statuary, as well as bottles and pottery. Archaeological excavations are ongoing, and volunteers are welcome to help with the dig on Saturdays (be sure to call ahead). Entry to the mission is via the gift shop, which has a nice selection of religious artifacts, including handcrafted rosaries from around the world. Open daily 9–4:45. Adults $3, seniors and students $2, children $1.

Rancho de los Penasquitos (858-484-7504; Canyon Side Rd., San Diego, CA 92129). This 1823 adobe ranch house was constructed as part of San Diego County's first Mexican land grant. It was built for the commander of the San Diego Presidio, and expanded in 1862 for the niece of prominent San Diegan Pio Pico, California's last Mexican governor. On weekends guests can tour the ranch house, and throughout the week visitors are welcome to hike the 3,700-acre preserve that surrounds the home. Admission is by donation. Open daily 8–sunset.

Rancho Guajome Adobe (760-724-4082; 2210 N. Santa Fe Ave., Vista, CA 92083). This beautifully preserved 22-room Spanish–Mexican adobe ranch house in Vista, just east of Carlsbad, dates from 1853 and is one of the best remaining examples of the prosperous ranchos that thrived in north county during the 19th century. Throughout the year there are festivals that showcase skills that were needed to survive in early California, such as calf roping, acorn milling, and basket weaving. Open for tours Saturdays and Sundays. Note that tours are cancelled during rain or after storms big enough to cause muddy conditions. Adults $3, children $1.

San Pasqual Battlefield State Historic Park (760-737-2201; 15808 San Pasqual Valley Rd., Escondido, CA 92025). Eight miles south of downtown Escondido, this historic park marks the spot of the decisive December 6, 1846, battle of the Mexican American War (which is recreated annually by volunteers). A visitor center points out landmarks. Admission is free. Open Saturday and Sunday 10–5.

Museums

Escondido History Center and Heritage Walk (760-743-8207; 321 N. Broadway, Escondido, CA 92025). Located in Grape Day Park, this complex of historical buildings includes the charming Bandy Blacksmith Shop, a pretty Victorian house, Escondido's first library building, the 1888 Santa Fe Railroad Depot along with a train car, and an antique windmill. The restored structures were saved from demolition on other sites, and were moved to the History Center for visitors to enjoy. Open Tuesday–Saturday 1–4. Admission free.

Guy B. Woodward Museum (760-789-7644; 645 Main St., Ramona. CA 920065). Stroll through Ramona's pioneer past at this small collection of weathered old wooden buildings, including a jailhouse, blacksmith shop, and a cowboy bunkhouse that looks like it is straight from a Hollywood western. Inside the Verlaque House onsite, the oldest home in Ramona, you'll find more than 2,500 vintage photographs of the original settlers of Ramona, as well as a collection of several hundred antique dresses and accessories. Open Thursday–Sunday 1–4. Admission $3.

Theater

California Center for the Performing Arts (760-839-4138, 800-988-4253; 340 N. Escondido Blvd., Escondido, CA 92025). Built to be the cultural center of the north inland county, the California Center for the Performing Arts is a sprawling campus that includes performance halls, classrooms, display spaces, and public art in the form of large outdoor sculptures. In addition to an elegant 1,500-seat concert hall, there is a 400-seat theater, a visual arts museum, art and dance studios, and a meeting hall for community outreach programs. The Center has hosted nationally recognized entertainers, including Olivia Newton John, the Bolshoi Ballet, and singer Kris Kristofferson. Each year in late December the Center hosts the award-winning San Elijo Dance and Music Academy's production of *The Nutcracker*, directed by renown dancers Ben and Lauri-Michelle Houk and featuring lush costumes, imaginative scenery (kids will love the noisy battle scene), and live music provided by the San Diego Civic Youth Orchestra.

Cygnet Theatre (619-337-1525; 6663 El Cajon Blvd., San Diego, CA 92115). Cygnet is a small, provocative theater company with an intimate performance space near San Diego State University. The company performs avant-garde pieces as well as puts a new spin on traditional works.

Mystery Café Dinner Theatre (619-544-1600; 1081 Camino del Rio S., Ste. 223, San Diego, CA 92108). Funny, interactive mysteries are performed at the **Imperial House Restaurant** (505 Kalima St., San Diego, CA 92101); be prepared to roll up your sleeves and help figure out whodunit. Playing Friday and Saturday.

Nightlife

Hot Monkey Love Café (619-469-4113; 6875 El Cajon Blvd., San Diego, CA 92115). A unique performance venue that features live music and dancing in an alcohol-free environment, this family-owned and managed club welcomes music lovers of all ages to enjoy rock, salsa, jazz, and folk music. Although you won't find bar beverages at this Bohemian hangout, you can purchase tasty smoothies and specialty coffees.

In Cahoots (619-291-1184; 5373 Mission Center Rd., San Diego, CA 92108). In Mission Valley, this is one of the most popular western nightclubs close to the city, with a huge dance floor and a lively DJ. Free dance lessons are offered Tuesday–Saturday. Cover charge varies.

Seau's (619-291-7328; 1640 Camino del Rio N., Ste. 1378 San Diego, CA 92108). Former professional football player for the San Diego Chargers, Junior Seau's sports-themed grill serves burgers, pasta, and sandwiches in this Mission Valley venue, but the real draw is the sports bar: Watch your favorite teams on 60 television monitors and the largest projection screen in San Diego, and keep your eyes open for local sports legends, who are known to frequent Seau's.

Seasonal Events

February is grapefruit season, and what better way to celebrate the dieter's favorite than the **Borrego Springs Grapefruit Festival** (760-767-5555) with music, food, crafts, and children's activities. And while you're in the desert this month, check out the wildflowers in **Anza-Borrego Desert State Park** (760-767-4684). Blooming times vary, depending on rainfall, but peak viewing season is only for two or three weeks, so make sure to call ahead.

The picturesque mountain town of Julian isn't just for apple pie; in May check out the **Julian Wildflower Show** (760-765-1857), which showcases a display of wildflowers that were gathered within a 15-mile radius of the town. And while you're in the neighborhood, swing by Ramona for the **Annual Ramona Air Fair** (760-789-1311) at the quaint Ramona Airport. Admission is free to see aircraft demonstration "fights," hot air balloons, music, and fireworks.

June is the start of the **Park at Dark** (760-747-8702) at the San Diego Wild Animal Park in Escondido; the park stays open during evening hours and presents special shows and live music. This is also a good time to check out the nocturnal animals on display.

To celebrate the founding of the first mission in California, the Mission San Diego de Alcala in mid-July, the **Festival of the Bells** (619-281-8449) features the ringing of the Alcala tower bells. Then head for the hills in Julian for the **Julian Gold Rush PRCA Rodeo** (760-765-1857), a full-scale event featuring barrel racing and bull roping.

Check out the parade of pre-1970s hotrods held on Friday nights throughout September during **Cruisin' Grand** (760-745-8877) in downtown Escondido. Beginning in mid-September and continuing through early November, the **Annual Julian Fall Apple Harvest** draws street-clogging crowds to this little town in the Cuyamaca Mountains to sip cider, sample some of the best apple pies available outside of my mother's kitchen, and stock up on the crisp crop straight off the trees. And in late September catch the annual **KGB Sky Show** (www.101kgb.com), a spectacular fireworks extravaganza choreographed to rock music held at the Qualcomm Stadium in Mission Valley.

Keep your eyes on the skies in mid-October for the annual **Air Show** (858-577-4099) held at the Miramar Marine Corps facility and featuring the famous Blue Angels precision flying team as well as other aeronautic acrobats; grandstand seating is pricey and sells out quickly, but blanket seating is free. If you're looking for a quieter activity, head to Escondido for the **Mum Festival at the Wild Animal Park** (760-747-8702); the colors of autumn come alive here in a brilliant display of chrysanthemums. Also this month, be sure to catch the annual **San Diego Asian Film Festival** (858-565-1264). And if you want to enjoy an old-fashioned Halloween, don't miss the **Pumpkin Patch** at Bates Nut Farm in Valley Center, east of Escondido (760-749-3333; 15954 Woods Valley Rd., Valley Center, CA 92082), where you'll find acres of pumpkins, a hay maze, horse-drawn buggy rides, and special activities for children.

In November, El Cajon hosts the charming **Mother Goose Parade** (619-444-8712) on the Sunday before Thanksgiving, a nationally televised parade that features more than two hundred floats, bands, and equestrian demonstrations.

In early December, head to Escondido for the annual re-creation of the **Battle of San Pasqual** (760-737-2201) at the San Pasqual Battlefield State Historic Park; watch as costumed historians interpret Mexican General Andrés Pico's battle with General Stephen Watts Kearny. **Christmas in the Village** (619-462-3000) in La Mesa celebrates the holidays the old-fashioned way: With carolers, horse-drawn carriage rides, and a festive outdoor market. Don't miss the **Wild Animal Park Festival of Lights** (760-747-8702) at the San Diego Wild Animal Park in Escondido, when the always lovely gardens transform into a holiday fairyland with more than 100,000 lights; there is even a sledding hill with real imported snow for the winter-deprived youth of San Diego to enjoy. Finally, football fans will not want to miss the **Pacific Life Holiday Bowl** (619-283-5808) held in Qualcomm Stadium at the end of the month, a postseason football game between two college teams from the PAC 10 and the Big 12 that is preceded by the **Pacific Life Holiday Bowl Parade** held along the downtown waterfront and featuring giant inflatable balloon characters, marching bands from across the country, and floats.

RESTAURANTS AND FOOD PURVEYORS

Restaurants

Much like the lodging options, restaurant options are heavily weighted in this area to large chains. It's easy enough to drive down the main corridors and see national favorites, but there are a few San Diego originals to be found, and many of these are old-time favorites.

LA MESA

CASA DE PICO
Owner: Diane Powers
619-463-3267
www.casedepico.com
5500 Grossmont Center Dr., La Mesa, CA 91942
Open: Daily
Price: Moderate
Cuisine: Mexican
Serving: L, D
Credit Cards: AE, D, DC, MC, V
Handicap Access: Yes
Reservations: No
Parking: Mall parking lot

For nearly three decades, Casa de Pico was the popular anchor restaurant in the Bazaar del Mundo, the colorful outdoor Mexican market in Old Town San Diego. In 2005, however, for reasons few locals understood (and fewer agreed with), owner Diane Powers lost her lease, and the Old Town dining area was rethemed as the old-western Plaza del Posada by the out-of-town vendor who underbid Powers. Many long-time San Diegans lamented the loss of what was the venue of important family celebrations throughout the years. However, all is not lost: After exhausting her legal options, Powers picked up the restaurant and moved to the edge of the Grossmont Center Shopping Mall in La Mesa (turn left into Entrance #3 of the mall and you'll find Casa de Pico on your immediate right). Although the La Mesa location cannot compete with the ambiance of Old Town, the new restaurant is nevertheless a colorful, lively space inside, with large murals on the walls and Mexican crafts throughout. Friendly servers, strolling mariachis, and a "tortilla lady" in the front churning out hundreds of paper-thin handmade tortillas all remind visitors of the legacy of the Casa de Pico. But let's face it: People come to Casa de Pico for one reason: the unbelievable food. The buttery *carne asada* seasoned with lime and wrapped in tortillas fresh off the griddle takes Mexican food to a higher realm, as does the Mexican chopped salad with grilled chicken, black beans, avocados, and cilantro-lime dressing. For big appetites—or for people who have a hard time deciding among favorites—the *macho grande* combination is an excellent choice, with *carne asada*, a chicken taco, cheese enchilada, tamale, and chili relleno. The fish-bowl-sized margaritas are as delicious in this new location as they ever were, especially the creamy mango variety. Even though Casa de Pico isn't the same outside of Old Town, this is still one of my favorite Mexican restaurants in the city. Judging by the crowds that continue to pack into Casa de Pico, San Diegans agree. Sombreros off to Powers, who once again proves you can't keep a good woman—or a good restaurant—down.

The relocated Casa de Pico maintains a festive atmosphere, despite its location in a megamall.

CHEF AXEL EUROPEAN BISTRO

Chef: Axel Dirolf
619-460-7942
www.chefaxel.com
7097 University Ave., La Mesa, CA 91941
Open: Wednesday–Saturday; Sunday for brunch only
Price: Moderate
Cuisine: German and Continental
Serving: L, D
Credit Cards: AE, D, MC, V
Handicap Access: Yes
Parking: Street

Before opening this bistro in east county, Chef Axel cooked for the likes of the U.S. Olympic team and British and Saudi royalty, as well as for fine restaurants and resorts throughout Europe. Despite the exalted client list, food in this bistro is comforting and simple, prepared to highlight the fresh ingredients and ever mindful of tradition. You'll find a nice selection of German wine and beer, along with German specialties that are a mix of familiar recipes and modern interpretations. To start consider the pan-fried sauerkraut cakes served with house-made sausages and pickles, or the Black Forest prosciutto, tomato, and mozzarella salad. Take it from Julie Andrews in *The Sound of Music*: Schnitzel is a favorite thing. Chef Axel serves tender, pan-fried pork cutlets with a traditional light breading, "hunter style" with a creamy mushroom sauce, "gypsy" style with peppers and paprika sauce over the top, or topped with ham and melted Swiss cheese. To accompany your meal, choose from homemade spaetzle (German flour dumplings), savory red cabbage, or tangy German-style potato salad. Other options include roasted rack of lamb, German beef roulade, and simply prepared fresh fish. Whatever you order, save room for the homemade apple strudel for dessert. There is also a deli onsite, where you can purchase sliced meats and cheeses, a wide variety of handmade sausages (turkey bratwurst, Bavarian veal sausage, classic frankfurters), and seasonal specialties like spicy pfeffernuss cookies and stollen.

MISSION VALLEY
ADAM'S STEAK AND EGGS

Owner: Ted Samoris
619-291-1103
1201 Hotel Circle S., San Diego, CA 92108
Open: Daily
Price: Inexpensive
Cuisine: American
Serving: B
Credit Cards: AE, D, DC, MC, V
Handicap Access: Yes
Reservations: No
Parking: Lot

A breakfast-only restaurant (open until 1 PM on the weekends) that has been a local favorite since 1962, Adam's is a homey place to enjoy a relaxing first meal of the day, featuring American and Mexican breakfast classics. The dark-wood-paneled walls and country décor are worn, as is the exterior, and it stands apart from the many tourist-oriented dining options in the Hotel Circle area, where this restaurant (and **Albie's** next door) is located. Although tourists are welcome, locals predominate; don't come if you're in a rush, because the place is generally crowded, you may have to wait for a table, and the service can be a little slow when it's busy. The wait staff is exceptionally friendly here, though, and the food is a good value for the money. The signature steak and eggs—or the Mexican variety of the same, *carne asada* and eggs—is generously proportioned and served with a good cup of coffee. Other options are the flapjacks served with smoky bacon and the *huevos rancheros* (eggs served on top of corn tortillas and sauced with *pica de gallo*). Regulars swear by the corn fritters.

ALBIE'S BEEF INN

Owner: Ted Samoris
619-291-1103
1201 Hotel Circle S., San Diego, CA 92108
Open: Monday–Saturday
Price: Moderate
Cuisine: American
Serving: L on weekdays; D
Credit Cards: AE, D, DC, MC, V
Handicap Access: Yes
Reservations: No
Parking: Lot

Adjacent to **Adam's Steak and Eggs** and next door to the Travelodge Motel in Hotel Circle, you'll find this kitschy, clubby 1960s-era steak house and piano bar, which offers an open mike and nightly sing-alongs. Clad in warm pine paneling and decorated with black leatherette chairs and banquettes and a giant taxidermied sports fish, the interior looks like it's straight out of a Doris Day and Rock Hudson flick—slightly frayed around the edges but comfortable. The dining room at lunchtime is heady with testosterone, as men's men knock back a few and power down beef like they did in the days before we knew about cholesterol. For dinner start with bar favorites like shrimp cocktail, potato skins, and fried calamari. For the main course, expect traditional meat-and-potato staples like filet mignon wrapped in bacon, aged prime rib, and lamb with mint jelly. You'll also find a few fresh fish dishes, prepared to your specifications. Side salads arrive in a big communal bowl, undressed, for you to serve yourself family style, and expect a large, whole carrot as a side with just about everything. Finish off with a tasty four-layer chocolate cake or a slice of creamy New York cheesecake. This place is certainly doing *something* right, because the loyal clientele has been coming back for nearly 40 years.

Superstar Chef Gaven Kaysen of El Bizcocho gained international fame as the U.S. representative for the prestigious Bocuse d'Or in 2007.

RANCHO BERNARDO
EL BIZCOCHO
Chef: Gavin Kaysen
858-675-8550
www.ranchobernardoinn.com/bizcocho
17550 Bernardo Oaks Dr., Rancho Bernardo, CA 92128
Open: Daily
Price: Very expensive
Cuisine: Continental
Serving: D, Sunday brunch
Credit Cards: AE, D, DC, MC, V
Handicap Access: Yes
Reservations: Recommended
Parking: Valet or nearby lot

Talented young chef Gavin Kaysen has breathed life back into "El Biz," the signature restaurant at the **Rancho Bernardo Inn** (see pages 209–210). In addition to the stellar service for which the restaurant has always been known, thanks to Kaysen now guests can enjoy some of San Diego's most creative food here as well, in a quiet, romantic dining room that looks more like a beautifully decorated private dining space than the public space that it is. The menu changes seasonally, but Kaysen promises to keep his signature appetizer throughout the year: Chilled Maine lobster is winningly paired with avocado, sweet brioche, peppery sprouts, and an aromatic vanilla and orange vinaigrette. However the menu morphs, count on perfectly fresh seafood, lamb, and veal. Diners can order courses à la carte to create their own experience or put themselves into the capable hands of the chef and choose among three tasting menus—a vegetarian-based menu, a seafood-based menu, and a "grand" menu that features a combination of shellfish and red meat. Excitement piqued at the El Bizcocho in January of 2007, when Kaysen was chosen from among more than five hundred contestants to represent the United States at the prestigious Bocuse d'Or cooking competition held in Lyon, France, where 24 of the world's best chefs engaged in a culinary battle of epic proportions in the great gastronomic capital. Although Kaysen didn't place in the top three, he garnered worldwide attention for El Bizcocho.

SAN MARCOS AND ESCONDIDO
HACIENDA DE VEGA
Owner: Alonzo Vega
760-738-9805
www.haciendadevega.com
2608 S. Escondido Blvd., Escondido, CA 92025
Open: Daily
Price: Moderate
Cuisine: Mexican
Serving: L, D, and Sunday brunch
Credit Cards: AE, MC, V
Handicap Access: Yes
Reservations: No
Parking: Two lots on either side

This beautiful 1.6-acre property is lushly landscaped with bougainvillea vines and palm trees and is accented throughout with sparkling water fountains. The main restaurant is housed in a 1930s adobe hacienda, but if the weather permits, forgo the charming interior and sit outside on the enormous outdoor dining patio, circling a pool-sized pond and a waterfall that seems

The Hacienda de Vega has a charming small dining room.

to flow right out of the roof of the restaurant. The quiet grounds, the sounds of flowing water, and the breezes rustling through the palm fronds are transporting. Recipes are traditional, homestyle Mexican—highly authentic and more like meals you'll encounter in Mexico than many of the Americanized Mexican restaurants throughout the city. The Sunday brunch at Hacienda de Vega is a tremendous value: For $16, you get an all-you-want plate of nine different side dishes (including delicious handmade corn tortillas, spicy shredded chicken, barbeque beef, tomato-sauced scrambled eggs, and refried beans) along with a huge serving of your breakfast entrée of choice. The scrambled eggs with chorizo should be called chorizo with eggs, because this dish is so stuffed with spicy sausage! For lunch and dinner, consider the *sampler del patron* for two, which includes a selection of tostadas, two *sopes* (stuffed tortillas), and two quesadillas—plenty enough for dinner, especially when paired with a specialty margarita. A lighter choice is the *ensalada de jicama*, a tossed combination of Mexican jicama, tangerine, mixed greens, and roasted almonds, topped with a tangy citrus dressing. Specialty entrees include the *filete de Vega*, a grilled filet mignon topped with chile sauce and served with potatoes and zucchini; the *pollo poblano*, a boneless chicken breast served with a rich, dark chile sauce; and tequila shrimp, sautéed in a spicy salsa and served with tortillas over white rice.

INDIA PRINCESS

Owner: Jesse Singh
760-744-7599
www.indiaprincess.com
1020 W. San Marcos Blvd., San Marcos, CA 92069
Open: Daily

Price: Moderate
Cuisine: Northern Indian
Serving: B Sun., L Mon.–Fri., D Mon.–Sun.
Credit Cards: AE, D, MC, V
Handicap Access: Yes
Reservations: Not necessary
Parking: Adjacent lot

The rustic wood and exposed-brick and stucco exterior proclaim a western theme that reminds visitors of Old California, but as soon as you step inside and catch the smells of exotic spices heavy in the air, you won't expect cowboy food. The interior is a little dark and uninspiring, but once the food arrives, it hardly matters. The servers are extremely gracious and will remember your favorite dishes from visit to visit. To start, your waiter will bring you an appetizer of *papadum*, a thin spicy wafer, served with wickedly hot onion chutney. You'll want to wash this down with something right away, lest your tongue spontaneously combust. Start out with a mango *lassi*—a refreshing (sweet) drink made from yogurt and mangoes—or a *chai*—hot tea brewed with milk and spices. The range of vegetarian entrees is impressive. There are also plenty of fish, lamb, and chicken offerings. The chicken *tikka masala* is arguably the best in the city— with large chunks of tandoori-cooked chicken breast smothered in a complex tomato-based sauce flavored with dozens of sweet and savory spices. The *palak paneer* is a soothing companion; creamed and pureed spinach is served with fresh chunks of yogurt cheese, and the dish is lightly flavored with cardamom. Chicken and lamb tandoori are aromatic and juicy, and the curries are creamy and well-balanced. You can customize any dish when ordering to get the appropriate level of spiciness. Finish with *kulfi*, an Indian ice cream made from sweetened condensed milk and either mangos or pistachios. If the dishes are dauntingly unfamiliar, try visiting India Princess for lunch during the week or for brunch on Sunday, when they serve a moderately priced buffet (with all dishes labeled) so that you can discover your own favorites.

MARIETA'S
Owner: Salvador Lopez
760-752-1765
www.oldcalrestaurantrow.com/marietas
1020 W. San Marcos Blvd., San Marcos, CA 92069
Open: Daily
Cost: Inexpensive
Cuisine: Mexican
Credit Cards: MC, V
Serving: L, D, Sunday brunch
Handicap Access: Yes
Reservations: Reservations suggested for large parties
Parking: Lot

Located in the Old California Restaurant Row in San Marcos, Marieta's is a family-run operation, and the friendly service makes you feel welcome right away with fresh tortilla chips and salsas. There is a full bar, and margaritas here are a good value. The house specialties range from *enchiladas del mar*, shrimp wrapped in corn tortillas and smothered in a tangy green tomatillo sauce—to *carnitas* (a Mexican-style pork roast) to *barbacoa*, tender chunks of beef simmered in a spicy barbeque sauce. You can also custom order a combination featuring your favorite items. Their handmade tamales (pork or chicken) and their shredded beef tacos are standouts. Meals are served with rice and possibly the best refried beans in the city. Finish with homemade flan (a firm custard in caramel sauce) or a *churro*, the Mexican version of a donut. From 9 to 11 AM on Sundays Marieta's features a brunch that includes any of their standard breakfast items (e.g., *huevos con chorizo*, chorizo sausage scrambled with eggs, or omelet Marietas with avocado and cheese—all served with rice, tortillas, and their signature beans) plus fresh fruit and your choice of juice, coffee, or champagne for an extremely reasonable price. You will not walk away hungry.

SAND CRAB CAFÉ
Owners: Sandy and Rita Crabbe
760-480-2722
www.sandcrabcafe.com
2229 Micro Pl., Escondido, CA 92029
Open: Daily
Price: Moderate
Cuisine: Seafood
Serving: L, D
Credit cards: D, MC, V
Handicap Access: Some
Parking: Lot

A little bit of the Low Country in San Diego County, the Sand Crab Café is incongruently located inland, on the Escondido–San Marcos border, hidden in the middle of a light industrial park. (Call ahead for directions or you probably won't find it.) The place is not much to look at on the outside, but don't let that worry you: Inside you'll find a friendly and funky neighborhood bar and restaurant, with butcher paper on the tables and maritime memorabilia hanging from the ceilings and tacked to the dark paneled walls. Each table comes equipped with a big galvanized bucket to toss in shells, a roll of paper towels, and wooden mallets to pound out the crabs. There are a few landlubber choices, including a kids' menu featuring traditional fare, but the point of this place is seafood. Try the fried clam strips, prepared fresh and served with several dipping sauces, or the spicy and thick seafood gumbo. For the main course, be sure to order a combo that includes stone crab claws, shrimp, tiny slipper-tail lobsters, Louisiana-style sausage, boiled new potatoes, and corn on the cob. Be prepared: Your server will dump it out directly on your table; make sure to use the plastic bib provided, because you *will* need it for this

messy, highly interactive meal. If you have room for dessert, try the gooey, chocolaty Snickers cheesecake or the sweet, crunchy apple burrito. The lovely owners, Rita and Sandy Crabbe (yes, these are their real names—the place is named after Sandy) will encourage newcomers to sign their guest register, and you'll walk away with a bumper sticker that says, "I got crabs at the Sand Crab Café."

THE FAR EAST: JULIAN AND RAMONA
JULIAN CAFÉ AND BAKERY
Owner: Cara Teeter
760-765-2712
2112 Main St., Julian, CA 92036
Open: Daily
Price: Inexpensive
Cuisine: American
Serving: B, L, D
Credit Cards: AE, MC, V
Handicap Access: No
Reservations: No
Parking: Street (very limited on weekends)

Housed in a historic 1872 building that originally served as a general store, this homestyle café packs them in on the weekends; there is almost always a line out the door, especially for Sunday breakfasts. Inside cowboy chic mixes with country kitsch; there are rawhide candle holders, horseshoes on the walls, and vintage photos everywhere. You'll be served soft drinks in glasses shaped like cowboy boots, and the wooden tables are branded. The food is straightforward and served in large portions. The "chili in the saddle" is a thick and delicious concoction of mildly spiced shredded beef and bean chili served in a bread basket—though only the heartiest of appetites will want a full portion. Other specialties include barbeque beef ribs, fried chicken, and meatloaf made with turkey and Italian sausage—all served up with soup or salad, homemade mashed potatoes, and fresh bread. But do not lose sight of why so many folks make the drive up the mountain to Julian: The pie. Slices are served up hot and with ice cream, whipped cream, or cheddar cheese. Apple pie is the classic choice, but if you're in town during the fall, don't miss the apple-pumpkin pie with a buttery crunch topping. If the line is too long to get into the café, order a pie to go from their sidewalk window.

Food Purveyors

Breweries and Pubs

Gordon Biersch (619-688-1120; 5010 Mission Center Rd., San Diego, CA 92108). Admittedly, Gordon Biersch is a West Coast chain, but this large outpost in Mission Valley deserves mention nevertheless. Gordon Biersch specializes in German beers, and brews change with the season, but expect to find their popular golden bock year round. Sandwiches, hot wings, and other pub food are also available, and there is complimentary valet parking on site.

San Marcos Brewery and Grill (760-471-0050; 1080 W. San Marcos Blvd., San Marcos, CA 92069). This inviting brewery and restaurant is located in Old California Restaurant Row in San Marcos. On tap you'll find a variety of microbrewed ales made on the premises; the restaurant is expansive, and the menu features huge salads, burgers, and pasta dishes, as well as a variety of appetizers (the hot wings are meaty and delicious). The service is a little slow, and sometimes a little unfriendly, but if you like handcrafted beers, the place is worth a visit anyhow.

Stone Brewing Company (760-471-4999; 1999 Citracado Pkwy., Escondido, CA 92029). Consistently rated in the top 10 breweries by RateBeer.com, this brewery distributes beer around the county, but you can find it straight from the source at the Escondido location. There are complimentary tours daily, which are followed by tastings.

The San Marcos Brewery is in the quaint Old California Restaurant Row in San Marcos.

Coffeehouses

Ciao Bella Caffe Bar and Ristorante (619-337-0238; 5263 Baltimore Dr., La Mesa, CA 91942). Purchase specialty hot drinks like the spicy Mexico mocha or chai latte, Italian sodas, and creamy fruit and chocolate smoothies and enjoy music and dancing in the evenings at this La Mesa favorite. On Mondays and Saturdays sign up for tango lessons, or come Tuesdays and Thursdays for swing dancing.

Old California Coffee House (760-744-2112; 1080 San Marcos Blvd., Ste. 176, San Marcos, CA 92078). This cozy coffee house in San Marcos features single-origin coffees, a wide variety of teas (yerba mate, tisanes, flavored black and green teas), fruit smoothies, and whole fruit and vegetable juices. You can snack on brownies and scones, or eat a more substantial lunch (try the pesto-veggie wrap on a garlic and herb tortilla). Enjoy your treats inside the small interior or on the pretty outside patio.

Packards (760-789-4262; 680 Main St., Ramona, CA 92065). On Main Street in Old Town Ramona, you'll find Packards in what used to be an old gas station. The small outdoor patio is decorated with vintage metal signs. Inside you'll find a few varieties of coffee, as well as a huge selection of homemade—and gigantic—scones, like lemon-poppy seed and cherry almond.

Pizza, Burgers, and Dogs

Etna's Restaurant and Pizza House (619-280-3067; 4427 El Cajon Blvd., San Diego, CA 92115). Soft sweet crust, tangy sauce, and generous toppings have helped make Etna's pizzas among San Diego's favorites. But the delicious calzones are what really draw the crowd. These giant pizza turnovers are stuffed with cheese, meat, and veggies and are a real bargain.

Johnny B's Burgers and Brew (619-464-2465; 8393 La Mesa Blvd., La Mesa, CA 91941). Casual bordering on dive-ish, Johnny B's is a San Diego favorite for inexpensive burgers (try the hickory bacon burger), beer, and yummy onion rings. For less than $6 on weekdays, you can get a lunch special that includes a burger, fries, and a draft (or root beer).

Venice Pizza House (619-283-2333; 3333 El Cajon Blvd., San Diego, CA 92104). Consistently voted by local newspapers and magazines as among San Diego's favorite pizza, Venice Pizza House has been delivering fresh pies for more than 50 years. The vegetarian is loaded with crisp veggies and features a sweet crust.

Woodstock's Pizza (619-265-0999; 6145 El Cajon Blvd., San Diego, CA 92115). College students love pizza, and Woodstock's near San Diego State University loves its college students; you'll find SDSU memorabilia, pictures, and banners throughout. Try the garlic chicken on a wheat crust for something different.

Z Pizza (858-689-9449; 10006 Scripps Ranch Blvd., Ste. 102, San Diego, CA 92131). Create your own pizzas from more than 40 toppings, or go with specialties like the Thai pie with spicy chicken, peanut sauce, carrots, and cilantro; or the "Berkeley veggie" made with soy cheese.

Specialty Markets

Bates Nut Farm (760-749-3333; 15954 Woods Valley Rd., Valley Center, CA, 92082). In addition to being the best place to buy fresh-roasted nuts to grind into your own personalized blend of butters, as well as superior apples, in the fall Bates hosts one of the largest pumpkin patches in San Diego County, complete with horse and buggy rides, a

There's almost no brand of old-fashioned confection the Candy Basket in Julian doesn't carry.

hay maze, and arts and crafts activities for children. (Be forewarned; parking is night-marish during pumpkin season; plan to come early.)

Bharat Bazaar (760-744-7499; 844 W. San Marcos Blvd., San Marcos, CA 92078). This Indian market in San Marcos sells hard-to-find Asian spices, delicious packaged Indian meals, and even offers up the latest videos from Bollywood.

Candy Basket (760-765-0785; 2116 Main St., Julian, CA 92036). Step in and be awed like—well, a kid in a candy store—at the wooden barrels full of old-fashioned treats such as horehound, Sen-Sen, Walnettos, and Mary Janes, as well as a staggering variety of salt-water taffy, homemade fudge, and flavored licorice.

Chino Farms Vegetable Stand (858-756-3184; 6123 Calzada del Bosque, Rancho Santa Fe, CA 92067). Tom Chino and his parents before him have grown exquisite produce since the mid-1940s, and the goods are available for purchase only at this stand—the very same produce that is featured on the menus of the finest restaurants around the city. Famous chefs such as Alice Waters of Chez Panisse in Berkeley and Wolfgang Puck of Spago in Los Angeles swear by the Chino's produce, and foodies from around the world flock to the ultra-wealthy Rancho Santa Fe neighborhood to shop for the most *beautiful* produce straight off the farm. Look for heirloom tomatoes in season, jewel-like straw-berries, baby artichokes, a bewildering variety of lettuces, and bell peppers in almost every color of the rainbow. Closed on Mondays.

Sweets and Treats

Dudley's Bakery (800-225-3348; 760-765-0488; 30218 Hwy. 78, Santa Ysabel, CA 92070). On the road to the mountains, you'll find Dudley's Bakery off Highway 78 in Santa Ysabel, about 15 miles from Ramona. This is the place to get a wide variety of freshly baked breads, including Irish brown bread, jalapeno cheese, and their famous date nut raisin bread. They also offer low-carb loafs of sun-dried tomato and whole grain wheat. If you develop a Dudley's habit, they'll ship to locations throughout the country. Lines are long on the weekends, and they are closed Tuesday through Thursday.

King Leo Confections (760-765-2264; 4510 Hwy. 78, Julian, CA 92036). King Leo has been making hand-crafted confections for more than one hundred years, and specializes in fudge and candy canes. For less than $3 you can purchase a 12-ounce box of soft peppermint sticks that probably won't make it down the mountain.

Miner's Diner and Julian Drugstore (760-765-3753; 2134 Main St., Julian, CA 92036). Belly up to the marble bar and order an old-fashioned "phosphate" fountain drink, in flavors ranging from sarsaparilla, cherry, vanilla, and chocolate, or have a famous Tommy's hot brownie sundae loaded with chocolate fudge sauce. While you're here, enjoy the vintage memorabilia, including an old cruiser bike and license plates from around the country.

Mom's Pies (760-765-2472, 2119 Main St., Julian, CA 92036). Julian is famous for its apple pies; they grow the fruit fresh on nearby orchards, and there are a dozen or so bakeries just on Main Street. With such a wealth of options, it would seem difficult to choose a favorite, but in truth Mom's Dutch-style deep-dish pies are head and shoulders above their worthy competition: Buttery topping, plenty of cinnamon, not-too-sweet apples, and flaky crust make these pastries worth the drive. Buy whole pies to take home, or buy a slice to enjoy in their small, antique-furnished dining room. Bumbleberry pies (a mix of blueberries, blackberries, and strawberries) are also a treat, especially hot out of the oven and served with a scoop of vanilla ice cream.

Peterson's Donut Corner (760-745-7774; 903 S. Escondido Blvd., Escondido, CA 92025). This is reminiscent of those old-fashion donut shops where as a kid you would press your nose against the glass and marvel at the rows of neatly lined frosted, powdered, glazed, and cream-filled delights. Back then you could only pick one, but with the dozens of varieties available at Peterson's, there's no reason (aside from your waistline) to limit yourself these days. This shop, in business since 1981, sells muffins, pastries, and cream puffs in addition to its oversized donuts. (One maple bar could feed a small family.). Prices are rock-bottom, and they are open 24 hours a day, seven days a week.

Surati Farsan Mart (858-549-7280; 9494 Black Mountain Rd., San Diego, CA 92126). This Indian market in Mira Mesa specializes in Gujarati snacks and sweets; in addition to staples like *samosas* (stuffed deep-fried pastry pockets) and *dosas* (rice crepes wrapped around potatoes and onions and served with a veggie soup), you'll find more unusual items like *panipuri* (puffy whole wheat shells stuffed with spicy potatoes and beans), refreshing sweet and salty *lassi* drinks, and *barfi*, an Indian fudge flavored with nuts, mangos, watermelons, or chocolate.

Taquerias

La Cocina (760-789-8332; 681 Main St., Ramona, CA 92065). Located in a historic storefront in Old Town Ramona, La Cocina serves up family-style Mexican food at shockingly low prices. The flauta is huge and stuffed with juicy shredded beef, and the refried beans taste like someone's Grandma made them—simmered in a pot all day and with lots of love.

Los Primos (760-735-8226; 1348 W. Valley Pkwy., Escondido, CA 92027). Part of a local chain of restaurants, Los Primos sells fresh, healthier versions of traditional Mexican food. Their *carne asada* tacos are stuffed full of chopped meat, *pica de gallo*, and guacamole, and they are served on soft corn tortillas—with barely a touch of grease. Open 6 AM–11 PM, you can satisfy your Mexican food jones pretty much whenever you want.

Señor Panchos (760-734-6655; 1909 W. San Marcos Blvd., San Marcos, CA 92069). Look for the old green train in the supermarket parking lot and you've found Los Panchos, a small taqueria that sells traditional Mexican food prepared quickly. The shredded beef tacos are stuffed so full of meat, cheese, and garnishes that the crispy shell generally breaks in half before the whole taco can be eaten. You'll also find carnitas, burritos, and tortas (Mexican toasted sandwiches).

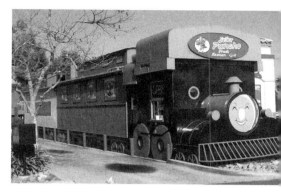

Señor Panchos sells authentic Mexican plates to go.

THEME PARKS AND ZOOS

SAN DIEGO WILD ANIMAL PARK

760-747-8702
www.sandiegozoo.org/wap
15500 San Pasqual Valley Rd., Escondido, CA 92027
Open: 9 AM daily; closing varies seasonally
Admission: Adults: $28.50, children: $17.50, parking $8

The famous San Diego Zoo's east county site, the Wild Animal Park is a 2,200-acre wildlife preserve located 30 miles northeast of San Diego. It's designed to give visitors a chance to observe animals in their native habitats, so enclosures are kept as natural as possible, and animals in expansive field exhibits roam freely and mingle with other animals they would encounter naturally. More than three thousand animals call the park home, including almost 50 species that are endangered. There are miles of trails winding through the beautifully landscaped grounds—which include approximately 4,000 species of plants, more than 250 of which are also endangered—and dozens of exhibits and guided hikes.

If you've been to the Wild Animal Park in the past, you might remember an electric monorail that wound its way around naturalistic field exhibits. Alas, the Wagasa Bush Line Railway is no more; in mid-2007 the park revamped the transportation system, and now visitors instead board the "African Express," a 100-passenger jeep-like vehicle that leaves the railways behind and drives right into the wide-open enclosures, bringing guests as much as 300 feet closer to the animal exhibits. The animals themselves have been shifted around a bit as well, to create a new "Journey into Africa" experience meant to mimic a safari.

Because the enclosures are expansive and animals can move about as they like, each "African Express" tour is a little different. Morning tours are generally more satisfying, because the animals have been recently fed and the temperatures are cool enough to keep them active. But regardless, you're sure to see giraffes, elephants, gazelles, zebras, rhinoceros, mountain goats, and dozens of other rare and endangered animals. Although the setting is natural, predators are kept at bay—in other words, the lions, tigers, and cheetahs in the park do not mingle with the animals that would be their prey in the wild.

Other not-to-be-missed exhibits in the park include the Lion Camp, where visitors view lions through a glass wall at exhibits designed to allow the animals to come closer than they otherwise could in a traditional enclosure; Condor Ridge, a trail that leads visitors through a habitat created for animals indigenous to North America, including the California condor, whose recovery from near extinction has been one of the great success stories of animal conservation; Lorikeet Landing, where you can stroll through a simulated Australian rainforest aviary filled with lorikeets—the friendly wild parrots from down under—which will land on your hands, shoulders, and even your head, especially if you purchase a cup of nectar to feed them; and the children's petting zoo, filled with docile deer and other small animals.

For an additional charge, you can take part in such adventures as the Photo Caravan Safaris, where you'll board a small off-road vehicle and drive even deeper into the enclosures to feed animals and take up-close photos; the Balloon Safari, where you'll ride a tethered hot-air balloon to get an unbeatable view of the park from 400 feet up; or overnight **Roar and Snore** camping, where you'll have a chance to actually spend the night in the park (see below).

RECREATION: THE GREAT OUTDOORS

The east county has more open space than any other area within San Diego County, which means plenty of opportunities to fish, hike, camp, and otherwise get away from the crowds on the coast.

Camping

Green Valley Falls Campground (760-765-0755; off 79 N, 15 miles south of Julian).
Located within Cuyamaca Rancho State Park, the Green Valley Falls Campground is surrounded by great hiking, including an easy loop that goes to the seasonal Green Valley Falls, with trailheads beginning in the campground itself. You'll also find horse trails onsite, as well as fishing. Sadly, the horrific 2003 fires that swept through Southern California burned throughout the rest of the park, and although the campground was mostly untouched, the once heavily forested mountain that surrounds it is now charred. First come, first served. No hookups, $15.

Roar and Snore Sleepover at the Wild Animal Park (619-718-3000; 15500 San Pasqual Valley Rd., Escondido, CA 92027). Even if you think you're not the camping type, falling asleep to the sounds of lions roaring and waking to the sun rising over a savannah full of giraffes and gazelles will make a convert out of you. Bring your own sleeping bag and the Wild Animal Park will set you up with a premier camping spot on grassy Kilima Point, overlooking the park's Africa Field Exhibit. You'll be assigned a preassembled tent, ranging from a basic model that sleeps up to six or an upgraded premium model with a queen-sized platform bed and safari-themed décor. This is a pricey adventure, and doesn't include the cost of admission to the park—which is required—but you'll be treated to a campfire program; a tour of the park at night; dinner, snacks, drinks, and a hot breakfast in the morning. Book well in advance. Per-person prices start at $135.

> **Gold in the Hills of Julian**
> In 1870, rancher Fred Coleman discovered gold in a creek in the Cuyamaca Mountains. That year more than 1,500 pounds of the precious ore was discovered in the area, and it wasn't long before the hills were overrun with prospectors. During the gold rush, more than $5 million in gold was mined from the Cuyamaca Hills near what is today Julian. But the boom lasted fewer than five years, and by 1876, most of the mines were closed. Visitors to Julian can still get a glimpse into the early California mining life at the **Eagle and High Peak Mine** (760-765-0036; 2320 C St., Julian, CA 92036). Guests will take a guided tour through hard-rock tunnels—bring a jacket, because the tunnels are chilly!—and view the now-bereft diggings.

Woods Valley Campground (760-749-2905; 15236 Woods Valley Rd., Valley Center, CA 92082). A small pond and petting zoo at the front of this campground in northeast county is tremendous fun for children, but try to secure a quiet camp site near the back of the campground; the resident rooster in the zoo doesn't understand the concept of dawn and sometimes crows all night long. There are two streams running through the campground, as well as beautiful oak and sycamore trees throughout, but little grass to speak of. Campfires are often restricted because of the dry vegetation. Tent and RV sites, $31–$45.

Fishing

Dixon Lake (1700 N. La Honda Dr., Escondido, CA 92025). Located in northeast Escondido, Dixon Lake has become famous as the site of the largest catch and release of a largemouth bass (25.1 pounds); as bass-fishing aficionados know, this astounding catch isn't strictly "official" because it was foul hooked and because it was released before the weight could be independently verified. However, that monster bass still makes its home in the lake, and hundreds of hopefuls show up regularly to try to lure it back to the record books. Dixon Lake also has an abundance of trout and catfish. There are rental boats available, but arrive early, because the number is limited. No private boats are allowed.

Santee Lakes (9040 Carlton Oaks Dr., Santee, CA 92071). Actually a grouping of seven small lakes, the Santee Lakes recreation area offers less by way of fishing than it does recreation. The main draws are the camping and picnicking, plus you'll find five playgrounds throughout the park, including a "sprayground" with water fountains to run through (especially welcome in the hot summers in east county). However, if you want to get your fishing feet wet without a big commitment, Santee Lakes offers day passes that waive the requirement for a California fishing license.

Golfing

Golf courses are plentiful in the east county, thanks to rolling hills and expansive acreage in this part of San Diego. Some of the nicest courses are adjacent to the lavish Native American gaming casinos in the area, which means there's plenty to do after the 18th hole as well.

Barona Creek Golf Club (619-387-7018; 1000 Wildcat Canyon Rd., Lakeside, CA 92040). Part of the Barona Casino complex, *Golfweek* magazine has rated Barona as the fifth-best modern golf course in California. The rugged terrain and scenic beauty of Barona are different from other courses in the county, and well worth the drive east. Green fee: $50–$110.

Carlton Oaks Lodge and Country Club (619-448-4242; 9200 Inwood Dr., Santee, CA 92071). Pete Dye designed this challenging 18-hole course, which features beautiful landscaping and extensive water hazards. Green fee $55–$80.

Maderas Golf Course (858-451-8100; 17750 Old Coach Rd., Poway, CA 92064). This beautiful inland course winds through natural creeks, forests, and cliffs—as well as three human-made lakes and five landscaped waterfalls. A challenging and exciting course, Maderas was designed in late 1999 by Johnny Miller and Robert Muir Graves. Green fee: $175–$195.

Rancho Bernardo Inn (858-675-8500; 17555 Bernardo Oaks Rd., San Diego, CA 92128). A San Diego favorite for more than 40 years, the old-style Rancho Bernardo course has deceptively sloped greens, a well-maintained course, and plenty of serenity. Green fee: $90–$115.

Riverwalk Golf Club (619-296-4653; 1150 Fashion Valley Rd., San Diego, CA 92108). Centrally located in Mission Valley, the Riverwalk Golf Club was the site of the San Diego Golf Open back in the 1950s; more recently, the course has been redesigned by Ted Robinson Sr. and his son Ted Jr. You'll find 27 holes with lots of water features and well-maintained greens. Green fee $95–$120.

Sycuan Resort Golf Club (800-457-5568; 3007 Dehesa Rd., El Cajon, CA 92019). Formerly Singing Hills, these two 18-hole championship courses wind through old-growth trees and offer challenges for seasoned golfers. Green fee: $34-80.

The walk up Mt. Woodson outside of Ramona is rigorous and scenic.

Hiking

Scrub-punctuated hills, massive boulders, and wild prickly pear cacti are abundant in the east county, and trails in this area will give hikers a taste of what early San Diego must have been like, before concrete and asphalt paved over the natural—and stark—beauty.

Mission Trails Regional Park (8300 Father Junipero Serra Trail, San Diego, CA 91942). Several short trails link together, so visitors to the Mission Trails Regional Park can take a short half-mile hike or make a day of it. Hike along the San Diego River on Father Junipero Serra Trail, which terminates at the Old Mission Dam; then connect with the Kwaay Paay Summit Trail for a more challenging climb that will have you scrabbling to the summit of Cowles Mountain (pronounced "coals"—really; most native San Diegans get this wrong).

Mt. Woodson East (from I-15 south, take 78 east to Main St.; from I-15 N, exit Scripps Poway Parkway, and turn left onto 67 N to Main St.; from Main St., go north on 67 about 5 miles). Pick up the marked trailhead off Highway 67, close to the Forest Fire station sign. A short dirt pathway meanders through a thick oak forest and after about a quarter of a mile it joins the main asphalt trail that runs through the boulder-strewn hills. This out-and-back 3.6-mile trail is a strenuous walk up, gaining about 1,200 feet in elevation, but even a half-hour hike will reward you with unparalleled views of Ramona and the surrounding mountains.

SHOPPING: EVERYTHING UNDER THE SUN

Large shopping malls abound in the east county; one of the best is the upscale **Fashion Valley Center** (619-688-9113; 7007 Friars Rd., San Diego, CA 92108); nearby **Westfield Mission Valley** (619-296-6375; 1640 Camino del Rio N., San Diego, CA 92108) comes in a close second, and you'll find innumerable big-box centers clustered between the two. Further east, check out **Westfield Parkway Plaza** in El Cajon (619-579-9932; 415 Parkway Plaza, El Cajon, CA 92020) and **Grossmont Center** in La Mesa (619-461-0630; 5500 Grossmont Center Dr., La Mesa, CA 91941).

Antiques and Collectibles

Antique Mall (619-462-2211; 4710 Palm Ave., La Mesa, CA 91941). Various vendors set up shop in the Antique Mall, where you'll find Depression glass, period furniture, and an interesting collection of vintage wedding dresses.

Aubrey Rose (619-461-4832; 8362 La Mesa Blvd., La Mesa, CA 91941). Not only will you find everything related to tea for sale here—including cups, pots, and cozies—but you can also indulge in the beverage. The Aubrey Rose has several tables available in the store to enjoy a spot of tea with a homemade scone or a plate of finger sandwiches. You can even take etiquette lessons (for children and adults), to learn how to curl your little finger just so when sipping.

The McNally Company Antiques (858-756-1922; 6033 Paseo Delicias, Rancho Santa Fe, CA 92067). Since 1978, owners Connie and Bill McNally have specialized in antique silver, as well as 17th- and 18th-century fine furnishings from Europe. Hours fluctuate, so be sure to call ahead.

Squash Blossom Trading Company (760-788-2353; 738 Main St., Ramona, CA 92065). Several antique shops line Main Street in Old Town Ramona, but Squash Blossom is my favorite. The owner is always on the look-out for collections she loves, and turnover is fast. Look for Native American and Mexican folk art and furniture, as well as vintage papers like valentines from the 1920s and turn-of-the-century postcards.

Time and Treasures (619-460-8004; 8326 La Mesa Blvd., La Mesa, CA 91941). An eclectic and high-quality collection of fine grandfather and case clocks are displayed in this small, beautiful shop.

Books and Music

Blue Meannies Records (619-442-5034; 1164 El Cajon Blvd., San Diego, CA 92021). As the name implies, this El Cajon store used to be devoted to everything pertaining to the Beatles; now it's gone mostly heavy metal—although you can still find a few LPs featuring the Fab Four.

Old Julian Book House (760-765-1985; 2230 Main St., Julian, CA 92036). Look for an eclectic collection of rare and used books in this comfortable, casual store—and don't miss Cocoa the cat, who spends most of the day napping in a basket out front.

Yellow Book Road (619-463-4900; 7200 Parkway Dr., La Mesa, CA 91942). Specializing in children's books, Yellow Book Road also caters to educators, with teacher supplies and guided-reading level books. The store was a La Mesa institution for more than two decades, but in 2006 it was relocated and is now under new management, although many of the knowledgeable and friendly sales staff moved with the store. This is still one of the best places to find eclectic and hard to find children's titles.

Find everything ballet themed at the San Elijo Dancewear boutique in San Marcos.

Just for Fun

The Birdwatcher (760-765-1817; 2775 B St., Julian, CA 92036). A block behind Main Street in Julian, this large store sells a huge variety of bird feeders, bird seed, bird houses, wind chimes, and books on ornithology.

The Bouncing Bead (619-460-2323; 8341 La Mesa Blvd., La Mesa, CA 91941). Strands of beads, bowls of beads, and cases of beads greet you on entering the Dancing Bead, including glass and metal specimens, semiprecious stones, and freshwater pearls in a rainbow of colors. Classes are offered onsite, so you'll know what to do with your treasures once you've selected from among the thousands of options.

San Elijo Dancewear (760-891-0220; 1635 Rancho Santa Fe Rd., Ste. 104, San Marcos, CA 92078). This small store tucked into a light industrial park at the border of San Marcos and Carlsbad sells designer dance wear and ballet gift items. You'll also find owner Kelsey Steinmetz's own line of pretty and utilitarian fashions, called Flaunt Body Wear, featured throughout the shop.

The Tijuana Cultural Center in the Zona Rio has unmistakable architecture.

8

Tijuana

South of the Border and Left of Center

Ask most San Diegans about Tijuana, and they are likely to tell you that it is a bawdy border town with little appeal except as a haven for underage drinkers looking for trouble and free-wheeling adults who don't necessarily agree with the U.S. vice laws. Although its reputation for debauchery is well deserved, the Tijuana of today has much more to offer. The large city is culturally rich, with a vibrant arts community, myriad international influences, and unique recreational activities. There are several major universities in the area that draw scholars from throughout Mexico and beyond, and fine dining and comfortable lodging. Best of all, even though border crossings are congested (the San Ysidro crossing is the busiest in the world), the city of Tijuana is less than a half an hour from downtown San Diego. It is possible to visit for a day (or even a few hours), which is certainly the easiest way to explore a new country. Come here with your eyes wide open, and you're sure to leave with an appreciation of Tijuana hospitality and a deeper understanding of the Mexican culture and lifestyle.

Despite the physical proximity to Southern California, Tijuana is a different world. There is a growing middle-class and a robust upper class in this border city, but wander a few blocks off the beaten tourist path and you'll see evidence of poverty everywhere. Panhandling is not as ubiquitous as it once was; tourist areas have been sanitized in the past decade, and local officials (and savvy shopkeepers) chase off vagrants. Still, expect to see poor individuals of all ages wandering the streets near the border selling small trinkets to tourists. If you drive into and out of the city—and thus get stuck waiting in the inevitable traffic coming in to the United States that backs up miles from the border—you'll even see people walking *between the lanes* of the highway asking for money or selling chewing gum or small bags of nuts.

Visitors venturing beyond the main tourist areas will likely see families living in conditions that will appall most Americans, and venturing too far off the beaten tourist path can be downright dangerous. Drug trafficking is a fact of life in this border town, and despite recent crackdowns by Mexican authorities, there are sometimes fatal repercussions for those who become embroiled in this illegal business.

Thankfully, most tourists will never see this side of the city. There are two main neighborhoods (called *Zonas*) in Tijuana where you'll want to concentrate your time: The first is the main downtown thoroughfare, which consists of the 10 or so blocks along the Avenida Revolucíon; this is called the Zona Centro. The second is clustered around Avenida Paseo

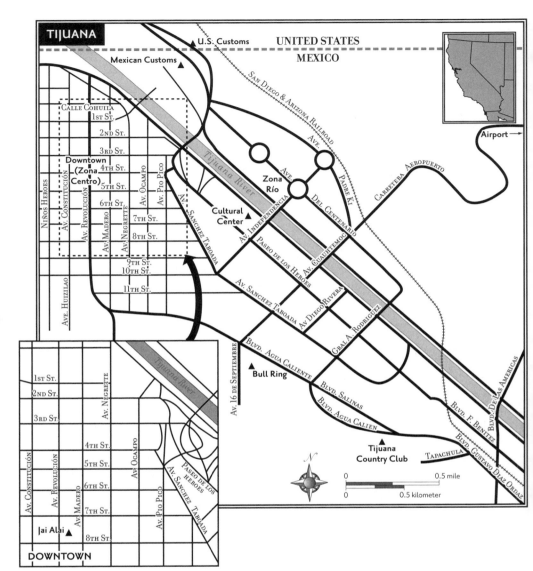

de los Héroes—another main thoroughfare, decorated with statues of Mexican historical figures and one incongruous statue of Abraham Lincoln. This area is called the Zona Rio and is the financial district of the city. The dense downtown area has numerous shopping opportunities, as well as many lively and eclectic restaurants and bars—and although you can pick restaurants that are nearly indistinguishable from those north of the border, you can also find places you'd never see in the United States. For the adventurous, there are delicacies that are likely unknown to most Americans (e.g., ant eggs in garlic butter or crispy fried worms). The Zona Rio is home to the fascinating Tijuana Cultural Center and the expansive Plaza Rio Shopping Mall, as well as several upscale dining choices and accommodations; this is also where you'll find appealing clubs and bars. Stay away from the Zona Norte (near the border and west of Av. Revolucíon), which is Tijuana's red light district, a haven for drug dealers and prostitutes.

You'll find locals in Tijuana are generally very polite and accommodating hosts, and most people try hard to please. Many folks in the tourist areas know passable English—and don't seem annoyed at having to speak a foreign language in their own country. If you get lost, chances are a friendly soul will steer you in the right direction. Don't be shy about using taxis in Tijuana: Cab drivers are often great (and reasonably priced) tour guides, and they will happily show you the city, make restaurant recommendations, and take you to the best shopping. Be sure to negotiate a price first; cabs near the border have a set fee ($5) to take visitors to downtown or to the Zona Rio, but once outside this restricted area will usually charge much less for their time.

SAFETY FIRST

It is extremely unlikely that a U.S. citizen within the tourist areas of Tijuana will run into serious trouble. With a little caution and common sense, you will probably have an uneventful, enjoyable visit—and your appetite might be whetted for additional travel throughout Baja California.

To play it safe when in Tijuana, leave an itinerary and a copy of your passport and drivers' license with a friend in the United States (in case you lose your paperwork). Always carry a photo ID; starting in 2008, U.S. citizens will be required to have a valid passport to cross back into the United States from Tijuana by land. U.S. citizens must have valid passports to enter Mexico via airline or cruise line. Make sure you also have on your person emergency contact information. Don't bring along unnecessary items, such as your airline tickets, expensive jewelry or electronics, credit cards you won't be using, or excess cash. Travelers checks are the safest mode of payment, and are widely accepted (although not every hotel and restaurant will accept them; call ahead to be sure). There is no need to convert them to *pesos*. If you plan to stay in Mexico longer than 72 hours, or you plan to venture farther south than Ensenada, make sure you obtain a tourist permit at the Mexican Consulate in the United States (619-231-8414).

Avenida Revolucíon in downtown is quiet on weekdays and bustling on weekend nights. Photo courtesy of Jon Preimesberger. Used with permission.

Simple Phrases in Spanish

ENGLISH	SPANISH	PRONUNCIATION
Hello	*Hola*	Oh-la
Please	*Por favor*	Pour-fah-vor
Thank you	*Gracias*	Grah-see-us
Excuse me	*Lo siento*	Low-see-en-toe
How much does this cost?	*Cuánto cuesta?*	Qwan-toe-quest-a?
Take me to Zona Rio	*Lléveme a Zona Rio*	Yay-va-may a zone-ah Rio
(to downtown)	(*a Zona Centro*)	(a zone-a sentro)
Where is the border?	*Dónde esta la frontera?*	Dohn-day es-tah la fron-tara?
Do you speak English?	*Habla usted inglés?*	Ah-bla oo-sted een-glace?
I don't understand.	*No entiendo.*	No in-tee-en-doh
What time is it?	*Qué hora es?*	Kay or-ah es?

As in any big city, know where you're going. Carry a good map, and don't venture into dicey areas (i.e., the Zona Norte). Know a few simple phrases in Spanish; although many shopkeepers and most waiters and hotel staff in the tourist areas speak English fairly well, don't count on everyone you encounter being bilingual.

If you ever find yourself in trouble in Tijuana, call the **State Secretariat of Tourism of Baja California** (664-973-0424, or dial 078 from any local telephone, including most cell phones; also see their Web site at www.discoverbajacalifornia.com). Operators speak English, and the visitors assistance hotline is open 24 hours a day.

Access for Disabled Persons

Tijuana has some wheelchair access, but in general the city wasn't designed for disabled travelers. Curbs are high and uneven throughout the city, and in the Zona Rio there are wide holes and deep cracks in many of the sidewalks. Wheelchair ramps (when they exist) are too steep to be useful, and many restaurants do not have adequate restroom facilities. Many more restaurants and bars are accessible only via a flight of stairs. Crosswalks aren't well marked, and many major intersections (especially around traffic circles in the Zona Rio) don't even have crossing signals.

In this chapter I have omitted the usual handicap access line in the information blocks for lodging and restaurants, because standards vary so widely. A hotel or café in Tijuana may claim to be accessible, even though restroom doors are not wide enough to accommodate wheel chairs, for example, and thus calling ahead isn't sure to solicit reliable information about accessibility. To verify before you travel that your preferred destinations will have appropriate accommodations, check the Web site for the **Information for Disabled Travelers** group at www.access-able.com.

Legal Issues

Remember that while traveling in Tijuana, U.S. citizens are subject to Mexican law. If you cross the law, you'll be subject to the Mexican criminal justice system, which generally refuses to grant bail to foreigners. Don't take chances: Avoid all activities that could get you into trouble while in Mexico (e.g., possession of illegal drugs and firearms and driving while under the influence of alcohol or drugs). A Mexican jail is the last place you want to be. If you *are* arrested, be sure to call the U.S. Consulate in Tijuana (664-622-7400) at your first opportunity.

Serious encounters with the law while in Tijuana are extremely unlikely, but if you are driving across the border with American license plates, there is an increased chance that you will run into local traffic enforcement officials. Police officers in Mexican border towns have been known to stop obviously American drivers under slim pretext, to extract a small (or not so small) bribe. The scenario might go like this: The officer asks to see the tourist's driver's license, poses a few simple questions, and then tells the driver that to save her or him the time to drive to the station (the official protocol for traffic infractions), the officer would be happy to collect the fine owed. The amount quoted is usually steep. Although corruption within Tijuana law enforcement has been cleaned up enormously in the past several decades, the record is not spotless. If you are pulled over for a traffic violation, ask for (and write down) the officer's name and badge number. Then go directly to the police station to pay whatever fine you have been assessed. If you are guilty of the infraction, your fine will likely be much less than what will be solicited by a corrupt officer. If you are not guilty, tell the officers at the station so and try to dispute the charges. *Never* offer an unsolicited bribe when stopped by Mexican law enforcement.

If you are driving a vehicle over the border, make sure you first purchase Mexican auto insurance, even if your U.S. company promises to cover you abroad. Mexican authorities often will not accept or recognize this insurance. (See chapter 2 for more details about auto insurance.) Understand that traffic is usually intense, and many driving in the city are aggressive about getting around the congestion, so even good drivers put themselves at additional risk for accidents in Tijuana.

If you're driving south beyond Tijuana, note that Mexican federal police sometimes set up roadblocks heading toward Rosarito and Ensenada to conduct random searches for illegal drugs and firearms. You must comply with these searches or risk being arrested.

If you purchase prescription drugs in Tijuana (an increasingly popular thing to do, given the discounts available in Mexico—and you'll find pharmacies everywhere), you must have a valid doctor's prescription to carry the medicines back into the United States.

Eating and Drinking in Mexico

Tourist-grade restaurants in Tijuana offer clean, reliable food, and by law all hotels and restaurants must serve ice made from purified water, so visitors needn't be anxious about partaking of the excellent frozen margaritas available at nearly every bar and grill in the city. But even when exercising care, you might pick up an intestinal bug. Mexicans call this *turista*, known to many Americans as Montezuma's Revenge (diarrhea and sometimes nausea). If you are prone to stomach ailments of this kind, choose your restaurants carefully, avoid unfamiliar ingredients (for example, skip the fried worms and the haberno gravy), and drink in moderation. An ounce of prevention is in order as well: A spoonful or two of Pepto Bismol is an excellent prophylactic. Whether it actually prevents *turista* or if it's just psychological insurance, it tends to work.

Stick with bottled water and sodas (sold on most street corners), and think twice about eating food prepared by street vendors. The taco stands selling small bundles of meat and fresh tortillas smell heavenly, and the fruit stands offering luscious and colorful cut mangos, pineapples, and watermelon are hard to pass by, but understand before you indulge that the sanitary standards for these vendors are not always optimal. Play it safe by ordering food in sit-down restaurants, and buy unpeeled fruits from local markets, which you can then wash with bottled water and peel and slice yourself.

MONEY

Although the official currency of Mexico is the *peso*, American dollars are widely—and gladly—accepted. Large stores will take major credit cards and travelers checks as well. Of course, smaller shops, kiosks, and stands in the open-air arcades will only accept cash, and they won't be able to break large bills. Note that it is common in Mexico for stores and restaurants to add on a 5 percent surcharge for credit card purchases, so be sure you ask before you whip out that plastic.

Although it isn't necessary to deal in *pesos*, exchanges can be made at banks throughout Tijuana, or for a nominal fee, most banks in Southern California can exchange small amounts of dollars for *pesos* (although it is a good idea to call in advance to make sure they have the currency on hand). Most major banks in Tijuana are open from 9 to 4. ATM machines are scattered throughout Tijuana (in many shopping malls as well as in banks). Be careful of these machines, however; they aren't as reliable as they are north of the border.

If you are dealing in *pesos*, take the time to familiarize yourself with the coinage. Tiny silver-colored coins are *centavos*, and 100 *centavos* makes 1 *peso*. Coin *pesos* come in denominations ranging from 5¢ to $50. Paper *pesos* come in denominations of 10, 20, 50, 100, 200, 500, and $1000. If you pay in *pesos*, you will most certainly get change back in *pesos*. If you pay with U.S. dollars, you may get change in *pesos*, dollars, or a combination of both. The exchange rate fluctuates daily; for current information, check the Mexico online Web site at www.mexonline.com/mexicanpeso.htm.

Although shopping is duty free in Tijuana (up to an $800 limit), the Mexican government tacks on a 10 percent value-added tax on many goods and services and an additional 2 percent on hotels. Some resort hotels in the state of Baja add an additional "service tax"; these fees are not included in quoted rates, so be sure to inquire when booking accommodations.

Note that tipping is slightly less in Tijuana than is expected in the United States: In fine restaurants, tip waiters between 10 and 15 percent. Cab drivers do not expect tips; this is figured into their prearranged fares

LODGING

Most first-time visitors to Tijuana will make it a day trip, but if you've been here before and are eager to see more of the city—or if you plan to party into the wee hours and need a place to sleep it off—there are several comfortable lodging options available in the city to enable you to extend your stay. Note that standards of luxury are different in Tijuana than they are in San Diego, and so what might be considered a "five-star" hotel in Tijuana might not pass muster north of the border. On the other hand, there are both comfortable and luxurious accommodations to be had—and they generally cost 25 to 50 percent less than a comparable room in San Diego. Note that it's acceptable throughout Tijuana to ask to see a few accommodations before you agree to a room—and this is generally a good idea, given the difference in guest rooms within the same property.

CAMINO REAL TIJUANA HOTEL

Owner: Alejandro de la Vega
664-633-4000 or 877-215-3051; fax 664-634-3981
www.caminoreal.com/tijuana
Paseo de los Héroes No. 10305, Tijuana, BC, Mexico 22320
Price: Inexpensive to Moderate
Credit cards: AE, D, MC, V

Located in the Zona Rio and considered to be one of the finest hotels in the city, the Camino Real is located across from the Plaza Rio Shopping Center and within walking distance of excellent restaurants and bars (although the busy traffic circle in front of the hotel can be a challenge to navigate on foot). The open, airy lobby is sleek, adorned with marble and decorated in elegant, neutral colors. The large, modern guest rooms vary greatly in design; some boast vibrantly painted walls and some are decorated in more serene colors. Bathrooms are swathed in marble, and are also commodious. On the exclusive (and more expensive) sixth floor, guests are treated as members of the Camino Real Club, which offers concierge services, a complimentary breakfast in a glass-enclosed space with expansive views of the city, and cocktails and appetizers in the evenings. On request, the staff will bring coffee or juice to your room as part of a wakeup service. The lobby bar features nightly live music, and there is also a tequila cantina on the property. The colorful and festive onsite restaurant **Azuelejos** serves buffet meals, and has theme nights offering Mexican specialties as well as Italian and Argentinian recipes. The hotel offers many package deals that represent a real bargain, including a bullfight package in season that comes with often hard-to-come-by tickets.

GRAND HOTEL TIJUANA

Manager: Rocio Duran
866-472-6385; fax 664-681-7000
www.grandhoteltijuana.com
4500 Agua Caliente Blvd., Tijuana, BC, Mexico 22420
Price: Moderate
Credit Cards: AE, MC, V

The sleek architecture of this 32-floor twin-towers hotel is visible throughout many parts of the city, and is conveniently located on the golf course at the Tijuana Country Club; rooms overlook the course, as well as offering commanding views of the city from higher floors. But note that the location is a

The Camino Real Hotel in the Zona Rio is fronted by a statue of Cuauhtémoc, an Aztec emperor.

bit too far from the heart of the Zona Rio to walk to many places off the property. The 422 guest rooms are decorated with colorful fabrics and clean-line furniture—although carpets and bedspreads are worn a little thin, and the overall look is of decades past. Rooms come with a minibar and cable TV in both English and Spanish. The amenities are extensive and include onsite restaurants and discos, a race and sports betting lounge, a large pool, tennis courts, a fitness center, a car rental office, a shopping arcade, and a movie theater. Efficient and helpful bilingual front desk staff will assist guests in finding their way around the city (and the large property) and will arrange for complimentary pickups from the airport. A complimentary continental breakfast is included. Another welcome feature is the large underground parking structure, which is monitored 24 hours a day—although because it is not exclusive to hotel guests, it can fill up, especially when the hotel is hosting an event.

HOTEL LUCERNA

Owner: José Encarnación Kabande Dabdub
664-633-3900
www.hotel-lucerna.com.mx
10902 Paseo de los Héroes, Tijuana, BC, Mexico, 22320
Price: Moderate
Credit Cards: D, MC, V

Part of a small chain of accommodations throughout Mexico, the Hotel Lucerna is a modern property with a large, inviting pool and nicely landscaped grounds. Located in the Zona Rio, this is a good option for business travelers. The hotel is 10 miles from the airport and 5 miles to the border; it is relatively close to the Tijuana Cultural Center, the Plaza Rio Shopping Center, the bullring (via taxi), and many of the classier clubs and bars. There is a business center onsite, with copiers, fax, and computers, and each of the rooms include data ports.

Guest accommodations are quite varied in size and design, but are clean, albeit a little timeworn. Rooms come with a complimentary fruit basket and bottled water, and air conditioning is in good repair (not something travelers can always count on in Tijuana—and it can get hot here in the summers, so it's a necessity for most of us). The Rivoli Restaurant on site specializes in international dishes, and has a pretty outdoor patio dining area; the El Aqueducto Restaurant and Bar serves up a morning buffet with American and Mexican breakfast specialties. Also on the property is the 10902 Bar, which frequently has live music.

PUEBLO AMIGO

Manager: Gerardo Delgado
664-624-2700; fax 664-683-5032
www.hotelpuebloamigo.com
Via Oriente 9211, Tijuana, BC, Mexico 22320
Price: Inexpensive
Credit cards: AE, MC, V

Step into the expansive, welcoming lobby at the Pueblo Amigo near the border and you'll find high ceilings and impressive chandeliers. Befitting its name, the staff are friendly and helpful, and most are bilingual. The 108 guest rooms are basic— spacious, clean, and functional but rather stark; wireless Internet connections are available in most rooms. The hotel is located in the Zona Rio, near the Pueblo Amigo center, but is actually closer to the border than the main tourist draws of this area (the Cultural Center and Plaza Rio). However, the popular bar and grill **Señor Frogs** (see page 246) is nearby. If you're looking to gamble, you need go no farther than the bingo gaming machines onsite; the hotel also offers a sports booking lounge. For added safety and comfort, there is 24-hour security, 24-hour room service, and a water purification plant onsite ensures that it's safe to brush your teeth straight out of the tap. The popular **El Patio Restaurant** specializes in pre-Hispanic food, which is increasingly popular throughout Baja.

REAL DEL MAR GOLF RESORT AND COUNTRY CLUB

Manager: Raul Mendoza
664-631-3670 or 800-346-3942; fax 664-631-3677
www.realdelmar.com
Km. 19.5 Ensenada Scenic Rd., Tijuana, BC, Mexico 22320
Price: Moderate
Credit Cards: A, MC, V

As one would expect from a country club, this lodging option offers a chance to get away from it all. Contemporary Mexican architecture and a beautiful and luxurious golf course make this resort, between Tijuana and Rosarito (see chapter 2), a favorite with San Diegans. The popular 18-hole professional golf course is lushly landscaped, and from several holes you have incredible views of the Mexican Coronado Islands and the surrounding Pacific Ocean. The Moorish-style hotel property offers full amenities, including a pool, tennis courts, Jacuzzi, onsite restaurant, bar, basketball courts, and a full-service spa. The spa offers fitness classes such as tae bo, kickboxing, and yoga, and guests can treat themselves to a sauna, massage, facial, or a full-body wrap. A continental breakfast is available in the morning, as is beer and wine in the late afternoon. This property is now owned and managed by the Marriott chain, which maintains the Real del Mar with the same care guests can expect of Marriotts north of the border.

CULTURE

Increasingly in the United States, chain restaurants, stores, and even hotels are indistinguishable from city to city. The great joy in Mexico is that visitors will not find cookie-cutter establishments. In Tijuana in particular, annual religious festivals, exotic spectator sports, and eclectic nightlife offer new experiences for most travelers.

Historic Places

Old Tijuana Cathedral (at Calle 2 and Av. Constitución). This timeworn cathedral offers a glimpse into the spiritual rituals of Mexicans in Tijuana. Inside you'll find numerous religious statues, where the faithful regularly bring fresh flowers and leave written petitions for divine intervention. Because this continues to be a place of worship, no flash photographs are allowed, and appropriate attire is required (no shorts or bare arms). Sidewalk vendors nearby sell both religious and superstitious items.

Plaza Santa Cecilia (First St. and Av. Revolucíon). Saint Cecilia is the patron saint of musicians, and this open square named after her is generally crowded with mariachis waiting to be hired for a single song or longer interludes. This is an especially lively place on the weekends, and there are several places on the plaza to buy a snack or a beverage and enjoy the entertainment.

Tijuana Arch and Monumental Clock (First St. and Av. Revolucíon). This is a relatively recent addition to downtown Tijuana, and so can't really be considered a historic monument, but its distinct design is visible even from north of the border and defines the Tijuana skyline. Look for a tall metal structure that resembles a half bicycle wheel and you're there.

Museums

Tijuana Cultural Center (664-687-9600;
9350 Paseo de los Héroes, Tijuana, BC,
Mexico, 22320). This extensive cultural
complex in the Zona Rio neighborhood
comprises an Omnimax theater (the
architecture of which you can't miss—it's a
giant sphere), with at least one film a day
in English; an outdoor space called the
Caracol Archaeological Garden, filled with
reproductions of Toltec, Olmec, and Aztec
artifacts; the CECUT Theater, a 1,000-seat
performance hall that presents dance and
music performances by regional artists
and regularly hosts performances by the
Mexican National Symphony and Ballet
Folklórico; and the Museum of the Califor-
nias, with exhibits and a permanent collection that illustrates the history of Baja,
including pieces from the pre-Hispanic
era to the modern day. There is a very nice
bookshop selling books primarily in
Spanish, as well as fine Mexican arts and
crafts. Well worth a visit, this attraction is

El Arco *in Tijuana marks the start of the
downtown tourist area.*

popular with Mexican schoolchildren during the week and attracts tourists from both
the United States and throughout Mexico on the weekends. Open Tuesday–Sunday,
10–6. Adults: $4.50, children and senior citizens $2.50. Omnimax films are an
additional cost.

Tijuana Wax Museum (664-688-2478; Calle Primero #8281, Tijuana, BC, Mexico 22000).
This collection of 80 or so lifelike (and life-sized) wax figures is a little weird, but where
else can you get a photograph standing next to Elvis, Michael Jackson, Mother Teresa,
and Pancho Villa? Squeamish folks should skip the depiction of an Aztec sacrifice and
the Chamber of Horrors. The museum is located in the old Chamber of Commerce
Building one block east of Avenida Revolucíon. Open daily 10–7. Adults $2.

Nightlife

Nightlife in Tijuana ranges from rowdy cantinas to crowded discos to downright obscene
venues, and there are literally hundreds of bars scattered throughout the city. Most San
Diegans stick to the classier clubs in the Zona Rio, but there are many fun choices in downtown as well. Note that there are strict dress codes for most dance clubs in Mexico: No flip
flops, no shorts, no grungy beachwear. Clubs generally don't get into full swing until close
to midnight, and they stay open late—generally until 5 AM. Streets are well lighted and, on
weekends, usually crowded, so it's easy to bar hop on foot, especially in downtown, where
clubs are clustered closely together.

Americans will be delighted to find that alcohol is quite a bit less expensive in Tijuana;
although prices vary, it isn't unusual to find two-for-one cocktail specials, and bottles of
Coronas generally go for $2 or so.

The legal drinking age in Tijuana is 18. Underage patrons are not to be admitted into dance clubs, even if they don't intend to drink—and even if they are accompanied by adults. Local law enforcement has cracked down on clubs that don't observe the legal age in the past few years, so that the legal restrictions are generally enforced.

Baby Rock (664-634-2404; Calle Diego Rivera 1482, Tijuana, BC, Mexico 22320). A young, hip crowd lines up nightly to dance to the pulsing beat of rock music in Spanish and English in this well-attended disco. The cover charge varies, and dress codes are strictly enforced. This is extremely popular with American college students, and can be over-whelmingly packed during spring break.

Hard Rock Café (664-685-0206; Av. Revolución 520, Tijuana, BC, Mexico 22000). You won't find anything different about this Hard Rock in downtown Tijuana from those you'll find in the rest of the world: loud music in the background and an eclectic collection of rock and roll memorabilia by way of décor. But if you want to party in Tijuana and you're a little squeamish about the independent local bars, this is a relatively benign alternative. Open daily 11 AM to 2 AM.

Iguana Ranas (664-685-1422; Av. Revolucíon at Calle 3, Tijuana, BC, Mexico, 22000). In the heart of downtown, this rowdy bar and grill attracts a young, boisterous crowd every day of the week. In fact, although most bars in Tijuana don't heat up until midnight, this one seems to have a party on constantly. Note that the bar's reputation has suffered in the past few years because of alleged violence, so keep your wits about you.

Maria Bonita (664-633-4000; Paseo de los Héroes 10305, Tijuana, BC, Mexico 22320). Part of the Camino Real Hotel in the Zona Rio, this new, upscale bar is a quiet place to enjoy drinks in a less frenetic environment than you'll find in many locales in the city.

Rodeo Santa Fe (664-682-4967; Bea Rapida 9, Tijuana, BC, Mexico 22320). In the Pueblo Amigo shopping center in Zona Rio near the border, this bar and dance club offers up a real indoor rodeo at midnight. You'll also find dancing at this expansive three-level,

The Caracol Archaeological Garden at the Tijuana Cultural Center features a copy of an Olmec artifact believed to represent the head of a king.

Iguana Ranas downtown is a colorful bar and grill.

Wild-West-themed club. Open Thursday through Saturday and Monday 9 PM–4 AM. Cover charge $4.

Señor Frogs (664-682-4958; Av. Paseo Tijuana, Tijuana, BC, Mexico 22320). This famous bar in Plaza Pueblo Amigo in the Zona Rio is always packed, and seems to be equally popular with tourists and locals. The grill serves an international menu. Come Sunday afternoon and be treated to "Frogslandia," with live entertainment, face painting, and piñatas—all meant to entice families. Open daily noon until 2 AM.

Viva Mexico! (664-634-3065; Ave. Diego Rivera No. 19, Tijuana, BC, Mexico 22320). In the Zona Rio, this restaurant and cantina is a loud, crowded nightspot, with live Mexican music nightly, a *long* happy hour (5:30–9:30), and inexpensive cocktails all the time. Open daily at 1 PM; closing times vary.

Seasonal Events

Carneval is celebrated in Tijuana the nine days before Ash Wednesday; this colorful, rowdy festival features costumed parades and plenty of music and food. Look to Avenida Revolución for the heart of the action.

Throughout Mexico during Easter week, ***Semana Santa*** is celebrated; a quaint custom at this time is to break *cascarones*—colorful paper eggs filled with confetti—over the heads of loved ones. This is a popular time for vacations for Mexicans, which means increased traffic in Tijuana.

In April the Tijuana Cultural Center hosts the **International Dance Festival** (664-687-9600), with performances by dance companies from Southern California, Baja California, and the interior of Mexico.

Although **Cinco de Mayo** is perhaps bigger in San Diego than in Mexico, you'll still find plenty of fiestas in Tijuana to celebrate the defeat of the 1862 French invasion of Mexico; look for street fairs throughout downtown and Zona Rio, including music, food, and parades.

July 11 is an important date for Tijuana: The city was founded on this day in 1889, and citizens commemorate the event with street fairs throughout downtown and parties in just about every bar in the city.

In late August or early September, the *Feria de Tijuana* (Tijuana Fair) is held at the Agua Caliente Racetrack (664-633-7300); similar to fairs north of the border, you'll find carnival thrill rides, games, and food booths.

In early October, visit the **Annual Expotequila Tijuana** (664-608-9326), where you can try some of the hundreds of tequilas showcased, sample Mexican food, and enjoy mariachi music and traditional ballet folklorico dancing. In late October, head to the **Tijuana Beer Fest** (664-638-8662), sponsored by Consorcio Cervecero, producer of Tijuana Beer, which features the creations of 15 microbreweries, as well as live music and food. Also this month at the Tijuana Cultural Center is the **Hispanic American Guitar Fest** (664-687-9600), where renowned guitar players from around the world come to play at this two-week musical event.

Day of the Dead (*Día de los Muertos*) on November 1 and 2 is similar to All Saints Day, and is observed with offerings such as food and liquor as well as papier-mâché skeletons, which are left at the gravesites of the dearly departed. You'll find stores throughout the city selling Day of the Dead crafts. And come to the Tijuana Cultural Center this month to enjoy the **National Theater Festival** (664-687-9600), where theater companies from throughout Mexico perform.

SPECTATOR SPORTS

Because of a prolonged labor dispute, the fast-paced sport of jai a lai is no longer played in Tijuana, but there are still a number of interesting sports in the city that you won't find north of the border.

Bullfights

From May through September, bullfight fans from around the world flock to two famous bullrings in Tijuana to watch famous matadors in a colorful, bloody spectacle imbued with tradition. Bulls bred specially for fighting (although not trained or encouraged in any way to be particularly ornery) are fought to the death in a gory display. This can be tough for Americans to watch, but at least the bulls killed in the ring don't go to waste: They are immediately butchered, and the meat is sold for consumption. A few miles east of downtown you'll find *El Toreo de Tijuana* and about 6 miles west of downtown is the *Plaza de Toros Monument*, also known as **The Bullring-by-the-Sea**. The latter facility can accommodate 25,000 spectators. Ticket prices vary, based on how close you sit, whether you sit on the sunny or shady side of the arena, and how popular the matador is, but expect to pay anywhere from $15 to $70. Purchase tickets in advance at the bullrings, because the events often sell out. Festivities usually begin at 4 PM. Call for schedules and ticket information in Tijuana at 664-685-2210. You can purchase tickets through the U.S.-operated **Ticket-Master** agency in San Diego (619-220-8497) or through **Five-Star Tours** (619-232-5049; 1050 Kettner Blvd., San Diego, CA 92101).

Greyhound Racing

Agua Caliente Greyhound Track (664-633-7300; Blvd. Agua Caliente and Tapachula 12027, Tijuana, BC, Mexico 22420). Agua Caliente, known in Mexico as *Hipódromo Caliente*, just a few miles east of downtown, started out life in 1929 as a horse racing track, and in its heyday regularly lured the glitterati from Hollywood. The track ran the first North American "Hundred Grander" (a horse race whose prize was $100,000) back in the 1930s, and it played host to famous thoroughbreds like Seabiscuit. But sadly, thanks to another prolonged labor dispute, horses no longer run at Caliente, and instead greyhounds race nightly at 8 PM and on most weekend afternoons. Pari-mutuel wagering takes place onsite, and seating in the grandstands is free.

RESTAURANTS AND FOOD PURVEYORS

Restaurants

Mexicans generally enjoy leisurely meals— rather than grabbing food on the go (despite all those food carts around town, which mainly proffer snacks). Given the complexity and labor intensity of preparing Mexican cuisine, it is no wonder folks take the time to enjoy their food. In Tijuana and across the country, the midday meal is generally the main one of the day, and locals usually sit down around 2 or 3 in the afternoon. Suppertime is a lighter affair, generally served after 9 (and often much later).

CAESAR'S

664-688-2794
Av. Revolucíon at Calle 5, Tijuana, BC, Mexico, 22000
Open: Daily
Price: Moderate
Cuisine: Mexican, steaks
Serving: L, D
Credit Cards: MC, V
Reservations: No

On the second floor of the weathered Hotel Caesar, in the heart of downtown Tijuana, Caesar's was a popular gambling and drinking destination for wealthy Americans back in the 1920s and 1930s. Legend has it that this is the restaurant where the famous salad of the same name was invented by Chef Caesar Cardini, back in 1924. According to this folklore, Caesar whipped up the salad, made with Romaine lettuce, parmesan cheese, chunks of bread, anchovies, lemon juice, and coddled eggs (not raw eggs, as U.S. chefs generally use) to please hung-over costumers who were looking for something light and different. Today the famous salads are prepared tableside in big wooden bowls in a theatrical presentation that uses the original recipe. Not a fan of salads? You can get delicious lobster here, as well as a variety of Mexican specialties. Note that despite a deceptively G-rated atmosphere up front, there is a strip club in the back, which is accessible from inside the restaurant.

CHIKI JAI

Owner: Francisco Monje López
664-685-4955
www.sdro.com/chikijai
1388 Av. Revolucíon, Tijuana, BC, Mexico, 22000
Open: Daily
Price: Moderate
Cuisine: Spanish and Mexican
Serving: L, D
Credit Cards: No
Reservations: No

Chiki Jai celebrates the art of bullfighting in the décor of its cozy dining room.

This tiny downtown eatery has been specializing in Spanish cuisine since 1944, served in a cozy and charming dining room decorated with a bullfighting theme. Start with spicy Spanish chorizo or salty prosciutto, both of which are excellent accompaniments to Chiki Jai's homemade bread served with Roquefort cheese. Entrée specialties include authentic Spanish paella studded with shrimp, tender stuffed calamari in squid ink sauce, or rare tuna steak seasoned heavily with fresh cilantro. Finish with a light dessert of quince with cheese or Spanish-style rice pudding. The restaurant has a beautiful bar in the back and a nice selection of beer and wine.

CIEN AÑOS

Chef: Victor Balbuena
664-634-3039
www.cieninfo
Calle José María Velazco 1407, Tijuana, BC,
Mexico 22010
Open: Closed Sunday
Price: Expensive to very expensive
Cuisine: Mexican
Serving: L, D
Credit Cards: MC, V
Reservations: Necessary

Situated close to the border, this fancy restaurant is one of the best (and most well known) in town—and it can be hard to secure a table because of its fame. The restaurant specializes in authentic Mexican recipes that date back to pre-Spanish days, and they use some mighty unusual ingredients. "Fear Factor" devotees will feel right at home ordering treats like ant eggs in garlic butter, fried tripe, or steamed beef tongue. A Mexican delicacy that requires a *little* less fortitude is the *huitlachoche*, which is a grayish fungus that grows naturally on corn. Try it in the *medallones en salsa chipotle*, a dish with beef filets in a smoky sauce. But you needn't be gastronomically adventurous to enjoy dining here: The delicate and seasonal squash blossom soup is a fragrant treat, and the *pollo sinfonia en rosa*, a chicken breast bathed in a slightly sweet walnut and chipotle sauce is delicious and not at all scary. Another favorite is the *camarones azteca*, shrimp prepared with mushrooms, cactus, and chili sauce. The restaurant offers free valet parking.

LA CASA DE MOLE

Owner: Herminia Hamador
664-634-6920
Paseo de Los Héroes 10511, Tijuana, BC,
Mexico 22320
Open: Daily
Price: Moderate
Cuisine: Mexican
Serving: B, L, D

Credit Cards: None accepted
Reservations: No

Mole (pronounced "mow-lay") is a complex, richly flavored sauce that is used in Mexican cuisine as a dressing for meats and fish, and it is used in traditional cooking throughout the country. Moles include what are normally considered sweet spices like cloves and cinnamon, and they are often flavored with nuts and dark chocolate—although the results are not generally sweet but rather tangy and sometimes spicy, depending on the addition of chiles. At the festive and friendly La Casa de Mole, you can try just about every kind of mole imaginable, made with owner Señora Hamador's family recipes. Don't miss the sesame seed sauce paired with chicken and the chili-almond sauce paired with absolutely anything. The restaurant often features live piano music and strolling mariachis, and the atmosphere is family friendly. Note that the place closes at 9 PM, before the rowdies come out to play.

LA COSTA

Manager: Juan Manuel Flores
664-685-8494
8131 Calle Seventh Galaena, Tijuana, BC,
Mexico 22000
Open: Daily
Price: Moderate
Cuisine: Seafood
Serving: L, D
Credit Cards: MC, V
Reservations: Recommended on weekends

This quiet, elegant restaurant just behind the Mexicoach station in downtown has been a favorite with locals and Californians since 1967. This is by far the best place to get fine seafood in Tijuana, served in refined and restrained surroundings. Folks from San Diego have been known to drive across the border just to indulge in Mexican lobster. La Costa serves up this special-occasion shellfish eight different ways. You can also choose among 20 different shrimp dishes and sample squid and octopus—either deep-fried or pickled into ceviche. Other specialties include the king crab Rockefeller, with a spinach and cream sauce; and the so-called fountain of youth, a cornucopia of ceviche, shrimp, and oysters. La Costa sometimes has abalone on the specials menu, a delicately flavored white-flesh mussel that is almost never sold north of the border—and can rarely be found in Mexico anymore, either, thanks to overharvesting. It's usually the most expensive item on the menu, but well worth trying.

LA DIFERENCIA

Chef: Juan Carlos Rodriguez
664-634-7078
www.ladif@telnor.net
Blvd. Sanchez Taboada 10611-A, Tijuana, BC, Mexico 22320
Open: Daily
Price: Expensive
Cuisine: Traditional Mexican
Serving: L, D
Credit Cards: AE, D, MC, V
Reservations: Recommended

The food at this elegant restaurant in the Zona Rio *is* different. Strange, many might say. The restaurant features unusual gourmet items prepared according to pre-Columbian, Mayan, and Aztec recipes. Culinary dare devils will delight in dishes like pork skin casserole with cracklings cooked with jalapenos, onions, and tomatoes; grilled crocodile filets served with a rich adobo sauce; or golden *sesos* tacos, corn tortillas stuffed with cow's brains. The previously mentioned fungus *huitlachoche* is offered here in numerous dishes, including stuffed in crepes and chilies and served with a squash-blossom sauce and in a cheese sauce served over chicken. This is truly a fine dining establishment with great variety, so there are plenty of familiar alternatives, like salmon filets in a sweet and sour mango sauce or roasted chilies stuffed

with filet mignon. Courteous, professional wait staff will help you navigate the menu (which is printed in English), so you're sure to find something with which you're comfortable ordering. The restaurant offers a full bar with an extensive wine list.

TIA JUANA TILLY'S

Owner: Mariano Escobedo Lavin
664-685-6024
www.tiajuanatillys.com
Av. Revolucíon 701, Tijuana, BC, Mexico 22000
Open: Daily
Price: Inexpensive to Moderate
Cuisine: Mexican
Serving: B, L, D
Credit Cards: MC, V
Reservations: No

This very popular bar and grill is famous with American tourists, both because of its convenient location in the Zona Centro and because of its reputation as a wild bar. The place started out life as the café for the jai a lai arena next door, which as previously mentioned has been closed for several years because of a labor dispute. There is an adjacent booking lounge, and televisions showing sporting and racing events allow patrons to keep track of their bets. Tilly's has amazing fresh chips and salsa, which you can enjoy at the bar or with your meal. For more substantial fare, try the chicken fajitas served with homemade tortillas; cheese fondue accented with chorizo and peppers; or the *carne asada*, marinated grilled flank steak served with rice, beans, and a stuffed pepper (although the steak can be a little fatty). As noted, this is also a night-time hotspot, so if you want to avoid loud music and crowds, come before 9 PM. The doors close at midnight during the week and 3 AM on weekends, so if you're looking for a party, come for a late dinner and the action will find you.

Tia Juana Tilly's downtown is both a restaurant and a happening night spot. Photo courtesy of Jon Preimesberger. Used with permission.

Food Purveyors

Breweries and Pubs

El Torito Pub (664-972-4020; 643 Avenida Revolucíon, Tijuana, BC, Mexico, 22000). Located on the second floor above the corner of Third Street and Avenida Revolucíon, El Torito sells cold bottles of Mexican beers like Corona and Tecate for under $2. You can also buy yummy Mexican appetizers like small tacos.

Tijuana Brewery Company *(La Cerveceria)* (664-638-8662; Blvd. Fundadores 2951, Tijuana, BC, Mexico 22550). Located in the Zona Centro, this microbrewery began production in 2000, after studying beer-making techniques in the Czech Republic. The brewery imports their hops and malts from the Czech Republic as well. They offer three brews: *morena*, which is a dark lager; *guera*, which is a pale lager; and *bronca*, a pale ale. In addition to beers, *La Cerveceria* also serves small-portioned meals here known as *botanas*, which include delicious *chiles rellenos* (chilis stuffed with cheese or meat and battered and fried until they are golden and crispy). Tours of the facility are sometimes available.

Specialty Markets

Gigante Supermarket (corner of Third St. and Av. Revolucíon). Downtown, at the corner of Third Steet and Avenida Revolución, this store really is gigantic, and it's open 24 hours a day. You can buy a large assortment of fresh fruits, freshly baked goods (including colorful Mexican pastries), and inexpensive spices, in addition to standard grocery store fare.

La Villa del Tabaco (664-68-3920; 865-15 Av. Revolucíon., Tijuana, BC, Mexico 22000). I have no affection for tobacco products, but if *you* fancy a stogie, this little cigar lounge and espresso bar in downtown (between Second and Third Sts.) is worth

> **L.A. Cetto Winery**
>
> (664-685-3031; Cañon Johnson 2108, Tijuana, BC, Mexico, 22130) The Baja wine industry has taken off in recent years, and L.A. Cetto—one of the finest wineries in the region—has a branch in Tijuana, housed in a restored 80-year-old facility. The company grows its grapes in the Baja California wine country to the south, and bottles the wine in Tijuana. There are tours through the bottling plant in both English and Spanish, and wine tastings are available with or without the tour. Excellent reds can be had for less than $10 a bottle. Open weekdays 10–5:30; Sat. 10–4 (although hours are subject to frequent change; call ahead for current tour schedules). Tasting $2.

a stop. It sells Cuban cigars, which are illegal to possess in the United States; brands include Cohiba, Montecristo, and the prestigious Habanos. Stay too long and the very air will put hair on your chest. It is illegal to take Cuban cigars back into the United States, so consume them here, along with a strong shot of Mexican espresso. (Note that you will find what are billed as Cuban cigars throughout Tijuana; a good majority of these will actually be Mexican. This is one of the few places in town where you're sure to get the real deal.)

Mercado Hidalgo (Av. Independencia at Ave. Sánchez Taboada, Tijuana, BC, Mexico, 22000). Approximately five blocks east of Avenida Revolución, this is Tijuana's biggest farmer's market, with stalls selling fruits, vegetables, and even some souvenirs. This is a great place to get a glimpse of the real Tijuana, because the Mercado Hidalgo is patronized almost exclusively by locals. Come in the morning for the greatest selection.

Sweets and Treats

El Popo Market (Second St., between Niños Heroes and Constitucíon, Tijuana, BC, Mexico, 22000). Many of the outside stalls in this colorful market sell Mexican candies like *dulce de leche* (a milk sweet that tastes like caramel), candied papaya, and walnut marzipan. The bittersweet chocolates throughout Mexico are unusual and are often flavored with strong spices like cinnamon and chili peppers. This is also a good place to buy typical Mexican housewares like grinding stones and tortilla presses.

Sanborns (664-684-8958; Av. Paseo de Heroes 10130, Tijuana, BC, Mexico 22320). Across from the Plaza Rio Tijuana (see Shopping, page 255), Sanborns is a strange combination of department store, coffeeshop, and restaurant—and sells just about everything, from perfume, chocolates, boots, and jewelry. This is also one of the best places to buy bakery items; Mexican pastries are more colorful and usually less sweet than their American counterparts, and they go extremely well with a cup of frothy Mexican hot chocolate (which is traditionally flavored with cinnamon).

RECREATION: THE GREAT OUTDOORS

Beaches

The pollution is such that visiting beaches in Tijuana is just not a good option (although stubborn surfers will come anyway). Local San Diegans often head south to Rosarito Beach (see chapter 2) or even farther, to Ensenada.

Buy delicious cookies by the pound at Sanborns.

Fishing

There is a ban on commercial fishing around the Mexican Coronado Islands, which means that sports fishing in this area is particularly good. Expect to catch bonito and seabass throughout the year, and some larger sports fish in the summer. Most excursions are booked out of San Diego (**Fisherman's Landing**, 619-221-8500; 2838 Garrison St., San Diego, CA 92106; **H&M Landing**, 619-222-1144; 2803 Emerson St., San Diego, CA 92106). Anyone 16 or older must have a Mexican fishing license. Most excursions into Mexican waters include a day license, but be sure to ask. Even people just out for the ride aboard a vessel carrying fishing equipment must be licensed. Licenses are available for the day, week, or for a full year, and can be purchased at tackle shops and, strangely enough, many Mexican insurance companies near the border. They can also be purchased by mail from the California-based office of the **Mexico Department of Fisheries** (PESCA; 619-233-4324; 2550 Fifth Ave., Ste. 15, San Diego, CA 92103) or from the **Discover Baja Travel Club** (619-275-4225; 3089 Clairemont Dr., San Diego, CA 92117; or online at www.discover-baja.com).

The daily catch limit is 10 fish, with no more than five of the same species. This limit holds for divers as well, who may use only handheld spears. Visitors to Tijuana may not gather shellfish, including abalone, clams, lobsters, or shrimp. You may transport your legal catch back over the border into the United States, but you must first complete a California Declaration of Entry form (get these at the border or at any international airport). You may be asked to show your Mexican fishing license at the border, and you need to be able to identify the fish you caught. Keep some part of the fish intact, rather than packing anonymous filets.

Golfing

Real Del Mar (664-631-3401, 800-662-6180; Km. 19.5 Tijuana-Ensenada Tollroad,
Tijuana, BC, Mexico 22655). About 10 miles south of Tijuana, off Mexico 1-D, this par-72
beautifully landscaped 18-hole course is challenging to golfers of all levels, and offers
lovely views of the ocean and beyond to the Mexican Coronado Islands; several holes are
into stiff head winds. Green fee: $70.

Tijuana Country Club (888-217-1165; Blvd. Agua Caliente 4500, Tijuana, BC, Mexico
22420). Designed in 1948 by Allister McKenzie for golfers of all skill levels, this is a
secret favorite by many old-time San Diego golfers. There is little water here, but lots of
challenging sand traps. It is easy to get a tee time, and the costs are reasonable. You'll
find the course next to the **Grand Hotel Tijuana** (see pages 234–240). Green fee: $35.

Surfing

Before the worst of the pollution—or perhaps before the worst effects of pollution were
understood—many California surf legends got their start riding the big-break Tijuana
waves. But despite concerted efforts by U.S. and Mexican officials, overflows in the surrounding canyons contaminate the Tijuana River, which flows directly into the ocean (after
crossing the U.S. border). The waters south of the border (and on border beaches in San
Diego as well) have caused significant health problems for residents using the beaches,
especially children.

Despite the pollution today, Mexican surfers—and some old-timers from California—
head to the point breaks between Tijuana and Ensenada. The largest swells come from the
west–northwest starting in October through May. If you're game to try the waters, at least
make sure the surf is up: For updated information, check www.surfline.com.

SHOPPING: EVERYTHING UNDER THE SUN

Even if you do not intend to buy, it's next to impossible to avoid at least browsing through
the wares of the hundreds of small vendors. Especially downtown on Avenida Revolucíon,
entertaining salespersons entreat visitors to examine the goods and proclaim them the best
(although a good portion of the items on display are identical from stall to stall). Bargaining
is expected in the open-air arcades, and a good rule of thumb is to expect to pay about half
the original asking price. Some finer stores will discount items slightly (by about 20 percent), but generally if the price is marked on the item in a store, this is the price you should
expect to pay, particularly in the Zona Rio, where haggling isn't encouraged. Shopping
downtown is not a spectator sport; you have to put on your knee pads and be prepared to get
a little roughed up. It can be fun—and it can be extremely annoying—but if the thrill of a
deal excites you, there is no better place to test your shopping savvy and bargaining wits.

A boon to serious shoppers is that Tijuana is a duty-free shopping zone. You can pay with
U.S. dollars, Mexican *pesos*, travelers checks, or credit cards (but obviously, do not give
credit card information to street vendors). U.S. residents are allowed to purchase up to
$800 worth of goods duty-free, which can include one liter of alcohol (which you can only
bring back over the border legally if you're 21 or older), one hundred cigars (although not
Cubans, which are illegal in the United States), and two hundred cigarettes. Plants, produce, and animals are prohibited from crossing from Mexico into the United States, and a
valid doctor's prescription must accompany any legal drug purchases. Be sure to keep all
receipts, to verify the value of your purchases.

Recently the state of Baja California (in which Tijuana is located) has instituted an Out-standing Host Program, which encourages local businesses to deal fairly and politely with tourists and to help visitors identify the most reliable, honest merchants, restaurants, bars, and so forth. Look for their logo at the entrance of businesses if you are in doubt, and check the Web site at www.discoverbajacalifornia.com/various/outstanding_host.html for a list of these local businesses.

Clothing

El Vaquero (664-685-5236; Av. Revolución 1006; Tijuana, BC, Mexico 22000). A trip to Mexico is not complete without purchasing leather goods—in fact, the smell of leather hits you the moment you walk through the ubiquitous vendor stalls or almost any border store. This is a reliable establishment with good quality leather jackets, purses, and shoes. You can even pick up a saddle!

Plaza Rio Tijuana (Paseo de los Héroes 96 and 98, Tijuana, BC, Mexico 22320). Located in the Zona Rio, close to the Cultural Center, Plaza Rio Tijuana is the largest shopping mall in Mexico, with more than 125 specialty and department stores, restaurants, a 14-theater movie complex, banks and money exchanging, and even an enormous grocery store (**Comercial Mexicana**). This is a shopping mall much as you would find north of the border—except the prices can be as much as 25 percent less for the same designer items.

Duty-Free

Although Mexico itself is a duty-free shopping zone, there are even opportunities on the U.S. side of the border to buy duty-free goods. The catch is that you have to carry whatever you buy into Mexico (even if you turn around and bring it right back), and the total receipts are included within an American's $800 duty-free allowance.

UETA (619-662-2028; 5775 Camiones Wy., San Ysidro, CA 92173), which has an outlet you'll pass en route from the U.S. border parking lots to the San Ysidro border, has a wide selection of imported perfumes and upscale cosmetics (e.g., Lancome, Dior) and liquors (e.g., Dom Perignon, Chivas Regal). UETA has its own parking lot, if you're driving across.

Baja Duty Free (877-438-8937; 4590 Border Village, San Ysidro, CA 92173) is also near the border and carries perfumes and liquor, as well as a wide selection of tobacco products and leather accessories. Note that because these items must be purchased and then taken over the border into Mexico, American guests are still limited to 1 liter of alcohol, one hundred cigars, and two hundred cigarettes. Note that even though the prices at these duty-free stores are good, and the selection is varied, you're likely to find many of the same items in Tijuana.

Native Handicrafts

Hand Art (664-685-2642; 1040-B Av. Revolucion, Tijuana, BC, Mexico 22000). In busi-ness at this location for more than 50 years, you'll find hand-embroidered tablecloths, napkins, and placemats, as well as fine imported laces crafted into table runners, doilies, and delicate shawls. Closed Sunday.

Mallorca (664-688-3502; Calle 4 at Av. Revolución, Tijuana, BC, Mexico 22000). Mallorca displays beautiful housewares and wrought iron creations for the home and garden.

The Silver Mine (664-685-5731; 1188 Av. Revolución, Tijuana, BC, Mexico, 22000). Taxco, located southwest of Mexico City, is known for fine sterling silver; this shop in down-

Inexpensive and colorful Mexican pottery can be found throughout Tijuana. Photo courtesy of Joanne DiBona, San Diego Convention and Visitors Bureau. Used with permission.

town specializes in high-quality silver designs, many of which are hand-crafted. Look for Mexican fire opals as well as turquoise and amber pieces. Onsite designers will create unique jewelry to order.

Tolán (664-688-3637; Av. Revolución 1471, Tijuana, BC, Mexico 22000). Between Calles 7 and 8 downtown, this beautiful store has a wide selection of folk art, from Day of the Dead collectibles to architectural pieces such as doors and armoires. You'll find relatively inexpensive Talavera pottery, as well as a nice selection of Mexican tiles that would cost twice as much north of the border. They also carry museum-quality pieces by internationally recognized artists.

Open-Air Markets

Up and down Avenida Revolucíon and its side streets and throughout Tijuana you'll find open-air markets, also known as *arcades*, where local entrepreneurs set up tiny stalls selling everything from cheap plastic toys and papier-mâché puppets to fine silver jewelry and leather goods. Other typically Mexican items to look for include colorful, hand-woven blankets (perfect for spreading out on the beaches in San Diego); huaraches (comfortable Mexican sandals); marble and onyx chess sets; ornately embroidered dresses; stained glass; and hand-painted knick knacks. You'll be sure to see plenty of black velvet paintings as well.

Bargain for anything without a price tag, and as noted earlier, expect to pay half of the original asking price. You'll find that these stalls carry very much the same merchandise, so shop around a little to get a good idea of what items should sell for—and don't be alarmed if a merchant whose wares you've passed by begins to follow you down the street in a last-ditch effort to close the deal. You'll find a block full of spirited vendors selling clothing, crafts, and pottery at **Mercado de Artesanias** (at Calle 2 and Av. Negrete).

Balboa Park Tower near the Old Globe Theater downtown.

9

Handy Facts

What You Need to Know

Surprises can be the most memorable parts of a vacation. But it never hurts to be prepared, in case one of these unexpected adventures turns unpleasant. What follows is a brief guide that may help you resolve problems or answer questions once you arrive in town. I've also included a bibliography on San Diego and Tijuana, so that if you're so inclined, you can do a little research ahead of your visit. Use this page as a quick reference to find what you need:

AMBULANCE, FIRE, AND POLICE

As with any U.S. locale, the only number you need to remember in an emergency in San Diego is 911. You'll instantly reach an operator who will put you through to the correct agency. To reach the police in nonemergency situations, call 619-531-2000. For the Poison Control Center, call 800-876-4766.

In Tijuana, for emergencies call 068 for the fire department; 060 for the police; 066 for the Red Cross; and 078 for tourist assistance. The General Hospital's number is 664-684-0922. You can reach the Highway Patrol at 664-682-5285.

Del Mar is one of the priciest zip codes in the county, thanks to miles of picturesque shoreline.

AREA CODES, TOWN GOVERNMENT, AND ZIP CODES

Area Codes

Downtown, Uptown, Mission Valley, Coronado, and Chula Vista: 619
Mission Beach, Pacific Beach, La Jolla, Del Mar, Solana Beach: 858
Encinitas, Carlsbad, Oceanside, Escondido, Ramona, Julian: 760
Tijuana: 664

You must dial 1 + the area code to make local long distance calls in San Diego from one area code to another, even if the distance is only a few miles. Local long distance rates apply, and additional long distance service fees may be tacked on when dialing from a hotel phone.

When calling Mexico from the United States, dial 011 + 52 + the area code + the local number. While in Tijuana, there is no need to dial the area code (664) to make local calls. When calling the United States from Mexico, dial 00 + 1 + the area code + the number. For directory assistance while in Tijuana (in English or Spanish), call 078.

Zip Codes

Carlsbad	92008, 92009	La Jolla	92037
Chula Vista	91910, 91911, 91914	La Mesa	91941, 91942
Coronado	92118	Pacific Beach	92109
Del Mar	92014	Point Loma	92017
Downtown	92101	Oceanside	92054, 92057
Encinitas	92024, 92027	Tijuana	22000, 22320
Escondido	92025, 92029		

BIBLIOGRAPHY

Architecture
Hines, Thomas S. *Irving Gill and the Architecture of Reform: A Study in the Modernist Architectural Culture.* New York: Monicelli Press, 2000.

Johl, Karen. *Timeless Treasures: San Diego's Victorian Heritage.* San Diego, CA: Rand Editions, 1982.

Sutro, Dick. *San Diego Architecture: From Missions to Modern: A Guide to the Buildings, Planning, People and Spaces that Shape the Region.* San Diego, CA: San Diego Architectural Foundation, 2002.

Autobiography and Biography
Fletcher, Edward. *Memoirs of Ed Fletcher.* San Diego, CA: Pioneer Printers, 1952.

Fuller, Theodore W. *San Diego Originals: Profiles of the Movers and Shakers of California's First Community.* Pleasant Hill, CA: California Profiles Publications, 1987.

Innis, Jack Scheffler. *San Diego Legends: The Events, People, and Places that Made History.* San Diego, CA: Sunbelt Publications, 2004.

MacPhail, Elizabeth C. *Kate Sessions: Pioneer Horticulturist.* San Diego, CA: San Diego Historical Society, 1976.

———. *The Story of New San Diego and Its Founder Alonzo E. Horton.* San Diego, CA: Pioneer Printers, 1969.

Cultural and Political Studies
Davis, Mike, Kelly Mayhew, and Jim Miller. *Under the Perfect Sun: The San Diego Tourists Never See.* New York: The New Press, 2003.

Hawthorne, Kristi. *Oceanside: Where Life Is Worth Living.* Virginia Beach, VA: Donning Company, 2000.

Holtzclaw, Kenneth M., and Diane Welch. *Images of America: Encinitas.* Charleston, SC: Arcadia, 2006.

Pryde, Philip R. *San Diego: An Introduction to the Region.* 3rd ed. Dubuque, IA: Kendall/Hunt Publishing, 1992.

Urrea, Luis Alberto. *Across the Wire: Life and Hard Times along the Mexican Border.* New York: Doubleday, 1993.

Fiction
Chandler, Raymond. *Playback.* New York: Houghton Mifflin, 1958.

Jackson, Helen Hunt. *Ramona.* Rev. ed. New York: Signet, 1988.

Matheson, Richard. *Somewhere in Time.* New York: Tor Books, 1980.

———. *What Dreams May Come.* New York: Tor Books, 1998.

Nunn, Kem. *Tijuana Straits.* New York: Simon and Schuster, 2004.

Shelby, Jeff. *Wicked Break.* New York: Dutton Books, 2006.

Wambaugh, Joseph. *Lines and Shadows.* New York: Bantam Books, 1995.

Wolfe, Tom. *The Pump House Gang.* New York: Bantam Doubleday, 1999.

Films
Anchorman: The Legend of Ron Burgundy (2004). Will Ferrell portrays a 1970s-era newscaster based loosely on local television personalities; an outdoor scene was shot at the San Diego Zoo.

Citizen Kane (1941). Interiors and exteriors of this Orson Wells classic were filmed in Balboa Park, and animals from Kane's menagerie were from the San Diego Zoo.

Fast Times at Ridgemont High (1982). Cameron Crowe went undercover at local Clairemont High School (southeast of La Jolla) and based this comedy in part on his observations. Some outdoor scenes were filmed in the city.

Top Gun (1986). Starring Tom Cruise, this movie about the real-life Top Gun program based at the Naval Air Station Miramar (now the Marine Corps Air Station Miramar) was filmed predominately in San Diego.

Traffic (2000). This Academy Award winning film about the narcotics trade, starring Benicio Del Toro, was filmed in large part in San Diego and Tijuana.

Geology and Biology

Abbott, Patrick. *The Rise and Fall of San Diego: 150 Million Years of History Recorded in Sedimentary Rocks*. San Diego, CA: Sunbelt Publications, 1999.

Beauchamp, Michael R. *Flora of San Diego County, California*. San Diego, CA: Sweetwater River Press, 1986.

Schad, Jerry. *Afoot and Afield in San Diego County*. Berkeley, CA: Wilderness Press, 1992.

Unitt, Philip (Ed.). *The Birds of San Diego County*. San Diego, CA: San Diego Society of Natural History, 1984.

History

Carlin, Katherine Eitzen, and Brandes, Ray. *Coronado: The Enchanted Island*. Coronado, CA: Coronado Historical Society, 1987.

Carrico, Richard L. *Strangers in a Stolen Land: American Indians in San Diego, 1850–1880*. Sacramento, CA: Sierra Oaks Publishing, 1987.

Daly-Lipe, Patricia, and Barbara Dawson. *La Jolla: A Celebration of Its Past*. San Diego, CA: Sunbelt, 2002.

Dana, Richard Henry. *Two Years before the Mast*. Rev. ed. New York: Signet Classics, 2003.

Engstrand, Iris W. *San Diego: California's Cornerstone*. San Diego, CA: Sunbelt Publications, 2005.

Engstrand, Iris W., and Ray Brandes. *Old Town San Diego: 1821–1876* San Diego, CA: Alcala Press, 1976.

Ewing, Nancy H. *Del Mar: Looking Back*. Del Mar, CA: Del Mar History Foundation, 1988.

Gaslamp Quarter Association, Gaslamp Quarter Historical Foundation, and San Diego Historical Society. *Images of America: San Diego's Gaslamp Quarter*. San Diego, CA: Gaslamp Quarter Association, 2003.

Profitt, T. D., Jr.. *Tijuana: The History of a Mexican Metropolis*. San Diego, CA: San Diego State University Press, 1994.

Salcedo-Chourré, Tracy. *California's Missions and Presidios: A Guide to Exploring California's Spanish and Mexican Legacy*. Guilford, CT: Globe Perquot Press, 2005.

Photography

Hendrickson, Nancy. *San Diego Then and Now*. San Diego, CA: Thunderbay Press, 2003.

Hudson, Andrew. *Photo Secrets: San Diego. The Best Sights and How to Photograph Them*. San Diego: Photo Tour Books, 1998.

Lawson, Greg. *Fine as San Diego*. Oakana House, 2006.

O'Connor, Colleen. *Faces of San Diego*. Chicago: Arcadia, 2001.

Recreation

Joyce, Alice. *Gardenwalks in California: Beautiful Gardens from San Diego to Mendocino*. Guilford, CT: The Globe Pequot Press, 2005.

Tobias, Todd. *Charging through the AFL: Los Angeles and San Diego Chargers Football in the 1960s*. Paducah, KY: Turner, 2004.

Wegener, Tom, and Burke, Bill. *Southern California's Best Surf: A Guide to Finding, Predicting, and Understanding the Surf of Southern California*. Redondo Beach, CA: Green Room Press, 1989.

Earthquake Preparedness

Although major earthquakes are extremely uncommon in San Diego, we live near several seismic hot spots, including the San Jacinto and the Rose Canyon faults, which produce tremblers every now and then and have the potential for catastrophic quakes. Small quakes usually last only a minute or so and do little more than rattle the windows—although it is always wise to take precautions even in what appears to be an insignificant episode, in case the trembler turns into something more serious. The U.S. Federal Emergency Management Agency (FEMA) recommends that in an earthquake you "drop, cover, and hold on"—in other words, drop to the ground, take cover under a sturdy table or desk, and hold on to it until the earthquake subsides.

Should you find yourself in the aftermath of a major quake, the American Red Cross counsels that you check yourself and others in your party for injuries; locate and then put out any small fires that may have been triggered by the quake; inspect your dwelling for

Under the historic Scripps Pier.

damage—and get out if you have any concerns about the structural integrity of the building. Note, however, that if your accommodation remains safe, you are better off remaining indoors. If you're inside, check for gas leaks, watch out for loose and broken plaster that could fall, and avoid broken windows and mirrors. If you're outside, stay away from fallen power lines, which can be deadly, and avoid spilled chemicals. Use telephones only in emergencies; as other recent natural disasters have shown us, the communications infrastructure can become overloaded quickly, and tying up lines unnecessarily may prevent emergency and rescue workers from doing their jobs. Use a portable radio to tune into safety advisories and to get more information. And expect aftershocks from major quakes. These can be almost as strong as the original earthquakes and can cause already compromised structures to fail completely.

It's wise to carry emergency supplies with you, even while traveling in your vehicle, including a first aid kit, a flashlight, extra water and food, a portable radio, extra batteries, and a whistle. The current California governor warns that in a large natural disaster, such as a major earthquake, survivors in the state may be on their own for as long as three days. Make sure you have emergency water and food supplies on hand. For more information on earthquake safety, download and read the online booklet "Steps to Safety," published by the Southern California Earthquake Center, at www.scec.org/education/public/safetysteps.html.

HANDICAP SERVICES

Public transportation is barrier-free in San Diego (and into Tijuana), and fares on San Diego buses and trolleys are a fixed $1 for all those with disabilities. City buses are equipped with wheelchair lifts, and drivers will provide assistance as necessary. Many of the rental car agencies in town offer hand-controlled cars, although most companies require between 48 to 72 hours advance notice to ensure that an accessible vehicle will be available.

All major attractions and most restaurants and hotels in San Diego are wheelchair accessible; this is not always the case in Tijuana. Please refer to the information bars throughout this book for San Diego establishments and call ahead for specific information. And to have questions about accessibility answered and to obtain up-to-date information on services in the city, call or check the Web site of **Access Center of San Diego** (619-293-3500; www.2isd.org) or **Accessible San Diego** (858-279-0704; www.asd.travel). Although Tijuana is less accessible, you'll find most of the better restaurants, hotels, and attractions are also working hard to serve visitors with handicaps.

HOSPITALS

The following hospitals have 24-hour emergency room care, with physicians on duty. As in any U.S. locale, call 911 in an emergency. In Tijuana, call 060 for police assistance.

CORONADO HOSPITAL (CORONADO)
619-435-6251
250 Prospect Pl., Coronado, CA 92118

SCRIPPS MEMORIAL HOSPITAL (LA JOLLA)
858-626-4123
9888 Genesee Ave., La Jolla, CA 92037

SCRIPPS MEMORIAL HOSPITAL (ENCINITAS)
760-633-6501
354 Santa Fe Dr., Encinitas, CA 92024

SHARP MEMORIAL HOSPITAL (SAN DIEGO)
858-939-3400
7901 Frost St., San Diego, CA 92123

UCSD MEDICAL CENTER (HILLCREST)
619-543-6400
200 W. Arbor Dr., San Diego, CA 92103

MEDIA

Major Newspapers and Magazines
Frontera (newspaper, Tijuana)
La Prensa San Diego (newspaper)
North County Times (newspaper)
San Diego (magazine)
San Diego Business Journal (newspaper)
San Diego Daily Transcript (newspaper)
San Diego Reader (newspaper)
San Diego Union Tribune (newspaper)

San Diego Radio Stations

FM Stations

KBZT, 94.9	KIOZ, 105.3	KSON, 97.3
KFMB, 100.7	KMYI, 94.1	KUSS, 95.7
KHRM, 92.5	KPBS, 88.3	KYXY, 96.5
KHTS, 90.3	KPLN, 103.7	XHTS, 93.3
KIFM, 98.1	KSDS, 88.3	XTRA, 91.1

AM Stations

KFMB 760	KLSD 1360	KOGO 600

San Diego Television
KBNT, Channel 17 (Spanish)
KFMB, Channel 8
KGTV, Channel 10
KSND, Channels 7, 39
KUSI, Channel 9
XETV, Channel 6

Professional Sports in San Diego			
SPORT	TEAM NAME	VENUE	CONTACT INFORMATION
Baseball	Padres	Petco Park	www.padres.com; 877-374-2784; 100 Park Blvd., San Diego, CA 92101
Football	Chargers	Qualcomm Stadium (formerly known as the Jack Murphy Stadium)	www.chargers.com; 619-280-2121; 9449 Friars Rd., San Diego, CA 92108

REAL ESTATE

Most visitors to Southern California are shocked by housing prices, which are among the most costly in the country. In 2006, the median home cost in San Diego County was more than $490,000. This translates to between $300 to $400 a square foot for suburbs that have no immediate access to the beach, and as much as $1000 a square foot for beachfront or ocean view properties.

If you come to San Diego and find yourself yearning to own a piece of paradise, like so many people do, call the **San Diego Association of Realtors** (858-715-8000), which will refer you to licensed agents. You can also check out real estate Web sites for photographs and other specifics on current listings (a good source is www.realtor.com) or peruse the *Union Tribune*, the Sunday real estate section of which is helpful in tracking new construction and finding existing properties for sale.

RELIGIOUS SERVICES

All major religions are represented in San Diego, and many services are offered in languages other than English. To find particular religious services, check the USA Worship Here Directory under San Diego, at www.worshiphere.org/CA/SanDiego.htm.

ROAD SERVICE

Nothing can ruin a vacation faster than getting stranded on the freeway or stuck in a beach parking lot. For emergency road service, members can call the American Automobile Association at 1-800-222-4357. Numerous local tow companies offer 24-hour assistance as well. Beware of tow trucks that come without being called first; such trucks troll the freeways for stranded motorists and often charge exorbitant towing rates. Get a quote in writing before you allow any company to move your vehicle.

SMOKING PROHIBITIONS

Many people in San Diego are downright hostile toward smokers, and the state law backs us up. It is illegal to smoke inside restaurants or bars, as well as outdoor patio dining establishments. You may not smoke in outdoor stadiums (although there are designated smoking areas well away from the crowds), and it is illegal to smoke within 30 feet of an entrance to any public building—although this isn't a well-observed law. Many hotels ban smoking altogether. And as of 2006, smoking was also banned on public beaches throughout the county. Interestingly, the casinos run by Native American tribes (see chapter 7) are an exception, because they are not subject to state regulations and allow smokers almost free rein in the public areas.

In Tijuana, smoking is illegal in public places such as municipal buses, banks, city offices, and theaters—although you'll find a lot more second-hand smoke south of the border, regardless of regulations. By law at least 30 percent of restaurant space in Tijuana is to be designated as nonsmoking.

TOURIST INFORMATION AND ON-LINE ADDRESSES

Information Center	Description	Telephone	Web site
Art + Sol	Online visual and performing arts information	NA	www.sandiegoartandsol.com
Baja California State Secretariat of Tourism	Baja Tourism	664-973-0424	www.turismobc.gob.mx
Chula Vista	Convention and Visitors Bureau	619-425-4444	www.chulavistaconvis.org
Coronado	Visitor Center	619-437-8788	www.coronado visitorcenter.com
North County Convention and Visitor's Bureau	Convention and Visitors Bureau	760-745-4741	www.sandiegonorth.com
Tijuana Convention and Visitors Bureau	Tijuana Tourism	664-683-1405	www.tijuanaonline.org
Travelers Aid Society	Travelers aid (San Diego and Tijuana)	619-295-8393	www.travelersaid sandiego.org
Union Tribune SignOn San Diego online information	Online events information	NA	www.signonsandiego.com

WEATHER AND WHAT TO WEAR

Weather

There is rarely cause for complaint about the weather in San Diego and Tijuana: Temperatures generally stay comfortable all year long, with a daytime average of 70 degrees Fahrenheit (21 degrees Celcius), and there is usually low humidity (although the past several summers have brought a few muggy weeks). As a general rule, neighborhoods close to the coast are cooler in the summer, often with heavy morning and evening fog during late summer and early fall, and these same neighborhoods are subject to year-round morning clouds. In late spring and early summer, the prevailing weather is so gray at the beaches that the phrase "June Gloom" was coined to describe the ubiquitous clouds. Inland neighborhoods, which tend to be sunnier, can reach temperatures of more than 100 in the middle of summer, and drop to the 40s and even 30s in winter evenings—although it rarely dips below freezing in the valleys. Even during summer months, it can get chilly at night, especially if you're near the ocean.

The area gets very little precipitation (an average of about 10 inches a year), and this almost always comes during our "rainy season," between December and March. We average nearly 150 clear days a year. The mountains sometimes get snow in high elevations, but we don't see flurries in the city or along the coast. Starting in September and stretching into early December, we're subject to Santa Anas, which are strong, hot, dry winds that blow through for several days at a time. These unfortunately coincide with fire season, and although populated areas generally have little cause to worry about wildfires, occasional fire storms compromise air quality. For example, during the catastrophic fire season of 2003, local schools closed for a week and children and elderly people were advised to stay inside and avoid physical activity.

Average Temperatures (in degrees Fahrenheit)

	Low	High
January	50	66
April	56	69
July	66	76
October	61	74

Shelter Island is an ideal place to get out and enjoy San Diego's nearly perfect weather.

San Diego's cadre of surfers hit the waves almost every day of the year. Photo courtesy of Jon Preimesberger. Used with permission.

Average Total Precipitation (in inches)

January	2.28	February	2.04	March	2.26
April	0.75	May	0.20	June	0.09
July	0.03	August	0.09	September	0.21
October	0.44	November	1.07	December	1.31

Weather Reports

For up-to-date weather reports, call 619-289-1212. For beach reports and surf conditions, call 619-221-8824.

What to Wear

The stereotype of "laid-back" Californians is apt when considering dress codes. Casual clothing like jeans, shorts, and t-shirts are common at all local beaches, attractions, and most restaurants and events, especially those located near the shores. Downtown restaurants and clubs are more formal, as are pricier establishments throughout the area. A jacket for men and a smart dress or pantsuit for women will suffice for all but the fussiest places. Be sure to pack a bathing suit, no matter the time of year you're visiting, and flip flops or sandals for walking on the beach. And don't forget a light sweater in the summer, especially if you'll be near the beach at night. A light jacket will do for the colder months; there is no need for a heavy coat, boots, or gloves, even if you come during what ought to be the dead of winter. A good pair of sunglasses will stand you in good stead as well; the glare of the sun is stronger here than in northern locales. In Tijuana, casual clothing is also appropriate; however, note that nightspots require dressier clothing than San Diego counterparts, so pack a little black dress (or the suit and tie equivalent) if you plan to hit the nightclubs south of the border.

The ever-changing downtown skyline, as seen from the Ferry Landing in Coronado.

10

IF TIME IS SHORT

The Best of the Best

To see the major attractions in San Diego and Tijuana, you need two or three weeks—and to really get the full flavor of the area, you'll need a few years. I heartily recommend a lengthy stay, which will give you opportunity to explore the north county, inland cities, south bay, and venture into Mexico. But if you only have a day or two, concentrate on downtown and La Jolla, and you won't be disappointed. Below are my favorite choices for lodging, cultural attractions, restaurants, and recreation. Some are budget suggestions—but most are not; all are representative of the relaxed, outdoor lifestyle that the faultless weather and sparkling coastline allow San Diegans.

LODGING

The Grande Colonial (858-454-2181; 910 Prospect St., La Jolla, CA 92037) is as close to a perfect hotel as I've ever found. The historic structure is ideally located near the La Jolla Cove, so staying here means you are never more than a quick walk from charming beaches, boutique shopping, fine dining, and eclectic galleries. The large, airy rooms are elegant and calming, and the onsite restaurant (**Nine-Ten,** 858-964-5400) is one of the best in the county.

The new Keating Hotel promises to be one of the hottest properties in the Gaslamp Quarter.

Hotel del Coronado (619-435-6611; 1500 Orange Ave., Coronado, CA 92118). If you can't decide between staying at the beach and staying downtown, this glamorous property presents the best of both worlds. Fall asleep to the sounds of the waves lapping just out-side the window of your guest room, and then wake up and head over the Coronado Bridge and into the hot downtown scene to enjoy its museums, nightlife, and fine dining.

The Keating Hotel (619-814-5700; 432 F St., San Diego, CA 92101) is a treat for

To find the Alcazar Garden in the back of the Mingei Museum in Balboa Park, visitors need to explore beyond the main thoroughfare of El Prado.

the senses, with dazzling Italian high style, futuristic audio and visual systems, sleek bathroom appointments, European refinement, and a prime location in the Gaslamp Quarter downtown. This pricey newcomer is destined to be one of the finest small hotels in the country.

CULTURAL ATTRACTIONS

Balboa Park (north of downtown; accessed from the Laurel Street Bridge on the west and Park Blvd. on the east). If the Smithsonian Institution is America's attic, then Balboa Park is San Diego's backyard. Thanks to the Spanish rococo architecture, acres of botanical gardens, and more than a dozen museums, Balboa Park is one of the best places to unwind and enjoy San Diego's blue skies and warm breezes. Plan to catch a play at the **Old Globe Theater** (619-234-5623); the summertime outdoor Lowell Davies Festival Stage is an especially romantic venue to enjoy a Shakespearean comedy.

Mission San Luis Rey (760-757-3651; 4050 Mission Ave., Oceanside, CA 92057). San Diego traces its cultural roots to the Spanish missions, and this King of the Missions is the best opportunity to see original Spanish architecture and view artifacts from both the early padres and the Native Americans who preceded them. Although Oceanside is the northernmost neighborhood in San Diego, if you take the Coast Highway (Hwy. 101) up, getting there will be half the fun.

San Diego Zoo (619-234-3153; 2920 Zoo Dr., San Diego, CA 92112). Even if you only have time to see the panda and koala bears, ride the skyline gondolas over the gorilla exhibit, and take a quick hike through the Monkey Trails, don't miss this amazing oasis in the heart of downtown. This zoo isn't world famous for nothing.

RESTAURANTS

Café Chloe (619-232-3242; 721 Ninth St., San Diego, CA 92101). Fine dining for breakfast, lunch, dinner, or even just a cup of tea in this jewel box bistro in the East Village of downtown is a relaxing experience that underscores the civility and sophistication of the revitalized city center.

Jack's La Jolla (858-456-8111; 7863 Girard Ave., La Jolla, CA 92037). Choose any of the three immaculately decorated restaurants under Jack's roof and you'll enjoy superior, imaginative food served in a fresh, vibrant setting that touches the essence of La Jolla.

Osetra: The Fish House (619-239-1800; 904 Fifth Ave., San Diego, CA 92101). Urbane interior design, a premier location in the Gaslamp Quarter near Horton Plaza, and imaginative, explosive flavors make Osetra a downtown standout. The "wine angels" provide free entertainment as well.

Rubios (locations all over the city). If you want to understand San Diego cuisine, you have to try a fish taco. Rubios serves up the very best of this inexpensive signature food, which captures in one delightful corn-tortilla-wrapped package the Mexican influence on this coastal community.

NIGHTLIFE

BellyUp Tavern (858-481-8140; 142 S. Cedros Ave., Solana Beach, CA 92075). The expansive dance floor, plenty of billiards tables, and the enormous bar at the BellyUp attract an eclectic crowd of locals who have been coming here for live music and good company for decades.

Croce's Restaurant and Jazz Bar (619-233-4355; 802 Fifth Ave., San Diego, CA 92101). This long-time local favorite isn't trendy anymore, so you won't have to wait behind velvet rope lines to make your way inside, but owner Ingrid Croce has created an inviting atmosphere to enjoy live music, fine wine, and surprisingly good food.

La Jolla Shores offers long expanses of sand and swimmable waves.

Surfers paddle out at sunset at Swami's Beach in Encinitas.

RECREATION

Coronado Municipal Golf Course (619-435-3121; 2000 Visalia Row, San Diego, CA 92118). Duffers can't go wrong at this course. You'll find one of the most inexpensive rounds of golf in the city *and* enjoy some of the loveliest views of the harbor and down-time skyline in the process.

La Jolla Shores (off Vallecitos St.). The prettiest beach, in the prettiest neighborhood, La Jolla Shores is the San Diego beach scene at its laid-back, buffed-out best. Enjoy some of the calmest, most swimmable waves in the region, stroll along the pristine shoreline, or just pull up a corner of cliff and watch the sunset.

Swami's Beach (off Hwy. 101, south of the Self-Realization and Fellowship Center) in Encinitas has big waves and hundreds of surfers who know what to do with them. Come to this relatively hidden beach during low tide and check out the tide pools as well.

Torrey Pines State Reserve (off Hwy. 101, north of La Jolla). Choose any of the hiking trails at this state park and you'll get awe-inspiring views of the ocean and a glimpse into the native habitat of Southern California, which has been nearly obliterated elsewhere because of urban sprawl.

General Index

Lodging by Price and Location

Dining by Price

Dining by Cuisine